Pandora's Trap

Pandora's Trap

Presidential Decision Making and Blame Avoidance in Vietnam and Iraq

Thomas Preston

ROWMAN & LITTLEFIELD PUBLISHERS, INC.
Lanham • Boulder • New York • Toronto • Plymouth, UK

Published by Rowman & Littlefield Publishers, Inc.
A wholly owned subsidiary of The Rowman & Littlefield Publishing Group, Inc.
4501 Forbes Boulevard, Suite 200, Lanham, Maryland 20706
http://www.rowmanlittlefield.com

Estover Road, Plymouth PL6 7PY, United Kingdom

British Library Cataloguing in Publication Information Available

Library of Congress Cataloging-in-Publication Data

The hardback edition of this book was previously cataloged by the Library of Congress
as follows:

Preston, Thomas, 1963–
    Pandora's trap : presidential decision making and blame avoidance in Vietnam and
Iraq / Thomas Preston.
        p. cm.
    Includes bibliographical references and index.
    1. Bush, George W. (George Walker), 1946– 2. Johnson, Lyndon B. (Lyndon
Baines), 1908–1973. 3. Political leadership—United States—Case studies. 4. Blame—
Political aspects—United States—Case studies. 5. Presidents—United States—
Decision making—Case studies. 6. Iraq War, 2003- —Decision making.
7. Vietnam War, 1961–1975—Decision making. 8. United States—Politics
and government—2001–2009—Decision making. 9. United States—Politics and
government—1963–1969—Decision making. 10. Presidents—United States—
Biography. I. Title.
E903.3.P75 2011
973.931092—dc23

                                                              2011023267

ISBN: 978-0-7425-6263-9 (cloth : alk. paper)
ISBN: 978-0-7425-6264-6 (pbk. : alk. paper)
ISBN: 978-1-4422-1215-2 (electronic)

♾™ The paper used in this publication meets the minimum requirements of American
National Standard for Information Sciences—Permanence of Paper for Printed Library
Materials, ANSI/NISO Z39.48-1992.

Printed in the United States of America

This book is dedicated to my parents, George F. and Velma K. Preston.

And to my sister, Ænid Kay Poteete.

Contents

Preface

When the first hardback issue of *Pandora's Trap* was published in 2011, the long shadow of the Bush administration's decision-making on Iraq, its misuse of intelligence and blame avoidance strategies, were still being felt as the Obama administration sought to address the continued instability in Afghanistan and move towards an eventual withdrawal. The war in Afghanistan, begun long before the Iraq invasion, had become an object of profound policy neglect as the focus of the Bush White House shifted to removing Saddam Hussein in March 2003. And the period of relative calm that lasted nearly four years after the initial overthrow of the Taliban in 2001, when a focused allied effort to strengthen the Karzai government might have stabilized the country and allowed for an early military withdrawal, was allowed to slip away as the lion's share of U.S. attention moved to Iraq. The long occupation and immense expense of the operations in Iraq sapped away at the political support for the war, not only within the American public, but in those of allied governments as well. Adding to this was the growing awareness of the manipulation and misuse of intelligence by the Bush administration to justify the war, and the controversies over both the missing WMDs in Iraq and its purported ties to Al-Qaeda and 9/11 (which never existed). As the second Bush term was winding down with the U.S. in its sixth year of occupation in Iraq, the Afghanistan situation was greatly destabilized (along with the stability of neighboring Pakistan), calling into question whether that conflict was winnable as well. The two wars in Iraq and Afghanistan had become inseparable because of the policy directions taken over the previous eight years by the Bush administration. Neither occurred in a vacuum and each was impacted by the other. The decision to invade Iraq and the subsequent occupation stole much of the attention and resources away from resolving the Afghan situation, which was allowed to fester and eventually reignite. As Obama took office in January 2009, the final wind-down of the Iraq war and the rapidly deteriorating situation in Afghanistan and Pakistan landed on his doorstep. These were the continuing consequences of the previous administration's broader 'War on Terror' which had been fought on many fronts, not all of whom had received equal care and attention.

There was also another simple reality that was plainly obvious as Obama began his first term: *whoever* the president was who followed after George W. Bush was going to inherit a distrust and skepticism (from the U.S. public, allies, and the international community) regarding *any* future calls for intervention, especially those based upon U.S. intelligence assessments. The political environment post-Bush had been altered, and the freedom of action for future administrations was inevitably more constrained than it had been post-9/11. The Pandora's Box of regime change opened by Bush unleashed political consequences that continued to reverberate into 2014—and in all likelihood into the administrations of future presidents as well. American foreign policy has been constrained (for good or ill) - and the options available for U.S. presidents to actively engage abroad in meaningful ways, use force if necessary, marshal domestic and international support, and our international credibility—are greatly weakened. Policy does not occur in a vacuum, and these lingering effects have worked to seriously constrain the Obama administration's foreign policy approach in shackles not easily cast aside.

The current crisis in Syria, with its ongoing civil war and use of chemical weapons on civilians, illustrates the dilemma facing the White House. War-weariness among the American public is such that strong majorities oppose any intervention in Syria, despite administration efforts to rally support for limited military strikes on the Assad regime (with no U.S. boots on the ground) to punish and attempt to deter further use of chemical weapons on civilians. Internationally, U.S. claims of intelligence clearly showing Assad's responsibility for the sarin gas attacks was greeted by many with a skepticism drawn from the Iraq case, making it easier for Damascus and her ally Iran to make the argument that this was merely history repeating itself against the innocent. And though the American intelligence assessment was supported by those of other countries intelligence services as well (the French and British in particular), and a U.N. investigation that implicitly supported these findings, a clear consequence of Iraq is that the 'bar of proof' internationally has now been set extremely high. Washington no longer enjoys the benefit of the doubt. Further, while some supporters of a more muscular Syrian intervention (like Republican senators John McCain and Lyndsey Graham) continue to argue for a far more robust policy approach than the Obama administration is currently proposing, there is strong opposition within Congress and the public to any actions that could involve the U.S. in yet another war in the Middle East. War weariness, much as it did post-Vietnam, has become a serious constraint on significant American involvement or resort to force.

The domestic political realities were clear enough to Obama that rather than use his commander-in-chief powers to order limited retaliatory strikes on Syria (thereby opening himself up to the inevitable partisan attacks from Congressional Republicans and to opposition from within his own party), he mirrored a strategy used by President Dwight Eisenhower during the Dien Bien Phu crisis of 1954 (Preston 2001). Though Eisenhower could have ordered strikes to assist the French against the Viet Minh, he instead approached Congress regarding their support (knowing it did not exist without a willingness from other allies to intervene as well). This allowed Eisenhower, who was not enamored with the idea of American intervention in Indochina, to avoid blame for a decision that would lead to a French collapse by shifting the responsibility to Congress and allies (like Britain) who were equally reticent (Preston 2001: 86-94).[1] Similarly, sensing the gathering politics of blame on his political horizon, Obama chose to outmaneuver his opponents by shifting responsibility and blame onto Congress as well—sharing with them a firm grasp on the lightning rod. Though opponents were quick to charge Obama with shifting positions on a 'red-line' in Syria and asking for congressional permission that weakened presidential prerogatives, in reality, the White House was simply recognizing a changed political landscape post-Iraq that had already placed significant constraints on American foreign policy and weakened the hand of any president.

And this dynamic has not been limited to Syria. The domestic politics surrounding the debate over intervening in the Libyan civil war in 2011 led to an American involvement that was limited mostly to providing logistical support (such as aerial refueling) and intelligence to NATO allies (like Britain and France) who conducted most of the combat operations. There was no support domestically for a more active engagement, and certainly not for U.S. boots on the ground—though partisans still decried Obama ceding leadership to Europeans for the operation. Subsequent tragedies like the attack on the U.S. consulate in Benghazi that resulted in the deaths of U.S. embassy officials (including Ambassador J. Christopher Stevens) quickly became the object of partisan debate domestically, riding on an undercurrent of distrust in government statements and intelligence that had been given currency by the previous Bush administration's actions. Efforts by the Administration to rally international support for greater sanctions against Iran's clandestine nuclear program also had substantial credibility hurdles to clear post-Iraq, with American intelligence assessments of the Iranian program being greeted skeptically by some in the Arab world as another attempt to justify a war.

Suspicions and a lack of trust in the Administration's use of (and justifications for) the use of drones over Pakistan and Yemen, with origins in the past conduct of U.S. policy, also served to undercut Obama's ability to engage Haqqani and Taliban operatives more aggressively. Clearly, from the current crisis in Syria through American foreign policy approaches towards Libya, Iran, Pakistan, and Afghanistan—the long-shadow of the Bush administration's opening of Pandora's box in Iraq has continued to have serious consequences for policy and constrained the options available to the White House.

The impact of this changing policy environment is one that the leadership style of Barack Obama is particularly attuned with given the stark differences between his style and those of both George W. Bush and Lyndon Johnson. Like those predecessors, Obama came into the presidency with limited foreign policy experience/expertise, although he (unlike the others) did serve on the Senate Foreign Relations Committee during his time as a senator. In this regard, he was similarly dependent upon expert advisers, though he possessed more interest and background on foreign affairs than either Bush or Johnson. And while no modern president rivals LBJ's need for personal involvement and control over the policy process, Obama has shown a strong pattern of personal engagement and a desire for 'hands-on' involvement—standing in sharp contrast to the far more delegative Bush. [2]

But where the major difference between Obama and his predecessors lay is in his general cognitive complexity, his need for broad information and sensitivity to the surrounding policy environment. Obama scores very high in measures of complexity, while Bush and Johnson are both far lower on this trait.[3] The impact this has upon leadership style is quite profound, especially in terms of how a president makes use of his or her advisory arrangements. Leaders high in complexity tend to see the world in 'shades of grey' and are less ideological and rigid in their belief systems than their more 'black-and-white' counterparts. This also results in high needs for broad information search (for that which *both* agrees *and* disagrees with prior views or policy), the populating of inner circle advisory groups with diverse advisers with a broad range of views and perspectives, and a willingness to more easily alter course in the face of new information or negative feedback (Preston 2001). While the Bush and Johnson administrations tended to exhibit inner circles comprised of advisers with similar ideologies, views, and policy preferences, Obama surrounded himself (like Lincoln) with a 'team of rivals'—a diverse group of advisers (both Republican and Democrat) whom he did not expect to always agree with each other or himself (Goodwin 2005).[4]

As a result, the operation of Obama's White House inner circle and advisory arrangements has been one that broadly gathers information, incorporates dissenting views and feedback that is *both* supportive and not supportive of existing policy (or presidential views), and which actively monitors the surrounding policy environment (with antennae up) to see what is possible, and where the pitfalls of policy lay.[5] It is an adaptive approach to policy based upon information search and feedback, not one driven by an ideological preconception of the world which only seeks confirming information while ignoring negative feedback inconsistent with those beliefs. In this, there is a marked difference between the Obama and Bush styles. It results in a cautious approach to foreign policy making that does not lend itself to rapid decisions, one that seeks to carefully ascertain the 'lay of the land' before taking precipitous steps—and one that is intensely frustrating to those seeking fast, decisive policy making based upon rigid 'principles' regardless of the surrounding context. For a future president with a less sensitive style like Bush's, the changing constraints on American foreign policy might be ignored—even though the consequences from misjudging or failing to recognize that context won't be mitigated (see the period between 2003-2008 in Iraq, for example). But for Obama, ever sensitive to the surrounding environment, the changing constraints and reduced freedom of action post-Iraq are seldom ignored and greatly influence his foreign policy making.

So as the final draw-down of U.S. forces in Afghanistan proceeds towards the 2014 target date for withdrawal, the Syrian crisis continues to unfold, and the largely unforeseen (and difficult to predict) consequences of the Arab Spring movements throughout the Middle East pop up on America's radar, the reverberating echoes of the lid of Pandora's box being pried open in March 2003 will continue to be heard. What began as direct consequences from that event for Afghanistan have now permeated outwards, like the ripples on a pond once a stone has been cast, to impact American foreign policy far into the foreseeable future. And the story leading up to these events is an important one to understand, not only for illuminating how the current policy environment and constraints on American leaders came about, but as a lesson to future leaders and practitioners regarding the ways in which style, the use of intelligence, and blame avoidance strategies can come to compromise U.S. national interests and policy making. That tale begins in chapter one of *Pandora's Trap*.

Thomas Preston
September 2013

Acknowledgments

As with all research endeavors of this size, I am deeply indebted to a great many people whose advice, support, reactions to earlier drafts, and patient tolerance made this project possible. Certainly, my wife, Frances, and two sons, Tobias and Samuel, deserve special mention for (once again) accepting my need to work on weekends—despite my promises post-tenure to abandon the practice. I am also indebted to my home institution, Washington State University, for its generous sabbatical support over the past year, and to the U.S. State Department, the J. William Fulbright Program, and the Fulbright New Zealand Program for my 2010 Fulbright Senior Scholar Award. Both proved essential in giving me the time and financial support to finish this book. In addition, I would like to express my great appreciation to the large number of individuals who generously gave of their time to discuss their insights and experiences with me. Although many of these individuals throughout the government must remain unnamed due to the sensitive nature of their previous jobs or current assignments, I will forever be in their debt for helping to pull back the curtain from the inner workings of the Bush administration in Iraq and providing me with their honest, unvarnished perspectives. Of those that can be recognized, I would like to express my deep thanks to several former senior policy makers from the Bush and Johnson administrations who granted interviews to discuss their insights with me: Richard Armitage, Lawrence Wilkerson, Paul Pillar, David Kay, James Woolsey, Robert McNamara, McGeorge Bundy, Clark Clifford, Paul Warnke, Harry McPherson, George Christian, Paul Nitze, George Elsey, Arthur Schlesinger Jr., Walt Rostow, and Richard Neustadt. For those both named and unnamed, you know who you are, all my thanks. I am also grateful to my friends and colleagues for their observations, comments, and support for this project, at all of its various stages: Asthildur Bernhardsdottir, Paul 't Hart, Barton Kropelnicki, Arjen Boin, Eric Stern, Margaret Hermann, Jon Johansson, Martha Cottam, Charles Hermann, Bruce Livingston, Mark Lay, Ken Yusko, Mark Axworthy, The Institute for the Study of Intercommunal Conflict, Mele Wendt, and all the Fulbright New Zealand staff in Wellington. Finally, a special thanks to my wonderful (and patient) editor at Rowman & Littlefield, Jon Sisk, for helping to guide this book to fruition.

1

Introduction

History appears poised to confirm what most Americans today have decided—that the decision to invade Iraq was a serious strategic blunder. No
one, including me, can know with absolute certainty how the war will be
viewed decades from now when we can more fully understand its impact.
What I do know is that war should only be waged when necessary, and the
Iraq war was not necessary. Waging an unnecessary war is a grave mistake. But in reflecting on all that happened during the Bush administration,
I've come to believe that an even more fundamental mistake was made—a
decision to turn away from candor and honesty when those qualities were
most needed.

—Former White House Press Secretary Scott McClellan (2008: xiii)

THE PANDORA'S BOX OF "REGIME CHANGE"

Since the ancient Greek poet Hesiod's first mention of the Pandora myth in
his epic poem, the *Theogony*, around the seventh century BC, many versions
of the famous story have appeared. The basic theme surrounding most of
these suggest that after being angered by the theft of fire by Prometheus, who
gave it as a gift to mankind, Zeus devised a grim punishment in the form of
Pandora ("all gifted"), the first woman, who was created and given gifts from
all the gods (curiosity from Hera; beauty from Aphrodite; cunning, boldness,
and charm from Hermes; musical talent from Apollo; etc.). Despite being
warned to accept no gifts from Zeus by his brother Prometheus, the dim-
witted Epimetheus accepted Pandora, fell in love with her, and was wed—
prompting Zeus to provide a "wedding present" or "dowry" to Pandora in the

form of a box. Within this beautiful, ornate box, Zeus had commanded Hades to gather from the darkest places of the underworld all of the evils of disease, hunger, cruelty, greed, hate, old age, and the rest that he could find and bind them within. Upon presenting the outwardly splendid gift, Zeus warned both Epimetheus and Pandora that the box should *never* be opened! But being unable to control her curiosity for long, Pandora opened the lid of the box to peek inside and unleashed all of the dark evils imprisoned within it to afflict the world of men, managing only to prevent "hope" itself from escaping. Later versions of the story have Pandora subsequently releasing hope from the box to give comfort to mankind—though one might question whether "misplaced hope" could also be among those other human ills that had rightly been placed within Zeus's trap. Over time, the story of Pandora's box has come not only to represent the dangers of misplaced curiosity but also to refer to all sources of unexpected, extensive troubles that are unleashed inadvertently by mankind upon itself when the long-term consequences of short-term actions are not adequately considered or warnings heeded.

For many within the Bush administration, who came into office in January 2001, a metaphorically similar ornate, beautifully crafted box was presented to the president as a "housewarming present" by neoconservatives who were enamored with both its radiant appearance and promise of easy solutions to many of the vexing foreign policy problems facing the new White House. Carved majestically upon the lid of this wondrous chest were glistening, golden words filled with promise: *regime change*. And for those who had spent years crafting the box, it was *the* answer. The images engraved along its sides depicted a blueprint for a fundamental reshaping of the world, to one in which democratic regimes replaced dictatorships and leaders like Saddam Hussein were consigned to the "dustbins of history." And like Pandora, President Bush would find it impossible to resist the growing temptation to open the box, despite warnings against doing so from Republicans like Brent Scowcroft, academic experts, congressional Democrats, European allies, the UN, and many others.

For unbeknownst to the Bush administration, and the crafters of regime change, lurking within that particular box were immense consequences waiting to be unleashed upon the world; costs on the order of trillions of dollars spent on the conflict and a massive ballooning of federal deficits (when the White House refused to raise taxes during wartime); immense levels of human suffering, from the thousands of American combat dead (and tens of thousands of wounded) to the hundreds of thousands of Iraqis who would eventually be killed or wounded in the conflict; a substantial tarnishing of America's reputation abroad (among both allies and world public opinion) as it pursued a unilateral policy in Iraq outside of the United Nations through a small "coalition of the willing"; a failed presidency for George W. Bush, as the protracted nature of the Iraqi conflict (and lack of WMDs) led a sizable majority of Americans to view the Iraq War as a mistake, bringing to the president historically low poll numbers as he left office in 2009. And even more disastrously, a catastrophic strategic reversal in Afghanistan and Pakistan, as the shift of focus to Iraq in 2003 led to a policy of profound neglect that squandered years of relative peace and stability in the region that could have been used to build up the Afghan central government and security forces under President Karzai. Instead, the Taliban and Al Qaeda were allowed to regroup, and the Karzai government (lacking adequate Western support) proved ineffectual in providing security and became increasingly discredited among an Afghan public tired of conflict and endless promises of better times to come.

And like Pandora's story, the only thing that remained in the box for the Bush administration was "hope," which the White House and its supporters clung to fervently as the ills unleashed by the decision to invade Iraq became manifest. The politics of "blame avoidance" became increasingly necessary to counter the growing domestic and international criticism of the Iraq policy and to maintain political support at home. Moreover, this particular type of hope (that WMDs would be found, that regime change would go smoothly, that the insurgency would die out quickly) was of the kind that would prove to be worthy of inclusion by Zeus in Pandora's trap. It was a hope that would be held on to by supporters of regime change and many neoconservatives with a tenacity usually reserved for only the most deeply held religious beliefs of the truly devout, preventing and delaying the administration from reconsidering or readjusting policy in the face of clear evidence of failures or reversals in Iraq. And importantly, it would play a key role in the perceptions of policy makers regarding the evidence, their "framing" of the security environment, and their use (and misuse) of the intelligence available (about both WMDs and Saddam's connections to Al Qaeda) during the fateful run-up to the war.

Indeed, the true consequences of the Bush administration's falling into "Pandora's trap" are yet to be fully appreciated or felt. The reality now facing American policy makers as they seek to marshal public and allied support for continued efforts in Afghanistan is that the war weariness produced by seven years of war in Iraq (along with the economic, human, and political costs inflicted) makes it difficult (if not impossible) to sustain or obtain increased support for operations in that region. Even by February 2008, the director of national intelligence, Mike McConnell, was reporting to a Senate panel that Al Qaeda had regained strength within its refuge in Pakistan and was steadily improving its ability to recruit, train, and position operatives capable of carrying out attacks inside the United States.[1] By the time President Barack

Obama announced an end to U.S. combat operations in Iraq in August 2010, having drawn down American forces to under 50,000, he would be forced to simultaneously oversee a massive deployment of over 100,000 troops to Afghanistan in an attempt to salvage the deteriorating strategic situation there and in neighboring Pakistan. That the Obama administration now faces a renewed insurgency across Afghanistan, the need for massive U.S. troop increases, and a severely weakened Karzai government are in no small measure a direct consequence of our lack of focus upon that country (in military, political, and economic terms) while we focused on Iraq. So while we may never know with certainty what would have happened in Afghanistan had the Bush administration remained on task, and not shifted its wandering gaze to Iraq by lifting the lid on "regime change," it is now no longer possible to see the two conflicts as being unrelated. Instead, the outcome of the conflict in Afghanistan is now inexorably linked to that fateful decision in 2003 to invade Iraq, with the ghost of that earlier decision haunting every continuing effort in Afghanistan and Pakistan for the foreseeable future.

A POST-9/11 POLICY ENVIRONMENT
THAT ALLOWED RESTRUCTURING

But what was it that set this chain of events into motion? And how was it that George W. Bush, who campaigned on a platform of *avoiding* foreign entanglements in 2000, eventually ended up presiding over the most far-reaching and costly foreign military commitments abroad since Lyndon Johnson's decision to fully intervene in Vietnam in 1965? To these questions, it is useful to note the observation by Fred Greenstein (1969), who suggested that a key factor in determining how important leaders themselves would be in determining policy outcomes (when compared against institutions or the broader political environment) involved the degree to which constraints would exist that would limit their freedom of action, and "the extent to which the environment allows *restructuring*" by that leader. In other words, there are times when either the policy environment or basic institutional realities and power distributions in the political system constrain even the most powerful political leaders, limiting their ability to implement drastic policy changes or make significant policy impacts. But on some occasions, the political environment may be more favorable toward leaders, constrain their actions far less, and allow quite dramatic policy changes to occur.

A good example of this phenomenon is the differing influence over policy and freedom of action possessed by U.S. presidents in the foreign versus domestic policy arenas. In the foreign policy realm, the president has the advantage of controlling through the executive branch all of the primary organs of foreign policy (like the State and Defense Departments, the intelligence community, etc.), as well as possessing the "commander-in-chief" role regarding the military. Although Congress is involved in ratifying treaties, declaring war, and setting budgets, presidents have a great deal of freedom of action to set foreign policy, negotiate with other states, and even use military force abroad with limited constraints. This differs markedly from the domestic policy realm, where the White House must deal with Congress and other actors who have much more of an ability to constrain its policy-making ambitions.

Yet even accepting this greater freedom of action in foreign affairs, it is difficult to imagine any recent president (George W. Bush included) who could have gotten congressional approval and public support to invade and occupy both Afghanistan and Iraq in the absence of a game-changing 9/11-style event. It was the traumatic terror attacks of 2001 that transformed the political environment and allowed a political path to be opened for proponents of regime change to pursue their desire for rectifying the past mistake of 1991, when Saddam Hussein was left in power. The "war on terror" provided the impetus for President Bush to confront an "axis of evil" and state sponsors of terror, like Iraq, and argue for the adoption of the Bush doctrine and a war of preemption against Hussein. In Greenstein's terms, the events of 9/11 fundamentally altered "the extent to which the environment allowed restructuring" by removing many of the political obstacles that would have normally constrained it.

Still, such environment-changing events do not typically happen in a vacuum. Just as containment policy during the Cold War laid the groundwork for the Gulf of Tonkin incident to open the way for Johnson in Vietnam, the fashioning of the message of regime change and the focus upon Iraq had begun long before Bush's 2000 election campaign and 9/11. Those crafting the regime change doctrine included prominent neoconservatives and think tanks, many of whom would later play key roles within the new administration and assist in lifting the lid of the box. For example, Paul Wolfowitz and Zalmay Khalilzad cowrote a 1997 *Weekly Standard* article calling for Hussein's overthrow, and both continued to push for regime change over the coming years in publications and congressional testimony. Indeed, Wolfowitz argued American policy had been ineffective primarily because it had been too weak, relying upon an international community who were by nature followers, and that only strong leadership and unilateral action by the United States would provide the necessary direction for effective collective action against Iraq (Mann 2004: 236–37). In 1998 a neoconservative group called the Project for a New American Century released an open letter to President Clinton calling for abandonment of the existing containment strategy against Iraq and its replacement by a policy of regime change—a letter signed by several future members of the Bush administration, including Wolfowitz, Khalilzad, Donald Rumsfeld, Richard Armitage, John Bolton, Robert Zoellick, and Elliott Abrams (Mann 2004: 238). Under pressure from congressional Republicans and besieged by the Lewinsky scandal, Clinton signed the Iraq Liberation Act in 1998, and by 2000 the Republican Party platform called for "full implementation" of the act and the removal of Saddam from power.

Yet, while still warning of the dangers of not standing up to Iraq, Bush's 2000 presidential campaign shared an eerie similarity to that of LBJ (who campaigned as a "peace candidate" against Goldwater in 1964) by criticizing Clinton's nation building and internationalism. During a speech at the national convention of the Veterans of Foreign Wars in Milwaukee in August 2000, Bush argued that his administration would "be far more reluctant to risk foreign military entanglements," would scale back U.S. deployments overseas, and would withdraw troops from Bosnia/Kosovo, and he accused Clinton of "committing the U.S. to military confrontations where no clear national interest was at stake" and "requiring the military to shoulder too many responsibilities with too few resources."[2] And like Johnson, who within a year of winning the election was making fateful decisions to intervene in Vietnam, Bush would within a year be not only occupying Afghanistan but moving inexorably toward war with Iraq.

THE FOCUS OF THIS BOOK

What accounts for the path that U.S. foreign policy has taken over the past twelve years? How important was President Bush's personality and leadership style in setting up the inner-circle dynamics leading to the administration's mode of decision making, uses (and misuses) of intelligence, and blame-avoidance strategies? How important were these factors in the decision to go to war with Iraq in the first place, in the treatment of the WMD issue, or in the subsequent prosecution of the war? And just how appropriate is the application of the often used (and misused) Vietnam War analogy to the conflict in Iraq? To what extent are there important parallels between the Bush administration's policy making in Iraq and that of Johnson in Vietnam, and are there important differences? For students of American foreign policy, presidential decision making, and the dynamics of blame avoidance, the answers to these questions not only provide greater understanding and explanation of these past cases but help us to further develop theoretical approaches and analytical capabilities for future leaders. Moreover, it is hoped this book will be of value to future practitioners as well, who might learn from the dysfunctional nature of the advisory and policy-making dynamics within the Bush and Johnson administrations in order to avoid similar pitfalls in their own decision making.

What this book is *not* intended to be is a simple rehashing of the events surrounding Bush's march to, and subsequent conduct of, the war in Iraq, which has already been visited in great depth by numerous scholars (e.g., Mann 2004; Bamford 2005; Isikoff and Corn 2006; Packer 2006; Ricks 2009), including most notably, Bob Woodward (2002, 2004, 2006, 2008). Instead, this book focuses more specifically on how Bush's leadership style shaped the structuring and use of his advisory system, how this affected Iraq policy making and use of intelligence, and how "blame avoidance" often played out within the administration. This should assist us in developing a more robust framework illuminating the tactics and strategies of blame avoidance often used by leaders facing controversial or protracted conflicts.

In addition, this book looks far more critically than previous ones at the appropriateness of the "fit" of the analogy between Vietnam and Iraq (Brigham 2006; Campbell 2007). In previous work, I've examined Johnson's leadership style and decision making during Vietnam (Preston and 't Hart 1999, 2001) and interviewed many of his former advisers, including McGeorge Bundy, Robert McNamara, Walt Rostow, Clark Clifford, Harry McPherson, George Christian, and Paul Nitze. It was this background as a Johnson scholar that led to my seeing important parallels and similarities, as well as differences, between Johnson's style and use of advisers in Vietnam and Bush's in Iraq. Although analogies are always imperfect, with no two historical events ever matching one another completely, in this case, on some critical leadership style and advisory levels, there are powerful parallels that cannot be ignored.

During the writing of this book, I interviewed many individuals who worked throughout the government during the Bush administration, who were involved firsthand either in Iraq decision making or in the gathering and use of the intelligence underlying the justifications for the war or its later conduct. Among the senior-level officials interviewed "on the record" were Richard Armitage, Lawrence Wilkerson, David Kay, Paul Pillar, and Norman Mineta. However, it should be noted that to obtain access (and the necessary candor) from a substantial number of officials, it was unavoidable that many interviews be conducted "on background" only, with the understanding that their identities would not be cited or revealed. This was especially important for those staff within various parts of the bureaucracy who remain in public service. While not ideal from an academic transparency standpoint, it was absolutely necessary in order to obtain firsthand accounts by observers of the decision dynamics that played such an important role in Iraq policy. Every effort has been made by the author to corroborate background information obtained through such interviews with testimony from other participants (both on and off the record). But it must be understood, while there are a substantial number of "on the record" interviews, where I cite anonymous officials in the text, in *no case* were these individuals elsewhere directly acknowledged as assisting with this project.

In the next chapter, the leadership styles of two Texans who occupied the White House (Lyndon B. Johnson and George W. Bush) are explored and compared to one another. How did each structure their advisory systems, use information and advice, and deal with dissent over policy within their inner circles? And for those making comparisons between the decision-making dynamics that occurred within the presidential inner circles dealing with Iraq and Vietnam, to what extent are there similarities (as well as important differences) between the leadership styles of Bush and Johnson? And how might these style characteristics have influenced the decisions made by both administrations? Moreover, how important were the foreign policy advisers surrounding each president?

In chapter 3, the increasing importance of "the politics of blame avoidance" in shaping how administrations sell policy options to the public and manage policy reversals is explored. Political leaders have great interest in taking "credit" for good policy outcomes, when everyone is happy with a crisis response or policy decision—no matter how central they were to bringing about the praised action or outcome. At the same time, leaders have an even *greater* interest in "avoiding the blame" for bad outcomes, major policy reversals, or poor crisis responses. And the new political environment facing policy makers, replete with 24/7 news cycles and immensely venomous partisan politics, forces leaders to be even more focused upon the politics of blame avoidance than was necessary in earlier times. Various strategies and tactics of blame avoidance frequently used by politicians will be outlined and discussed with an eye toward how these were applied in either Iraq or Vietnam.

The opening of Bush's own Pandora's box in Iraq is the focus of chapter 4, with the decision making and use of intelligence and advice leading up to the war in Iraq after 9/11 being examined in more depth. Chapter 5 continues this exploration of how these dynamics morphed as the war continued, with special attention paid to the impact Bush's own style had on inner-circle dynamics and blame-avoidance strategies. In many respects, Bush's leadership style (much as Johnson's had forty years earlier) exacerbated the president's own weaknesses and failed to provide him with an advisory system that could compensate and prevent the kind of insular, closed-off advisory dynamics and bureaucratic politics that characterized both conflicts.

After this examination of the Iraq case, chapter 6 revisits the oft-used Vietnam analogy to explore how appropriate it really is to discussions of Iraq decision making. What are the important similarities (and differences) between the Vietnam conflict and the war in Iraq? While there are significant differences between the two conflicts, and caution is in order when applying the Vietnam analogy to Iraq, it is also inappropriate to completely dismiss it as lacking parallels. A number of similarities, particularly in terms of leadership styles and uses of advisers across the two presidents, are explored—along with the observations of a number of Bush advisers (who saw both similarities and differences) during interviews with the author. The chapter concludes with a discussion of the important role played by presidential leadership style on foreign policy decisions (whether in cases like Iraq and Vietnam, or current ones like Afghanistan) and how inner circles function. To what extent has applying the Vietnam analogy to Iraq assisted or clouded our understanding of the Iraq case? And more importantly, how do the politics of blame avoidance help or hinder leaders in both maintaining their "political" health and making good policy choices? Further, do "protracted conflicts" (and the difficult political situations they create) lend themselves even more readily to a focus on blame-avoidance strategies? The chapter ends with a series of recommendations for practitioners, including a warning to future policy makers to more carefully consider the long-term consequences of satisfying one's short-term desires by lifting the lid to any new Pandora's trap.

2

A Tale of Two Texans: The Leadership Styles of George W. Bush and Lyndon Johnson

For those seeking the "echoes" of Vietnam within the Iraq conflict, one of the most inviting comparisons involves the strong similarities between the presidential leadership styles of George W. Bush and Lyndon Johnson. Though the two men were obviously *very* different temperamentally and ideologically, and followed quite different paths to the presidency, they had a great deal in common regarding their leadership styles and how they structured and utilized information and advice within their inner circles. Moreover, these shared style characteristics led to some very similar policy dynamics in both Iraq and Vietnam that are worth exploring in more depth as we consider the appropriateness of the Vietnam-Iraq analogy in later chapters.

To begin with, both lacked substantial foreign affairs experience prior to entering office, though Johnson had received some exposure during his Senate career. But even those surrounding Johnson acknowledged he had little true background or interest in foreign policy, and that his actual expertise (and passion) were reserved for domestic policy (McPherson 1972; Preston 2001). In contrast, Bush had virtually no exposure or interest in foreign affairs prior to entering the White House, and his lack of background was so substantial it required the now famous "tutoring" lessons by Condoleeza Rice during the 2000 campaign (Bruni 2002; Mann 2004; Kessler 2007). For both men, one consequence was that each would be *heavily dependent* upon expert policy advisers within their inner circles (Preston 2001). These experts played critical roles by "framing" (or explaining the nature of) the policy environments for both presidents, influencing their perceptions of the situation and the character of available policy options. While still making the "final decisions" on policy matters, both would fall into a pattern typical for less experienced leaders of delegating substantial amounts of policy formulation and implementation tasks to their subordinates (Preston and 't Hart 1999; Preston 2001; Woodward 2004, 2006). And each found themselves forced to deal with foreign policy crises early in their presidencies, forcing them away from their natural "comfort zones" in domestic policy. For Johnson, the deteriorating situation in Vietnam, the accepted doctrine of containment, and the stark political realities facing any Democrat showing weakness in standing up to communism during this time period forced his attention away from his Great Society programs toward Indochina. For Bush, the terror attacks of 9/11 fundamentally changed the "nature of the game" for his administration, permanently refocusing his attention toward the "war on terror" and a near constant emphasis on foreign policy.

Another similarity was a shared tendency to view the world in relatively simple, absolute, black-and-white terms—a characteristic typically resulting in leaders developing rather closed advisory systems not open to a broad range of information, advice, policy feedback, or gathering of opposing viewpoints (Preston 2001). Leaders viewing the world this way tend to be more ideological and less willing to be pragmatic and compromise on policy issues. They often rigidly adhere to policy lines they believe are correct and are slow to adapt to changing circumstances (which is hardly surprising given their low monitoring and information search in the surrounding policy environment). They usually surround themselves with a "comfort zone of true believers"—advisers and confidants who share similar perspectives on policy or the world more generally. As a result, it often takes tremendous policy reversals or deteriorating circumstances before they reflect upon or adapt to the situation, or before dissident policy views can obtain a hearing within their inner circles. Indeed, this description of Johnson and his advisory group's dynamics during the Vietnam War has long been described by those who have studied his presidency in depth (e.g., Berman 1982, 1989; Burke and Greenstein 1991; McNamara 1995; Preston and 't Hart 1999; Preston 2001). Moreover, similar patterns of inner-circle dynamics have been observed by those who have more recently focused on the Bush administration during the war in Iraq (e.g., Clarke 2004; Isikoff and Corn 2006; Draper 2007; Woodward 2006; McClellan 2008).

In both cases, the similarities in style across the two presidents resulted in shared weaknesses (or dysfunctions) within their advisory systems, leading to quite similar problems for each White House. And it is this parallel between presidential styles that provides one of the strongest echoes reverberating across the gulf between Vietnam and Iraq. But before delving into these two styles in more depth, it is necessary to understand these in terms of leadership style more generally—and how the personal characteristics of leaders tend to shape their decision making and use of advice.

UNDERSTANDING PRESIDENTIAL LEADERSHIP STYLE

Over the past several decades, an extensive literature on leadership and personality has developed within the field of political psychology, one which focuses not only on "measuring" the personal characteristics of leaders but on linking these to specific "types" of styles and patterns of decision making (Preston 2001; D. Mitchell 2005; Dyson 2006, 2009; Kille 2006; Schafer and Walker 2006). Moreover, a wide variety of techniques for assessing political leaders "at a distance" have been developed and applied to both U.S. and foreign leaders (e.g., Winter 1987; Smith et. al. 1992; Hermann 1999; Feldman and Valenty 2001; Post 2003; Schafer and Walker 2006). These sophisticated techniques are used not only in academia, but also extensively within government analytic communities for understanding and predicting the likely behavior of foreign leaders. These at-a-distance approaches generally focus on the personal characteristics of leaders (usually using content analysis of interviews, speeches, writings, etc.) that have been shown through extensive psychological research to have connections to how those leaders actually behave in real-life decision contexts (e.g., how they use information or deal with personal relationships or dissent, how much they insist on personal control). In fact, utilizing the Leader Trait Assessment (LTA) technique developed by Margaret Hermann, research by scholars has shown clear links between the scores on individual LTA measures (such as a leader's need for power, conceptual complexity, self-confidence, etc.) and specific types of leader styles, uses of advisers, and decision-making dynamics (Kaarbo and Hermann 1998; Preston and 't Hart 1999; Hermann et. al. 2001; Preston 2001, 2008; Taysi and Preston 2001; D. Mitchell 2005; Dyson 2006, 2009; Kille 2006).[1] Far from being purely journalistic exercises giving life to "impressions" about leaders (with little evidence behind them), these studies enjoy a lengthy track record of solid empirical support for the validity of the measures themselves and (based on archival studies) clear links between leader measures and specific behavioral correlates in the real world (Preston 2001; Kille 2006; Dyson 2009).

For this book, the style typology developed by Preston (2001) will be employed not only to demonstrate important similarities between the two leaders' styles but to also highlight areas of difference. Based on their LTA scores, both presidents will be assigned style "types" within the model. The typology lays out detailed expectations for each style type, predicting how leaders with differing styles will vary in their structuring and use of advisory systems. Moreover, these styles not only provide clues to the strengths a particular leader may have in the policy-making arena but highlight areas of potential weakness or vulnerability for that leader.

The first style dimension, the leader's "need for control and involvement in the policy-making process," involves a combination of a leader's "need for power" and their "prior experience in (or exposure to) the policy area" in question (see table 2.1 below).

As the psychological literature on power suggests, individuals with progressively higher power needs tend to be increasingly dominant and assertive in groups, insisting upon greater personal control over subordinates, the policy process, and decisions (Adorno et al. 1950; Donley and Winter 1970; Winter 1973, 1987; Winter and Stewart 1977; Etheredge 1978; Hermann 1980a, b; Fodor and Smith 1982; McClelland 1975; House 1990). These patterns have also been found in studies of modern U.S. presidents, where higher power

Table 2.1. Leader's Need for Control and Involvement in the Policy-Making Process

	Prior Experience in / Exposure to Policy Area	
	High	*Low*
High **Need for Control/** **Involvement in Policy Process (Need for Power)** **Low**	***Director*** • Decision making centralized within inner circle • Prefers direct control and involvement in policy process • Tendency to strongly advocate own policy views, frame issues, and set specific policy guidelines • Relies more on own policy judgments than those of subordinates in final decisions	***Magistrate*** • Decision making centralized within inner circle • Prefers direct control over decisions, but with limited need for direct involvement throughout policy process • Sets general policy guidelines, but *delegates* policy formulation and implementation to subordinates • Relies more on views of subordinates than own in final decisions
	Administrator • Decision making less centralized and more collegial • Requires less direct control over policy process and subordinates, leading to enhanced roles for staff • Actively advocates own policy views, frames issues, and sets specific policy guidelines • Relies more on own policy judgments than those of subordinates in final decisions	***Delegator*** • Decision making less centralized and more collegial • Requires little to no direct control or involvement in policy process • Enhanced roles for subordinates, along with substantial delegation of policy formulation and implementation • Tendency to rely on (and adopt) views of expert advisers in final policy decisions

Source: Adapted from Preston 2001: 16–17.

needs lead to more hierarchical advisory arrangements, more personal engagement and less willingness to delegate to subordinates, and the tendency to centralize decision making into tight inner circles (Preston 1996, 2001). The leader's prior experience in (or exposure to) the policy area drives patterns of leader interest or engagement in the policy-making process. It has long been observed in the U.S. presidential literature that leaders tend to be more personally engaged and active in policy areas they have personal interest or experience in (Barber 1972; Cronin 1980; George 1980; Neustadt 1990). Similarly, the expertise literature suggests that the more background experience possessed by an individual, the more heavily engaged they will be in policy making and the more assertive they will be in pushing their own judgments or views within decision groups (Shanteau 1992; Stewart and Stasser 1995; Wittenbaum et al. 1998; Tjosvold et al. 2001).

The second dimension of style, the leader's "sensitivity to context" (encompassing their general need for information in decision tasks and their awareness of constraints in the surrounding policy environment), involves a combination of the leader's "cognitive complexity" and their "prior experience in (or exposure to) the policy area" in question (see table 2.2 below). Complexity is not a measurement of IQ or intelligence, nor does it relate to political sophistication, but is merely a reflection of how much individuals tend to differentiate within their environments—ranging from those who see the world in very black-and-white, absolute terms to those who see the shades of grey (Hermann 1999, 2003; Preston 2001). Do you tend to see multiple perspectives to issues, or do you see things as either right or wrong, true or false (you're either with us or against us)? Scholars have long noted that as individual complexity increases, people show greater needs for information, prefer systematic over heuristic processing, and become more capable of dealing with complex decision environments—especially when these demand new or subtle distinctions (Suedfeld and Rank 1976; Suedfeld and Tetlock 1977; Hermann 1980a, 1980b; Tetlock 1985; Wallace and Suedfeld 1988; Vertzberger 1990). Individuals with higher complexity generally prefer broader collection of information, seek out greater diversity of perspectives and viewpoints among advisers, demonstrate more attentiveness to feedback from the environment, and employ analogies (for understanding and framing their policy environments) far less frequently than their less complex counterparts (Preston 2001; Taysi and Preston 2001; Preston and Hermann 2004; Dyson and Preston 2006; Preston 2008). Leaders' prior experience in (or exposure to) the policy area also impacts sensitivity to context, since individuals who have experience working a policy area (and who possess more detailed knowledge about it) are more likely to be attentive to information "about that particular issue," be sensitive to what information is relevant, and

Table 2.2. Leader's Sensitivity to Context

	Prior Experience in / Exposure to Policy Area	
	High	*Low*
High **Conceptual Complexity**	***Navigator*** • High general need/search for information from policy environment and for *broad-ranging advice* • High sensitivity to external constraints on policy making (Respecter) • Advisers selected based on expertise, competence, and diversity of viewpoints • Limited use of analogies and stereotypes to frame decision environment	***Observer*** • High general need/search for information from policy environment and for *broad-ranging advice* when making decisions • Sensitive to external constraints on policy making (Respecter) • Advisers selected based on expertise, competence, and diversity of viewpoints • Limited use of analogies and stereotypes to frame decision environment • Limited personal interest/experience leads to heavy dependence on expert advice
Low	***Sentinel*** • High personal interest in policy, but *low general need* for information and advice when making decisions • Relatively insensitive to external constraints on policy making (Challenger) • Advisers selected based on loyalty and ideological fit over expertise/competence. • Limited, narrow information search emphasizing advice/data deemed relevant for leader interests • Seeks to guide policy along path consistent with own personal principles, views, or past experience • Heavy use of analogies and stereotypes to frame decision environment	***Maverick*** • Low need for information and advice; extreme dependence on subordinate advice • Largely insensitive to external constraints on policy making (Challenger) • Advisers selected based on loyalty and ideological fit over expertise/competence • Decisions driven by own idiosyncratic policy views, ideology, and principles • Heavy use of analogies and stereotypes to frame decision environment

Source: Adapted from Preston 2001: 22–23.

have greater comfort levels for involvement in policy making (Khong 1992; Levy 1994; Preston 2001). Those sensitive to context also tend to "respect" constraints existing in their policy environments and attend to situations more intently in looking for openings where the "environment might allow restructuring" (Greenstein 1969). Their antennae are "up" and actively monitoring the policy environment, looking for the right moment. On the other hand, those less sensitive to context tend to challenge constraints—either because they are not adequately perceived to be constraints (due to their more closed information and advisory systems) or because their more absolute views of the political world (whether based on religion or ideology) construct "alternative versions" of reality that replace the existing one. As a result, it takes a far more negative feedback to break through in order to capture their attention and force changes in behavior—whereas sensitive "respecters" are quick to change course or modify policies based on such feedback (Preston 2008).

Individuals differ in terms of how much they tend to focus on task accomplishment—that is, achieving their goals as opposed to maintaining personal relationships with others (Hermann 1980a, 1999). This is known as the task/interpersonal orientation (Cottam et al. 2010). In terms of sensitivity to context, those high in task needs place greater emphasis on feedback from the environment that helps them achieve their policy goals or effectively implement policy (while placing far less concern on maintaining follower morale, worrying about constituencies, etc.). In contrast, those more interpersonally oriented are far more sensitive to information and feedback that helps them maintain such important personal relationships.

These two main dimensions of leadership style (need for control and involvement in the policy process and sensitivity to context) combine to provide a more nuanced view of how presidents will structure and utilize their advisory arrangements within inner circles (Preston 2001). But more importantly, they help us begin the task of comparing the leadership styles of George W. Bush and Lyndon Johnson by laying out areas where we would expect to find similarities between the two men, and where there should be differences. And clearly, there were substantial ones between the two Texans, with Johnson's incredible levels of personal self-confidence and need for control over his policy environment standing in stark contrast to Bush's less assertive personality.[2] On the other hand, both shared a lower complexity and more absolute view of the world, along with a lack of prior experience in the foreign policy arena. Given these characteristics, George W. Bush would be expected to manifest the *Delegator-Maverick* style in foreign policy matters, while Johnson would show a *Magistrate-Maverick* style (Preston 2001). Moreover, given his highly delegative style, it would be expected that Bush's inner circle and advisory arrangements would be highly influenced by the style of his key adviser, Vice President Dick Cheney, who essentially ran the White House transition and played the leading role in staffing positions. Unlike his less engaged, more delegating boss, Cheney had a *Director-Sentinel* leadership style (high power, task, and prior policy experience, but lower complexity) that would be expected to create tighter hierarchies and inner circles than Bush's style. Such a dominant role by advisers would not be seen in the Johnson White House, where LBJ insisted upon direct, personal involvement and control over policy, while sharing Bush's dependence on expert advisers.

THE LEADERSHIP STYLE OF LYNDON JOHNSON—
THE *MAGISTRATE-MAVERICK*

In reflecting on the leadership style of Lyndon Johnson, one of the truly signature elements has to be his immense self-confidence and need for personal control over his surrounding political environment. He was a dynamo, a "force of nature" in the political arena, an individual who felt that he could almost, through sheer personal willpower, convince anyone to move in his desired policy direction. It is a description that all who experienced the famed "Johnson Treatment"—LBJ's preferred one-on-one, "up close and personal" style of interaction in which he invaded one's personal space while using the entire range of emotions, humor, and threats to sway his victim to his position—would attest (McPherson 1972; Kearns 1976; Califano 1991; Clifford 1991). And this personal aura of dominance was not lost upon subordinates around Johnson, who would later recount the nature of the "presence" he cast about himself. His former special counsel Harry McPherson fondly recalled Johnson as "a hell of a leader," a "hell of a man," who was "a bull in a field full of heifers!" (Preston 2001: 137). This self-confidence was magnified in the domestic policy arena, where Johnson's true policy expertise and personal interests lay, but even in foreign affairs, where his touch was less sure and his dependence upon expert advisers more profound, it remained. As Paul Warnke later observed:

> Lyndon Johnson was a man of immense self-confidence . . . in a way that Carter or Clinton couldn't begin to approach. When Carter walked into a room, you didn't say, *"There is the, by God, President of these United States!!!"* With Johnson, you had no hesitation about that! . . . It was a natural confidence. And he had a lot of confidence in his foreign policy advisers. And I think that part of this was that he thought that John Kennedy was a foreign policy expert. And he kept President Kennedy's foreign policy team. And he thought that they were in total command of the situation. And he found it very, very difficult to figure that they may have been wrong. (Preston 2001: 145; emphasis Warnke)

Herein lies the problem for leaders who lack policy background or expertise themselves (like Johnson or Bush)—they depend upon foreign policy advisers to help them understand that realm and shape policy options to deal with it, but simultaneously lack the personal expertise to judge the quality of the advice or policy recommendations they receive. This weakness can sometimes be compensated for by leaders who have a high sensitivity to context (who gather lots of information and divergent advice from many different sources through open advisory arrangements). But for less sensitive leaders, the dependence upon experts becomes even more pervasive given their limited information search and the narrower range of advice gathered by the closed, insular advisory arrangements they favor. In table 2.3 below, the characteristics expected of Johnson's advisory system given his *Magistrate-Maverick* style are laid out.

These inner-circle dynamics, driven by Johnson's *Magistrate-Maverick* style, were seen throughout his presidency and certainly impacted the ways in which Vietnam policy was discussed and formulated (Preston and 't Hart 1999; Preston 2001). As expected for a leader with this style, Johnson preferred formal, hierarchical arrangements that centralized decision making into a small inner circle ensuring his own decision authority and personal control over policy—which during his senate majority leader days had led fellow senators to refer to him as a "dictator" (McPherson 1972; Preston 2001). Even in foreign policy, where he lacked expertise and was forced to rely on expert advisers, Johnson still insisted on personal control. Robert McNamara, his former defense secretary, recalled LBJ's often "autocratic style" in foreign affairs, while former secretary of state Dean Rusk observed that as far as Vietnam was concerned, Johnson was "his own desk officer," with "every detail of the Vietnam matter" being "a matter of information to the President" (Preston 2001: 139). Indeed, Joseph Califano (1991: 25–26) later noted that Johnson "wanted to control everything" and "his greatest outbursts of anger were triggered by people or situations that escaped his control." And as Paul Nitze observed (1989: 261), Johnson not only demanded "absolute loyalty" from his aides but "felt a need to wholly dominate those around him."

This need for control influenced how Johnson tended to use advisers and the settings where he made decisions on policy. Given his *Magistrate* style, it is unsurprising Vietnam policy making took place largely within the famous "Tuesday Lunch" group of close, loyal inner-circle advisers (consisting

Table 2.3.   The *Magistrate-Maverick* Foreign Policy Leadership Style of Lyndon Johnson

Magistrate	*Maverick*
• Decision making centralized within inner circle	• Low need for information and advice; extreme dependence on subordinate advice.
• Prefers direct control over decisions, but with limited need for direct involvement throughout policy process	• Largely insensitive to external constraints on policy making (Challenger)
• Sets general policy guidelines, but *delegates* policy formulation and implementation to subordinates	• Advisers selected based on loyalty and ideological fit over expertise/competence
• Relies more on views of subordinates than own in final decisions	• Decisions driven by own idiosyncratic policy views, ideology, and principles
	• Heavy use of analogies and stereotypes to frame decision environment

mainly of Rusk, McNamara, NSC Adviser McGeorge Bundy, and sometimes
the chairman of the Joint Chiefs of Staff [JCS] and the director of the CIA),
rather than in much larger National Security Council (NSC) settings. Indeed,
LBJ saw the Tuesday Lunch format as having the advantage of maintaining
secrecy, of being a loyal group that "never leaked a single note" (Kearns
1976: 319–20).

Coupled with this strong need for control over policy was Johnson's more
Maverick style of lower sensitivity to context, which further reduced the
sweep of his advisory system and the type of feedback and advice it would
pick up from the political environment. While Johnson was an immensely
intelligent man, he tended to see the world in fairly absolute terms, and
though gathering tremendous amounts of information, he was very selective
in the types of information he sought out (Preston 2001). It was not the broad
gathering of information, of pros and cons, of diverse viewpoints, that more
sensitive leaders (like Kennedy or Eisenhower) might seek out, but a more focused search primarily for information, feedback, and advice that would help
him accomplish whatever task he had set his mind on (Preston 2001). One
of the best illustrations of this tendency is a story told by McPherson (1972:
172–73), who was working as a Senate staffer for LBJ during the period he
was considering running against Kennedy for the presidential nomination in
1959:

> One afternoon on the Senate floor, I sat at Johnson's desk, looking for a memo-
> randum among the roll-call slips and other debris of a week's work. I found a
> thick hardbound document labeled "Indiana." I opened it and read a detailed
> analysis of Indiana politics, with comments on important political figures, labor
> leaders, citizen's groups, and so on. . . . Obviously, Kennedy had left the docu-
> ment behind by mistake. For a moment, I considered taking it to Johnson . . .
> so that he might see how sophisticated and thorough the Kennedy campaign
> was and emulate it. But . . . Johnson would never launch such an extensive
> intelligence operation. His world was embodied in roll-call slips, the memos to
> senators, the reminders to speak to chairmen about bills in their committees. I
> called a page and sent "Indiana" back to Senator Kennedy.

When this story was later brought up during an interview, McPherson
answered my query with a response illustrating quite vividly the desire by
Johnson for detailed information, but only that which would assist him in
achieving a policy goal:

> Take the electoral thing. . . . If that had been "Texas," Johnson, he would have
> wanted *five books* like the one I found!!! One on the politics, and one on the
> potential supports, and one on the breakdown on voters in different areas, and

one on what issues were important to who! But, he really had a very different interest in things like that than Kennedy. He wanted to know very specific information about things he was trying to accomplish, like, who needed what in the Senate if he wanted to pass an appropriations bill, or something like that. But, he didn't want some broad paper on how the whole policy worked or broad, brush-stroke stuff. (Preston 2001: 149; emphasis McPherson)

Thus, Johnson's information search was typically highly selective, focused on gathering things that would be instrumental in achieving policy objectives or goals, and gathered using a fairly closed advisory system favoring loyal advisors who agreed with his policy views. Those outside of the Tuesday Lunch inner circle, and especially those critical of Vietnam policy, were shut out of policy deliberations by Johnson (McPherson 1972; Berman 1982, 1989; Nitze 1989; McNamara 1995; Preston 2001). And while he would sometimes reach out for advice from an "informal network" outside of the White House inner circle, the individuals involved (Clark Clifford, Abe Fortas, etc.) were selected based on both their perceived loyalty to him and their support of his policies (Clifford 1969: 6). Thus, the access of truly divergent or critical views into Johnson's inner circle was highly constrained. Instead, the focus was on gathering supportive information, material assisting in accomplishing policy tasks or helping to sell things politically. Advisers who were critical of Vietnam policy or expressed reservations (like Hubert Humphrey, Bill Moyers, McPherson, Nitze, or McNamara) suddenly found themselves in Johnson's "dog house" and were "uninvited" to policy meetings dealing with Vietnam (McPherson 1972; Preston 2001). Indeed, upon returning from a trip to Vietnam in 1967, and seeking to avoid a renewed trip to Johnson's dog house, McPherson wrote a memo critical of current policy, but which "at the end put in a couple of sentences again stating that I supported what we were trying to do in Vietnam and that it was really necessary" (Preston 2001: 163). Noting that Johnson often saw "people's doubts about the war as disloyalty," McPherson observed that if he hadn't added those few supportive sentences at the end, the President wouldn't have accepted the report and he'd have just gotten silence (Preston 2001: 163).

Clearly, as we look back at Johnson's Vietnam decision making, the elements discussed in this chapter so far (i.e., his intense need for personal control, the tight inner circle of like-minded and loyal advisers, the tendency to view dissent as disloyalty, the closed advisory system and highly selective information search) have long been remarked upon by Johnson scholars as playing a critical role in events (Berman 1982, 1989; Burke and Greenstein 1991; Preston 2001). Moreover, former Johnson advisers themselves have also emphasized many of these same style elements as playing important roles in how the decisions and policies on Vietnam were made—and why the administration found itself floundering during that long, protracted conflict (McPherson 1972; Nitze 1989; Clifford 1991; McNamara 1995).

THE LEADERSHIP STYLE OF GEORGE W. BUSH:
THE REAL MAN VS. THE CARICATURE

As we move to a discussion of George W. Bush, and compare his style to Johnson's, we must first address a significant problem. One of the biggest challenges for scholars studying the Bush presidency is separating the extreme caricatures of the man (which became a standard for comedians and late-night talk show hosts alike during his time in the White House) from his actual persona, which had *both* positive and negative attributes. The real Bush was genuinely well liked by most of his staff, evidenced a great deal of charm on an interpersonal level, was seen as very loyal to those around him, was strongly driven to do what he "believed was right" on policy, and though not intellectually brilliant, was usually described by colleagues as being far more "street smart" than his detractors often suggested.[3] As former White House press secretary Scott McClellan (2008: xii) observed, "Bush is self-confident, quick-witted, down-to-earth, and stubborn, as leaders sometimes need to be. His manner is authentic, his beliefs sincere." At the same time, however, it is also true that Bush became the most deeply unpopular president in modern American history according to public opinion polls and presided over an administration marked by an exceptionally high number of controversies (over the Iraq War, treatment of detainees, torture, the response to Hurricane Katrina, etc.) and scandals (Abu Graib, the outing of Valerie Plame, the political firing of federal attorneys, the manipulation and misuse of intelligence prior to the Iraq War, etc.). There have been many books written that have essentially portrayed Bush as a "figurehead" or "puppet" of neocons, like Karl Rove, or others (Ivins and Dubose 2000; E. Mitchell 2000; Moore and Slater 2003), with many focusing on magnifying this portrait to make scathing political attacks (Franken 2003, 2005). In many respects, this caricature of Bush, like Will Farrell's comic portrayal of the president on *Saturday Night Live*, has largely come to represent for many what the former president was like.

Unfortunately, defenders of the Bush administration, in response, often routinely fall into the trap of dismissing any criticisms of his presidency as biased (despite obvious shortcomings any dispassionate analyst would acknowledge), which is just as distorting as critics falling into the trap of "demonizing" Bush and his advisers far beyond what the evidence supports. Indeed, defenders tend to paint *extremely* rosy portraits of the president's leadership style, his decisiveness and impeccable decision making, and downplay any powerful role for the advisers themselves around him (Cheney, Rumsfeld, Rice, or the neocons) in shaping policy (Greenstein 2002, 2003; Burke 2004; Hughes 2004; Moens 2004; Renshon 2006). These types of interpretations of Bush were, of course, quite prominent early on in his administration—before subsequent patterns became more apparent that contradicted these earlier impressions.

For example, Renshon (2006: 107–8) argues the Iraq War was essentially "leader-driven"—with Bush not being guided by neocon advisers but instead playing the principle role in the decision making. While acknowledging Bush's stark worldview, his resilience to criticism from others, and his propensity for ambitious, high-risk strategies, Renshon generally portrays these qualities as strengths rather than weaknesses. As a result, Renshon quickly falls into the trap of equating the overall policy "vision" or approach being espoused by the administration as representing the true "inner Bush," whereas in reality it represents only an amalgam of interactions between many interested parties, inner-circle advisers, and the president. It is probably true that this overall policy approach generally matches Bush's own personal views—he is not a puppet. But this interpretation ignores the role interactions *between* Bush and his advisers played in shaping his overall policy. And in the view of many who have worked in the administration, Bush's own very general ideological views served only as a basic foundation upon which expert advisers later constructed distinctive policy approaches.

Similarly, Moens (2004) attempts to give Bush himself (and his disciplined management style) primary credit for organizing the efficiency of the 2000 White House transition, despite the fact it was Vice President Cheney who ran the transition! Indeed, Moens goes to rather extreme lengths in minimizing the importance of Cheney, Rumsfeld, Rice, and others in the Bush White House and, quite unconvincingly, attempts to paint a portrait purely consistent with the "spin" originating from the administration itself and partisan allies—one of Bush leading the way, making all the decisions, being completely in command of all the facts and policy nuances, bringing his advisers along with him through his masterful leadership, and soon—an image largely divorced from the reality of most subsequent reporting of his inner circle's actual operations.

Obviously, a common "theme" across many of these competing views involves either the "political spin" accompanying the *blame-avoidance strategies* of Republicans (who seek to minimize any negative assessment of the magnitude of the policy reversals, shortcomings, or scandals during the Bush years, for obvious reasons) or the *blame-assignment strategies* of Democrats (seeking to magnify the administration's shortcomings and pin these to the

GOP more generally). Within the heavily shelled no-man's-land between these warring trenches, it is difficult for any research to avoid labeling. The bottom line for scholars is simply this: *any* analysis of the Bush administration's policy making will be controversial due to this context, as will any treatment of Bush's personality and leadership style. And given what happened during the administration's tenure in office, objective analyses of the Bush presidency are, realistically, often going to be quite critical of either policy outcomes or the process by which decisions were made—a reality that makes any of them vulnerable to the blame-avoidance strategy of "discrediting the source" of the criticism by detractors.

However, for us to learn from history and better understand the dynamics of presidential decision making, it is critical we resist this impulse. This book deals with a highly controversial policy case and seeks to understand not only how Bush's leadership played a role in shaping his advisory system and the ways that it functioned during Iraq decision making, but also the types of blame-avoidance strategies adopted to deal with policy reverses. It makes an effort to contrast this against the experience of a previous president, LBJ in Vietnam, in order not only to give a richer understanding of these elements but to critique the applicability of the Vietnam analogy to Iraq (which often plays a leading role in blame-assignment strategies used by Bush opponents). That this volume's analysis of Bush's handling of Iraq decision making is often quite critical is really secondary to the main objective of seeking to improve our understanding of presidential decision making and leadership and the dynamics of blame avoidance.

THE LEADERSHIP STYLE OF GEORGE W. BUSH—
THE *DELEGATOR-MAVERICK*

In looking at the personal characteristics of George W. Bush, it is useful to note that, like Johnson, Bush saw the world in absolute, black-and-white terms and had hardly any prior experience or exposure to foreign affairs before entering the White House. In this, one can see that both Bush and Johnson share a *Maverick* style (see table 2.4 below) as far as their sensitivity to context. On the other hand, Johnson and Bush differ quite markedly regarding their needs for personal control and involvement in the policy process. While Johnson was extremely high in his personal need for power and task accomplishment, Bush was more interpersonally oriented (placing far more emphasis on maintaining personal relationships) and was much lower in his need for control. As a result, Bush falls into the *Delegator* category (see table 2.4 below), heightening the importance of key, influential advisers around him in policy making.

Table 2.4. The *Delegator-Maverick* Foreign Policy Leadership Style of George W. Bush

Delegator	*Maverick*
• Decision making less centralized and more collegial	• Low need for information and advice; extreme dependence on subordinate advice
• Requires little to no direct control or involvement in policy process	• Largely insensitive to external constraints on policy making (Challenger)
• Enhanced roles for subordinates, along with substantial delegation of policy formulation and implementation	• Advisers selected based on loyalty and ideological fit over expertise/competence
• Tendency to rely on (and adopt) views of expert advisers in final policy decisions	• Decisions driven by own idiosyncratic policy views, ideology, and principles
	• Heavy use of analogies and stereotypes to frame decision environment

This becomes critically important as we consider the amalgam of Bush's quite hierarchical, centralized advisory structures existing alongside his highly delegative style—a setup that at first glance would seem out of place. However, for leaders requiring less personal policy engagement, who lack their own policy expertise, it is the *nature* of their delegation to subordinates that plays the critical role in shaping their subsequent inner-circle structures. For Bush, the trusted adviser to whom he delegated much of the transition-related organization and staffing of the White House was Cheney, his eventual vice president. Unlike Bush, Cheney's personal style was very control-oriented, and he developed perhaps the most powerful vice presidential staff organization in history to assert his control over policy. Cheney falls into the *Director-Sentinel* style of leadership—one emphasizing high control and engagement along with moderate to low sensitivity to context.

For the *Delegator-Maverick* Bush, the selection of a more hands-on, directive vice president was quite complementary to his style, allowing him to focus more on the personal side of the presidency (while Cheney focused more on the task side). As a result, Cheney (along with other subordinates) were allowed to play quite powerful policy-making roles in the administration, and given their loyalty and ideological fit with Bush, served to provide policy substance (or flesh) to the President's own preexisting ideological policy views. They would not push Bush in different policy directions than he was already predisposed to agree with, since they shared his deeply conservative perspectives. And they certainly didn't "control" him as detractors often suggest. However, they served to "frame" (or explain) the policy environment for him and largely formulated the "types" of policy choices the President would choose from during the decision process. As will be seen during our discussion of Iraq policy making, this had the consequence of limiting dissenting policy views and isolating the White House within a closed advisory system housing an insular inner circle at the top. It would encourage subordinates, who had been delegated substantial freedom of action, to compete with one another for influence with the President over policy (e.g., the vice president's office or Rumsfeld's Department of Defense competing with Powell's State Department over Iraq policy). Given Bush's style and the inner-circle advisers he selected, the policy-making dynamics seen within his administration over Iraq (and many other areas) were quite consistent with what would have been predicted (Preston and Hermann 2004; Preston 2008).

THE IMPORTANCE OF LOYALTY IN THE BUSH INNER CIRCLE

One quality that certainly played a major role in defining Bush's interpersonal style was the heavy emphasis placed by the president upon loyalty—both in the expectation that staff would be unfailingly loyal to him and in his own belief that he should reward that loyalty with loyalty in return. It was a tendency the younger Bush shared with his father; it was a Bush family standard (Dowd and Friedman 1990; Moens 2004; Draper 2007). It represented a kind of "social contract" for Bush, a two-way street of responsibilities between those he worked closely with and himself. As even the most ardent supporters of the administration acknowledge, within the president's inner circle, loyalty and absolute fidelity to White House policy were an unquestioned component (Burke 2004; Moens 2004). Indeed, Moens (2004: 2) observed that Bush not only thought and acted in terms of "values," but viewed all politics as "personal," with loyalty being the essential "glue" between him and his inner-circle advisers.

While laudable on a personal level, the downside of such an emphasis on loyalty is that leaders tend (as a result) to surround themselves with political or policy "doppelgangers" who never provide healthy criticism or challenges to policy (or the leader). The higher the degree to which loyalty is emphasized by leaders, the more likely they are to become insulated inside a phalanx of supporters and detached from a more healthy process, whereby negative (and potentially useful) feedback might reach the inner circle. It has been noted that many of the advisers surrounding Bush, even if they did influence the "specifics" of policy, did not markedly differ from the president's own predispositions (in terms of ideology, worldview, etc.). What they generally tended to add was flesh to the skeleton, not create the skeleton itself—with Rove, for example, being described by Heclo (2003: 34) as providing experience and merely "complementing" Bush's own political mind. Among leaders seeking the warm cocoon of loyalty within their inner circles, one often also sees a lower comfort zone for any dissent that does occur. As Gellman (2008: 79) observed, "Bush generally hated it when advisers disagreed, demanding that they get their acts together. . . . Bush valued not only consensus, but finality," which meant that once he had made up his mind, he expected all controversy to cease, so "getting to him at just the right time" was "extremely important."

An emphasis on loyalty also results in leaders often selecting subordinates for roles based more on that dimension than upon their competence, expertise, or prior experience dealing with a given issue or policy area. This is often coupled with a slow response to making personnel changes, an ineffective blame-avoidance response when loyal, yet unqualified subordinates become political liabilities due to their ineffective or incompetent handling of policy problems. For Bush, this resulted in hanging on to Secretary of Defense Rumsfeld long after his mishandling of the Iraq War had become a major political liability in 2006, provoking even former senior military leaders to publicly criticize him. It also led Bush to stand firmly behind former FEMA director Michael Brown during the Hurricane Katrina response and, much to his detriment, express publicly the belief that "Brownie" had done "a heck of a job"—despite obvious evidence to the contrary (Preston 2008). Indeed, as one exasperated senior administration official observed, "the president thinks cutting and running on his friends shows weakness," even though politically it would have been the smart move to make (Baker 2007).

This emphasis on loyalty also contributed to the degree to which the administration was unusually (even extraordinarily) "tight" with regard to "staying on message" and limiting its leaks to the press—although the White House *was* very adept at *intentionally* leaking information for policy-advocacy or blame-avoidance purposes (as will be seen in later chapters). Of course, Bush's own personal preference for emphasizing loyalty was reinforced by advice he received prior to taking office—with the Heritage Foundation warning him in 2001, for example, to "make appointment decisions based on loyalty first and expertise second."[4] Certainly, the more ideological the leader, the more likely they will want to surround themselves with loyal "true believers," and the new administration would be one of the more ideologically driven in modern times (Preston 2001; Draper 2007). Moreover, Bush's own preferences for loyalty and keeping leaks under control was reinforced by the experiences of both Cheney and Rumsfeld during their years in the Nixon and Ford administrations, where both participated in leaks of information to undercut rivals, while observing the damage such leaking could do to an administration (Cockburn 2007). For all of these reasons, as Thomas and Wolffe (2005: 36) drolly observe, like Robert De Niro's ex CIA officer in *Meet the Parents*, Bush had a "very small circle of trust." McClellan (2008: 140) later recalled that this applied to Bush's interactions abroad as well, since "there was nothing that angered the president more than a world leader who violated private assurances he made . . . if Bush gave his word to a foreign leader, that leader could take it to the bank—and Bush expected the same in return."

Unfortunately, equating "conformity with existing policy" with loyalty on the part of advisers has the dampening effect of allowing dissenting advice over policy to be dismissed by the broader group without much reflection. This dynamic took shape within both the Bush and Johnson inner circles. As former assistant secretary of state Richard Armitage later acknowledged during an interview regarding how often dissent was seen as disloyalty,

> That was pretty prevalent. Powell and I felt this was the height *of loyalty*! We weren't disagreeing. We knew what he wanted to do! But, if you're gonna do X, and I don't think X (for instance the war in Iraq) was immoral. We had all those UN resolutions with us saying Saddam Hussein was a terrible guy. So I didn't feel this was a matter of principle. For me, I want it done a different way. And we raised issues, all along the way! Issues to be resolved before we did it. Not issues to be used as a roadblock. But they were misinterpreted as roadblocks.[5]

In an echo of Vietnam inner-circle dynamics that occurred during the Johnson administration, different bureaucratic actors or advisers who disagreed with Bush and his inner circle's views on Iraq were not only dismissed but viewed with hostility as opponents. As Armitage noted, "Tenet, the CIA, and the State Department were the hated enemies of the White House. They hated us! Because sometimes the intelligence didn't comport with whatever the bullshit the White House wanted to come up with. Or we would raise issues. So we were both seen, for different reasons, as not being on the team."[6] When it was observed that people might use the phrase *cherry-picking of information* to describe that kind of dynamic, Armitage replied: "That's fair. Yeah. That's fair. By the way, I'm thrilled they dropped us out of meetings! It speaks very well of us. For instance, on detainees and abuse, water-boarding. We were not even told there were meetings. Why? Because we raised objections."[7]

THE NEED FOR CONTROL AND
INVOLVEMENT IN THE POLICY PROCESS

Bush reveled in seeing himself as "The Decider" who made all the tough, final policy decisions, almost channeling his own, inner Harry Truman to model his leadership image upon (Woodward 2002). And it is certainly true that Bush often (though not always) made the final call on policy matters within his inner circle, much as Truman made the final decisions after staff brought him questions to be decided (Preston 1997, 2001). But such "deciding" does not necessarily require active presidential engagement in the policy-making process preceding the decision point (where policy formulation and the fashioning of options take place), nor does it preclude a heavy reliance on the leader's part upon expert advisers to frame the policy environment and provide options to decide amongst. Certainly in the case of Truman, these earlier elements were delegated to subordinates (like Secretary of State Dean Acheson), who would fashion policy and lay out the options for the president to decide on—while still preserving his final "yea" or "nay" (Preston 1997, 2001). This was similarly the case with Bush, who retained the final decision authority but delegated much of the policy formulation tasks to his tight inner circle of advisers. As McClellan (2008: 154) observed, the President "liked to compartmentalize information within the White House. There were regular meetings between the president and the vice president, or Andy Card or Karl Rove, that were strictly private." Indeed, in terms of the "tightness" of Bush's inner circle, Thomas and Wolffe (2005: 33) remarked that he "may be the most isolated president in modern history, at least since the late-stage Richard Nixon." But unlike Nixon, who insisted on retaining a great deal of personal control over policy, Bush tended to delegate. And this would have a significant effect on policy making, as Powell's former chief of staff, Lawrence Wilkerson, later observed during an interview:

Here's the point where I think he really failed, in a major sense! Not only was he a president who *believed* in being aloof from the details, being the "great decision maker" as he himself has said. The guy who makes the big ones. And then leaves them alone for execution. Not only was that his nature . . . he was also lazy in my view. Intellectually, and what I would call execution-wise. And he'd say, "My decision's made! It's sacrosanct!" A certain amount of hubris and arrogance associated with this too. "No one would *dare* not carry out my decision the way I have conceived that decision!" But he may not have even articulated the way he conceived of that decision. He just made the decision. You know? And then the bureaucracy went out and did what it damned well pleased, usually with its own predispositions and its own biases, and so forth. And the president had no *attentiveness* to that execution.[8]

And just as would sometimes happen during the Truman administration, where bureau-political competition between lower-level subordinates would determine how policy decisions were implemented (Preston 1997), this would also happen with the delegative style of Bush. As Wilkerson observed:

A great case in point was when the brouhaha occurred over who made the decision to disband the Iraqi Army down to the lowest private. Well, the president had made the decision just a week or two earlier that the Iraqi Army would not be disbanded any further than battalion—about six to nine hundred men—those units would be kept intact. The brigade commanders, the division commanders, and their staffs maybe will go away, but the battalions and their people would stay, and they would form a new Iraqi Army. That's the decision the president made! Well, a couple of weeks later, without telling anybody, Jerry Bremer issues an order disbanding the Iraqi Army down to the lowest private. No one *knew* who made that decision! And the president *himself*, as far as I know, has made the same statement! I listened to him one day in an interview, and I think what I heard him say was, "'I don't know who changed that decision.'"[9]

Indeed, as Packer (2006: 146) noted, even the selection of Bremer to replace Garner in Iraq in the first place did not come from the president, but as Bush himself noted, "I didn't choose him. . . . Rumsfeld chose him." Of course, such statements suggesting the president was out of the loop on such key decisions could also be part of a blame-avoidance strategy. In accepting this possibility, Wilkerson acknowledges what may have happened:

The decision was made by the president, in full view of the other principals: secretary of state, secretary of defense, and others. The vice president went back into the Oval Office, talked the president out of it, went back and told secretary of defense, who told Feith, who told Bremer. And so it was done. That gave the president plausible deniability, and the vice president, of course, is hidden in his "secret, undisclosed location." And so you had it done, and the president was complicit, but no one knows. And even the president now is putting out the story that, you know, *he* didn't even know that his decision was reversed.[10]

While possible, it's hard to state with certainty this was, in fact, a use of the blame-avoidance tactic of "plausible deniability" by Bush. Instead, off-the-record descriptions of the president by many former White House officials, and other colleagues who knew him well, tend to provide more support for an explanation based on his general lack of interest in details and delegation to subordinates. Indeed, former assistant secretary of state Armitage recalls that Bush's style was highly delegative and not focused on policy details:

I'll give you a couple of examples. . . . The president wanted to get out of the ABM Treaty. We wanted the Treaty of Moscow. Powell said, "I can get ya this. I can do this! Just keep the animals off my back basically." And the president, "okay." But he wasn't interested in the details, he was interested in the result, and we got it. We get to war planning and what-not, the president would always say to the generals, whoever they were, "You get what you need? You have what you need?" And they'd say, "yes" or "I need this." Generally, they'd say, "yes sir!" because Mr. Rumsfeld had browbeat them so much. But he wasn't interested in the, what's it gonna be used for, etc. Part of it, I think, was what he's read about Vietnam. That Vietnam was run from the president's desk and all that, and you let the generals fight the war. It's gotta be both. The president commits young men and women to battle and then he wants to be sure that he's fighting in the best possible way. And Mr. Bush, in my view, took a very, too much hands-off view. But it was a reaction to what he sees during Vietnam as too much interference by the president. So no, he wasn't steeped in details.[11]

The resulting combination of a president who saw loyalty as the first and foremost quality in advisers and who wanted to be a decisive "decider," while tending to delegate substantially to subordinates, is what characterized the Bush *need for control or involvement in the policy process*. While questioning whether Bush's national security adviser, Condoleezza Rice, really did an adequate job of calibrating for the president's "headstrong style of leadership" or "appreciate the need to keep his beliefs in proper check," McClellan (2008: 128) observes:

Overall, Bush's foreign policy advisers played right into his thinking, doing little to question it or to cause him to pause long enough to fully consider the consequences before moving forward. And once Bush set a course of action, it was rarely questioned. That is what Bush expected and made known to his top advisers . . . there would be no hand-wringing, no second-guessing of the policy once it was decided and set in motion.

But how do we reconcile the view of Bush as "The Decider" versus the image of him as a leader heavily influenced (or dominated) by the views of his inner-circle advisers—two competing images around which much of the literature on his presidency revolves? Essentially, it could be argued that these debates between these two poles miss the fundamental point. Bush could be "in charge" of the final decisions and have similar worldviews to his inner-circle advisers, yet still be dependent upon their judgment and expertise in formulating policy approaches and deciding upon courses of action. This is the difference between the caricature of a "puppet" (which no doubt was incorrect regarding Bush) and the more accurate depiction of a leader lacking experience in substantive policy areas who delegated to expert advisers and was dependent upon their guidance during the policy-making process. In this, Bush was hardly dissimilar from Bill Clinton, Johnson, or Truman in the foreign policy realm—who leaned heavily upon their foreign policy experts (Preston 2001).

Indeed, Bush entered the White House as, arguably, the least experienced or knowledgeable about foreign affairs of any modern American president! Not only had he not traveled abroad to any significant degree (lacking even a passport until only a few years prior to his presidential run); he possessed no real prior experience or knowledge of foreign policy matters. This lack of knowledge required a "crash course" under the tutelage of Rice during the campaign to compensate for this obvious weakness during the debates and in speaking with reporters. Soon the campaign focused on emphasizing how Bush would surround himself with experienced policy experts if elected, men like Cheney, who had served in many capacities in Washington. Experienced advisers like Rice, Powell, Rumsfeld, and others were described as individuals likely to play key roles in the new administration—roles that would compensate for the public's concerns about Bush's own relative inexperience. As Wilkerson observed, this emphasis on surrounding Bush with experienced advisers was critical, because "it allowed everybody to believe that this Sarah Palin–like president—because, let's face it, that's what he was—was going to be protected by this national-security elite, tested in the cauldrons of fire."[12]

As would be expected for an inexperienced leader, Bush delegated substantial authority to subordinates and loyal inner-circle policy experts. During foreign policy meetings, Bush "often deferred to Cheney" on issues (Draper 2007: 114), a pattern he often repeated even in domestic affairs (where he also had limited substantive experience)—with former treasury secretary Paul O'Neill recalling that Bush "seemed to be limited in his knowledge of most domestic issues" (Suskind 2004: 88). Indeed, for O'Neill, the problem was

> this President's lack of inquisitiveness or pertinent experience . . . meant he didn't know or really care about the position of the U.S. government. It wasn't just a matter of doing the opposite of whatever Clinton had done, which was a prevalent theme throughout the administration. This President was starting from scratch on most issues and relying on ideologues. . . . Not an honest broker in sight. (Suskind 2004: 126)

For O'Neill, it was clear Bush often ceded significant authority over policy to others and was "signing on to strong ideological positions that had not been fully thought through. But, of course, that's the nature of ideology. Thinking it through is the last thing an ideologue wants to do" (Suskind 2004: 127). As McClellan (2008: 85) observed, because the president lacked "a deep background in foreign policy, Bush counted on a team of foreign policy heavyweights with diverse expertise to help him formulate policy based on his guiding principles, such as freedom, a strong military, and free trade." Unfortunately, having a team of heavyweights with diverse expertise only helps to compensate for closed advisory systems if they also possess diverse viewpoints and perspectives. And this the Bush inner circle lacked, with the exception of Powell, who generally was ignored and whose influence was minimal when compared to core advisers like Cheney, Rumsfeld, and Rice.[13]

BUSH'S SENSITIVITY TO CONTEXT AND
USE OF INFORMATION

The *Maverick* style of Bush, with his low sensitivity to context and limited, highly selective information search, is pretty well documented and reinforced by interviews with many former advisers, staffers, and individuals who briefed him (see table 2.4 above).[14] As would be expected, Bush's inner circle was one in which diversity of view and wide information search was severely constrained. Advisers tended to share very similar views (both politically and ideologically), and typical of closed advisory systems, those with policy views or perspectives that challenged the prevailing ones within the core group were either ignored or never granted access. Where information search occurred, it was often highly selective and sought out only material supporting existing policy or assisting in implementing or selling it politically. The *Maverick* style is also quite idiosyncratic, and certainly Iraq policy was driven from a basic foundation, an absolute view of the world, based within Bush's own personal, ideological beliefs. While it is true Bush was extremely dependent upon advisers to provide the details and substance to the formulation of policy, it is equally true the basic directions that Iraq policy took were not divergent from the president's own personal views or beliefs. In this way, again, it is inaccurate to characterize him as a puppet of the neocons. Though they influenced his thinking and suggested paths to follow, these roads were not ones Bush was disinclined to take. Typical of simple, black-and-white belief systems, leaders possessing them tend to be more decisive and confident in their own idiosyncratic policy choices and see no need to search for lots of additional information or alternative viewpoints. After all, if you already see the world in terms of "you are either with us or against us," and you know what is "right or wrong" or "true or false," the decisions are much more straightforward in your mind. And you don't need to gather information that challenges those absolutes. For the *Maverick* Bush, these elements played a central role in how Iraq policy was developed and later implemented—and governed much of the inner-circle dynamics governing the policy debate.

Certainly, Bush's general pattern fits perfectly into that description. As McClellan (2008: 127) observed, "Bush has always been an instinctive leader more than an intellectual leader. He is not one to delve deeply into all the possible policy options—including sitting around engaging in extended debate about them—before making a choice. Rather, he chooses based on his gut and his most deeply held convictions. Such was the case with Iraq." Indeed, Woodward (2002: 342) remarked that during interviews "the president spoke a dozen times about his 'instincts' or his 'instinctive' reactions, including his statement, 'I'm not a textbook player, I'm a gut player.' It's pretty clear

Bush's role as politician, president, and commander in chief is driven by a secular faith in his instincts—his natural and spontaneous conclusions and judgments. His instincts are almost his second religion." This style of gathering information and making decisions has the tendency to often short-circuit policy debate and reduce circumspection on the part of leaders. As Baker (2007) notes, this certainly appeared to be the case with Bush:

> Bush walls himself off from criticism. He does read newspapers, contrary to public impression, but watches little television news and does not linger in the media echo chamber. He does a very good job of keeping out the extreme things in his life. . . . He doesn't watch Leno and Letterman. He doesn't spend a lot of time exposing himself to that sort of stuff. He has a terrific knack of not looking through the rearview mirror.

This insensitivity to context also contributed to a tendency many former administration officials noted during interviews—of a president relatively incurious (intellectually) about policy details beyond "big picture" or "broad brushstroke" treatments of subjects. For example, former treasury secretary O'Neill remarked that whether in large or small meetings, Bush tended to be relatively unresponsive and behave differently than had previous presidents he had served under who actively engaged during briefings (Suskind 2004: 57–58). Relating his own experience briefing Bush on a detailed memo he had written on the economy, he noted the president showed no outward expressions (positive or negative), asked no questions at all, leading O'Neill to wonder if "the President didn't know the questions to ask" (Suskind 2004: 57–58).

For inner-circle advisers (or others) who briefed Bush frequently, while he often engaged more than O'Neill experienced, it still took the more limited form typical of leaders who don't look at the minutia. Richard Clarke (2004: 243) notes that "Bush was informed by talking with a small set of senior advisers" rather than casting his net more widely for advice, and that "early on we were told that 'the President is not a big reader' and goes to bed at 10." As a result, the type of advice Bush sought from his inner circle, or those who briefed him, did not lend itself to broad information gathering or a focus on the details of policy. McClellan (2008: 128) recalled that Bush believed "it's important for his advisers to think about specific actions in terms of larger, strategic objectives—how they fit into the bigger picture of what the administration seeks to accomplish." As Clarke (2004: 243) would later note:

> It was clear that the critique of him as a dumb, lazy rich kid was somewhat off the mark.When he focused, he asked the kind of questions that revealed a

results-oriented mind, but he looked for the simple solution, the bumper sticker description of the problem. Once he had that, he could put energy behind a drive to achieve his goal. The problem was that many of the important issues, like terrorism, like Iraq, were laced with important subtlety and nuance. These issues needed analysis and Bush and his inner circle had no real interest in complicated analyses; on the issues that they cared about, they already knew the answers, it was received wisdom.

As one former White House official who worked for Bush for over two years observed, "With argument comes refinement, and there was none of that. . . . It's fine to say he's a big-picture leader and doesn't get bogged down in the details. But that's another way of saying he's lazy—not physically lazy, but intellectually lazy."[15] McClellan (2008: 46) recalls during campaigns, "Bush dealt with the pressures remarkably well. He made time to clear his head, work out, and get a good night's rest . . . understood the importance of pacing himself. . . . He also had a great ability to stay focused on the big picture and not worry about the 'process' stories—day-to-day analysis of the minutiae of the horse race that the press likes to report but which often has less interest among the general public." Indeed, Draper (2007: 416) observes "most of all, Bush evinced an almost petulant heedlessness to the outside world."

This detachment from context, and application of a strategy avoiding information and details to manage stress, certainly would not be one advocated by most business schools for future CEOs. Indeed, it is far more common for books on leadership in business to emphasize flexibility and gathering a variety of different kinds of information in order to make optimal decisions. Instead, according to several former White House officials, Bush generally preferred "short conversations—long on conclusion, short on reasoning," which often served to short-circuit the kinds of inner-circle policy debates that would have fleshed out problems (Thomas and Wolffe 2005: 37). It was often noted that in subtle ways, Bush did "not encourage truth-telling or at least a full exploration of all that could go wrong" on policy matters, and seldom asked the kind of probing questions that would open up discussions to examine such matters (Thomas and Wolffe 2005: 37). A similar observation was made by Dr. David Kay, the former chief UNSCOM inspector in Iraq, who briefed Bush several times on the search for Iraqi WMDs:

I briefed him directly twice on what was going on in Iraq. . . . And usually when you give a briefing you know where all the holes are in your own briefing. There's no briefing that doesn't have holes when you're dealing with something as complex as Iraq. And so you're prepared for the tough questions. Or you at least know that they're coming. In his case, he just expressed confidence. I remember the first time, which was the morning national security brief, which had the president, the vice president, secretary of defense, the director of the CIA, Andy Card (who was then chief of staff). . . . Secretary of State wasn't there for that briefing . . . and all he said afterwards was essentially, "What else can we do for you?" . . . Everyone who is dealing with a complex issue, and particularly if you go to the White House, everyone has their own agenda. Their own sets of issues. Things are *never* as good as you'd like the people to believe they are. And so, you expect . . . I expected greater curiosity and skepticism from the president. And I got a lot less than I'd gotten when I was doing my own graduate work, or certainly than I gave my own graduate students when they would come in with it. And it was just not at that level, it was just a lack of intellectual curiosity as much as anything else. The questions, even later on, tended to be questions that went to, sort of personality issues, not to the deep factors that might be involved.[16]

Comparing Bush to Clinton, whom he also served under, Clarke (2004: 243–44) observed that not only were there "innumerable differences between Clinton and Bush . . . the most telling . . . was how the two sought and processed information," with Bush wanting "to get to the bottom line and move on" while "Clinton sought to hold every issue before him like a Rubik's Cube, examining it from every angle to the point of total distraction for his staff." In this comparison, one sees the difference between how the complex, highly sensitive to context Clinton sought out information (Preston 2001) and the pattern typical of less sensitive leaders like Bush. As McClellan (2008: 145–46) later observed:

Bush is plenty smart enough to be president. But . . . his leadership style is based more on instinct than deep intellectual debate. His intellectual curiosity tends to be centered on knowing what he needs in order to effectively articulate, advocate, and defend his policies. Bush keenly recognizes the role of marketing and selling policy . . . but his advisers needed to recognize how potentially harmful his instinctual leadership and limited intellectual curiosity can be when it comes to crucial decisions.

It should be emphasized again this notion of *sensitivity to context* is completely unrelated to intelligence or IQ in leaders and refers merely to how much they tend to differentiate in their environments and attend to information. Indeed, Harry Truman's less-sensitive-to-context style was augmented by tremendous, basic "common sense" and intelligence. Lyndon Johnson could be accused of being many things, but unintelligent would certainly not be among them. But like these former presidents, Bush possessed a less sensitive, big-picture focus driven by a commitment to his own idiosyncratic policy beliefs (Preston 2001). As Kay would later observe in recounting his experience briefing Bush on the problems impacting the search for WMDs in Iraq, his general style of information gathering was definitely not detail oriented:

> Certainly in my case, and what I observed, it was *very* broad-brush. It was like, ten thousand feet above the details. . . . At one stage, I certainly appreciated this because I was trying to pick apart something that was very complex and I didn't know exactly what the shape of this elephant was either. . . . I remember coming back . . . in October, and talking to him. And . . . things were *not* going well in Iraq on the security problem. And that was affecting how we carried out our activities of discovering. And he was concerned about *safety*, but he wasn't concerned about *what does that mean*? What are the broader implications? . . . I remember describing to him that one of the hurdles we had in trying to find weapons of mass destruction was the vast amount of looting that took place immediately after the war. And he didn't show any curiosity at all in the extent of the looting, why it might have taken place, all of that . . . issues that for me, were of great concern. . . . I didn't find . . . someone across the table that seemed to be that interested in it.[17]

Indeed, Armitage recalled that Bush was "pretty street-smart. He's probably pretty smart. But he doesn't look around corners, in my view."[18] And as one senior official who played key roles in the 9/11 and WMD Commissions observed, this lack of interest in information (and divergent views) may be related to the "lesson" that Bush took away from the electoral defeat of his father, the belief that it occurred primarily because "he wasn't *enough* of a decider! He was *too* inclusive. He sought too many conflicting views."[19] In fact, when Senator John McCain was asked by Brent Scowcroft if Bush had ever asked his opinion on policy, McCain admitted, "No, no, he hasn't. . . . As a matter of fact he's not intellectually curious. But one of the things he did say one time is . . . 'I don't want to be like my father. I want to be like Ronald Reagan'" (Woodward 2006: 407–8). While Henry Kissinger liked Bush personally, he told colleagues it was not clear the president really knew how to run the government. One of the big problems, he felt, was that "Bush did not have the people or a system of national security policy decision making that ensured careful examination of the downsides of major decisions" (Woodward 2006: 407–8).

Given his absolute views of the world, there was almost a belief on the president's part that the "policy clarity" provided by these beliefs alone would allow his Iraq policies to succeed (and reduced his tolerance of information questioning that view). As a result, Bush had "little patience for briefings," often telling briefers to "speed it up, this isn't my first rodeo!" (Woodward 2008: 408). Indeed, as Woodward (2008: 407) reported from an interview with David Satterfield, who served as senior adviser on Iraq to Secretary of State Rice:

> If Bush believed something was right, he believed it would succeed. Its very rightness ensured ultimate success. Democracy and freedom were right. There-fore, they would win out. Bush . . . tolerated no doubt. His words and actions constantly reminded those around him that he was in charge. He was the decider.

In fact, Satterfield recalled "it was difficult to brief him because he would interject his own narrative, questions or off-putting jokes," which meant "presentations and discussions rarely unfolded in a logical, comprehensive fashion" (Woodward 2008: 408). Moreover, Woodward (2008: 431) noted that for Bush, "his instincts are almost his second religion," and as a result, he "didn't want an open, full debate that aired possible concerns and considered alternatives. He was the 'gut player,' the 'calcium-in-the-backbone' leader who operated on the principle of 'no doubt.'" And this had implications for the types of advisers Bush wanted around him, with the president noting to Woodward (2008: 431) that "I don't need people around me who are not steady. . . . And if there's kind of a hand-wringing going on when times are tough, I don't like it." In fact, one former aide remarked that no matter how many people Bush consulted, he heeds only two or three (Baker 2007). A similar concern was expressed by Brent Scowcroft, who worried "the White House was taking the wrong advice and listening to a severely limited circle" of like-minded advisers on Iraq, especially Cheney (Goldberg 2005: 57).

Indeed, the influence on Bush's thinking by his inner-circle advisers was far more complex than just the standard neocon influence often suggested to have played a key role. Undoubtedly it was important. But not all of the play-ers within the inner circle were neoconservatives. Agreeing with Scowcroft's interpretation, Wilkerson observed that he didn't even think Bush himself was really a neocon:

> I think there was an unholy alliance there between hyper-nationalists like Cheney and Rumsfeld, neocons like Feith, Bolton, Wolfowitz . . . although Paul's in a category all by himself. And Bush's tendency to be evangelical and to be a hyper-nationalist himself if rubbed the right way. I think that all came together in this unholy conglomeration of decision making that haunts us still.[20]

The less complex lens through which Bush viewed his environment, com-bined with the president's own quite personal, idiosyncratic beliefs (including his evangelical views), merged with those of hyper-nationalists like Cheney and neoconservatives like Wolfowitz to greatly shape Iraq policy. During a White House meeting on the Middle East with scholars and theologians, participants saw these characteristics in play in shaping how Bush viewed the world. One noted, "Bush seemed smarter than he expected," but that the discussion about the Middle East took on a predictable, low-complexity flavor with "much of the discussion focused on the nature of good and evil, a perennial theme for Bush, who casts the struggle against Islamic extremists in black-and-white terms" (Baker 2007). Similarly, Michael Novak, a theologian who participated, later remarked "it was clear Bush weathers his difficulties because he sees himself as doing the Lord's work" (Baker 2007). Indeed, Wilkerson noted that "I don't think you can get at Bush and his decision-making style, and some of the decisions he's made, without thinking about the evangelical aspect, without thinking about the spiritual aspect, in the sense that he gets advice from a 'higher authority.'"[21] But again, even those who worked for Bush quickly acknowledge the president's views were more complicated than simply his religious beliefs. As Wilkerson notes:

The president did listen to a lot of voices. He had *predispositions*, if you will, and those predispositions if they were not fed by some of the voices—reinforced, confirmed by some of the voices—then the tendency was to quicker rather than later turn those voices away, or off, or not listen. . . . If the advice being rendered didn't fit, more often than not, with preconceived notions, then that began to taper off in its importance and . . . his listening began to taper off too. Plus, the preconceived ideas were very hard to penetrate. Some have said, the most revealing remark about him was when he said he listened to a "higher father." And that had a lot to do with those preconceived notions. . . . [But] it's my firm view . . . buttressed by some experience up close and personal, but more, my thirty-five years in the government and understanding how these things work bureaucratically. That oftentimes, the predisposition was influenced not by God, but by Dick Cheney. And the fact that Dick Cheney is the most unprecedentedly powerful vice president we've ever had. Steeped in defense, and military-industrial complex, congressional issues. The president isn't. He's the gray eminence, if you will, the president isn't. He's the guy whose done foreign policy before, national security policy, the president hasn't. He's the guy that goes into the Oval Office after everyone else has left and gets the last bite at the apple. So, I think a lot of the president's predisposition was not necessarily, exclusively the vice president's influence, but if there was a single influence that *hardened*, and that might be a better word, rather than created that predisposition, it was the vice president. The secretary of state put it this way to me one time: "Bush has a lot of shoot-from-the-hip, cowboy hat, buck-skin inclinations. The vice president knows how to bring those out." . . . The vice president astutely recognized that and then used that "shoot-from-the-hip," that "you're with us or against us" type predisposition to reinforce a much wider perspective on an issue or a foreign policy. So it wasn't like the president didn't have any complicity in this. He was predisposed, perhaps, to listen to the piper.[22]

Even as the Iraq situation was spinning out of control in mid-2007, and Bush was forced to remain heavily focused on Iraq policy, he still refused to second-guess himself. As Irwin Stelzer, a senior fellow at the Hudson Institute who met privately with Bush during this time, noted, "You don't get any feeling of somebody crouching down in the bunker. . . . This is either extraordinary self-confidence or out of touch with reality. I can't tell you which" (Baker 2007). Similarly, Kissinger found Bush "serene" and of the view that "he feels he's doing what he needs to do and he seems to me at peace with himself" (Baker 2007).

As one senior administration official later observed, Bush clearly "is a very self-confident man, which in the view of many, including myself, is both his greatest strength and his greatest weakness" when it comes to policy making.[23] Not only did Bush like "to appear to be the Decider," the official noted, but his sense was the president "*believes* himself to be the Decider," and this was used "as a reference point" for him. [24]

BUSH'S INTERPERSONAL STYLE

One of Bush's foremost strengths has always been his engaging, charming personal style—a basic likability, which both friends and political opponents acknowledge. Those who know Bush remark that he "finds being around people invigorating and uplifting" (McClellan 2008: 40). Even during his student days at Harvard, Draper (2007: 29) observed that the "young Bush's particular genius—the facility for wiping out in milliseconds the distance separating himself from total strangers," was one that drew other boys to him through the use of an uncanny ability to generate "instant familiarity" through "remembering their names (or if one's surname twisted the tongue, assigning a nickname), flinging arms around shoulders, acute eye contact, a gruff yet seductive whisper." Indeed, Draper (2007: 29) notes, "formality never suited him—he wasn't really a prince, just a senator's grandkid—so George W. swept it aside." McClellan (2008: xi) notes Bush possessed a "disarming personality" and observed "much of what the general public knows about Bush is true. He is a man of personal charm, wit, and enormous political skill." Yet as McClellan (2008: 242) also notes, this great skill was also a double-edged sword:

> Bush likes familiarity and does not like change, especially . . . to key staff members he has come to trust and rely on. This had led to a close bond between Bush and a number of us senior staffers. . . . It's a great personal strength . . . that he is able to inspire such loyalty. But . . . it is also a potential source of weakness.

Bush's discomfort with change makes it difficult for him to step back from the bonds he develops and make clear-eyed decisions about what is best.

Wilkerson also noted the *very* high emphasis placed by Bush on personal relationships, his quickly "giving you a nickname" followed by the "hail Fellow, well met!" and "all that good Texas stuff!"[25] Agreeing, Armitage recalled Bush "was a big nicknamer, and everybody's got a nickname. I was Tiny for instance. And he likes that. I mean we used to joke, call it locker-room talk, but he's kind of that way. The dynamic of talking with the President—he wasn't intimidating in his manner or anything of that nature."[26] Since advisers were selected based on their perceived loyalty and ideological fit, there was also not a lot of direct conflict during meetings with the president (though there was often tremendous bureaucratic conflict between various department heads outside of Bush's sight competing for policy influence). But Bush's own interpersonal style preferred to avoid conflict, as Armitage recalled:

> Generally there wouldn't be huge fights. There is one funny story, and I'm front and center in it. In Bob Woodward's first book, he talks about a meeting we had after the operations had started in Afghanistan, and Rumsfeld said X, George Tenet said Y, and I looked at the two of them, and the president said, "Tiny, what's your problem?" And I said, "Mr. President, I think what you just heard is FUBAR!" And then he agreed. Now he didn't say right there, "Yeah, it's FUBAR." But he told Condi to get it fixed because I was right. But instead of saying . . . "Hey, wait a minute. Let me have *your* understanding, George. Let me have *your* understanding, Don. Okay, I don't agree with either of you; here's what we're gonna do." That was done kind of afterwards. He didn't like the head-on collisions.[27]

Avoiding head-on collisions can also be accomplished by excluding outside players who disagree with policy from having access to the inner circle, where their views might upset the group's harmony. For example, while Scowcroft was appointed chairman of the president's Foreign Intelligence Advisory Board in the first term, he wasn't consulted on plans for Iraq and (after he publicly criticized the policy) was not reappointed at the end of 2004 (Goldberg 2005: 58). Observing that the White House "ignores ideas that conflict with its aims," a colleague of Scowcroft noted he was "not the only person to be frozen out," a clear reference to James Baker and other officials who also expressed reservations about Iraq policy (Goldberg 2005: 58).

Another consequence of avoiding head-on collisions and open conflict within inner circles (especially ones where loyalty is emphasized) is a reluctance to fire close subordinates. For Armitage, this element within Bush's style was nowhere seen more clearly than in the handling of Rumsfeld and the degree to which the White House stuck with him long after he had become a political liability. According to Armitage:

> To be a great leader, you need three primary attributes. You gotta have a vision which people can believe in. He had that. Whether you agree with it or not. . . . So that part of leadership he got right. But a leader demands, in various ways . . . execution of that vision. And then, right alongside of execution he demands accountability. So vision, execution, accountability. Mr. Bush had . . . vision. He didn't have any demand for execution; he didn't hold anyone accountable. . . . I was asked, not so long ago, what I thought of the firing of Mr. Rumsfeld. And I described it as a national tragedy! It came five and a half years too late! [*laughs*] So, you know, he didn't man the execution, didn't man the accountability.[28]

Another puzzling aspect of Bush's interpersonal style was the disconnect between what those close to him observed versus the public perception derived primarily from his public speaking. As Wilkerson observes, this difference was quite stark:

> The first thing that comes to my mind is the difference between the President Bush in front of the American people and the international community, and the President Bush one-on-one in the Oval Office. The one-on-one in the Oval Office was charming, on his brief, very polished. . . . And then, the President Bush that appeared at the podium, whom I had to watch all the time, because the secretary charged me with watching his speeches. Making sure that the secretary knew what he'd said, particularly when the secretary wasn't in town. . . . So I listened with an attentive ear . . . not just to the words, but to the way he delivered and everything . . . the contrast was so stark . . . it got to be by 2003 absolutely painful for me to turn the TV on and watch his speech. Because he was so inept. He used the bully pulpit so poorly. . . . I'll never understand the difference between the President Bush I met up close and personal . . . and the President Bush I consistently saw speaking to the American people and the international community. Bumbling, fumbling—is the way I would explain the latter. On his brief, polished, and charming is the way I would explain the former.[29]

THE KEY ADVISERS IN THE BUSH INNER CIRCLE

For *Delegator-Maverick* leaders like Bush, the nature of the key advisers surrounding them play a major role in the subsequent patterns of their decision making and exert a strong influence on the leader's policy preferences. Such leaders depend on their experts to provide the roadmap by which to navigate the policy terrain, and to frame (explain/define) the nature of that policy environment and the options available to deal with problems. Because the leader doesn't insist upon personal control and involvement, advisers take the lead in formulating and constructing policy options and implementing decisions made by the leader. For Bush, those key advisers included, first and foremost, Cheney, Rumsfeld, Rice, and Powell. Added to these heavyweights were others like Paul Wolfowitz and Stephen Hadley (who would play more limited roles), but for the most part, it would be this relatively small group who would "map" the policy terrain for Bush. And significantly, even within this small inner circle, the influence of Powell would be greatly diminished by the overwhelming presence of Cheney and Rumsfeld.

Though Larson (2003: 7) notes that "good judgment is not necessarily associated with academic knowledge or theoretical expertise," and there have been many presidents lacking policy expertise who still made good, commonsense judgments, it is equally true this has a great deal to do with the advisers surrounding them and the quality of their advice. Truman had the good fortune of being surrounded by advisers like Dean Acheson, George Marshall, Averill Harriman, and others who helped compensate for his inexperience and less sensitive, "shoot from the hip" style (Preston 2001). Johnson, who inherited Kennedy's inner circle, was not as fortunate with McNamara, Bundy, and Rusk—who like the Bush inner circle, failed to adequately provide alternative perspectives on his Vietnam decision making (Preston and 't Hart, 1999, 2001). Indeed, both McNamara and Bundy, in interviews with the author, later noted "we didn't serve the president very well!"[30] Like Johnson before him, Bush would depend upon a similarly small, loyal inner circle for his Iraq decision making.

Vice President Cheney

Almost universally, when interviewing former Bush administration officials, one individual is seen to clearly stand out in terms of both his influence with the president and his ability to shape policy on Iraq—Dick Cheney. Even while the Florida ballot dispute continued in the aftermath of the 2000 presidential election, Cheney was put in charge of the transition by Bush and began vetting potential staff for the new administration. As Gellman (2008: 52) notes, not only did Cheney have a "preeminent role" in the nominations and appointments, but this preeminence "did not stop with the transition." Indeed, as McClellan (2008: 137) acknowledges, while "the relationship between Vice President Cheney and President Bush has always been clouded in mystery to some extent," the reality was "it was a very close one," with the two spending "considerable time together in private meetings, their discussion largely kept confidential." Even during the transition, those working for the Bush team saw stark differences between the management styles of Bush and Cheney—differences that would eventually (due to Cheney's key role in the transition) merge together to shape the new White House advisory system. One top transition aide remarked that while Bush favored "a flat hierarchy and gives authority to a wide range of underlings," Cheney's style was that of a "chain-of-command kind of guy" and was more "tightly controlled" with "very clear lines of authority and responsibility."[31] Indeed, comparing Cheney and Bush, the aide remarked that while both had "a tendency to hub and spoke," it was the Vice President who had the "smaller wheel."[32] And Cheney was much more "hands-on" in his style, demanding a high degree of personal engagement on policy-making tasks. As Gellman (2008: 55–57) observed, while vice presidents traditionally have joined presidents at "policy time" if the president desired,

> Cheney intended to get involved sooner, long before the moment of decision. By "reaching down," a term that recurs often in interviews with his aides, Cheney set himself up to shift the course of events while deferring to Bush's prerogatives at the top. Cheney would exert a quiet dominance over meetings in which advisers framed their goals, narrowed options, and decided when— or whether—to bring them to the president. Cheney's presence unavoidably changed the tone and often the outcome. . . . It required a healthy dose of boldness for anyone at the table to press a disagreement very far.

Similarly, McClellan (2008: 85) recalls the heavy involvement of the vice president on White House policy making, with the president being heavily dependent upon (and seeking out) Cheney's advice on a wide range of topics (but most especially on national security and foreign policy matters). Bush showed great deference to Cheney, whose counsel was usually offered in private, and the vice president and his top advisers "were included in all presidential policy briefings, world leader meetings, congressional meetings, and the like" (McClellan 2008: 85). This view of the Bush-Cheney relationship is supported by many former officials interviewed by the author, who agreed the vice president and his staff played dominant roles on issues like Iraq policy. One senior official noted Cheney would "always sit on the other side of the table" from Bush, and whatever he had to say to the president, he said to him personally in private.[33] Moreover, Cheney "had a separate organization that was quite loyal to him," and "the White House, the presidential side, didn't always know what the vice presidential side was doing."[34]

Agreeing that Cheney influenced policy "enormously" and to a great extent "called the shots," another senior White House official observed that this was always done "in a very quiet way."[35] As Armitage recalled:

> What brought us difficulty was the vice president made his staff into almost another bureaucracy. It's like having a whole other department to deal with! They

aligned themselves with the neocons, and did things that I *know* Mr. Rumsfeld didn't understand. And then he would be in with the President all the time, I'm reliably informed, saying [*in a Cheney-like whisper*], "Armitage, Powell. They're not on the team. You see the questions they raised today? That's designed to keep you from being able to do that. They're raising the difficulties!" While the rest of them were singing this is gonna be a cakewalk, and they'll throw flowers at us. So, over time, on anybody. This president or any president. That would wear to have a guy who sees you six, seven times a day coming in privately to say [*in a Cheney-like whisper*], "You're not on the team!"[36]

Responding to the observation that this undercuts the ability of any inner circle to see the full range of options available on issues, Armitage replied strongly, "Oh yes! Absolutely undercuts it! I mean, it's very devastating!"[37] Wilkerson agreed, noting this kind of access for Cheney meant even if "he was not always *successful*," the vice president "always got the last bite at the apple!"[38] As Richard Haas (who served as head of policy planning at the State Department) later observed, Cheney's methods actually gave him "three bites at the apple" on every decision: "There's the one with the president, when they're alone. That's the most interesting one, and we know the least about it. There's his participation in the principals committee meetings. And there's the staff role, from the deputies on down" (Gellman 2008: 54). As Gellman and Becker (2007: 1) note, given his involvement throughout the policy process, Cheney was often able to steer the preparation of options presented to Bush, and after accompanying him to his briefing, "before the president casts the only vote that counts, the final words of counsel nearly always come from Cheney."

Further, Cheney set up a powerful, influential staff within the Office of the Vice President that has no equal in presidential history. He established a "web of contacts" throughout the government, selected a personal staff who "possessed far more experience and force of will than their counterparts on Bush's staff" (Gellman 2008: 40). Cheney also had his staff appointed with very senior titles, giving them additional ability to punch above their weight. As Gellman (2008: 49) notes, "Some of Cheney's staffers followed the Libby precedent, acquiring presidential as well as vice-presidential appointments. Mary Matalin, who became Cheney's counselor, had the same rank . . . as her West Wing counterparts, Karen Hughes and Dan Bartlett." Indeed, few White House staffers were aware that during the first term, "many of their emails were blind-copied to Cheney's staff," with his aides eventually being called "The Watchers" by others in the government "for their habit of attending meetings and reporting back without disclosing the vice president's position" (Gellman 2008: 376–77). In fact, stealth was among Cheney's most effective tools, with interagency consultation, proposals, and information flowing into the vice president's office from around the government, but like a one-way valve, very little flowed out (Gellman and Becker 2007: 1).

The breadth of Cheney's organization allowed him to have a broad influence across the policy spectrum in a way that amazed other players in the administration. During interviews, time and again, officials would express bewilderment at the extent of the vice president's influence and the power his office had over policy.[39] Further, while most were highly critical of the poor performance of the NSC and Rice, many acknowledged the nature of the institutional factors working against her. Observing that the Bush NSC model was certainly not Eisenhower-esque, Kay observed:

> It's not anyone's model. I mean, I don't think there's ever been one like this. But it's not just the NSC. Quite frankly, pick almost any of the previous national security advisers to the president, none of them could have operated I think the way they did with a vice presidency like Cheney. And the Cheney-Bush relationship. And Cheney allowed to have a staff that had the right to see everything, gather everything, and had the time. I mean the mystery for me has always been, how in the hell does Cheney do everything he does! I mean he has good staff, with Addington and Libby and those people. They had their fingers in everything! We concentrate on Iraq, but they were doing energy policy and everything else simultaneously. It's a very amazing operation![40]

Yet it was such a powerful, influential organization primarily because of the confluence of a powerful, directly engaged vice president coupled with a delegative president willing to cede great swaths of policy terrain to his subordinate. That Cheney was not a political threat to Bush undoubtedly helped to ease any reticence Bush might have felt in delegating to his vice president. And as Gellman (2008: 49–50) observes:

> The first MBA president soon emerged as a manager who left a great deal to his subordinates, and who allowed disputes among his advisers to fester for months and years. . . . Until and unless Bush settled an argument, Cheney felt free—and even obliged—to use every advantage of his office to prevail.

Because of his role in the transition, and the appointment of officials throughout the administration, Cheney created a plethora of allies. His appointees ran many departments and agencies and were quite loyal, and through these networks, a "hidden-hand" influence was created. As Kay observed, in the past, vice presidents haven't been able to "advance your career and reward people in the federal bureaucracy," but Cheney had people in positions throughout the government who saw "their roles and careers being tied to the vice president."[41]

So not only did Cheney have an influence network with tentacles stretching throughout Washington, but those who bucked the vice president's office in far-flung departments or agencies might find their careers under fire by Cheney appointees leading their offices.[42] Indeed, Wilkerson has described Cheney's organization, especially in how it later became so closely coupled to Rumsfeld's Pentagon, as being a "cabal" within the Bush administration that set up structures bypassing the traditional policy-making process.[43] It was a reality attested to by many former administration officials throughout the government who were interviewed about the connection between Cheney's and Rumsfeld's offices.[44] As Wilkerson recalled:

It didn't necessarily bypass it so much as it set up an alternative to it. You let the standard one go on and be frustrated. Or think it's doing things. North Korea for example. Made a decision about the Six-Party Talks in the NSC with the president presiding. Jim Kelly takes off, across the Pacific, going to Beijing for the next round of talks. Gets to Hawaii. Lands for refueling and all of a sudden the secretary [Powell] gets a telephone call, and he has to call Jim Kelly and change the decision. Now Jim is in a straitjacket! Now Jim can't do any negotiating at all beyond the script he's got in his hand! How did that happen? The vice president made the call to the secretary. And does the secretary go pick up the phone and call the president and say, "Mr. President, did you *really* tell the vice president to reverse your decision?" No, he waits for a week or two, gets on a plane with the president . . . and gets the president alone and talks to him for a few minutes. And by that time, of course, Cheney had time to backfill. And the president says, "You know what, I thought that's what we were gonna do all along," or whatever, and brushes the secretary off. . . . Some of it's incompetence, no question about it! Some of it's lack of attention to detail, no question about it. But some of it is just *damn good* bureaucratic work by the vice president and his team! And he had a team across the bureaucracy in all the peep holes. NSC staff, State Department, led by Bolton, Defense, led by Feith and some would say by Rumsfeld. I'm sure that Paul [Wolfowitz] was always in sync with it.[45]

Combined, the Cheney and Rumsfeld axis could hardly help but dominate policy debates over Iraq. Cheney, with his personal influence with Bush and powerful staff, and Rumsfeld, with the immense clout of the Pentagon behind him (providing much of the raw intelligence on Iraq directly to the vice president's office for circulation within the White House), were an almost unstoppable force. Woodward (2008: 195) observes Cheney and Rumsfeld operated "as a kind of iron wall on defense and war policy that no one could get around," with the vice president continually praising and defending Rumsfeld to Bush and advising the president in private, away from the rest of the team. This resulted, according to Woodward (2008: 195), in no one being able to "challenge Cheney because no one knew exactly what he said to Bush," leading to the appearance that all of the president's decisions carried his VP's implied blessing.

And for the State Department and Powell, it was quickly apparent after 9/11 that the balance of power had shifted in the White House—and it would be doubly difficult to influence the direction of the policy debate. As Armitage recalled:

> For the first nine or so months before 9/11 . . . State Department felt we were laboring mightily to get decisions like smart sanctions, Treaty of Moscow, and all that. But we were prevailing. But after 9/11, the whole dynamic changed. I think the president himself felt that, "Ah! This is why I won the election! There was a reason to it. And I've got to respond to this grievous attack!" After that, things got much more difficult because, with Mr. Cheney, Mr. Rumsfeld on one side—a basically absent national security adviser—at least in terms of bringing things to a head. Which is what the president *wanted*! I'm not criticizing Dr. Rice for that in this case. I'm just saying, that's what the president wanted. And his decision-making style became one where decisions weren't generally rendered at the meetings. They were generally rendered later in some obscure, and sometimes even Byzantine fashion.[46]

Another characteristic of Cheney was a great suspicion and deep distrust of the U.S. intelligence community, especially the Central Intelligence Agency. After CIA estimates of Iraqi WMDs prior to the first Gulf War proved to be inaccurate and underestimated what Saddam had, Cheney brought his defense secretary experience (and biases) along with him into the vice president's job. Several intelligence officials interviewed recalled the degree to which Cheney (and his staff) would question analysis that didn't fit their own preconceptions—whether it be about Iraqi WMDs or a purported link between Al Qaeda and Saddam Hussein—especially when it raised questions or didn't support their policy preferences.[47] And important staffers to Cheney and Rumsfeld, Scooter Libby and Wolfowitz, shared Cheney's "congenital distrust of the CIA" (Isikoff and Corn 2006: 5). This distrust influenced the degree to which intelligence analysts, or the agencies themselves, were able to brief the vice president (and by extension, the president). Not only did Cheney's staff visit Langley prior to the Iraq War to push for analysis finding the things they wished to find—an experience a number of analysts found unsettling—but they didn't want caveats or analysis that didn't reach black-and-white conclusions.[48] John Maguire, an Iraq covert operations officer who often attended briefings with Cheney, recalls the VP often drilling in on substantive details during briefings, saying, "I want answers on this . . .

this is not acceptable," while noting that the "worst thing to do with Cheney was to hedge or to waffle" since "he didn't want to hear sentences that began, 'We don't know'" (Isikoff and Corn 2006: 4).

Indeed, when David Kay, the head of the Iraq Survey Group, would brief Cheney or members of his staff, there was always an emphasis upon his need to be using "non-CIA" sources and a dismissal of intelligence questioning the existence of WMDs.[49] As Kay recalls:

> Everytime I met the president, the vice president was in the office. And the vice president didn't ask a question, he showed great deference to the president. But in the meeting with Cheney, he was very challenging about: Have you done this? Have you done that? We've seen this. Have you run it down, he'd ask. Great skepticism about the failure to find them [WMDs]. . . . He was very detail oriented. He knew the briefs backwards and forwards . . . he was not using just CIA data. And a lot of what he was using we'd already run down and proven to be absolutely unsubstantial. But he was engaged, very engaged. As was Scooter.[50]

Cheney augmented "official" intelligence from the intelligence community with "unofficial" raw intelligence (that avoided the tyranny of analytic trade-craft) from Undersecretary of Defense Doug Feith's shop at the Pentagon.[51] This raw intel (which had been selectively gathered without any concern for corroborating evidence, verity of sources, or validity of its link to given hypotheses) was circulated by the vice president's office as if it had gone through the same careful analytic process as the rest of the output from the intelligence community.[52] For the purposes of advocating policy, or defending such policies politically, this pseudo-intelligence worked ideally—and it was often mixed together with more traditional intelligence products to provide multiple sourcings for rather dubious arguments (as with Curveball). Certainly a lot of Cheney's emphasis upon the use of such intelligence was driven by his strong belief that action had to be taken against Saddam in the wake of the 9/11 attacks. Indeed, as Woodward (2002: 346) notes, at a principals meeting at Camp David without Bush on September 6, 2002, "Cheney was beyond hell-bent for action against Saddam. It was as if nothing else existed."

Interestingly, though Scowcroft has famously suggested he "didn't know Cheney" anymore, as if he had somehow changed in recent years, Wilkerson had a very different take on whether Cheney had really changed:

> I've had people who've served in the Congress with him in the beginning who tell me . . . very eloquently in my view, "Dick Cheney has always been the same Dick Cheney you see now. It's just that before, he had adult supervision."

And they went through his life, where Donald Rumsfeld was once his adult supervision. Where Jerry Ford afforded some adult supervision. Where Colin Powell and George H. W. Bush wedged him between themselves and provided adult supervision. Then he gets into the White House as vice president, and he has no adult supervision at all. His tendencies to, for example, as he and Rumsfeld ganged up to get rid of Henry Kissinger in Gerald Ford's administration. His tendency to say, "A pox on your house if you want to talk about diminished American power!" "A pox on your house if you want detente with the Soviets!" "A pox if you wanna talk with evil!" "I'm right and the right and the rectitude of my rightness is that you never talk to evil, and that American power is not diminishing, it's growing! If it's diminishing at all it's because of turkeys like you!" Dick's always had that attitude. I don't know which one I subscribe to. Brent Scowcroft's *New Yorker* interview or this congressman. But this congressman made, he's from Oklahoma . . . made a very persuasive case for him, saying, "Dick's always been this way. Look at his voting records. He's always been this way. He's a hyper-nationalist! It's America first, second, third, and last. And if I say we need to do this, we need to do it, because it's for America!"[53]

Defense Secretary Rumsfeld

Another very influential, key adviser within the administration was Rumsfeld, who combined with Cheney to form a powerful double act within the inner circle. Rumsfeld and Cheney shared a long professional history, having worked together in the Ford administration thirty years earlier. They also shared strong conservative, nationalist views, though most who worked for both men argue they were not really neocons ideologically.[54] With his strong, "forward-leaning" personality, descriptions of Rumsfeld's style are plentiful among those who worked for him at the Pentagon or who interacted with him elsewhere in government.[55] Many note the degree to which he surrounded himself with a small group of loyal advisers and his penchant for disregarding intelligence that disagreed with his own beliefs (Cockburn 2007). He was well known for an extremely high need for control, extending even to personally vetting all promotions into the upper ranks of the military to weed out officers not sharing his policy views (Cockburn 2007: 110). Not only was this unprecedented for a defense secretary, but it played a role in neutering (through disincentives) the willingness of senior officers to take positions contrary to Rumsfeld's or speak truth to power (Cockburn 2007: 110). Certainly many former Defense Department officials, who had the job of briefing the defense secretary, knew what would happen if they presented or raised points conflicting with Rumsfeld's preferred policy views, often recounting the direct public rebukes and dismissive sarcasm that would follow.[56] Or the inevitable flurry of "snowflakes" (Rumsfeld's short memos or notes demanding further information—preferably the "right" information this time) showering down on parts of the Pentagon after such briefings.[57] Even prior to Iraq, there were indications Rumsfeld's style would serve to impede the flow of unvarnished, professional military advice or opinions up to the secretary, as one Defense Department consultant recalled:

I was having lunch at the Pentagon in late 2002 with a colleague in the officer's dining room, about forty feet from Rumsfeld's office, with seven other generals of various ranks. During the course of lunch, as we all talked shop and many complained about the difficulties of dealing with the civilian appointees, one general noted a very serious problem with a particular DoD program that was in big trouble. It was also a program the secretary was personally invested in and had strong views about. It was clear the problems being described were so serious it would ultimately compromise effectiveness if not fixed—but it was equally clear nothing was being done to remedy it. After a good ten minutes of complaints, one of the other generals, in mock seriousness, then enquired of the frustrated officer, "Well then, why don't you just walk down [*inclining his head toward the direction of the office forty feet away*], and tell Rumsfeld all about it?" This suggestion immediately provoked uproarious laughter all around the table among this group of senior generals—the idea was obviously so ludicrous—to actually take information that disagreed with Rumsfeld up to his office! As the generals then alluded to the snowflakes that would follow, I couldn't help but shake my head and think to myself, "This is not a healthy dynamic! This is going to eventually lead to some serious problems if the uniforms don't feel they can take honest (and accurate) assessments up to Rumsfeld!" What a mess![58]

This unwillingness to put oneself on the "firing line" with Rumsfeld would, in fact, later lead to many problems on Iraq policy making. One vivid example of this occurred when Bush secretly authorized Rumsfeld on November 21, 2001, to begin making plans to invade Iraq, resulting in an early December briefing by General Gregory Newbold, director of operations on the joint staff (J-3), to the secretary and senior Pentagon officials on existing war plans. In response to Newbold's briefing, calling for troop strengths equal to the first Gulf War, Rumsfeld dismissed those numbers as "absurd," arguing that "we don't need nearly that many . . . certainly no more than 125,000" (Cockburn 2007: 152). As Newbold later remarked, "Shame on us. . . . Here was a man with absolutely no concept of what was involved in mounting an operation of this kind" and none of the senior military officers present raised any objections (Cockburn 2007: 153). But Rumsfeld's emphasis on promoting only officers who were compliant or agreed with his positions not only served to reduce the chances alternative views or recommendations would reach the secretary; they reduced the chances they would reach the president's inner circle as well. Indeed, according to former high-ranking colleagues, two of Rumsfeld's choices for JCS chairman, Richard Myers (described as "not a man who looks for or enjoys confrontation") and Peter Pace (described as a "political general" ever sensitive to advancing his career), fit perfectly with Rumsfeld's style of seeking staff who were purely implementers of his views, not advocates (Cockburn 2007: 111). As Daalder and Destler (2009: 274) observed, Rumsfeld sought to completely control the policy process through a rigid insistence on the chain of command, succeeding brilliantly in eliminating the military as an "independent voice in policy deliberations," noting that

> General Richard Myers, the JCS chairman, achieved what he called a "mind meld" with Rumsfeld, so that they would always speak in the same voice during meetings at the White House. The general in charge of Central Command was no different. Asked by Bush during a meeting what he thought, General Franks replied: "Sir, I think exactly what my secretary thinks, what he's ever thought, what he will think, or whatever he thought he might think."

Moreover, as Woodward (2006: 316–17) observed, Rumsfeld's style was to emphasize caution, trust few people, and adopt a "rubber glove syndrome" whereby he tried not to leave his fingerprints on decisions—while adopting an abusive "prosecutor's interrogation style" that "diminished important people in front of others." Indeed, one senior defense official noted Rumsfeld's style not only created a dysfunctional dynamic within briefings but also rubbed off on subordinates (like Feith, Cambone, and Wolfowitz) in ways that added to the problem:

> I've been in meetings with Rumsfeld where there was a briefer. Rumsfeld talked back to briefer, and had very, very little interaction with anybody else. They kept their mouths shut. I know Chairman Pace would be sitting with his head down not saying anything. Not very participatory at all . . . it was a universal trait. There was no conflict resolution process. . . . I've seen undersecretaries violently disagree and go to war with one another, instead of taking it in to the boss. . . . They'd just let it fester. . . . It's so politicized that acknowledging we can't work out our differences is a problem. . . . I've been in meetings where five major organizations in DoD dealing with the Sec Def were saying, "We don't agree." And him chewing us out, essentially saying, "Here's the three options, Sir, pick one!" Him saying, "I'm not gonna do your job for you! You go back and come up with a solution!" So you come back with this watered down . . . there's a problem with that somewhere! Rumsfeld in particular, created an air of "I'm not interested in debates here." And it was funny, cause you could see Cambone and Feith almost become Mini-Mes in how they treated people. Abusive, short shrift. "I already know the answers, so let's just go through the

formality"-type of attitude. . . . Gates comes in and it's a different environment! You tend to reflect the personality of the person in charge. Distinctly different, far more collegial, ready to make a call. "Don't ask me for a decision if you don't want one, cause I'll give it to you!" So Gates was a significant difference . . . was willing to listen. Far more collegial![59]

Similarly, another senior NSC official, noting that Rumsfeld had a reputation for being very tough to brief and pretty blunt in meetings, recalled:

I had to brief on an extremely sensitive program prior to Iraqi Freedom. So I was here, Feith was right across from me, Chairman, couple of others. And he asked me a question. And he's very engaged. And I said, "Well, that's covered on the next page, Sir." And he looked down, and said, "What page is that?" And I hadn't put in page numbers! And that was one of his pet peeves! He looked at Feith and said, "This man has no page numbers!" And I felt like there was this kind of collective hush in the room! And Feith said, "Well, Sir, this is so sensitive we don't assign numbers." And he kind of giggled. Disarmed it. He loved the briefing, but his MA walked me out the door and said, "That was a dang good brief, the boss was really enthusiastic," and says, "Normally I would have had to carry the guy out with a shotgun blast in the chest because he'd left the numbers off!" So he goes, "I know it had to be a good brief!" [*laughs*] He had a habit of just shooting people in the head for the strangest things.[60]

Other military officers who participated in briefings with Rumsfeld recounted similar instances, as well as the secretary summarily ending briefings after they had only just begun and walking out of the room (without uttering a word) if he felt the briefer wasn't getting to the point or was providing material that ran contrary to his views.[61] Or cutting off briefers midbrief to suggest they needed to "get their facts straight" or "start covering the points that really mattered," sending them away to rework the presentation for next time.[62] Rumsfeld's subordinates, like Wolfowitz, Cambone, and Feith, would adopt similar styles with their briefers and staff—essentially vetting some of the types of briefs making it up to the secretary.[63] Not only did this severely limit the diversity of views considered by Rumsfeld, but it also severely constrained the range of options and viewpoints subsequently reported back to Bush.

As a seasoned, experienced Washington player quite savvy in his understanding of how the political game was played, Rumsfeld implicitly knew how to interact with the president, the importance placed by Bush upon loyalty, and how to package policy proposals to him. In fact, Rumsfeld shared with the president a penchant for "big ideas" and knew that "if you wanted the president's support for an initiative, it was always best to frame it as a 'Big New Thing'"—something Powell never did (Draper 2007: 282–83).

Rumsfeld was especially adept at playing bureaucratic politics, guiding (or blocking) policy proposals circulating within the administration to ensure his own or the Pentagon's interests. Even during his first run as defense secretary during the Ford administration, former senior White House officials recalled "he had a penchant for complicating the decision process . . . in throwing monkey wrenches into the works, not to alter course, but simply to impede" (Cockburn 2007: 38). This ability to bureaucratically outmaneuver other Washington actors allowed the Pentagon to play an increasingly central role in Iraq, sidelining other actors. When Bush signed National Security Presidential Directive No. 24 on January 20, 2003, for example, he did so "without hearing the strenuous objections" of the State Department, which had already developed plans for administering postwar Iraq while the Pentagon had not (Packer 2006: 120). It was a victory of bureaucratic maneuver by Rumsfeld and Cheney that had the effect of largely pushing the State Department (and Powell) out of a significant role.

Moreover, Rumsfeld, Cheney, and Bush all preferred to operate with a high degree of secrecy, a pattern which made the process difficult to penetrate for Powell and other actors, who were left to fight "rearguard" actions to influence policy.[64] This secrecy also prevented information sharing within the administration and short-circuited both debate and policy coordination. As Cockburn (2007: 177) observed, Rumsfeld "treated information as a weapon, to be hoarded as much as possible and shared only when necessary," a strategy that protected and maintained "the chain of command that made Rumsfeld, and only Rumsfeld, the link between the Pentagon and George Bush." It was a pattern that manifested itself in a routine refusal to share information with other agencies, and even extended to keeping the details of the Iraq invasion plan from the State Department and the military staff at NSC in the run-up to the war (Cockburn 2007: 177). As Wilkerson notes, this penchant for secrecy and control extended even to Rumsfeld's own deputy Wolfowitz:

> Paul used to have to call Rich Armitage in order to find out what the agenda was for deputies meetings, cause no one would tell him! That's pretty bad. When the deputy secretary of defense has to call the deputy secretary of state to find out what's going on![65]

National Security Adviser Rice

The junior member of the inner circle, Rice left academia to serve as a foreign policy adviser to then-candidate Bush during the 2000 elections. She became his tutor, and the two developed a close friendship and "comfort zone" with one another, eventually leading Rice to being named national security adviser. It was a personal relationship Rice greatly valued, and it served as her main avenue of influence within the new administration. Like Bush, Rice possessed a deeply religious, moralistic streak and, according to associates, was one of "the least reflective" people they knew, always having the "capacity to see the world she wants to see—as opposed to the world that actually exists" (Kessler 2007: 18–19). Rice was well known for being impatient and losing interest quickly with issues falling outside her narrow expertise— vintage Soviet politics (Alfonsi 2006; Kessler 2007). But above all else, she was intensely loyal to Bush, focusing almost exclusively as NSC adviser on carrying out his wishes and supporting his views. In fact, Woodward (2006: 100) notes that not only did other officials believe Rice was "running more and more interference for Bush" during policy discussions, some felt Rice believed "anytime someone wasn't ready to do immediately exactly what the president wants, it was almost disloyal."

With an eye toward maintaining the special bond with Bush and preserving her status, Rice was very judicious in how she engaged with others. Former CIA director George Tenet (2007: 138) notes that while Rice "knew the president's mind well," she also "tended to stay out of policy fights" with other senior advisers. As Draper (2007: 284) remarked, Rice saw her role as NSC adviser as that of "facilitator rather than opinion leader" and, valuing her access to the president, endeavored to "maintain it at all costs." This enabled Rice to be Bush's "information broker and sounding board, rather than the person who incessantly ruffled his feathers with opinions that he did not share" (Draper 2007: 284). Rather than do battle with the other inner-circle heavyweights, Rice, McClellan (2008: 145) notes, "was more interested in figuring out where the president stood and just carrying out his wishes while expending only cursory effort on helping him understand all the considerations and potential consequences."

In many respects, Rice was a perfect complement to Bush's interpersonal style. She provided the type of loyal, supportive, sounding-board adviser the president needed and a close confidant who would work to reduce any discordant notes being struck within the inner circle. The highly relationship-oriented Bush valued the loyalty and friendship Rice provided easily as much as she valued their bond in return. Playing her "cards close to the vest" while usually "saving her views for private discussions with Bush," Rice "complemented and reinforced Bush's instincts rather than challenged or questioned them" (McClellan 2008: 243). While "invariably" falling into line with Bush's thinking during meetings or discussions, McClellan (2008: 243) notes that "she wasn't actually shaping his thinking, she knew how to read him and how to translate his ideas, feelings, and proclivities into concrete policies."

Similar to Rumsfeld and Cheney, Rice also insisted on secrecy and personal control—a tendency that came into sharp relief when she became secretary of state during Bush's second term—centralizing control over policy making to shut out all but a handful of aides. Obsessed with leaks, Rice warned her staff not to "brief down" to lower-level aides about discussions, warned them not to return reporters' phone calls, and left even senior officials (puzzled over policy) looking for clues in her public statements (Kessler 2007: 26).

Of course, Rice's performance at NSC has been heavily criticized in the aftermath of the Iraq War, with many even within the administration itself viewing her as historically the worst NSC adviser ever![66] Certainly by the yardstick of previous NSC advisers, Rice's performance can be seen as severely wanting. As Daalder and Destler (2009: 261) observed, with such an inexperienced president, it was necessary for the NSC adviser to take the initiative, present all the logical alternatives, probe underlying assumptions, and perform the critical analysis necessary for reaching decisions—something that Rice didn't see as part of her responsibilities.

Richard Haass, who served as head of policy planning at the State Department, noted the NSC "is not just an honest broker" but must be "an honest balancer" (Packer 2006: 111). For Haass, part of the NSC adviser's job is to introduce arguments not held by people at the table, to explore whether there are better arguments not being represented—and "Rice, in charge of coordinating policy, proved more skillful at seconding the president than obliging him to consider the range of arguments and resolve them in a coherent way" (Packer 2006: 111). Yet even Armitage, who is critical of Rice's performance, recognizes that her unwillingness to engage in settling policy disputes and her style of managing the NSC were basically a consequence of Bush's own leadership style. As Armitage remarked:

> In a bureaucracy, the second best answer after yes is no. Because in a bureaucracy, if you don't win or lose the battle, and the decision is not rendered, then everybody gets back on the gerbil wheel and gerbils away again! So these things were not brought to a head. We'd fight the same fights day in and day out. And eventually, somehow, they resolve themselves in some bizarre fashion that wasn't fully explained ever. But I realized over time, although I was very critical of Dr. Rice originally, that Mr. Bush was the only nationally elected leader. He got the national security adviser *he* wanted. He didn't get the national security adviser *of the type* that I was familiar with. But he got what he wanted. He wanted a companion. A soul mate, and I mean that in a nicest way . . . rather than someone who was gonna make the trains run.[67]

Moreover, the distribution of power among key players within Bush's inner circle did not favor a powerful role for Rice and almost preordained that she could not adopt the strong NSC style necessary to help compensate for Bush's inexperience in foreign affairs. Reacting to the heavy criticism of Rice's performance by Armitage and others, one close friend and colleague in the administration argued the "blame Rice" interpretation was hard to completely accept:

> Because that theory suggests Rice should be stronger than the vice president. Because that's where that decision was coming from! That's where she was getting rolled. And I don't think *any* second-tier staff could trump a vice president. And certainly not Cheney. And Cheney carried Rumsfeld and Wolfowitz. So . . . you could have the strongest person in the world . . . he would have lasted three weeks and Cheney would have gotten rid of him! He kept her there because he *could* go over her. But I'm not sure you can blame her for that.[68]

Indeed, the same colleague noted that while Rice did have a close personal relationship and friendship with Bush that afforded her some influence, it was important to remember "that's not where he's getting his policy advice. . . . He's getting it from Cheney, Rumsfeld, from the guys that put him in the door, put him in that seat!"[69] And, as Wilkerson observed, this power imbalance within the inner circle created "facts on the ground" Rice had to adapt to:

> I think Dr. Rice was confronted with some inevitabilities that she recognized, perhaps before my boss did. One was how powerful the vice president was, and was going to be. Two, how much in league he was with the secretary of defense. And three, how often the president would ultimately wind up on their side. And she had a choice to make. She could discipline the national security decision making the way one envisions the role being played out properly. Or, she could more often than not, build her intimacy with the president by being on his side. And she chose that path. And she had her "eye on the prize" the whole time, to later become secretary of state. It got her to become secretary of state. I'm not saying that's bad, I mean, that's the way people at that level operate. But, I do think that made her role as national security adviser one of the *most* dysfunctional in the short history of that position.[70]

While noting Rice had performed a lot better as secretary of state, Paul Pillar, who served as national intelligence officer for the Near East and South Asia on the National Intelligence Council (2000–2005), observed, "There was not just a bad policy process on Iraq, there was *no* policy process on Iraq, none."[71] Agreeing that Rice was the worst NSC adviser in history, Pillar remarked that during the "most important foreign policy departure of the whole administration, and one of the most important departures this country has made in recent decades . . . we had *no process at all*! That's right in job number one for the National Security Adviser. *Make sure we got a process for an important national security decision!"*[72] But as Kay recalled, "I've told Condi personally that my experience is that the NSC has one boss, and that's the president of the United States, and your job is to protect him from everyone coming in with their own agenda and not telling him the truth . . . to help vet and put the information together," but she never saw that as her job.[73] This conceptualization of her duties as NSC adviser would play a significant role in Bush's eventual Iraq decision. As Kay, recalling a conversation with Bob Joseph, one of Rice's senior NSC aides, recounts:

> I had a long discussion with Bob, who told me I simply didn't understand how the NSC worked. That Condi didn't have the time, or the staff didn't have the time, to vet the evidence that came in, and that their job wasn't to do that. It was to more or less package it and put it in, and go back and get information the president and vice president wanted. So they weren't out there. . . . The NSC saw its role as making the case for WMD, not figuring out whether that case was accurate or not. So this NSC I think had the most peculiar version. I mean, and in part, in Condi's defense, she had some very big obstacles out there in Donald Rumsfeld, and Powell, in a different way, nicer, but still a big force. And she was, after all, the junior staff member. And she saw her job as being the best friend to the president, not the best gatekeeper and analyst for the president.[74]

For Rice, there was nothing to be gained by engaging in the bureaucratic struggles between the vice president's office, DoD, and State over Iraq. Especially since she was "focused on ensuring that the president saw her as his best friend," and was "very sensitive to maintaining that relationship."[75] As NSC adviser, Rice "clearly believed that the president did not like conflict among his closest advisers," and so she didn't do things like arranging battles where "Rumsfeld and Powell go after each other, or Cheney."[76] Indeed, as Wilkerson notes, Rice was doing nothing more than playing a realistic political game indulged in by many at senior levels, especially those who don't enjoy overwhelming influence:

> I think bureaucrats, especially good, entrepreneurial bureaucrats, will figure out where the president's predilections are, and then shape their own views to those predilections rather than challenge them . . . to figure out where the president's going and use where he's going to make it look as if you've been successful in your efforts to persuade him. I don't think she challenges him very often. If she does anything, she persuades him.[77]

Rice's approach meant the NSC wouldn't play the information-gathering, vetting, devil's advocacy role it performed in other administrations (George 1980; Greenstein 1982; Burke and Greenstein 1991). It meant important decisions on Iraq and discussions on WMDs were quite narrowly focused and driven by the dominant views of Bush's inner circle. Upon returning from Iraq with his finding there were no WMDs, Kay noted Rice came close to implicitly acknowledging the flaws in the NSC process:

> After the last time I saw the president . . . in '04, she asked me the next day if I'd come by to talk to her, and I did. At this point I'd gone through this script about why WMD was not there, how the society had changed in such a way. And Condi said, "You know, I should have known that because that's exactly what happened in East Germany. That's the West German's joke, that they took over this powerful country and they couldn't even collect their own garbage. It'd been a Potemkin's village . . . and in many ways that's what Iraq was." And she said, "I should have known that." And I just wanted to say, "What did you think you were doing for the president, if you weren't challenging every evidence, every conclusion that came in against some sort of analytic process or standard?" Because if you don't, everything that moves through there is likely to be distorted because people all have their own agendas when they come to the president. . . . We had a situation where the vice president had his own national security operation. And they had an agenda that just wasn't the president's, and it wasn't truth, it wasn't. They viewed their job as to push forward an agenda. In the case of Iraq it had the objective of carrying out a military attack on Iraq, and that meant they had to have WMD and had to have links to terrorists.[78]

Similarly, Tyler Drumheller (2006: 44) at the CIA once briefed Rice on a rendition operation and noted her "chief concern was not whether it was the right thing to do, but what the president would think about it." Given his expectations of how an NSC adviser would normally operate, Drumheller "expected a big meeting, a debate about whether to proceed with the plan, a couple of hours' consideration of the pros and cons," but instead "got no direction, just an approving response and a 'We'll have to figure out how to tell the president' reaction from Rice" (Drumheller 2006: 44). Indeed, noting Woodward's criticism of Tenet for not going to Bush prior to 9/11 with intelligence suggesting an attack was coming, Daalder and Destler (2009: 265) observe he "might better have asked why Rice didn't do so?" Though Rice would later say the Tenet meeting "wasn't all that important," she still didn't call Bush, even when confronted by a threat briefing "that made people's hair stand on end" (Daalder and Destler 2009: 265).

In these examples, the shortcomings of the NSC process and Rice's performance as NSC adviser become obvious. For a president like Bush, who lacked a robust, open advisory system gathering lots of feedback from the environment and possessed an inner circle of like-minded advisers, such an NSC structure only exacerbated the weaknesses in his style. As one senior politician, who served in various capacities within the Bush administration, later remarked:

> Condi's always kind of surprised me . . . because I thought she would do more as an honest broker to keep the president informed and to try to keep him from being most influenced by the last person that saw him, or whatever. And almost everybody . . . and I've seen both players and talked to a lot of people who were a part of that immediate concentric circle around the president. Almost all of them fault Condi for not directing traffic better. There was a sense that she was, in that respect, too close to her boss.[79]

The Freudian slip of Rice once referring to the president as her "husband" during an interview aside, colleagues who know both well acknowledge the "real chemistry between those two" and her emphasis upon maintaining that relationship taking precedence over her NSC role or policy.[80] As one close friend of Rice noted:

> I think she *just* really likes President Bush as a person. I think they're friends. And I think she's still sort of "starstruck" with him. People are loyal to their friends. . . . Policy wasn't as important as that friendship.[81]

Finally, the question of how much Rice actually agreed with (or believed in) the neocon view on Iraq is a source of confusion for close associates. Though almost all agree maintaining her relationship with Bush was the main driver of her support for Iraq policy, few actually believed she was a neocon herself. Wilkerson, for example, argues as secretary of state, "you're seeing *now* how fundamentally she *did* disagree on some things. . . . I do think you're seeing Condi's more realpolitik approach to foreign policy and her underlying views . . . about using diplomacy in concert with other elements of national power, including military, come out more prominently."[82] Yet, while Rice pushed more moderate internationalist positions once she became secretary of state, a colleague who knew her well remarked, "Don't read too much into it. Condi is not a neocon. But she's not Colin Powell either" (Thomas and Wolffe 2005: 37). Or as Wilkerson remarked, rather tongue in cheek, when asked whether Rice was a neocon, "No, I think Condi is a realist who's been hit over the head by a neocon!"[83] Others note that her conversion to Bush's worldview was "rooted in her Christian faith, which leads her to see the world in moralistic terms, much as the President does" (Goldberg 2005: 59). Her "evangelical tone" regarding Iraq came into sharper focus during a heated dinner discussion with her former mentor Scowcroft in 2003, where her adoption of parts of the neocon perspective became evident to him:

She says "we're going to democratize Iraq," and I said, "Condi, you're not going to democratize Iraq," and she said, "You know, you're just stuck in the old days," and she comes back to this thing that "we've tolerated an autocratic Middle East for fifty years and so on and so forth," he said. Then a barely perceptible note of satisfaction entered his voice, and he said, "But we've had fifty years of peace." (Goldberg 2005: 59–60)

Importantly, when Rice left the post of NSC adviser to take over the State Department, nothing changed in terms of how the NSC operated because her deputy, Stephen Hadley, was appointed to replace her, and her views about the proper role for the NSC were mirrored in her successor (Woodward 2008: 8–9). A dysfunctional NSC remained dysfunctional.

Secretary of State Powell

Trapped even more than Rice by the "facts on the ground" in the new administration, and the powerful influences of Cheney and Rumsfeld, was the new secretary of state, Colin Powell. Being neither a neocon nor a hyper-nationalist, Powell, in an "ideal" setting, *could* have provided a moderate voice within the Bush inner circle, giving the president access to alternative viewpoints and advice. Throughout his career, and during his time working in previous administrations (Reagan, Bush Sr., and Clinton), Powell had always shown a cautious, pragmatic decision style that was largely nonideological and highly suspicious of the use of force to solve international problems (Powell 1995; Preston 2001). Moreover, he had a tremendous amount of prior foreign policy experience, making him (on paper at least) an equal to the other heavyweights within the White House. He was enormously popular with the American public and had been showcased during the election campaign as part of the experienced team that would shepherd the less experienced Bush through difficult foreign or national security policy issues. The fact he did not end up *playing* that role in the new administration raises an important point about leaders and their advisers—a "law," if you will, regarding why certain advisers end up being more influential than others. And it is simply this—*advisers are not all created equal, regardless of their titles, and serve at the pleasure of the leader, not the other way around.* As a result, the official positions held by an adviser, or even their background expertise, will matter little in terms of whether or not they will be influential with a given president. Instead, it is the leader's own "comfort zone" and personal predilections that determine this in the end—the leader's alone. And it is the Johnson and Bush administrations that provide two of the strongest examples (or illustrations) of this particular leader-adviser dynamic.

Robert McNamara, who served as secretary of defense for Johnson and Kennedy, was seen as a key inner-circle adviser to both presidents—and he was (Schlesinger 1965; Berman 1982, 1989; Preston 2001). However, what is often lost, especially in all of the criticism of McNamara's role in Vietnam policy making, is that he was not *equally influential* across the two presidencies. After McNamara's mea culpa on his role in Johnson's Vietnam decision making, and admission it had been the wrong decision (McNamara 1995), skeptics questioned how much he really had tried to change LBJ's mind, often noting, "he was *secretary of defense*, and was so powerful, how could he have failed to change Johnson's mind if he had really tried?" What this reaction fails to understand, however, is it is largely the *president* who decides whether and who to listen to within their inner circles! And, as noted during interviews with many former Kennedy and Johnson advisers, McNamara's influence with Kennedy had always been far greater than it subsequently was with Johnson.[84] This is nowhere seen more clearly than in the differing influences of McNamara and Secretary of State Rusk across the two administrations. Under Kennedy, McNamara (aside from Bobby Kennedy) was probably one of the president's closest advisers, one whose opinion he really listened to and took seriously, as compared to Rusk, whom JFK often referred to as "the Buddha" for his tendency to not express his views openly during meetings and desire to privately relay them to Kennedy afterward (Schlesinger 1965; Preston 2001).[85] For Kennedy, who wanted open sharing of information and debate, this was very frustrating—and it is quite likely Rusk would have been replaced had JFK lived to serve a second term (Schlesinger 1965; Preston 2001). In contrast, McNamara, according to many former Johnson advisers, was seen by LBJ as more "Kennedy's man" than his, and he never achieved the same kind of "closeness" with Johnson he had enjoyed with JFK.[86] Moreover, due to his style, the controlling Johnson loved that the loyal Rusk wanted to give him *private* information after meetings, leading to the secretary of state becoming LBJ's closest adviser throughout his presidency. Thus, you have the same men, holding the same bureaucratic positions—but each having *very different* influence relationships with their presidents.

For Powell, serving as Bush's secretary of state would, at first glance, have appeared to be a very powerful, influential position. But associates of Powell, even before the new administration took office in 2001, began to voice concerns about how influential the moderate Powell could really be within such a strongly conservative administration[87]—concerns later finding voice in former Treasury Secretary O'Neill's rueful observation that moderates like himself, Powell, and Christie Whitman had essentially been used as "cover" by the new administration to convince people it would be less ideological and more focused on seeking out common ground and best solutions than it really was (Suskind 2004: 130).

Such fears appeared to have been well grounded as Powell's initiatives were repeatedly blocked by other, more conservative advisers, and neoconservative positions on arms control treaties (like the ABM Treaty), on China and North Korea, and importantly on the need to confront Saddam gained traction (Woodward 2002; Mann 2004). Sharing the experience of Powell, O'Neill, after several of his own policy initiatives were hijacked or blocked, wondered about the broader inner-circle pattern of "either no process, or a truncated one, where efforts to collect evidence and construct smart policy are, with little warning, co-opted by the White House political team, or the Vice President, or whoever *got to the President* and said something, true or not, though in any case effective, that no one else was privy to" (Suskind 2004: 165). Indeed, as Wilkerson observed:

Powell really underestimated, badly, the vice president, the secretary of defense, and their ability to, as he said to me himself, half in jest, "rub the president's cowboy attitude." To get the right things out of him. I think he overestimated his *own* ability to prevent that. And so a combination of the underestimate and the overestimate came back to haunt him big time![88]

Close associates and friends of Powell note that while Wilkerson was publicly "more forward-leaning" than the secretary was willing to go, if you talked to Powell privately, "he will lean *way* far forward! I don't think they had any fundamental difference in how they saw it."[89] Powell's nonconfrontational style, one emphasizing professionalism and open discussion of issues, was ill equipped to deal with the more bare-knuckled, insider-politics style of Cheney and Rumsfeld in competing for the president's ear. Powell's deputy Armitage recognized the need to be more aggressive in seeking to influence policy but noted the "personal styles" of Bush and Powell were *so* different it made a close connection difficult:

I had become aware that Secretary Rumsfeld was spending a lot of time with the president. And our view was always, if he wants to see us, he knows where we live. You know, we got a bureaucracy to run. That was Secretary Powell's view. But then the secretary did start asking for weekly time with him, and he'd have an agenda list of things he'd put together himself. And then he'd go over to talk to the president. And he'd brief me when he came back. But Secretary Powell would not, quote, go locker-room, unquote. He wouldn't slap anybody in the ass with a towel. He doesn't do that! This is the *presidency*! It's not some frickin' Yale frat party! [*laughs*] In a way, I used to say, I felt the president was indeed much more at ease with me than he was Secretary Powell. Because with Secretary Powell in the room, it's kind of like, "you don't swear in front of your father!" And I was the same age as the president. I'm a lot rougher guy, came from a different side of the tracks—well, Colin did too. But, in that way, he was much more comfortable with me. And I wasn't a threat to the president. Powell was the most popular . . . and is today, still the most popular man in the country![90]

Indeed, this concern about Powell as a potential "political threat" to the president, as someone who had been seen as a potential presidential candidate, and who still enjoyed huge public popularity, probably also worked against developing a close, influential relationship with Bush. As Wilkerson observed:

Rove and some of the others were palpably afraid of Powell as a potential candidate. It used to boggle my mind! It's another study of how people can develop phobias that have *absolutely* no basis in reality. Powell had no inclination to run for elective office. And I thought had disabused everyone of that idea in 1995. But there was some fear of him, politically, especially in 2004. And especially after Bush had lost by 500,000 popular votes to Gore, and had won by such a method as a 5 to 4 decision in the Supreme Court. There was concern, political concern . . . his polls were in the stratosphere, like Mother Teresa's. Seventy percent, seventy-one percent. One poll was showing him in 2002 at eighty percent. They were jealous of that. Particularly the vice president.[91]

It also didn't help that the less experienced Bush did not enjoy being shown up by his cabinet officers, and that being loyal meant not making the president look bad publicly—*especially* when that cabinet member could also be a potential political opponent! Indeed, in reflecting upon the nature of Powell's own personal relationship with Bush, Wilkerson observed it was

very jealous. Very jealous I think. I think that was something the secretary failed to see as vividly as he should have! It was so apparent when President Bush announced Powell as his secretary of state that the secretary had screwed up. The President made about, you go back and look at it, three, four minutes worth of remarks. Powell got up and gave a tour de horizontal of the world! And I thought to myself, "Big mistake boss! Big mistake! You just put that little, short man in the background there in the photo. Look at his face! You just put him in the shadows. You don't ever want to do that with your president, no matter who he is!" [*laughs*] And, you know, that was there![92]

More significantly, at the same time advisers like Armitage were encouraging Powell to take stronger approaches vis-à-vis the Bush inner circle during policy debates, other senior Bush administration and State Department officials who attended these meetings noted that he didn't really engage:

No. There's the real Powell and there's the persona of how much clout he actually promotes. That he was out there, battling, etc. I never saw a battle! I mean, in too many meetings, Powell didn't say a word! Too many of them, to the president, to [various foreign leaders], Powell didn't say a word. Other meetings I would go to over at the NSC, there would be Armitage or it would be Marc Grossman. Powell was just absent! And yet, I'd come out of these meetings . . . and it'd be leaked to the press that Powell was battling. I never saw it! Unless it went on in meetings I didn't go to—or after a meeting or before a meeting—but I never saw it! I saw them just lie down, because they felt they couldn't win![93]

Certainly as the discussion within the Bush inner circle turned toward invading Iraq after 2001, Powell's influence vis-à-vis the other conservative advisers continued to diminish (Woodward 2002, 2004). While having strong personal reservations about the path of policy and its wisdom, Powell adopted the loyal soldier demeanor and supported Iraq policy, thereby avoiding McNamara's path of dissent in 1967–68 with Johnson (McNamara 1995; Woodward 2002, 2004, 2006). But while unable to alter Bush's path to war, Powell would still play the "providing cover" role alluded to by O'Neill during his speech to the UN—essentially giving the final "sales pitch" prior to the war in Iraq.

CONCLUSION

In looking at Bush's leadership style and the advisory dynamics it promoted within his inner circle, it is easy to see the parallels to Johnson's style and use of advisers in Vietnam. Though the two men were obviously *very different* in terms of personalities and worldview, they shared important similarities. Both were inexperienced in foreign affairs and, as a result, heavily dependent upon expert advisers to help frame the policy environment for them. The two men placed tremendous importance on loyalty among advisers and disliked dissent, surrounding themselves with like-minded subordinates. Both administrations had closed advisory systems largely impermeable to alternative viewpoints or criticism of existing policy, with information and advice being gathered from only a small section of loyal insiders or places where support for policy was already assured. For outside actors or negative feedback, it was a difficult path to gain access to either inner circle, to have a "day in court" before the president. And both presidents felt a "moral obligation" to pursue the paths they took and firmly believed they were right.

For LBJ, many former advisers noted he felt the "ghost of JFK" on his shoulders over Vietnam, believed his predecessor wouldn't have allowed the country to fall, and understood strategically (due to containment policy) and politically (due to the jeopardy failing would put *any* Democrat in versus Republicans domestically) that it was almost impossible to turn away.[94] For Bush in the aftermath of 9/11, he felt a "moral obligation" to pursue the war on terror to avenge the attacks, and he believed he had been placed in the White House by God to protect the American people from this menace. It ushered in a more straightforward, uncomplicated vision of the direction policy should pursue against not only terrorists and "rogue states" but any who supported them—"you're either with us or against us" (Woodward 2002, 2004). Certainly Rumsfeld, on the very afternoon of 9/11, was already telling JCS Chairman Myers to gather all the information he could on the attacks and judge whether it was "good enough" to justify targeting Saddam as well as bin Laden (Cockburn 2007: 9). Though not a perfect comparison—with one being a deeply conservative Republican opposed to "big government" and the other being a liberal Democrat known for the Great Society—in terms of their basic styles and use of advisers, the comparison certainly provides interesting parallels across Vietnam and Iraq.

Within the Bush administration, it led to selective use of information and intelligence—and the shutting out of feedback challenging policy. And while McClellan (2008: 129) confirms "the president and his leadership team believed that victory in Iraq could be achieved swiftly and decisively, and that the Iraqi people would then welcome and embrace freedom," it was equally true that a broad range of foreign and military think tanks (from the Council on Foreign Relations and the Center for Strategic and International Studies to the Rand Corporation, Army War College, and National Defense University) produced reports warning the reconstruction of postwar Iraq would require large numbers of troops for an extended period—reports that never "penetrated the Pentagon or the Oval Office" (Packer 2006: 113).

Among the advisers surrounding Bush, there was a narrowness and locked-in mentality that disturbed onlookers like Scowcroft, who saw the dysfunctional nature of the NSC (where Hadley wouldn't stand up to anyone and Rice had not been "up to the job"), where Rumsfeld had either broken or made puppy dogs out of his JCS chairmen (Myers and Pace) and had continued behaving as he had during the Ford administration, as "a wholly negative force" that was "enigmatic, obstructionist, and devious" (Woodward 2006: 419–20). To Scowcroft, who felt it essential to "continually challenge your own assumptions," it was clear the administration "wouldn't reexamine or reevaluate its policy" (Woodward 2006: 420). This pattern draws strong parallels to the advisory dynamics surrounding Johnson in Vietnam (Berman 1982, 1989; Preston 2001), where his inner circle was also not renowned for "continually challenging" their assumptions. Like Bush, Johnson was equally unable to draw upon his own foreign policy expertise to press advisers for alternative views or know where to look outside for other perspectives (as Kennedy or Eisenhower would have done).

The perceived "correctness" of their policy approaches, and the belief they were doing the "right" thing, also explains why both Johnson and Bush pursued the policies in the manner they did.[95] As Foyle (1999: 183–99) explains, across modern presidents, Johnson (like Truman and Reagan) believed public opinion was fickle and unpredictable and that the popularity of a policy should not be the determinant of their choice, but rather the president should just do what he thinks right for the country. As McClellan (2008: 15) observed, Bush believed "results matter most" and that "people judge leaders and history remembers them based on their success" more than on the means by which they achieved them. This logic—that the ends justify the means, that the eventual "correctness" of the policy would win out with the public (and critics would be silenced)—would play a key role not only in shaping the focus upon secrecy within the administration but also on its focus on public relations, staying "on message" with the media, and following strategies of blame avoidance in pursing their policies. It is to these strategies of blame avoidance that we turn to next.

3

The Politics of Blame Avoidance: Presidential Strategies for Surviving the Washington "Blame Game"

Typical accountability questions . . . include: What happened? Who and what caused this to happen? Who is responsible? Who should be sanctioned? Such questions . . . are typically played out through an array of official inquiries, investigative journalism, political "dirt" digging, parliamentary questions, legal investigations, victim and family campaigns, as well as lobby group interventions. Scrutiny often calls into question long-standing policies, the working of public institutions and the performance of political and bureaucratic leaders. . . . Given their positions . . . all actors involved in accountability processes will use a variety of strategies to argue their case and apportion blame. We refer to this [as] . . . the "blame game." (Boin et. al. 2008: 11)

From the moment the first hijacked plane struck the side of the north tower of the World Trade Center at 8:46 a.m., September 11, 2001, the world fundamentally changed, not only for the United States but for the Bush administration as well. The magnitude of the terror attacks themselves and the profound grief and anger they unleashed within the American body politic demanded a response—and posed a challenge few presidents have faced. It called for the president to demonstrate strength and resolve, to express sorrow and give comfort to the public. It also required the White House to quickly develop an effective response to the outrage, channel public anger, and be seen to strongly retaliate against those responsible by bringing them to justice. It was also an opportunity for a president whose election had been highly controversial (and ultimately determined by a Supreme Court decision) to show leadership and rebound from poll numbers generally showing him to be in the low fifties in public approval, during what would normally be his "honeymoon period" politically.[1] But more importantly, it marked the true beginnings of what would become one of the most complex and protracted crises in American foreign policy history, one whose consequences would continue to reverberate for more than a decade after the sparking event.

For while the 9/11 attacks, and the initial White House response, can all be seen as one policy case, and separate from all of the policies that followed, this actually obscures the true significance of the event. The emotive power of the imagery of the collapsing towers and the public demand for action made 9/11 a uniquely *transforming* event, profoundly changing the political environment. It removed constraints on political action, allowed wide latitude in moving forward, and kick-started policies unlikely to have been pursued otherwise. The attacks served as glue, binding together, interlinking, and justifying wide-ranging policy "responses" by the administration. The initial domino pushed over by Al Qaeda in New York led to Bush's nationally televised speech before a joint session of Congress nine days later declaring a "war on terror," followed by the October invasion of Afghanistan and overthrow of the Taliban.

The failure to actually capture bin Laden at Tora Bora, however, created tremendous political pressures on Bush, who now faced a seemingly endless conflict with a widely dispersed, nonstate terror group providing no convenient "return address" for retaliation. This greatly increased the temptation to pursue a *Casablanca*-esque solution to the problem (by "rounding up the usual suspects"), magnified by the strong ideological influence of neoconservatives (like Paul Wolfowitz) and those in senior positions who believed Saddam Hussein should have been removed from power after the first Gulf War (as did Cheney and Rumsfeld). The steadily collapsing row of dominoes soon moved beyond the original confines of Afghanistan, with Bush's State of the Union address in January 2002 proclaiming a new objective for the "war on terror"—rogue states who supported terrorists (Iraq, Iran, and North Korea), who together formed an "axis of evil" that must be confronted.

While the "axis of evil" provided opponents more easily located than the Al Qaeda leadership and allowed Bush to show strength of purpose to the public in response to 9/11, the war on terror itself was a double-edged sword. While a politically useful turn of phrase, communicating the president's tough, no-nonsense response, it was also a concept effectively imprisoning the White House within a "frame" requiring it to show to the public progress in "winning" that war. Thus, its utility as a blame-avoidance strategy was important, channeling public anger outward toward an external enemy (and away from questions of why the attacks had been allowed to happen in the first place, and Bush's performance prior to the event). The "war on terror" frame became not only how the public viewed and judged Bush's performance but the *primary lens* through which the White House itself viewed and formulated its response. As a result, pressure began to build, inexorably, almost as a pressure cooker building up steam, to take further action and show progress on the war on terror by moving against a target long in the crosshairs of the administration—Saddam Hussein and Iraq.

This domino would fall in March 2003, with the invasion and occupation of Iraq under the WMD premise, thereby unleashing further dominoes when WMDs were not found, raising the stakes for the administration's blame-avoidance strategies. The decision to invade Iraq not only brought a long, drawn-out conflict but ushered in a policy of disastrous neglect in Afghanistan. It squandered the period of relative calm between 2002 and 2006 (when the Karzai government could have been strengthened) and allowed the resurgence of the Taliban and Al Qaeda and destabilization of Pakistan. Now, long after Bush left office, the protracted crisis sparked by 9/11 continues to be felt, as President Barack Obama's administration finds itself immersed in a deteriorating situation in both Afghanistan and Pakistan, a growing insurgency, and a war on terror that continues unabated.

While one *could* argue all of these were separate policy events, they are nonetheless linked and interconnected by 9/11—and none would have likely occurred in its absence. No matter how much neoconservatives wanted to topple Saddam prior to 2001, in the absence of 9/11 it's difficult to imagine the Bush administration finding it politically possible to launch that invasion (or the one in Afghanistan). The administration's Iraq decision making (and subsequent blame-avoidance tactics) are only understood properly within the context of this much larger protracted conflict—the "war on terror"—of which it formed but a part.

THE POLITICS OF BLAME AVOIDANCE— STRATEGIES AND TACTICS

Within the crisis management literature, there is a growing body of research focusing on how political leaders or their governments "manage accountability" in response to "extraordinary" or "disturbing" events that unfold, and how they avoid the blame that tends to be apportioned as a result (e.g., Weaver 1986; Ellis 1994; Bovens and 't Hart 1996; Hood 2002; Hearit 2006; Boin et al. 2008, 2010; Hood et al. 2009). Indeed, as Boin et al. (2010: 706) observe, "When crises occur, something or somebody must be blamed—for causing the crisis, failing to prevent it, or inadequately responding to it." And for political leaders, these are extraordinarily dangerous times, because if they are unable to deflect the blame and avoid responsibility for policy reverses, their political survival (as well as their ongoing policy effectiveness) will be called into question.

For example, after publication of an official inquiry into the role of Dutch peacekeepers in the 1995 Srebrenica massacre in Bosnia, the entire Dutch cabinet was forced to resign in 2002 when blame settled on it (Brandstrom and Kuipers 2003). Similarly, Spanish Prime Minister Jose Maria Aznar's attempt to blame ETA (the Basque terror group) for an Al Qaeda train bombing in Madrid to reap political gains on the eve of national elections backfired, and he went on to suffer defeat at the polls when the truth about who was really responsible was uncovered (Olmeda 2008). Even when governments manage to survive reversal of their blame-game strategies, their previous public image of administrative competence and popularity can be severely damaged as a result. This was certainly the case for the Bush administration with its handling of Hurricane Katrina and its aftermath in 2005 (Preston 2008; Boin et al. 2010), as well as for the Swedish government and its ineffective relief efforts to assist Swedish nationals after the 2004 Boxing Day Tsunami (Brandstrom et al. 2008). For the Bush administration—which already was dealing with an increasingly unpopular war in Iraq, a 9/11 Commission Report not supporting a link between Saddam and Al Qaeda, and a WMD Commission failing to support the case that WMDs had been in Iraq— the mishandling of Katrina served as the final nail in the coffin of its public credibility (Parker and Dekker 2008; Preston 2008).

LEADER BLAME-AVOIDANCE STRATEGIES

Get Your Version of the Events Adopted and Deal with Inquiries

For political leaders, blame avoidance often involves a "battle to get their definition of the crisis accepted as the official account of events," a dynamic certainly seen in the Bush administration's early efforts to frame the need for war in Iraq as necessary due to Saddam's WMD threat or support for terrorism (Boin et al. 2010: 707). The administration's shrewd use of the national media (especially its main ally Fox News), and its focus upon "staying on message" and spinning events through things like Rumsfeld's frequent Pentagon news conferences, reflected an understanding of media importance in "framing" or providing "definitions" of policy to the public. In the aftermath of 9/11, advisers like Rove and White House communications director Karen Hughes focused on ensuring Bush got "full public attention and credit for being in charge of the battle against terrorism" (Mann 2004: 296–97). Indeed, numerous observers have emphasized the degree to which both the White House public relations and political campaign machinery blatantly used the imagery of the war on terror not only to push policy but to burnish the image and reputation of Bush as a "war president" to assist in his 2004 reelection (Rich 2006). As McClellan (2008: 95) observes, "we had an elaborate campaign structure within the White House that drove much of what we did. We were always focused on how to control the agenda, shape the media narrative, and build public support for our policies." But soon a problem common to managing blame avoidance in general would complicate the administration's handling of the Iraq conflict—the growing call for official inquiries. In such situations, leaders are often reluctant to cooperate by providing access to information or government witnesses. This can lead to stonewalling fact-finding efforts, pretending to cooperate but flooding inquisitors with truckloads of mostly tangential records, or seeking to place a positive spin on information provided to investigators (Boin et al. 2010: 708). Other strategies include front-loading tactics like "restricting the terms of reference of the investigation, hand-picking 'friendly' or malleable chairpersons, and limiting the time and resources made available" (Boin et al. 2010: 708). But caution is in order since such tactics may rebound upon leaders if inquiries are accused of being "tainted" by government manipulation—and "being seen to be compromising the search for 'the truth' may do considerable damage to public support for incumbent leaders and governments" (Boin et al. 2010: 708).

Many of these tactics would be seen in the Bush administration's attempts to deflect blame, as would the use of lightning rods (like blaming the CIA, or intelligence community as a whole) to explain the "strategic surprise" of 9/11—thereby focusing attention on the lack of information sharing and "stove-piping" among agencies, but not on the White House's ignoring of intelligence warning of attacks in the days running up to them (Ellis 1994; Clarke 2004; Pillar 2006; Parker and Dekker 2008). Similar blame would later be directed at the intelligence community for missing WMDs, despite the fact that "traditional" reporting from the agencies (and not from the Feith-run shop at the Pentagon) had questioned the administration's case early on (Woodward 2004, 2006; Pillar 2006; Rich 2006). Whether with the original 9/11 Commission, the WMD Commission, or the Iraq Study Group, Bush consistently resisted establishing fact-finding groups free to assess Iraq policy (and the intelligence underpinning it). As McClellan (2008: 117–18) recalled, the "president and his senior advisers had little appetite for outside investigations" and "resisted openness," believing investigations meant "close scrutiny of things they would prefer to keep confidential"—which if disclosed publicly "might cause political embarrassment for the president." The White House "lacked real accountability in large part because Bush himself did not embrace openness or government in the sunshine," which in an age of heightened media scrutiny and the internet is "ultimately self-defeating," merely delaying (but not preventing) the consequences (McClellan 2008: 118).

Regarding the formation of the 9/11 Commission, while Bush "was never willing to lead the charge in pursuit of potentially unflattering truths, the administration eventually concluded that an investigation of events leading up to the September 11 tragedy was inevitable" and finally acquiesced to the November 2002 formation of the commission (McClellan 2008: 188). As many former administration officials acknowledged, the White House supported the formation of the 9/11 Commission only grudgingly and, in the absence of the immense amount of public pressure generated in the media by the victim's families, would never have agreed to an independent commission.[2] It was only when such a commission became politically inescapable, and continuing to block it ran the risk of making it appear the administration had something to hide, that Bush reluctantly signed off on it.

A similar dynamic would appear with the later WMD Commission, which examined the intelligence behind the belief Iraq had WMDs prior to the 2003 invasion. As one senior participant in that commission later explained, the whole matter was "a very sensitive subject" for the administration, and "the whole commission wasn't put together voluntarily" but only after continuing political pressure being exerted on it as a result of coming up empty in the weapons search.[3] But while the 9/11 Commission had done "everything publicly," due to pressure from "surviving widows and other family members," the WMD Commission "did everything privately in a less formal way."[4] And as with any effective blame-avoidance strategy vis-à-vis fact-finding commissions, their "charge," or what they were allowed to investigate, was constrained by political agreement prior to its start. As one senior participant observed, this was due to both political realities (a highly partisan climate that would otherwise block it) and the need to get access to people who otherwise would not testify:

Our mandate did *not* include, and it was with our complete concurrence because it would have turned into a complete political football, if we had been evaluating the Executive Branch response . . . and Dan Bartlett, when he saw the report for the first time, after we'd just briefed the president . . . his comment was something to the effect that, "you didn't do a report on us, but this is the most critical thing that anybody has written about us!" In other words, he understood that although we didn't try to assess how the officials reacted, that was off-limits. We said it was off-limits, they said it was off-limits. Everybody who wanted to go for the jugular wanted that on the record, they wanted a record of that, never really understanding that we couldn't have gotten the candor from the community that was necessary to get a complete report, if it was gonna be. I kept saying, there's only a handful of people that can't investigate that, and that's this little group working on the WMD Commission. We pledged not to do that.[5]

Given the bipartisan construction of the WMD Commission, there was also a great deal of concern about not causing political "waves," and a reluctance to really "push" on issues that would step "over the line" into how the White House used intelligence. Or how more indirect pressures and manipulations might have been used to move assessments on Iraq in directions they desired. As another senior participant on the WMD Commission observed, "We would not have undertaken the assignment if that had been part of our task."[6] And while one commission member admitted taking "flak from my wife constantly, who says, 'you guys aren't going after them for ignoring contrary evidence,' we were from the beginning not going in that direction, but instead trying to do something constructive that looks ahead and analyzes why the intelligence piece came out as it did."[7] Moreover, the politics surrounding the commission report became an even bigger issue for members as the 2004 presidential elections loomed ahead:

> Remember, this was before a presidential election. And this was gonna be a *big* deal! And we decided that we were not gonna say a thing about it until after the election. There was plenty of open-source evidence for everybody to work with to come to a conclusion, and I think most people who look at it carefully draw the conclusion that they wanted this [the Iraq War] to happen. But the question remained: Was there any impropriety in what they did to force it to happen or to, in fact, corrupt the intelligence system? And we specifically asked every member of the NIE . . . as well as those who'd reviewed it for publication across the board. And with all the articles that have been critical of everything, including our report . . . no one has found a single instance . . . where someone said, "yes, I was forced." A number of people have come forward and said, "well, the atmosphere was such that we knew what they'd wanted. We knew what the solution was supposed to be."[8]

Republican control of Congress during most of the Bush administration served to prevent more aggressive fact-finding investigations from being launched on Capitol Hill in committee settings, greatly reducing the pressure that otherwise would have been placed on the White House by Democrats. And while deflecting some flak, neither the 9/11 nor WMD Commissions supported an Al Qaeda connection with Iraq, nor had the latter effectively exonerated the White House over its inflated WMD claims. As one former WMD Commission member observed, Bush was under "enormous pressure" since we had gone to war and "you said there was WMD, you said there was an Al Qaeda connection, and we . . . found that there was nothing to substantiate that either." As the Iraq War dragged on, calls for further reviews grew louder, eventually resulting in the congressionally appointed Iraq Study Group (ISG) in March 2006, cochaired by Republican James Baker (former secretary of state for the president's father) and Democrat Lee Hamilton (a longtime veteran of Congress).

For blame-avoidance purposes, the push by Congress for a bipartisan ISG allowed a group to be formed that could be seen as balanced, yet would (due to that bipartisan makeup) prevent strong attacks on White House policy. And though bipartisan inquiries can be argued by defenders to be more balanced and fair, they can also be used to effectively "water down" criticism of the party being investigated if there is a strong need to "maintain bipartisanship" within the group. Still, as one senior participant recalled, the Bush administration was worried about the potential of the ISG to criticize its Iraq policy:

> The ISG was put together by Congress. So that wasn't really a Bush vehicle. The WMD Commission was put together by the president, but it was, again, I have no qualms in saying categorically that he would never have asked for it but for the public pressure to come clean with this; it was that kind of pressure. The ISG was put together by the Congress on a bipartisan basis, and he was very worried.[9]

In fact, as another senior participant recalled, the situation was so politically touchy (much as WMDs had been), that the Republican cochair of the ISG, James Baker, actually asked permission from Bush before accepting the position.[10] This set the stage for some interesting dynamics as the ISG later moved toward wrapping up its investigations and interviews. Not only was Bush forewarned about the ISG report's contents prior to release, he was placed in the awkward position of accepting the report graciously, adopting some positions formally to appear "responsive" to the nonpartisan panel's efforts, while actively avoiding the appearance of capitulating to an outside group. Even if Bush eventually adopted many of the ISG's recommendations in practice, it would nevertheless create political vulnerabilities to do so directly after the report. And even with a bipartisan panel, the White House was very nervous about the report's findings.

> [Bush] was given a courtesy briefing on it by Jim Baker alone the afternoon before we presented it to him formally the next morning. So for that report, he was ready. He knew basically what was gonna be in it. . . . There was real concern on the part of the White House, and on the part of a lot of people in positions of power around the world. We got requests to have a second meeting with the president after we were finished with him! We'd like to meet with you again, the whole group, including Cheney, Rumsfeld, and Condi. Steve Hadley . . . Bill Clinton and his team wanted to come in and be heard. And then we got a request from Tony Blair to be heard. And then word that King Abdullah wants to be heard. . . . There was the perception that this was gonna dramatically change the whole status quo in the whole theater! I mean, the expectations for the report

were overblown! Having said that . . . if you were president of the United States, and had a group formed not at your request to critique your administration . . . because that's what you're asking them to do on Iraq . . . what we shouldn't be doing. It can't get much more critical than that. . . . If they come out with something that is clearly not consistent in its entirety with things you've already said, just as a matter of human nature, you're not gonna say, "I'm gonna do the whole thing!" John Kerry was running against him and did come out and say, "I'll do the whole report." You couldn't expect any president to say that! And it's my feeling . . . that he recognized what he's done is pretty much consistent with that whole report, including the surge. The truth of the matter is most of the other things, except for a couple of high-visibility things like direct negotiations with Iran . . . almost everything else in there was being done, but it wasn't being done saying, "we're complying, we're doing what they suggested."[11]

Use "Bad Guys" to Justify Policy or Deflect Blame

Of course, for strategies of blame avoidance and justifying existing political strategies or policies, few things are as useful to policy makers as the proverbial "bad guy." Indeed, as Wayne (2003: 103) observes:

> Presidents have them, use them, and consistently invoke their image. They serve as political foils, unifying figures, and fodder for the exercise of presidential power, and they provide at least the appearance of strong presidential leadership. . . . They are the enemies that every president has and needs, the people who allegedly cause the problems that presidents . . . are forced to address. . . . Invoking the image of a bad guy . . . helps focus people's attention, simplifies policy explanations, and helps the public determine right from wrong. It allows presidents to claim the moral high ground in political conflicts as well as justify the necessity for saying or doing something potentially controversial. Blaming the problem on a bad guy can make a complex issue more understandable to more people more quickly . . . reducing or removing nuance.

A perfect illustration of the use of the "bad guy" in crisis rhetoric to justify a drastic, controversial shift in policy direction is found in Bonham and Heradstveit's (2005) discussion of the evolution of the "Axis of Evil" metaphor and how this served to shift or "redefine" the debate over the proper focus of the war on terror away from being centered on bin Laden and Al Qaeda in Afghanistan and toward states that were unconnected with the 9/11 attacks (Iraq, Iran, and North Korea). Such "enemy images" have long played similar roles in foreign policy, with countries perceived through such frames being seen as degenerate and evil, and a threat against which states are justified to take extreme measures to protect themselves (R. Cottam 1977; M. Cottam 1994; Cottam and Cottam 2001). Moreover, as Wayne (2003: 105) observes, bad guys "contribute to the president's good-guy image," serving as a "unifying figure to dislike, a personification of evil, a reason for action, a point around which support can rally" that can "contribute to stature by elevating presidential actions, sometimes to heroic proportions." For blame-avoidance purposes, such bad guys can be either "foreign" ones (who serve the useful external enemy role) or "domestic" ones (who can be cast as opponents of your sensible policies, roadblocks to their success, or even enemies of the people). But while it is easy to see the political value of using bad guys to justify policy or deflect blame, Wayne (2003:104) also notes the clear downside to this strategy:

> Bad guys can also be dangerous to presidents who invoke their "evil" images. Their presence and perceived malevolent actions can serve to restrict vision, limit options, shorten time frames, expose decisional processes to public view, unleash emotions, impair analysis, and bind and inhibit future decisions and actions. . . . Too narrow a vision, too superficial an understanding, too emotional a reaction can adversely affect judgments.

For the Bush administration, it would have been difficult to find more of a bad guy than bin Laden, or an evil enemy after 9/11 more compelling than Al Qaeda for justifying policy: from toppling the Taliban to denying Geneva Convention rights by declaring captured fighters "enemy combatants"; from extraordinary rendition and "torture-lite" (water-boarding) to the need to overthrow Saddam. The White House employed the bad guy to justify policies and to deflect criticism when controversial moves (like rendition, torture, or warrantless wiretapping) became public (Woodward 2002, 2004, 2006, 2008). Moreover, the blame-avoidance tactic of justifying morally questionable actions by arguing they were essential to protect the public, prevent further 9/11 attacks, or defeat terrorism was frequently employed—effectively placing critics uncomfortably on the side of having to argue implicitly to undercut these public goods being provided by the policies in question.

Saddam long had played the bad guy role for American policy makers. His longstanding (and well-earned) reputation for brutality at home and aggression abroad made the threat posed by Iraq (with or without nuclear weapons) one the international community took very seriously. Added to this were Saddam's verbose threats to "burn half of Israel" with chemical weapons prior to the first Gulf War, his use of such weapons against the Kurds and Iranians (during the Iran-Iraq war of the 1980s), his invasion of two neighboring states (Iran and Kuwait), and his ready use of Scud missiles during both wars (Woodward 1991; Preston 2001). Though he did not, in fact, utilize the chemical or biological weapons at his disposal during the Gulf War (UNSCOM inspectors found such artillery shells and Scud warheads after the war), his refusal to cooperate with inspections and prior use of WMDs firmly established his threatening bad-guy image (Preston 2007). Further, Saddam's unwillingness to abide by UN resolutions after the war and the Oil for Food program were a useful lightning rod to divert blame away from the international community (including the US) for the hundreds of thousands of Iraqi civilians who died as a result of sanctions (Mueller and Mueller 1999).

And though the 9/11 and WMD Commissions both found no credible evidence linking Saddam Hussein and Iraq to Al Qaeda, the administration would continue to use this as a justification for taking action. In Bush's "Cincinnati speech" on October 7, 2002, he called Iraq a grave threat, didn't admit any doubts or dissents in the intelligence community, and talked about a partnership between Al Qaeda and Baghdad with "high-level contacts that go back a decade" (Isikoff and Corn 2006: 146). Similarly, during the run-up to the war in January 2003, Rice famously stated regarding Iraq that "facing clear evidence of peril, we cannot wait for the final proof—the smoking gun—that could come in the form of a mushroom cloud" (Isikoff and Corn 2006: 147). These threats posed by Iraqi WMDs and the country's purported links to Al Qaeda were repeated continually by administration officials like Cheney during speeches and appearances on news programs long after both claims had been dismissed as lacking support by independent commissions (Woodward 2004, 2006, 2008). Yet, from a blame-avoidance perspective, Saddam continued to provide the administration with some degree of political cover long after his death by allowing the defense of "even if there were no WMDs or Al Qaeda connections, the region and Iraq are better off without him!"

Use the "Hidden Hand" of Bureaucratic Obstruction to Block Policy without Leaving Fingerprints

Greenstein (1982) popularized the notion of the "hidden hand" style of presidential leadership in his study of Eisenhower, who maintained his popularity by the "illusion" of appearing to be above the political fray and not being involved in the making of unpopular decisions. So successful was this blame-avoidance strategy that until Greenstein published his book, the general picture of Eisenhower in the public mind was of a Reagan-esque figure largely uninvolved in policy who delegated substantially to subordinates like John Foster Dulles—an image that couldn't have been further from the truth (Ambrose 1990; Burke and Greenstein 1991; Preston 2001).

A cousin of this blame-avoidance strategy is one employed by Cheney and his staff to great effect. As Wilkerson explained, it was a tactic effectively blocking policy but leaving no damning fingerprints. When Assistant Secretary of State for East Asian and Pacific Affairs Jim Kelly set off for the Six-Party Talks with North Korea (after an NSC meeting in which Bush presided over the decision to send him on the negotiation mission), he made it only as far as Hawaii before being told he had to stick to a more limited script and could not actually do any negotiating beyond it.[12] This was, in fact, contrary to the decision taken at the NSC meeting, and for Wilkerson it was an example of Cheney's hidden-hand influence with the president, getting that "last bite from the apple" in private after the rest of the inner circle had gone home.[13] It was hidden and stealthy, and it left no traces other than the altered decision. And on Korea policy, Cheney's team effectively thwarted any initiatives the vice president disagreed with:

> They thwarted the process everywhere from the Policy Coordinating Group, chaired by Assistant Secretary Jim Kelly, all the way up to a couple of times in Principals, and then actually in one NSC meeting as I said. . . . Because the summary of conclusions reflected a decision that Jim Kelly was then not able to carry out. So they had different bureaucratic techniques and they fit them to the problem. And in most cases, they were successful.[14]

Where there was no need to actively thwart policy, Cheney's office merely monitored, especially in areas where there was already enough bureaucratic disagreement or difficulties to make policy decisions unlikely to emerge. In such cases, it was better to sit back, not engage in the process, and allow bureaucratic inertia to literally drag policy to a halt. As Wilkerson recalls:

> They took a totally unique approach to the Iran decision. They let the statutory process function, time and time again. Deputies meetings tee up the material. Principals meeting, once or twice they'd tee it up for the actual, formal NSC meeting. They never, as far as I know to this day . . . produced a national security decision document on Iran. It's all ad hoc. And what my view is—that the vice president, who had the most incredible network I've ever seen in the bureaucracy. Loyal. Had a vision. Had a strategy for executing that vision. And they were *ruthless* in following it! Walk over anybody! So they were way ahead of the rest of the bureaucracy. Rest of the bureaucracy was fumbling around trying to find its candle in the dark! They had everything going for them. And so, they smelled really quickly that there were a lot of divisions in the entire bureaucracy, particularly in State, Defense, Justice, Treasury, Commerce, about Iran. So they said, "Hmmm. Don't have to worry about this! There'll never be a decision in the process!" [*laughs*] And so they got what they wanted by default, which was no talks. They didn't have to frustrate that process; they just had to keep an ear to it. And if it ever looked like there might be consensus coming about, and the president might be responding . . . I'm sure they would have moved in and done something if it went against their views. But they didn't have to. They just let the process, and its inability to come to a decision, and the president's lack of desire to force it to, and I'm sure Cheney had something

to do with that too. So here we are, seven years plus, and we still don't have a document on Iran.[15]

Use Crisis Rhetoric Effectively

The effective use of "crisis" rhetoric is a blame-avoidance tactic seeking to create a *special context* (the crisis) within which a leader is justified in taking strong, controversial, and potentially unpopular decisions out of necessity. As already noted, Bush employed the concept of the war on terror to garner greater support for his policies and create a "war president" image. Describing something as a "war" in the American political system is a way to denote a different magnitude of seriousness with which one views the problem, whether it be a true armed conflict, a war on poverty, or a war on drugs. That there is often uncertain or ineffective follow-through on such "wars" does nothing to dampen the continued enthusiasm of officials for declaring such wars on public problems! It is a way to show you take a given problem seriously and are taking steps to address it (like appointing a drug czar), deflecting criticism that a serious, difficult problem to solve is being ignored.

For Bush, the war on terror—especially in the unique political environment after 9/11—created a *very* special context for action. It was not a use of crisis rhetoric to merely give the appearance of doing something, as declaring wars on problems often amount to, but it served as a key to open the door to dramatic policy actions (like invading Afghanistan and Iraq) while dampening criticism. During a war on terror, how could any politician (especially the Democrats) stand in the way of harsh measures against terrorists (like being sent to Guantanamo Bay), or really block a move against a dangerous, WMD-armed Saddam who was supporting terrorism? While objections were raised by opponents to some of Bush's actions and policy proposals, within the American body politic (and the contest for the acquiescence of the public) opponents found themselves cast as Sisyphus pushing an enormous boulder up a hill made increasingly steep by 9/11 rhetoric. As Kiewe (1994: xvi) observes, rhetorical presidents seeking to use crisis rhetoric are "image makers" who "seek the opportunity to define situations and to construct the reality they wish the public to accept," with crisis situations being particularly well suited to this task since they "allow presidents to communicate an image of decisiveness and determination" during events cast as "extraordinary, unique, and threatening."

This proved enormously effective in the first few years after 9/11, with Brzezinski (2007: 1) observing that the use of the phrase "war on terror" also created a "culture of fear" in America resulting in a "classic self-inflicted wound"—where "fear obscures reason, intensifies emotions and makes it easier for demagogic politicians to mobilize the public on behalf of the policies they want to pursue." From its use in getting congressional and public support for war with Iraq to Bush's reelection call to not change commanders midstream during a war, Brzezinski (2007: 1) notes these pervasive, yet imprecise dangers were "channeled in a politically expedient direction by the mobilizing appeal of being 'at war.'"

Avoid Negative Imagery by Reducing Exposure to the Media

Another effective blame-avoidance tactic is to lower one's profile on the public or media radar by avoiding (where possible) negative imagery being presented by the mass media. A famous example of this tactic was the effective control of the media during the first Gulf War, where the press corps was kept corralled on base in Saudi Arabia, not allowed to move independently in the war zone, and fed official briefings by military commanders as their main source of information. Arguably this was important for maintaining security during military operations and kept journalists safer than they otherwise would have been, but it also served to keep negative stories or images out of the Western press. As war presidents soon discover, public opinion is harmed by the ugly images inevitably occurring during wars—something Saddam understood when he allowed press images of the hundreds of civilians killed in a command bunker bombing in Baghdad out early in the war. During the one-hundred-hour ground war, it would be CNN images from the so-called highway of death—where columns of Iraqi forces retreating from Kuwait City were bombed by coalition forces, leaving imagery of charred Iraqi soldiers in their vehicles on television—that helped move George H. W. Bush to end the war (Bush and Scowcroft 1998; Preston 2001). During Vietnam, Johnson faced constant negative imagery on nightly network newscasts of flag-draped coffins arriving back at Dover, serving to highlight the costs of the conflict and channel blame back toward the White House. Such negative imagery in the media is akin to holding a golf club aloft during a thunderstorm for political leaders. Far from channeling blame away, it attracts and directs the blame directly downward, toward the wielder.

For the Bush administration, a number of blame-avoidance strategies to reduce negative imagery and press exposure were adopted. Recognizing the politically harmful blowback caused during Vietnam by such images, the Pentagon banned the media from showing (or taking) photos of flag-draped caskets arriving back at Dover from Iraq (McClellan 2008). Restricting such images was vitally important given the clear evidence that the increasing death toll among U.S. soldiers (and the general perception of lack of progress in Iraq) harmed Bush's public approval numbers and support for the war

(Eichenberg and Stoll 2006; Gelpi et al. 2006; Voeten and Brewer 2006). In many respects, this parallels a dynamic seen during Vietnam, where public opinion dropped from around 74 percent in favor of U.S. military involvement in Vietnam in 1965 to barely 50 percent in favor just prior to the Tet Offensive in December 1967 (Mueller 2005).

In addition to the problems posed by American casualties for public opinion, there was also a de-emphasis upon reporting (or collecting information on) civilian casualties in Iraq. Doing "body counts" of enemy combatants as a measure of progress had been discredited during the Vietnam War and with modern insurgencies was even less useful given the difficulty in separating out civilians from insurgents. More importantly, in the kind of urban conflict Iraq became, there was a grim inevitability to the reality that there would be high numbers of civilians killed as collateral damage by allied forces (or by militants themselves) or indirectly as a result of the breakdown of public infrastructure (such as medical services). As the war continued, estimates of Iraqi civilian casualties provided ammunition for critics of Iraq policy, and officials routinely tried to dismiss the higher counts as inaccurate or politically biased. This was particularly the case with the high numbers of civilian casualties being suggested by outside actors in 2006, ranging from the eighty to ninety thousand proposed by the online Body Count site (that merely counted press-reported deaths) all the way up to the controversial claim of over six hundred thousand by the British medical journal *Lancet* (based on interviews and statistical methods usually employed to determine the amount of "excess" deaths above the normal amount during flu seasons). Still, for blame-avoidance purposes, the most important casualties for the Bush administration, politically at least, remained those of U.S. soldiers. Indeed, as Mueller (2005: 50) observed, "what chiefly matters for American public opinion are American losses, not those of the people defended. . . . There is nothing new about this."

Further reducing his exposure to the media, Bush (whose performances during press conferences often revealed a lack of depth and understanding of the substance of policy matters beyond the broad brushstrokes) avoided such settings where possible, leaving it to subordinates like Rumsfeld to do battle with the press (McClellan 2008; Woodward 2004, 2006). By 2004 Bush had held only eleven solo news conferences, compared to twenty-three by Nixon and seventy-one by George H. W. Bush at the same point in their presidencies—easily the lowest count in history (Rich 2006: 161). In so doing, the administration employed an effective blame-avoidance strategy akin to that used by pilots during wartime—if you don't want to face flak, avoid flying over the enemy's gun emplacements.

Stay on Message and Repeat (Spin or Deny Bad News)

On September 21, 2001, the Presidential Daily Brief (PDB) (distributed to Bush, Cheney, Rice, Hadley, Rumsfeld, Wolfowitz, and Powell) informed them there was no evidence of Iraqi participation in 9/11 and "scant credible evidence" of any "significant collaborative ties" between Iraq and Al Qaeda, with Saddam actually regarding the terror organization as a threat to his own secular regime (Rich 2006: 230–31). This initial finding was seconded by the 9/11 Commission, along with continued reporting from the intelligence community.[16] Nevertheless, as a blame-avoidance tactic to disarm criticism, emphasizing Saddam as the bad guy while continuing to describe his connections to Al Qaeda was highly effective politically. Cheney continued to insist on such links (despite their being discredited) clear to the end of the Bush administration (Woodward 2004, 2006, 2008). Even when the inspector general at the Pentagon, Thomas F. Gimble, testified before Congress that captured Iraqi documents and interrogations of Saddam and his lieutenants had "all confirmed" there had been no cooperation between Iraq and Al Qaeda prior to the U.S. invasion, Cheney still appeared on Rush Limbaugh's radio show the same day repeating the allegation Al Qaeda was operating inside Iraq "before we ever launched" the war (Smith 2007: A01).

The blame-avoidance strategy of staying on message and repeating a charge (regardless of the evidence) is an age-old tactic infamously described by Nazi Propaganda Minister Joseph Goebbels as being that of the "big lie," noting that "if you tell a lie a thousand times it becomes the truth" (Thacker 2009). And one need only watch rival commercials during election campaigns, where dirt is flung regardless of its accuracy, to see the effectiveness of this tactic in both labeling your opponent as the bad guy and driving down their public support—while deflecting criticism from your own policies or stands. Repeated enough times, it becomes engrained in the public mind, easily recalled and difficult to remove—especially if listeners are relatively uninformed or lack easy access to information refuting such statements.

The power of "staying on message and repeating" is illustrated by polling numbers from 2002 onward continuing to show strong public belief in the link between Iraq and Al Qaeda, a link constantly reinforced by the administration. For example, according to a September 2002 CBS News poll, 51 percent thought Saddam was "personally involved" in 9/11 and 70 percent believed Al Qaeda members were based in Iraq (Rich 2006: 248). As the administration continued giving interviews linking Saddam to Al Qaeda in the run-up to the war, public opinion continued to respond, with an October 2002 Pew poll reporting that 66 percent of the public believed Saddam had helped the 9/11 terrorists (Rich 2006: 254). Only a few months prior to the war itself in January 2003, a Knight Ridder poll found 51 percent incorrectly believed one or more of the 9/11 hijackers were Iraqis, while 44 percent believed "most" or "some" were Iraqis (Rich 2006: 257). After Powell's UN speech making the case for war against Iraq, its possession of WMDs and likely links to terrorists, a CNN/*USA Today*/Gallup poll in February 2003 found 79 percent felt a "strong" case had been made for invading Iraq and 66 percent that a "strong" case for Iraq's "ties" to Al Qaeda had been made (Rich 2006: 264). That same month, a Pew poll found 57 percent of the public believed Saddam had helped the 9/11 terrorists (Rich 2006: 264).

Although criticism of these claims would eventually weaken this belief, for the purposes of pushing the policy of invading Iraq through politically, the steady drumbeat linking Saddam to 9/11 proved highly effective in marshalling support for the administration. Indeed, in March 2003, the month of the actual invasion of Iraq, an NYT/CBS poll found 45 percent believed Saddam was involved in 9/11 (Rich 2006: 266). So powerful was this residual belief, and the not too difficult to accept notion that Hussein was actually a "bad guy" (which no one would dispute), even the absence of WMDs would not be enough to completely undercut support for the White House. Indeed, after Bush's infamous Mission Accomplished photo op and speech in May 2003, a Gallup poll still found 79 percent of Americans believed the war with Iraq was justified even without conclusive evidence of WMDs (Rich 2006: 267–68). While the weight of the evidence began to change public perceptions (especially as the war became more unpopular from 2004 onward), the continuing effects of these repeated claims proved difficult to eliminate. Indeed, as Cheney continued these claims, a September 2007 CBS News/*New York Times* poll still showed 33 percent of the public believed Saddam was personally involved in the 9/11 attacks, with 40 percent of Republicans and 27 percent of Democrats falling into this camp.[17]

Discredit the Credibility of Opponents

This blame-avoidance tactic serves to deflect attention away from the substance of a criticism and toward the character or credibility of the critics themselves. During Vietnam, for example, Johnson often derisively referred to domestic critics who questioned or opposed the war as "Nervous Nellies" who obviously lacked the internal fortitude to deal with the hard policy realities faced by the White House (Wayne 2003). Dismissing political opponents as somehow being "unmanly" and lacking his toughness was a typical weapon in Johnson's rhetorical arsenal (Kearns 1976), while Nixon would argue criticism of his policies was based on a liberal conspiracy against him in the media (Greenberg 2003). But whatever the target, if bad news is being delivered or blame is being directed at you by a particular messenger, you "kill the messenger" politically by discrediting their character or motives.

An example of this tactic, which became a major controversy, was the "outing" of Valerie Plame's CIA cover by White House operatives (including members of Cheney's office) in retaliation for her husband, Ambassador Joseph Wilson's, public allegations the administration purposefully misled the nation into war with information about purported Iraqi purchases of uranium from Niger it knew were untrue.[18] On March 7, 2003, just days before Operation Iraqi Freedom was launched, IAEA Director General Mohamed ElBaradei told the UN Security Council the documents on which the Niger claim were based were forgeries, and the resulting intelligence about Iraqi uranium purchases were not credible and there was "no evidence or plausible indication" Iraq had revived its nuclear weapons program (McClellan 2008: 6). This was a major disaster in the making requiring blame avoidance; the idea Bush had made arguments for war based on inaccurate intelligence was one thing, but "if administration leaders deliberately chose to ignore the facts when assembling the case for war, and, even worse, if they knowingly dissembled in order to make the case appear stronger than it was, Americans might not be so forgiving" (McClellan 2008: 7). In May 2003 Nicolas Kristof of the *New York Times* published an article, based on an anonymous but credible source, stating that this had occurred regarding the purported yellowcake. That source was Ambassador Joseph Wilson, sent to Niger by the CIA in January 2002 to investigate the uranium allegations and reported back the documents showing the Iraqi effort were forgeries.[19] As McClellan (2008: 8–9) later acknowledged, Cheney's office immediately began efforts in late May 2003 to discredit Wilson, with Bush secretly declassifying key portions from the October 2002 NIE for Cheney and Scooter Libby to use in leaks to selected journalists. In addition, Libby, Armitage, Rove, and then press secretary Ari Fleischer also anonymously shared with reporters that Wilson's wife, Valerie Plame, was a CIA employee who helped arrange the trip to Niger—a felony release of classified national security information (McClellan 2008: 8–9). As McClellan (2008: 8–9) revealed, the purpose of the leaks was to "discredit Wilson" and undermine his public assertion (which was true) that he had been sent to Niger by the CIA after a request for information by Cheney.

When investigations began to uncover it had been officials within the administration itself who had leaked Plame's CIA identity to people like columnist Bob Novak, the blame-avoidance strategy was forced to shift to hiding and denying the evidence. In his memoir, McClellan (2008: 3–4), recounting his efforts to deny the story to the press (after being assured there was no White House involvement), reveals his frustration at finding later he had been deceived by Cheney, Libby, and Rove (who had allowed and encouraged him to repeat the lie).

Another tactic to discredit opponents is to claim to have superior information compared to the less informed critics. For example, in responding to the recommendations of the Iraq Study Group (many of which ran contrary to existing administration policy) in 2006, White House officials noted upon further review that they had concluded many of the key proposals were either "impractical or unrealistic" and, as White House Chief of Staff Andrew Card noted while referring to Bush's daily intelligence briefings, "The president by definition knows more than any of those people who are serving on these panels."[20]

Provide a Credible, Alternative Messenger to Rebut Criticism

Interestingly, the Bush administration also provides a good example of how you *counter* the tactic of discrediting your opponents—this time against critics making the charge the White House was a narrow, partisan, neocon-dominated group. Bush, who lacked foreign policy credentials himself, was certainly not the actor to make the case for the war in the face of such criticism, especially given a growing public impression of him as lacking knowledge and depth on issues. What the White House needed was an *alternative messenger*, someone who had both expertise and credibility to counter the image being painted by critics. For Bush, that messenger was Powell. As McClellan (2008: 5) notes, the choice of Powell to deliver the UN speech was driven by his "enormous bipartisan popularity, as well as his unquestioned honor and integrity," which made him the "most logical and persuasive person to help seal the case at home and abroad." It was a rationale Powell, along with most of his senior staff, were aware was at play.[21]

The administration also sought to provide the national media with credible, alternative messengers on Iraq policy and the war on terror in the form of a Pentagon "stable" of former senior military officers who served as analysts. As Barstow (2008) noted in a lengthy exposé published in the *New York Times*, these analysts were taken on tours of Iraq, given access to classified briefings by government officials, and provided "talking points" on the issues to support the administration's policies. Even when analysts doubted their veracity, they suppressed doubts for fear of losing their access, which greatly assisted their lucrative work on major TV and radio networks.

Of course, it was important to avoid the appearance these messengers were personally biased or were "put up to" making their arguments. And for a long time, this connection between the Pentagon and the military analysts was unknown. It became, as Barstow (2008) observed, part of a unified effort to provide credible, alternative testimony that by all appearances did not come from the White House—with Rumsfeld and his aides specifically instructing analysts not to quote briefers directly or describe their Pentagon contacts. In the lead-up to the war, they were given "talking points portraying Iraq as an urgent threat" (Barstow 2008). Pentagon officials noted, in a messaging triumph, that the media analysts were "taking verbatim what the secretary was saying" and repeating it over and over across the major networks (Barstow 2008). After obtaining access to Pentagon records detailing these operations, Barstow (2008) revealed internal documents repeatedly referring to these "message force multipliers" or "surrogates" who could be counted on to deliver "themes and messages" to the public. Further, these enlisted analysts were often used by the Pentagon as a "rapid reaction force" to rebut critical news coverage—all without a visible official fingerprint (Barstow 2008).

Use the "Hazy Memory" Defense

From Reagan claiming to have "no memory" of significant actions during the Iran-Contra Scandal to Clinton's lack of recall over inappropriate relations with a White House intern, the "hazy memory" defense is a blame-avoidance tactic frequently employed to deny responsibility. One illustration of this approach is found in the dispute between Tenet and the former chief of the European division at the CIA, Tyler Drumheller, over whether a warning was given about the dubious credibility of "Curveball"—the primary source behind many of the administration's claims about Iraq's WMD program. Although Curveball-originated material was being pushed by the Cheney-Rumsfeld group at every opportunity, even finding its way into Powell's UN speech (though he didn't realize it was the only major source for the claims), German intelligence (who held the individual) had warned it didn't view him as credible (Drumheller 2006; Rich 2006; Woodward 2006, 2008; Tenet 2007).[22] After no such weapons were found in Iraq and the questionable nature of Curveball became public, Tenet (2007) denied having been warned about the source's credibility problems. And during interviews with former administration officials, as well as colleagues and friends of Tenet who know him well, no consensus emerges as to whether they believe his defense or not—with several of Tenet's defenders noting he was often lazy in looking beneath the surface of issues, not even feeling the need to have a computer in his office.[23] For his part, Drumheller (2006: 10–11) noted he warned Tenet about Curveball by phone in February 2003 and also alerted his deputy, John McLaughlin, about the source during a January 2003 meeting.

Another example of the hazy-memory defense, according to former White House officials, is the way Bush would seek to avoid committing to certain statements of fact regarding policy or defend himself when earlier statements proved false.[24] McClellan (2008: 49–50) recalls Bush often fell back on the hazy-memory defense to protect himself from political embarrassment, rationalizing that "as long as he was not stating unequivocally anything that could be proven false," being evasive was not the same thing as lying.

Select a Lightning Rod or Scapegoat Reluctant or Unable to Defend Itself

Of course, a time-honored blame-avoidance strategy is to find an individual or organization reluctant or unable to defend itself to serve as a "lightning rod" or "scapegoat." For example, when prisoners were abused at Abu Ghraib, only soldiers (and one low-ranking senior officer) were eventually blamed and punished, while accountability for issuing the orders or setting into place practices actually fostering the environment leading to the abuse did not lead to consequences for senior ranks or Rumsfeld (Hersh 2004; Strasser 2004). Similarly, when FEMA Director Michael Brown was shown to be unqualified for his position and incompetent in his handling of the Katrina relief efforts in New Orleans, he was forced to resign, while those who appointed him in the first place avoided sanctions (Preston 2008). And when White House claims of a 9/11 link to Iraq or the existence of WMDs came unraveled after the war began, a predictable dynamic also occurred on schedule. As Drumheller (2006: 2) observed, "The CIA has always been a convenient lightning rod for the White House because its generals and foot soldiers are disinclined to come out to defend themselves. . . . I have grown increasingly angry at the way the CIA has been made a scapegoat for one foreign policy disaster after another." Responsibility for how the intelligence products were actually used, or how material might have been selectively sought out by the administration to support its policies, is seldom the focus. As one former senior-level intelligence official ruefully observed:

> Think about it from the perspective of everybody blaming you for 9/11, everyone blaming you for Iraq. No consideration that it might have been policy makers' interpretation of information. It just kept talking about one intelligence failure after another. If we think about it, are these really intelligence failures or are they failures at the policy level? Is it just because we have black-and-white thinkers who are ideologues that set up their own offices and make their own intelligence? That gets kind of lost in the discussion. So now you have people who have been smacked down, who've been told their failures. Who've been told, "Don't say anything that's gonna get you in trouble. Don't take a definitive stand anymore, because if you do, then you're gonna be held accountable and your feet will be in the fire." So this is what happens to intelligence! And you get crappy analysis![25]

As a consequence, analysts become even more gun-shy regarding language, trying to put caveat upon caveat into analysis to prevent being left holding the bag once again for policy makers seeking political cover. Analysts live in "fear of being wrong," worried about "what if you're wrong and somebody finds out that you were wrong—somebody acted on it because you were wrong."[26] And this could happen whether analysis was wrong or not in the end, since analysts have no control over how senior consumers eventually make use of the information or assessments sent to them (caveats or no). Indeed, when asked about whether what had happened to the CIA (in terms of taking the blame for WMDs and 9/11) had influenced how other intelligence shops functioned, one former senior intelligence official replied:

> Oh yeah! Absolutely! Clearly! See and that's the thing. In many ways, we saw the CIA always taking heat because [name of an intelligence agency redacted] is just a nonentity many times, no one really thinks about what they do or say, even though we were doing the same kind of analysis as CIA. So it was always like, let the CIA take the fall! [*laughs*][27]

Given the world in which the intelligence community operates, and the sensitive nature of their tradecraft and sources, they are almost the perfect scapegoat for policy makers. Not only can they not openly defend themselves, they also work directly for political leaders who use them as human shields when blame needs to be apportioned. So they are doubly unable to protect themselves. And the blame-avoidance tactic of, "If I had only known the facts, I would have made a different decision," requires a provider (or withholder) of information or advice to be identified. As a result, the intelligence community is almost tailor-made for use as a blame-avoidance lightning rod. As Drumheller (2006: 6) observed, "The truth, as all CIA officers know, is always several shades of gray. The truth is the White House, for a number of reasons, believed what it wanted to believe . . . [and] deliberately tried to draw a cloak over its own misjudgments by shining a light on ours." In the case of Iraq and the administration's actual use of intelligence—involving both its direct and indirect pressuring of the community to find the "right" answers vis-à-vis WMDs—the blame apportioned by later commissions (like the WMD Commission) landed squarely on intelligence officials and (as usual) ignored the actions of political officials. Indeed, responding to the question of whether the true failure should really be seen as one of White House leadership as opposed to merely one of an intelligence community failing, Paul Pillar observed:

> The main dynamic is indeed one of U.S. intelligence having traditionally been used as a scapegoat. And it has been politically inconvenient to apportion the

blame in other directions. The way the Silberman and Robb [WMD] Commission operated, for example . . . on this politicization issue they were punting on that! What was that one line they had? It sort of barely acknowledged it—"the policy makers had a strong interest in the issue." It didn't begin to capture it. Strong interest in the issue without policy bias would be if the policy makers go to the intelligence officer and say, "We are strongly interested in this issue. We want to place high importance on finding out exactly what happened. So I want you to leave no holds unbarred, look at all sides of the issue, ask questions from all sides of the issue. And give us your very best unvarnished judgment on this issue." It isn't even *close* to what the atmosphere was! It didn't even *remotely* resemble that! Everything was in *one* direction! So, to say, "interest in the issue" . . . doesn't *begin* to describe it! [*laughs*] And, yes, it's difficult and inconvenient to start apportioning blame in other directions, especially in the case of the Silberman and Robb Commission, which was appointed by the White House after all. You can't expect them to turn fire on the people who created them. Judge Silberman, I think at one point was asked, "Are you gonna really look at how the administration used the intelligence?" "Oh no, no way! It's quite clear . . . that's beyond our charter! Oh no, we wouldn't touch that with a ten foot pole!" Too politically sensitive! I point to that sometimes as sort of a point of comparison when somebody comes down hard on some intelligence themes, like Tenet in particular. I've been in committee hearings where Tenet was crossed, "Well, when the vice president says something publicly on X, Y, Z, and it disagrees with what your analysts are saying, what did you do? Did you go tell the vice president that he's all wrong?" So there's *that* expectation of officials who are fully employed by the executive branch of government? Whereas somebody like Silberman, who has senior status and a lifetime whatever . . . "Well, oh no, we're not going to touch that!" [*laughs*] I think that adds some perspective to the expectations![28]

Moreover, the kind of pressure that can be placed on analysts by policy makers to find a particular type of evidence is of a very subtle variety—which leaves few (if any) overt fingerprints. While the WMD Commission stated they found no evidence of pressure being placed on analysts, confidential interviews by the author with individuals throughout the intelligence community during this time generally confirmed the existence of a more subtle, pervasive influence.[29] Essentially, analysts recalled "the writing was on the wall" as far as what the administration wanted to hear on Iraq, and those who briefed senior White House officials would be queried hard on analysis questioning Al Qaeda links or WMDs in Iraq, with requests for further reviews often following.[30] Such "bounce back" is not seen by the analytic community as nonjudgmental, but an indication of skepticism on the part of policy makers—a skepticism often quite clearly communicated to briefers in the tone in which it was met.[31] Those who were present during visits made by Cheney, or more often his chief of staff, Scooter Libby, to CIA headquarters prior to the Iraq War noted how this was both exhilarating and intimidating to analysts—and could hardly help but elicit a desire to "tell them what they want to hear."[32] As Pillar observed regarding such visits:

> In terms of the way analysts react, it is a *major* event! A *major* event! Of course, just getting face time with somebody as senior as the *vice president* or Libby—is a *big* deal! So, how that face time goes is a big deal. One of the biggest feathers in an intelligence analyst's cap that they're gonna have on the table at the next promotion panel is, "Oh, there's a good word put in by the senior consumer for the estimate or the assessment that Sally wrote!" And boy, that's in the backs of analysts' minds all the time! Of course, heaven forbid the other thing, that "senior consumer X said he really thought that Sally wrote crock"! Whether you use *the p* word and call it pressure or not, in terms of how human intelligence officers react, any kind of analyst reacts, of course there was pressure.[33]

Not only does the intelligence community provide a convenient scapegoat for policies that go wrong, but Pillar's observations illustrate yet another blame-avoidance tactic often used by political leaders in connection with their lightning rods. The classic defense of "If my subordinate had really disagreed with my position/policies, they could have said something or objected—but they didn't." This puts the weaker subordinate, whose continued employment is fully in the hands of superiors, in the extreme position of having to vehemently, publicly object or resign if they disagree with their bosses' preferred policy course. This is analogous to opinions arguing that if Powell (or McNamara) had threatened to resign (or done so), it would have made a difference and changed the administration's policy direction. It sounds so simple, and immediately gives the superior an easy path toward blaming their decisions on subordinates who didn't "guide them back to the path" on the issue. But it also ignores the reality that presidential advisers in White House inner circles seldom dissent in such a dramatic, Hollywood manner—and wide-ranging interviews with former advisers to presidents from Roosevelt to Bush support this fact (Preston 2001).[34] Most presidential advisers can recall very few such instances, and almost always the actual dissent falls far short of a dramatic resignation threat or knock-down-drag-out fight.[35] It just isn't the way inner circles function. Moreover, with certain leaders, advisers have a much shorter leash for dissent or disagreement over policy than with others. For example, with Kennedy, Eisenhower, or Obama, advisers have the luxury of being able to express strong reservations and dissent during policy debates without being excluded from further discussions by the president (Preston 2001).[36] In contrast, for leaders like Johnson and Bush, these sorts of dissents effectively discredit the adviser and result in their exclusion from further policy discussions—whether it be by placement in LBJs "doghouse" and exclusion from Tuesday Lunch meetings, or through the effective "sidelining" of Powell's State Department from Iraq policy (Preston 2001).[37]

It's not only the White House that makes use of the intelligence community as a scapegoat to avoid blame. Fact-finding commissions, appointed by either presidents or Congress, often find using the community as a focus for blame avoids the more dangerous path of directing their gaze toward the actions of political leaders (especially when partisan politics are in play). As Pillar noted, a couple of things make intelligence on issues a convenient scapegoat for commissions:

> One is we're deflecting the politically sensitive aspect of something. It's worked. Republicans or Democrats, instead of firing at each other, you know, fire at somebody else. That was certainly true at the 9/11 Commission, where it was set up to maintain the bipartisanship. And Kean and Hamilton are trying to stay like Siamese Twins, despite things like the Republicans going after Jamie Gorelick. So one of the strong, strong concerns was . . . "Please don't have this torn apart in partisanship!" Well, what can they do? Well, it's the intelligence that was screwed up. Rather than picking apart what this or that administration did as a matter of policy. And then, of course, on the whole Iraq War thing. The political motivations are pretty clear.[38]

As one former senior member of the administration admitted, "the 9/11 Commission was a whitewash" because it had been set up to essentially avoid political controversy and not examine the actions of the political leadership itself.[39] And as another senior State Department official noted, "A real problem was the Hill, because that's where the oversight should be, but the Democrats rolled over. . . . They could have done more, could have been a good opposition, but they weren't!"[40] Even when criticism toward the community was softened, the function served by intelligence was deflecting blame from upper levels. As Isikoff and Corn (2006: 251) observed, as officials were "attempting to wiggle out of their definitive prewar statements," intelligence was the explanation for Wolfowitz, who in testimony before the House Armed Services Committee noted, "If there's a problem with intelligence . . . it doesn't mean that anybody misled anybody. It means that intelligence is an art not a science." Similarly, during a press briefing, JCS Chairman Myers remarked, "Intelligence doesn't necessarily mean something is true, it's just, it's intelligence, you know, it's your best estimate of the situation. It doesn't mean it's a fact" (Isikoff and Corn 2006: 251).

For political purposes, it can also be useful to find individuals who can be singled out as "examples of a bigger problem" within a larger group you wish to discredit. This blame-avoidance tactic is essentially one of creating an unwilling lightning rod to deflect criticism through discrediting the larger

group of which they are a part. And as regular viewers of the television channel Animal Planet can readily attest, it is far easier for predators to pick off
individuals who get separated from the herd than it is for them to take on the
larger group itself. Recounting his inadvertent conversion into a lightning rod
after having been invited to give an informal, unofficial talk to a university
class in early 2002, Pillar remembers:

> What I was talking about was terrorism. . . . And near the end of the talk . . . one
> of the students said, "Well, Mr. Pillar, you said at the outset of your talk that
> you were speaking as a private individual and not in your official capacity. But
> it sounds like you agree with most everything we're doing on counterterrorism."
> And I said, "Well, I do agree with a great majority of it. But if your question is
> do you want me to find areas where I would perhaps have a different slant," I
> said. And this happened to be just . . . after the "axis of evil" State of the Union
> address . . . one thing that really bothered me about that speech is how the whole
> issue of terrorism and weapons proliferation just got all mushed into one issue;
> it was totally a mistake. From the way I approach these issues as a scholar,
> that's not the way to do it. They're two different issues, they're different issues
> of reality, and if it were my speech, I wouldn't have squished them together!
> . . . Well, there was somebody in the class . . . who was the source of a leak to
> *Insight Magazine*, which is kind of a neocon version of the *National Enquirer*,
> which came out a few days later with the headline, "Senior Intelligence Of-
> ficial Blasts President's Speech!" [*laughs*] And this got subsequently replayed
> by editorial writers at the *Wall Street Journal* and the *Washington Times*, and
> one of the journal editorials had me giving a "public speech" at Johns Hopkins
> University devoted to attacking the president's policies! [*laughs*] One of the
> grillings I once got from Republican senators I got after one of these *Wall Street
> Journal* editorials! [*laughs*][41]

The targeting individuals in order to cast doubt on the credibility of intelligence products, or to question the motives of those individuals or agencies
themselves, was certainly a blame-avoidance tactic used by the White House
in response to damaging leaks in the run-up to the 2004 presidential elections. There had been a leak in early October 2004 of an intelligence estimate
the National Intelligence Council had written on Iraq in mid-2004 that was
"a pretty gloomy estimate, which in retrospect turned out to be pretty accurate."[42] Nevertheless, during a presidential election season, this kind of report
was quite damaging and required deflecting. As Pillar recalls:

> This was a matter of some controversy and the president said publicly, "Ah,
> they're just guessin!" About the same time, I had given a talk to a Civic Coun-
> cil on International Affairs session out in San Diego. . . . It was supposedly an
> off-the-record dinner conversation with about twenty people, and I was talking

about Middle Eastern stuff. Well, as of 2004, it was kinda hard to talk about the Middle East without talking about Iraq, kinda hard to talk about Iraq without saying some things aren't going very well lately! [*laughs*] This became the subject of a Bob Novak column, who identified me as leading an intelligence community insurgency against the White House and mentioned this talk as evidence of insubordination and undermining the president's policies, and so on. And it was all partly by way of discrediting the other leaked estimates. . . . "Okay, these are the people who came out with this gloomy stuff, things to say about Iraq! They're just a bunch of closet Democrats who are out to undermine the president." That was the whole message. So that got replayed again and again in various editorials. In fact, Novak [recently] had a column that mentioned it again. . . . This time his version was that I was "giving speeches across the country," quote unquote, attacking the president's policies! [*laughs*] So this is the way these things sort of get embellished in the retelling.[43]

Avoid Leaving Paper Trails

One way to avoid blame is to not leave incriminating evidence around that could later be used to assign it, like paper trails. During the Eisenhower administration, for example, when highly sensitive subjects were being discussed with his advisers—like covert American operations to overthrow Prime Minister Mossadegh of Iran in 1953 or President Jacobo Arbenz of Guatemala in 1954—the president insisted on purely oral discussions in which no physical notes would be taken (Preston 2001). This tactic serves to provide leaders with "plausible deniability" regarding actions or policies that later prove to be unsuccessful or controversial. This tactic also describes Cheney and his staff's visits to CIA analysts at Langley to "implicitly" apply subtle pressure on analysis, pressure that would not be linked later to any piece of paper or memo explicitly saying, "We want you to find this on Iraq." The problem of paper trails can also be applied to situations in which officials "go on record" with a report or memo at too early a stage in the policy process, which can place political pressure on an administration. In such cases, there is usually an effort to hold back such materials until a later date.

For example, in early March 2001, Tenet gave Hadley a list of expanded authorities the CIA was seeking in order to go after bin Laden (including authorization for operations to kill him without first trying to capture him)—a memo that NSC Senior Director Mary McCarthy requested Tenet take back, stating, "We need you to take back the draft covert-action finding. If you formally transmit these to the NSC, the clock will be ticking, and we don't want the clock to tick just now" (Tenet 2007: 144). As Tenet (2007: 144) would later reflect, "In other words, the new administration needed more time to figure out what their new policies were, and thus didn't want to be in a position someday to be criticized for not moving quickly enough on a critical intelligence community proposal."

The potential embarrassment when such memos are not pulled back (and something catastrophic like 9/11 occurs) is well illustrated when Richard Clarke, who at the time was the administration's chief counterterrorism adviser on the NSC, sent a memo covering a proposed strategy against Al Qaeda to Rice on January 25, 2001, asking for an NSC principals meeting that would never be called (Tenet 2007: 143). This paper trail of memos and meeting discussions between officials would later prove very embarrassing for the White House (and especially Rice, who can be seen dramatically failing in her job of gathering assessments from throughout the government to adequately inform the president) when the 9/11 Commission chronicled them in their report. On June 28, 2001, Tenet (along with several of his top assistants) met with Rice to warn her that "based on a review of all source reporting, we believe that Usama Bin Ladin will launch a significant terrorist attack against the U.S. and/or Israeli interests in the coming weeks" (Tenet 2007: 149). Again on July 10, Tenet and his staff (along with Clarke and Hadley) met with Rice, who was warned the signs were "unmistakable" that "there will be a significant terror attack in the coming weeks or months" (Tenet 2007: 151). As Tenet (2007: 152–53) recalls, Rice was warned "multiple and simultaneous attacks" by Al Qaeda were being planned to "inflict mass casualties against U.S. facilities and interests," and after questioning whether that was true, she finally agreed to put forward to Bush measures Clarke and others had previously submitted in March—a four-month delay (and meeting) which was never even mentioned by the 9/11 Commission in its final report, likely due to pressure on the commission not to embarrass (or examine the conduct of) administration officials.

Make the Argument That You Are "Looking Ahead" not "Dwelling on the Past"

Another blame-avoidance tactic to rebut criticisms of past actions emphasizes that you are "looking ahead" to deal with the real problems—not "dwelling on the past," where it is too late to change things. It has a pragmatic ring to it, demonstrates decisiveness and a focus on taking action to deal with a problem, while conveniently relegating past decisions or policies to the "not relevant in helping us deal with the current situation" category. For example, Cannon (2007: 67) notes when Ari Fleischer was asked about Bush's inability to cite what he had ever done wrong, he argued, "It's the foolish politician who looks backwards and wallows in his difficulties. A good politician looks forward. It's the difference between a pessimist and an optimist, between a loser and a winner, between Jimmy Carter and George W. Bush." Similarly, testifying before the Senate in February 2007, JCS Chairman Pace pointedly stated in his remarks, "This is not at all a finger-pointing exercise," in the clear hopes of preventing the hearing from becoming one while he was in the witness chair (Cooper 2007). Certainly, the call to avoid looking backward was relevant for the Department of Defense, given the State Department's argument that if the Pentagon had included it in postwar planning, Iraq might not be the mess it later became (Cooper 2007).

Emphasize You're Listening to Constituents to Demonstrate Willingness to Hear Criticism

Of course, when leaders find themselves under a great deal of criticism over their actions, it is often useful to emphasize that they are gathering more information or opinions, especially from constituents, in order to demonstrate flexibility or open-mindedness to change. This is one reason congressmen, who have critical votes coming up in Congress, or who have faced criticism at home for their position or votes on a topic, often announce they are going back home to "listen to the people"—thereby deflecting the charge they are isolated or out of touch with the public. A good example of this tactic can be found in the week after the Iraq Study Group report came out in December 2006, challenging existing policies in Iraq. Bush announced the beginning of an "Iraq war listening tour" and various semipublic meetings to be held with the military, Iraqi leaders, and administration officials—all intended to show he was "urgently working on a solution to the worsening instability of Iraq."[44]

Maintain "Order in the Ranks" by Punishing Defectors to Deter Criticism

A blame-avoidance strategy seeking to kill two birds with one stone is to deal harshly with internal criticism from within your administration (or by allies) in order to silence it, while also creating a deterrence effect that will hopefully self-censor other potential defectors in the future. This approach can also be seen in attempts to head off statements or publication of criticisms of policies before they can be made public, thereby setting a tone within organizations regarding what is acceptable or not to superiors. Examples would include numerous complaints about White House political interference on science matters in previously nonpartisan government health and scientific agencies. In one case, former Surgeon General Richard Carmona told a congressional panel in July 2007 that administration officials "repeatedly tried to weaken or suppress important public health reports because of political considerations," including not allowing him "to speak or issue reports about stem cells, emergency contraception, sex education, or prison, mental and global health issues," as well as delaying and watering down a landmark report on second-hand smoke.[45] Similar censoring actions were reported after the administration blocked officials from speaking about or including in reports scientific information supporting global warming science, since these were out of step with official White House skepticism on the subject (Gelbspan 2004; Revkin 2006; Bowen 2007).

In the case of Iraq, the focus was similarly on punishing (as well as discrediting) defectors. As noted earlier, one of the major reasons Valerie Plame was outed from her CIA cover was to retaliate against her husband, Ambassador Joseph Wilson, who had publicly attacked the White House claim that Iraq had bought uranium yellowcake from Niger. This had been an important assertion in Powell's UN speech justifying the war, and Wilson's op-ed in the *New York Times* had infuriated Cheney's office. By serving as an example, the strong action taken against her was likely to be noticed not only by colleagues but by others within the administration as well. However, for Pillar, what happened to Plame, and the strategy of retaliation against her, was just the tip of the iceberg in terms of how dissent was rewarded: "Oh sure, it was all part of the larger environment—a big, oppressive, suffocating environment that affected the work of a lot of the people in our organization."[46] Indeed, noting Plame's outing and the very public ways he himself had been singled out over rather innocuous talks, Pillar acknowledged how it effectively "signaled" to others the cost of dissent: "What's the deterrent effect on everybody else! It's impossible to measure that. But people observe and people draw conclusions."[47] Other former administration officials recounted the plight of other analysts who had drawn the ire of senior officials, like John Bolton, by not supporting his policy views on particular countries and were targeted for firing (in this case unsuccessfully) because of their analysis.[48]

For the Pentagon stable of former military officers serving as commentators on cable and news networks, their role in providing *credible alternatives* to critics also came with a price. As many of these analysts observed, "the administration has demonstrated that there is a price for sustained criticism. . . . You'll lose all access" to the briefings and insider opportunities that formed the basis of their consulting (Barstow 2008). And these briefings are the lifeblood of military analysts who are expected to provide current, insider commentary for the media! In September 2003 the Pentagon took their select group of media analysts on a tour of Iraq (just as the insurgency was gaining strength) and provided briefings spooling out "an alternative narrative, depicting an Iraq bursting with political and economic energy, its security forces blossoming," with no need for additional troops (Barstow 2008). One participant, General Nash of ABC, noted that the briefings "were so clearly 'artificial' that he joked to another group member that they were on 'the George Romney memorial trip to Iraq,'" a reference to the governor's infamous claim that U.S. officials had "brainwashed" him into supporting the Vietnam War during a tour there in 1965 (Barstow 2008). Several analysts noted even the mildest of criticism could draw stern rebukes and the fielding of calls from displeased Department of Defense officials only minutes after broadcast (Barstow 2008). Indeed, when one analyst dared to tell Bill O'Reilly on Fox News that the United States was "not on a good glide path right now" in Iraq, the repercussions were swift; he was "'precipitously fired from the analyst group' for his appearance" (Barstow 2008).

In April 2006 several of Rumsfeld's former generals went public in the so-called generals' revolt, issuing devastating critiques in the media of his wartime performance and the military strategy in Iraq, with a number calling for his resignation (Barstow 2008). In response, the Pentagon marshaled the commentator group to come to the secretary's defense, writing opinion pieces for newspapers and defending him on television with talking points emphasizing that Rumsfeld "consulted 'frequently and sufficiently' with his generals; that he was not 'overly concerned' with the criticisms; that [he was] focused 'on more important optics at hand,' including the next milestone in Iraq, the formation of a new government" (Barstow 2008). In Rumsfeld's case, however, these blame-avoidance tactics proved ineffective, as the credibility of the revolting generals exceeded his by that point. In essence, the Pentagon response wound up being more of a holding action that only saved Rumsfeld's job until after the November midterm elections.

Encourage Subordinates to Give Answers Supporting Your Positions in Advance of Your Decision to Provide Political Cover

Finally, an effective blame-avoidance strategy is to encourage—either overtly or, more preferably, subtly—subordinates to provide supporting evidence or agreement with potentially controversial decisions prior to your making them. This provides political cover for leaders, who can later point to this support in defense of their actions. For example, Johnson always wanted to be "the last man standing" on the official record, insisting all of his advisers explicitly state their support for a potentially controversial position (even if he agreed with them), before moving forward.[49] As former White House press secretary George Christian, recalled:

> He wants to be able to defend against any criticism and he doesn't want to be the first guy to throw in the straws, he wants to be the last one. . . . That was

Johnson. He was protecting his flanks and he was trying to make sure they all would stand up and defend him when he did this. They didn't have any escape hatch.[50]

Certainly, few leaders want to have press reports later surface about active dissent among their advisers over difficult, controversial policy choices. Though this could, in reality, be seen as a far healthier dynamic within advisory groups, where multiple and differing viewpoints have the freedom to be heard, politically this almost always is pitched by the media as disarray or indecisiveness. The reaction to the first book on the Obama administration's deliberations over the difficult Afghanistan policy situation it inherited from its predecessor, and the disagreements among staff over the direction to pursue, is a good illustration of this phenomenon (Woodward 2010). The appearance of a united front among advisers, on the other hand, communicates confidence and certainty on the part of an administration regarding its decisions. It was why the Bush administration paid such close attention to maintaining unity in its message to the public and a "veil of secrecy" over its internal policy deliberations. It was an effort McClellan (2008: 85–86) likened to a "permanent campaign" run by seasoned staff (like Rove and Hughes) who constantly focused on maintaining the administration's message and appearance of unity over policy.

Aside from having senior subordinates all on record in support of policy, another aspect of this blame-avoidance strategy is to encourage lower-level staff to provide information or analyses supporting or reinforcing the policy choice. The more it can be argued as having been impartial, objective, or nonpartisan in nature, the better—since the taint of any pressure upon lower-level staff can raise the issue of politics intruding upon analysis or a leadership cherry-picking only the information supporting its positions from among a basket of conflicting data. For lower-level analysts, who are dependent on higher ups for career advancement, one basic politicization approach was through "inconsistent review of analysis," with reports conforming to policy preferences having "an easier time making it through the gauntlet of coordination and approval than ones that do not" (Pillar 2006). Such subtle politicization is much harder to prove (as it leaves few fingerprints), especially if fact-finding commissions are likely to later investigate the process. As Pillar (2006: 21–22) observed, while the Senate Select Committee on Intelligence and the WMD Commission claimed to find no evidence analysts had altered or shaped their judgments in response to political pressure, "the method of investigation used by the panels—essentially asking analysts whether their arms had been twisted—would have caught only the crudest attempts at politicization." For analysts needing favorable attention from policy makers, it was clear well before March 2003 that analysis calling into question the decision to go to war would be frowned upon, while support would be welcomed (Pillar 2006).

This creates enormous pressure, as one former senior intelligence official observed, either to do "objective analysis" that is unlikely to be noticed and used, or to be a "butt kisser" who has essentially recognized the direction from which the wind is blowing:

> Yeah. There were the butt kissers, who I've seen give presentations on Iraq. And the butt-kissing part was about, "Look, I really see this connection," and "Look how special I am. I've found things." This guy I remember once whipped out this link chart. Okay, first of all, there's no discussion of what the links mean or the correlation, or have they really caught anything. It's just this, "I see this link between this and this," and he was briefing this stuff. And I walked out and I was in disgust! And I think, if I remember correctly, and I want to get this story right. He was the one who was, at the end of the day, one of the primary people feeding that other side of the story to the administration. And he was loving it! "Look at how much attention I'm getting!" So there were all types. There were analysts who wanted to be in the limelight. Who want to be important. And there were analysts who wanted to sit at their desk and do their work and show both sides of the story, or at least do as objective an analysis as possible. I mean, we were, I think on some level, to blame as well.[51]

Of course, the real danger for policy makers in encouraging such environments is they can become self-deceived by their own deception: "A policy-maker can easily forget that he is hearing so much about a particular angle in briefings because he and his fellow policymakers have urged the intelligence community to focus on it" (Pillar 2006: 24). Given the natural human tendency to attend more to information supporting one's own views, this constant reinforcement over time (especially when the process creating that environment is a subtle one) can create a self-fulfilling prophecy of sorts—where confidence in a policy direction grows due to a wealth of supporting information flowing in which their own actions helped to create. As Pillar (2006: 23) observed, for the intelligence community, it is like looking out at a field of rocks it lacks the resources to fully examine—but if policy makers continually ask for only particular rocks to be turned over, rather than allowing the intelligence community to use its analytic judgment, the process becomes biased. As a result, due to this overemphasis, analyses leave the impression that "what lies under those same rocks is a bigger part of the problem than it really is"—which Pillar (2006) argues is exactly what happened to the Bush administration over Iraq.

Even for analysts seeking to remain objective and maintain their focus on the broader field of rocks, the blowback from having (as organizations) failed to correctly identify threats in the past (whether it be 9/11 or WMDs in Iraq) led to a heavier emphasis on caveats and refusing to rule things out, even if the majority of evidence made the events extremely unlikely to occur. Such heavily caveated analysis becomes even easier to mine by motivated parties seeking support for policy positions not totally ruled out by the products, and they provided cover later for both the intelligence community itself (who can't be totally wrong given the caveats) and the policy makers (who can blame the analysis for being misled if the policy goes bad). Indeed, as Pillar (2006: 22) notes, on the issue of Iraqi WMDs, the "opportunities for bias were numerous" given the "differences between sound intelligence analysis," and the "flawed analysis actually produced had mainly to do with matters of caveat, nuance, and word choice." Various forms of pressure combined to encourage the intelligence community to further watered-down analyses to avoid the finger of blame. As one former senior intelligence official observed:

> That's where, I think, you see the watering down of things. It's incredibly hard to put anything on a PowerPoint slide that's going to go up to any policy maker without it being so heavily caveated now—with we might, we may, we surmise, we believe. There's no, this sort of definitive, "there is" anymore! You probably read the NIE that's come out. I mean, come on, what do they say? Seriously, they don't say anything. I think that's a major problem! And it's really affected the way we analyze intelligence, because no one's willing to step out and say, "My God, no, this is really what's happening!" So I don't know as a policy maker what you do with those kinds of things. When you're faced with . . . you're being brought information that doesn't tell you what to do. You know. It doesn't definitively say, "there is this here."[52]

Caveats can also take the form of throw-ins added to analysis going to policy makers to ensure (or improve the odds) they will at least consider or read a report in the first place. Unfortunately, such throw-ins also serve to greatly soften any critical message or data inconsistent with policy being communicated to policy makers—making them easier to dismiss or ignore. For example, Harry McPherson included overt statements supporting the war in Vietnam in his 1968 memos to Johnson that contained criticism of existing policy—since doing otherwise would have resulted in banishment to LBJ's doghouse and his report not being considered by the president (Preston 2001: 163). Within the Bush administration, a number of senior intelligence officials agreed that a similar "sugarcoating" dynamic was in operation regarding Iraq analysis:

> Another form of politicization . . . is the sugarcoating of what otherwise would be an unpalatable message. Even the mostly prescient analysis about the problems likely to be encountered in postwar Iraq included some observations that served as sugar, added in the hope that policy makers would not throw the

report directly into the burn bag, but damaging the clarity of the analysis in the process.[53]

Policy makers have a tendency to start translating these kinds of analyses, especially if they already have strong, definitive policy views themselves, into additional pieces of "what they want to hear."[54] In other words, psychologically, they see what they want to see and interpret the ambiguous information in the analyses as actually being consistent with their preferred policy views, instead of being neutral or contradictory (Cottam et al. 2010). It is a motivated kind of selective processing bias, one everyone is at risk of falling victim to in gathering information from their environments. A consequence of the blame-avoidance strategies adopted by policy makers and organizations, however, is they further encourage this bias by stacking the deck with even more supportive or ambiguous information than would normally exist.

CONCLUSION

Policy makers, by their very nature, *always* desire to claim as much credit for things that go well during their tenures as they possibly can. They would wish to be seen by their publics as personally responsible for the sun rising each morning if that were possible! At the same time, they have an even greater interest in avoiding criticism (as they advocate for certain policy paths to be followed) or avoiding blame and accountability if that policy subsequently goes south. In this respect, the Bush administration did not differ markedly from any other previous administration in American history, or from leaderships found in most countries around the world. But just as happened with Johnson during Vietnam, the Bush administration would find itself in a situation where the initial blame-avoidance strategies (and tactics for marshalling information and analyses to support policies) would collapse during the protracted conflict in Iraq. In many respects, it is *the very nature of protracted conflicts themselves*—that they go on for long periods of time without resolution—*that encourages the sort of questioning* (by the public, political opponents, or fact-finding commissions) *that leads to criticism and an undermining of blame-avoidance strategies*. The longer a light is held up against the darkness, the more it reveals the shadows and details. For political leaders, blame-avoidance strategies seek to create a darkness to conceal their actions from onlookers. Protracted conflicts, in contrast, slowly burn until they become brightly lit pyres driving away that darkness and casting things previously hidden into sharp relief.

4

Opening Pandora's Box: Blame Avoidance, 9/11, and the Push for War with Iraq

After 9/11, everything changed. Many foreign policy issues were now viewed through the prism of smoke rising from the World Trade Center and the Pentagon. For many in the Bush administration, Iraq was unfinished business. They seized on the emotional impact of 9/11 and created a psychological connection between the failure to act decisively against al-Qa'ida and the danger posed by Iraq's WMD programs. . . . There was never a serious debate that I know of within the administration about the imminence of the Iraqi threat. . . . Nor was there ever a significant discussion regarding enhanced containment or the costs and benefits of such an approach versus full-out planning for overt and covert regime change. . . . Had 9/11 not happened, the argument to go to war in Iraq undoubtedly would have been much harder to make.

—Former director of the CIA George Tenet (2007: 305)

In considering the run-up to the decision to go to war with Iraq in March 2003, it is impossible to minimize or downplay the impact the trauma of 9/11 had on the American body politic, or its role in effectively removing the political constraints that normally would have impeded such a policy. Twelve years earlier, President Bush's father had made the strategic calculation, following his victory over Saddam in the first Gulf War, that pursuing his enemy to Baghdad to overthrow him and occupy the country would run the enormous (and unacceptable) political risk of miring the United States in a quagmire likely resulting in large numbers of casualties, a rupturing of international support, and lengthy, protracted conflict (Bush and Scowcroft 1998). As a result, Saddam remained in power and became subject to years of UN sanctions, UNSCOM inspections, and a generalized policy of containment seeking to limit the threat his regime posed to the region. Though warned not to do so, and subjected to no-fly zones over Iraq, Saddam slaughtered the Shia in the south of the country (who had risen up in response to President George H. W. Bush's call for Hussein's overthrow), and the White House did nothing. After years of noncooperation and obstruction of their efforts, Saddam eventually kicked out international weapons inspectors, leading the Clinton administration to launch waves of cruise missile attacks during Operation Desert Fox in 1998. But when these failed to force Saddam to renew international inspections, there was never a point at which it was realistic for the White House to actually consider an invasion to topple Saddam from power. The slogan of "regime change" was adopted as a plank within the Republican Party platform, a result not only of a desire by Republicans to appear "tough on Saddam" for domestic political purposes, but also a consequence of intensive lobbying by prominent neoconservatives and think tanks around Washington calling for such action. Regime change was even accepted by the Clinton administration as official U.S. policy when the Iraq Liberation Act of 1998 was signed into law, something defenders of the Bush administration's Iraq invasion would later point back to in justifying the 2003 invasion. Yet for all the domestic "sound and fury" coming from the regime-change rhetoric, it still "signified nothing" until the morning of September 11, 2001—when the previous political environment facing policy makers ceased to exist as surely as had the permanence of those twin towers against the New York City skyline.

For Bush, the unfinished business in Iraq had long been something he felt needed to be addressed. As Draper (2007: 173) notes, Bush confided to a family friend in 2000 his view that "Dad made a mistake not going into Iraq when he had an approval rating in the nineties. If I'm ever in that situation, I'll use it—I'll spend my political capital." Upon taking office, his focus quickly turned to Iraq. In fact, after participating in Bush's first NSC meeting on January 30, Treasury Secretary Paul O'Neill was surprised by how much Iraq and the need to undermine Saddam took center stage—"ten days in, and it was about Iraq" (Suskind 2004: 75). At that meeting, a potential "blueprint" for regime change in Iraq, drawn up by three of Bush's top national security advisers (Richard Perle, Douglas Feith, and David Wurmser) five years earlier and titled "A Clean Break: A New Strategy for Securing the Realm" was discussed (Bamford 2005: 261–62). The centerpiece of their recommendations for "remaking the Middle East into a region friendly to Israel" was the removal of Saddam and his replacement "by a puppet leader friendly to Israel" (Bamford 2005: 261–62). By the time the meeting was over, O'Neill was convinced "getting Hussein was now the administration's focus" (Bamford 2005: 267).

At the following NSC meeting on February 1, where Powell pushed for "smart sanctions" on Iraq, the main focus remained building a case against

Saddam for regime change. O'Neill noted there was "never any rigorous talk" within the NSC questioning the premise that regime change would solve everything and transform Iraq into a new country; "it was all about finding *a way to do it*" (Suskind 2004: 86; emphasis original). Indeed, Bush's response was simply, "Fine. Go find me a way to do this" (Suskind 2004: 86). The neocon advisers behind the "Clean Break" report assumed influential posts: Perle became chairman of the Defense Policy Board (packing it with neoconservatives favoring action against Iraq); Wurmser moved into a top position at State (later becoming Cheney's top Middle East expert); and Feith became undersecretary of defense for policy at the Pentagon (Bamford 2005: 268). NSC deputies meetings convened frequently to work on Iraq policy, with the group presenting a proposed "liberation strategy" for Iraq to the NSC in August, focusing on overseas opposition groups in a phased strategy to undercut Saddam (Woodward 2004: 21).

Wolfowitz argued the U.S. military could be used to seize Iraq's southern oil fields, establishing a foothold (dubbed the "enclave strategy") from which opposition groups could rally the country to overthrow Saddam (Woodward 2004: 22). It was the beginning of a series of overoptimistic assessments regarding the ease with which Saddam could be overthrown, eventually leading to the 2003 belief that U.S. forces would be greeted as liberators by the Iraqi people, complete with candies and sweets. For Powell, Wolfowitz's idea "was one of the most absurd, strategically unsound proposals he had ever heard," but as Woodward (2004: 22) noted, "It was not clear where the off switch was or whether there was an off switch." Pushing back, Powell warned Bush that such operations would not be as easy as suggested and not to allow himself to "get pushed into anything until you are ready for it . . . or until you think there is a real reason for it" (Woodward 2004: 22). Bush simply told Powell not to worry about it; it was merely good contingency planning, and he was "in no hurry to go look for trouble" (Woodward 2004: 22).

Still, making the argument that Iraq was an immediate, "clear and present danger" was complicated (at least prior to 9/11) by the fact senior officials, including Tenet, Powell, and Vice Admiral Thomas R. Wilson, the director of the Defense Intelligence Agency, had publicly stated Saddam's military ambitions had been effectively constrained by the sanctions imposed after the first Gulf War (Isikoff and Corn 2006: 26). Indeed, Powell himself, during a visit to Cairo in February 2001, stated Saddam had "not developed any significant capability with respect to weapons of mass destruction," a point he expanded upon in testimony to the Senate in May: "The Iraqi regime militarily remains fairly weak. It doesn't have the capacity it had ten or twelve years ago. It has been contained. And even though we have no doubt in our mind that the Iraqi regime is pursuing programs to develop weapons of mass destruction . . . I think the best intelligence estimates suggest that they have not been terribly successful" (Isikoff and Corn 2006: 26).

At the same time, efforts by those opposed to a single-minded focus upon Iraq, like Richard Clarke, found it almost impossible to gain traction with the argument that Osama bin Laden and Al Qaeda might be the larger threat. Indeed, at an April 2001 deputies committee meeting, Clarke (2004: 231–32) recalled that rather than accept the well-established, proven link between Al Qaeda and the 1993 attack on the World Trade Center, Wolfowitz argued for an undiscovered Iraqi connection: "You give bin Laden too much credit. He could not do all these things like the 1993 attack on New York, not without a state sponsor. Just because FBI and CIA have failed to find the linkages does not mean they don't exist." For Clarke (2004: 231–32), this was just a "rehashing of Laurie Mylroie's theory of Iraqi involvement in the 1993 attacks that had long since been completely discredited" but which had become a popular belief among neoconservatives, especially those pushing for action against Iraq. And it created tremendous background noise obscuring signals already present in the environment warning of the growing danger posed by Al Qaeda. Clarke (2004: 235) recalled both he and Tenet "regularly commiserated that al Qaeda was not being addressed more seriously by the new administration." In fact, despite Clarke's repeated requests (beginning in January 2001) for an NSC principals meeting to discuss the threat of Al Qaeda, it took until September 4 for the meeting to finally take place, and it was "largely a nonevent" in which they passionately outlined the urgency of the threat while receiving only agreement from Powell and little interest from anyone else (Clarke 2004: 237). As Clarke (2004: 237–38) would later recall, "Rumsfeld, who looked distracted throughout the session, took the Wolfowitz line that there were other terrorist concerns, like Iraq, and whatever we did on this al Qaeda business, we had to deal with the other sources of terrorism." Unfortunately, in only seven days' time, Clarke's point about the threat posed by bin Laden's organization would be aptly demonstrated in the skies over New York and Washington. And the degree to which the administration had paid proper attention to these threats would become controversial, leading to the first major efforts by the White House to engage in a strategy of blame avoidance.

POST-9/11: LEADERSHIP STYLE, BLAME AVOIDANCE, AND THE SEARCH FOR THE USUAL SUSPECTS

The personal beliefs of Bush, his leadership style, and the composition of his inner circle would play a *central role* in determining how the administration responded to the events of 9/11—a response eventually leading to the invasion of Afghanistan in October 2001 and Iraq nineteen months later. Bush's style led to an inner circle closed off from advice running counter to the dominant views held by those closest to the president—and meant neoconservative arguments found an easier path into debates over a response than alternative viewpoints. For those seeking a stronger approach to Iraq, the events of September 11 fundamentally changed not only the nature and tone of the internal debate but also the overall receptivity of the external political environment to the message. As Perle later acknowledged, "the world began on nine-eleven"; it was an event that "had a profound effect on the president's thinking" (Packer 2006: 41). Throughout the bureaucracy, neoconservatives were in place who shared this focus and "could give the president's new impulses a strategy, a doctrine, a world-view" (Packer 2006: 41). It was *the makeup of the advisers surrounding the inexperienced Bush* that now mattered, or as Perle admitted, "if Bush had staffed his administration with a group of people selected by Brent Scowcroft and Jim Baker, which might well have happened, then it could have been different, because they would not have carried into it the ideas that the people who wound up in important positions brought to it" (Packer 2006: 41).

After the 9/11 attacks, the immediate response by many within the administration was to look toward Iraq rather than Al Qaeda as the perpetrator of the events. It was the beginning of a pattern in which, however far afield the dots stretched, the White House would eventually reconnect them into a pattern leading back to Saddam. As Clarke (2004: 30) recalled in the immediate aftermath of the 9/11 attacks:

> I expected to go back to a round of meetings examining what the next attacks could be, what our vulnerabilities were, what we could do about them in the short term. Instead, I walked into a series of discussions about Iraq. At first I was incredulous that we were talking about something other than getting al Qaeda. Then I realized with almost a sharp physical pain that Rumsfeld and Wolfowitz were going to try to take advantage of this national tragedy to promote their agenda about Iraq. Since the beginning of the administration, indeed well before, they had been pressing for a war with Iraq. My friends in the Pentagon had been telling me that the word was we would be invading Iraq sometime in 2002.

In fact, the *9/11 Commission Report* (2004: 334–36) would later recount the heavy emphasis placed by Bush, Rumsfeld, and Wolfowitz on Iraqi involvement in the attacks. Almost immediately, Wolfowitz began calling for a "broad campaign to cut off all the terrorists' support systems" as part of a broad strategy for "ending states who sponsor terrorism" (Mann 2004: 300). By September 12, Rumsfeld was already talking about "broadening the objectives of our response and getting Iraq"—with Powell pushing back, urging the focus remain on Al Qaeda (Clarke 2004: 30). After Clarke thanked Powell privately for making the argument, the secretary shook his head and remarked, "It's not over yet" (Clarke 2004: 31). Later that day, Rumsfeld, while complaining about a lack of decent bombing targets in Afghanistan, suggested bombing Iraq instead, which had better targets (Clarke 2004: 31). Indeed, during the afternoon of 9/11, Rumsfeld and others were already focusing their attention on Iraq for retaliation, with the defense secretary pushing to "sweep it all up . . . things related and not" in gathering information that might allow for a simultaneous attack on Saddam *and* bin Laden (Bamford 2005: 284–85).

In many ways, the "framing effect" provided by the preexisting beliefs of Bush's inner-circle advisers strongly influenced how they perceived the incoming information surrounding the 9/11 attacks. Though Clarke (2004: 30) notes the CIA had *explicitly* said Al Qaeda was guilty of the attacks by the morning of the 12th, the Department of Defense focus was already shifting toward other quarters—with Wolfowitz again emphasizing his previous view that only a state sponsor could have allowed bin Laden to carry out such a sophisticated, complicated operation, and like the 1993 attack on the Twin Towers, Iraq must have helped! And while Bush was not totally convinced, his own personal views on Iraq strongly pulled him toward a belief Saddam must *somehow* have been involved in the attacks. Indeed, on the evening of September 12, Clarke (2004: 32) recounted being approached privately by Bush with a request "to go back over everything" to "see if Saddam did this . . . if he's linked in any way." Though Clarke emphasized Al Qaeda was responsible, and that they had looked extensively into state sponsorship and never found any links to Iraq, Bush testily replied, "Look into Iraq, Saddam," and left (Clarke 2004: 32).

Rumsfeld again pushed for striking Iraq as well as Afghanistan during a September 13 NSC meeting, a position Powell and Bush opposed (Suskind 2004: 184). Arguing "any serious, full-scale war against terrorism would have to make Iraq a target—eventually," Rumsfeld tried to convince the president the 9/11 attacks presented an opportunity to go after Saddam immediately (Woodward 2002: 48–49). But initially at least, Bush seemed to respond more to Powell's counterargument that while Iraq might be a future problem, it was more important to focus on Al Qaeda, since that was where the American public was focused (Woodward 2002: 48–49). During a series of meetings of the war cabinet held at Camp David over the next few days, Wolfowitz tried to shift the focus of attention to Iraq and overthrowing Saddam (Suskind 2004: 187). Though the meetings ended with no decision on Iraq, there was talk about the broader war on terror (beyond Afghanistan), and that Iraq would be next, even though no one was willing to commit to an Iraq invasion at that point (Suskind 2004: 189). In fact, at one afternoon meeting at Camp David, Powell warned Bush it was important to go after bin Laden first and "not to lose focus" since the state sponsors of terror were not going anywhere and they would lose the coalition of allies being gathered if Iraq became the target (Woodward 2002: 86–87). Interestingly, Rumsfeld remained silent at the meeting, and Cheney, while expressing deep concern about Saddam and noting he would not rule out going after Iraq at some point, also recommended waiting, joining Powell in opposing action against Iraq (Woodward 2002: 88–91). Nevertheless, on September 17, immediately following Camp David, Bush signed an order directing the Pentagon "to begin planning military options for an invasion of Iraq" (Bamford 2005: 287).

Perle's Defense Policy Board worked to create a believable case linking Saddam to 9/11 and Al Qaeda—with Wurmser being charged with putting together a secret intelligence unit (the Policy Counterterrorism Evaluation Group) that would bypass normal channels and report directly to Feith (Bamford 2005: 287–89). Leading neoconservatives, including Perle, sent a letter to Bush urging him to "immediately focus on a war with Iraq regardless of whether he can show a connection" to the 9/11 attacks (Bamford 2005: 288). While Bush still resisted the calls to attack Iraq, his own beliefs were clearly in evidence during an NSC meeting on September 28, when he remarked that "many believe Saddam is involved. . . . That's not an issue for now. If we catch him being involved, we'll act. He probably was behind this in the end" (Woodward 2002: 167). Less than a month later, after an NSC meeting on November 21, Bush pulled Rumsfeld aside for a private one-on-one discussion and asked, "What kind of war plan do you have for Iraq? How do you feel about the war plan for Iraq?" to which Rumsfeld replied he didn't think it was current (Woodward 2004: 1; McClellan 2008: 127). "Let's get started on this," Bush replied, asking that Tommy Franks begin working on the war plans, while emphasizing the need to keep it secret and have the planning done so it "would not be terribly noticeable" (Woodward 2004: 2–3). Bush later acknowledged he didn't want many in on the secret since a leak would trigger "enormous international angst and domestic speculation. . . . I knew what would happen if people thought we were developing a potential or a war plan for Iraq" (Woodward 2004: 2–3).

Unknown to Rumsfeld, however, Bush had already spoken to Rice, telling her he was "planning to get Rumsfeld to work on Iraq," while noting Cheney "clearly saw Saddam Hussein as a threat to peace . . . and was unwavering in the view that Saddam was a real danger" (Woodward 2004: 4). For Cheney, "taking care of Saddam was a high necessity," which some colleagues felt bordered on a "fever" or even "a disquieting obsession" (Woodward 2004:

4). Indeed, Tenet (2007: 321) would later suggest the United States did not attack Iraq because of WMDs—and he doubted it was "even the principle cause"—but this had been the "public face" put on it rather than regime change. Even Wolfowitz was quoted in *Vanity Fair* in May 2003 that WMDs had been "settled on" because it was "the one issue that everyone could agree on" (Tenet 2007: 321).

MAKING THE CASE FOR WAR AND
THE SELECTIVE USE OF INTELLIGENCE (2002)

During his State of the Union address in January 2002, Bush, in his new role as "wartime" president, began making a stronger case for eventual action against Iraq. Telling the American people "our war against terror is only beginning," Bush specifically pointed to three states—Iran, Iraq, and North Korea—who he argued collectively constituted an "axis of evil" supporting international terrorism.[1] It was a powerful turn of phrase, bringing with it the imagery of the righteous struggle against the Axis powers of Germany, Italy, and Japan during World War II. More importantly, it communicated a new message, or reality, to the American people—that like World War II, the new conflict against terrorism would not be a short campaign but a lengthy one. For blame-avoidance purposes, this new message was increasingly important for the White House, which was now facing growing public impatience with the fact that while Afghanistan had been conquered with relative ease, bin Laden had escaped from Tora Bora in November (along with many of his senior lieutenants) and successfully gone into hiding.

The political problem facing the administration was essentially the same one faced by any leadership once it is forced to move away from more traditional, state-versus-state military operations (providing discernible "centers of gravity" and visible, easily located targets to attack) toward "asymmetric" combat operations against nonstate opponents like Al Qaeda. For leaders, the successful management of any crisis requires they continually demonstrate their competence and the effectiveness of their response efforts, as well as visible signs of progress to maintain confidence and support. If the desired target proved illusive and difficult to target, as bin Laden and Al Qaeda now were, what could be done to avoid blame? It was the same problem once faced by Johnson in battling the Viet Cong. How does one show progress in a war against opponents who remain hidden in the shadows, with no clear return addresses for retaliation? And without visible opponents (like states) having armies to defeat and cities to conquer, how do you demonstrate a decisive victory or progress in a "war on terror"?

Over the next thirteen months, the Bush administration increasingly turned its focus and political rhetoric toward more easily located "axis of evil" states—especially Iraq. By April stories circulated in the *New York Times* quoting unnamed "senior officials" acknowledging "that any offensive [against Iraq] would probably be delayed until early next year, allowing time to create the right military, economic and diplomatic conditions."[2] In early 2002 the White House launched an internal review of Iraq policy that agreed containment was no longer viable and a regime-change approach should be adopted (Mann 2004: 332–33). At the same time, prominent neocons led by Perle and James Woolsey publicly pressed the argument for war with Iraq in media appearances, seeking to build support (Mann 2004: 334–35). More importantly, the White House Iraq Group (known as WHIG) was set up "to coordinate the marketing of the war to the public," focusing on "how to set the agenda and influence the narrative," using "communications strategies and messaging grounded in the familiar tactics of the permanent campaign" (McClellan 2008: 142). As Isikoff and Corn (2006: 29) note, the WHIG was "in a selling mode," and when Rove produced polling data showing the public's doubts about an Iraq invasion, Bush exploded, "Don't tell me about fucking polls. I don't care what the polls say."

WHIG produced a highly effective messaging effort, with the famous rhetorical line the "first sign of a smoking gun might be a mushroom cloud" originating from this group. As Isikoff and Corn (2006: 35) note, "This hadn't been a spontaneous remark; it was the public debut of a carefully constructed piece of rhetoric. The smoking gun/mushroom cloud sound bite had been conceived by chief speechwriter Michael Gerson and discussed at a WHIG meeting just three days earlier." As McClellan (2008: 144) observed, the WHIG effort was part of a "political propaganda campaign to sell the war to the American people" and "was all part of the way the White House operated . . . and no one seemed to see any problem with using such an approach on an issue as grave as war." Even while the intelligence community questioned the threat posed by Iraqi WMDs or its connections to Al Qaeda, the unified White House message sought to strengthen those links and effectively drown out dissents. These included congressional testimony in March 2002 by the head of the Defense Intelligence Agency that "Iraq possessed only 'residual' amounts of weapons of mass destruction, not a growing arsenal," nor were any links to Al Qaeda mentioned (Isikoff and Corn 2006: 27). Nevertheless, the administration moved forward on the Iraq track, focusing its prodigious messaging skills on emphasizing the Iraqi threat as part of the war on terror and building political support for removing Saddam.

It was very clear, at least internally, that war was coming (though this would be denied publicly until 2003). In fact, Tenet (2007: 309) recalled that in July 2002, Richard Haass told him Rice had already warned him that "the decisions were made, and unless Iraq gave in to all our demands, war was a foregone conclusion." This version of events is supported by Wilkerson, who recounted a conversation he had with Haass (who was writing his own book on the war and wanted to ask Wilkerson a few questions):

> He asked me, "When did you think the decision to go to war was made?" And I said, "Well, Richard, I've read some of the things you've said, and I agree with you. I can't tell you where it was made!" And he said, "In July of 2002, Condi told me, 'This Administration is going to war. It's going to war.' And I came back, remember, and I told the staff." And I said, "Yeah, I remember that." And he said, "What you don't know is I went and told the secretary [Powell] . . . and the secretary said, 'Nuhh' and gave me the body language to support it that he believed I had misinterpreted Condi.' People have *told* me that Dick Cheney came to office going to war with Iraq, or waiting for the opportunity.[3]

Similarly, another senior State Department official noted by August 2002 that "it became very clear to me that they were gonna go to war," but there were hardly any plans set up for "reconstruction in the aftermath."[4] As the official recalled:

> I started asking around, about what plans there were for reconstruction in the aftermath. And very little was done. . . . We were told to write plans for it in secrecy. Or write contracts when you didn't have a budget, you couldn't have a budget until there was a declaration of, which had to go to the Hill, so it was all a very complicated, very stressful situation.[5]

Analysts working within the intelligence community, even by mid-2002, were commenting (at least internally) about the clear "vibe" those who were briefing senior administration officials were beginning to receive about Iraq—and the sense they were moving toward war.[6] Products presented to senior customers focusing on Iraqi WMDs or terror links were well received, while those questioning them (or raising broader issues of stability in the event of war) were criticized or sent back for further analysis.[7] This dynamic would increase in strength as time passed, as analysts became very much aware of "where the administration's gaze lay" and where they should focus their analysis if they wanted it to be noticed. Indeed, as Pillar noted regarding the "atmospherics of the situation" for the intelligence community:

> The mechanism is fairly clear. When it is clear to all what is expected. What is wanted and what is not wanted in terms of the substance in answers to questions. That affects the life of an analyst intelligence officer in many ways which go beyond just being stared down by some senior policy maker over a briefing table.

It affects the ease or difficulty with which draft analysis is approved or not approved as it goes through the process of review and coordination. Review by the analyst's own superiors . . . who are reading the same tea leaves and feeling the same environment, and who in many cases are the ones who are more likely to deal face-to-face with senior policy makers. So there's . . . a kind of "shift in the burden of proof." If an analytic line is going to be proposed that the analyst and his or her bosses fully realize will be quite consistent with what the consumers are looking for in one respect, it will be a relatively easier path to get from draft to finished paper that goes into somebody's production folder. If it is something that everyone realizes will be a source of discomfort for the consumer, that is a much different situation. The burden of proof is much higher. The scrutiny is much greater. The questions asked much tougher. The road from draft to having something in the production folder is much longer. And that's just one of the ways in which it's affected. The other ways are, you know, even if there isn't one judgment that was changed from X to not-X, it's all the ways of wording, of shading, of emphasizing, of caveating or not caveating. So much of the criticism about the ways in which some of the weapons-related assessments on Iraq were written were all a matter of caveats. Or the language was too strong here! And those are exactly the sorts of things where the atmospherics can make a difference on the infamous, ill-fated estimate on Iraqi unconventional weapons in Fall 2002. You've got scores of analysts around the community, in a dozen different agencies, who collectively are making judgments on scores of different things, not just specific, substantive points. But, alright, how are judgments going to be "worded." Or even how are things going to be "placed," which of course makes a difference in emphasis. And so on, each of these many, many little decisions that are tacitly made . . . the environment, the political atmosphere . . . makes a difference.[8]

And the administration was working diligently to alter that political atmosphere. On Capitol Hill, the White House had the advantage of Republican control over the House of Representatives, and the GOP was only one vote short of controlling the Senate (which they would take after the midterm elections). As a result, not only were the Democrats in a very weak position to oppose the administration's push toward war with Iraq (especially given the political tone after 9/11), but Republicans were not willing to be "watchdogs" over policy in their oversight committees. From a blame-avoidance perspective, this removed many of the political constraints greater accountability to external groups might have maintained—and gave the administration far greater freedom of action to pursue its Iraq policy. Indeed, once Republican control over both houses of Congress was attained, the administration had little reason to fear the kind of congressional investigations that might have taken place under Democratic control. Still, when Bush's own lawyers suggested he was not required to seek congressional approval for hostilities

against Iraq, Democrats warned "a more vigorous debate" would be necessary, and even Republicans "urged Bush to seek congressional backing."[9]
From a blame-avoidance standpoint, doing so was by far the wiser approach,
since policy reversals are far easier to weather if the initial decision is seen
to have been arrived at through legitimate, legal means—which an executive
branch constitutional fight over the right of Congress to declare war would
not have aided.

Further, the administration still held the political high ground in the debate.
After a September 4 meeting between Bush and congressional leaders, where
he asked for a resolution granting him authority to deal with Saddam quickly,
Isikoff and Corn (2006: 23) noted Senator Tom Daschle wondered whether,
in a post 9/11 climate, Democrats running for reelection could afford not to
support the resolution? Daschle also wondered whether Bush was cynically
pushing the Iraq threat as a "campaign gambit," pressing the president on
whether this could be put off till after the election, thereby taking politics
out of the decision (Isikoff and Corn 2006: 23). In response, Bush "looked
at Cheney, who shot the president . . . a 'half smile,'" after which he replied,
"We just have to do it now" (Isikoff and Corn 2006: 23). Even so, some senior Republicans were uncomfortable, including House Majority Leader Dick
Armey, who raised serious concerns at the meeting as well. Armey warned
about the potential dangers of going into Iraq, stating pointedly, "Mr. President . . . if you go in there, you're likely to be stuck in a quagmire that will
endanger your domestic agenda for the rest of your presidency" (Isikoff and
Corn 2006: 24). In response, Cheney curtly told him that it would be a good
idea if he didn't dissent from the president's position in public—which out of
deference, Armey agreed to do (Isikoff and Corn 2006: 25).

Interestingly, Cheney's response to Armey's concerns the United States
would be mired in Iraq showed a framing very apparent in the run-up to the
March 2003 invasion. Discounting the implicit Vietnam analogy in Armey's
comments, Cheney argued that the Iraqis were not only "going to welcome
us," but it would "be like the American army going through the streets of
Paris" (Isikoff and Corn 2006: 25). Cheney argued the Iraqi opposition
was ready to form a new government, and "the people will be so happy
with their freedoms that we'll probably back ourselves out of there within a
month or two" (Isikoff and Corn 2006: 25). However, this wishful thinking
on Cheney's part did not change the intelligence community's view of the
likely outcome. As Tenet (2007: 309) observed, while the administration emphasized our being greeted as liberators, what they "failed to mention" was
the intelligence community told them "such a greeting would last for only a
limited period," and "unless we quickly provided a secure and stable environment on the ground, the situation could rapidly deteriorate."

Yet the political climate in late 2002 was still very conducive, with Bush's public approval ratings strong and a majority believing Saddam not only was pursuing WMDs but had been involved in the 9/11 attacks (McClellan 2008: 120–21). The WHIG group had worked diligently to develop a marketing campaign for selling the Iraq War as "inevitable and necessary," with the script being "finalized with great care over the summer" in preparation for a fall launch, which Andy Card explained was necessary, "from a marketing point of view," since "you don't introduce new products in August" (McClellan 2008: 121). During an address to a Veterans of Foreign Wars meeting in Nashville, Cheney prepared the ground, arguing there was "no doubt" Saddam had WMDs and was preparing to use them against the United States and her allies, and that deliverable WMDs in the hands of terrorists or dictators (working together) "constitutes as grave a threat as can be imagined . . . time is not on our side . . . the risks of inaction are far greater than the risk of action."[10]

When Bush gave his "Cincinnati speech" on October 7, 2002, he called Iraq a grave threat, didn't admit any doubts or dissents in the intelligence community, and talked about a partnership between Al Qaeda and Baghdad with "high-level contacts that go back a decade" (Isikoff and Corn 2006: 146). Relying on the turn of phrase developed by WHIG, Bush called on Congress "to authorize the use of America's military" in a "historic vote," noting that "facing clear evidence of peril, we cannot wait for the final proof—the smoking gun—that could come in the form of a mushroom cloud" (Isikoff and Corn 2006: 147). Arguing confronting Iraq was "crucial to winning the war on terror," Bush noted how Saddam's regime "gleefully celebrated" the 9/11 attacks, and "on any given day" could give WMDs to terrorists to strike America "without leaving any fingerprints"—rhetoric making a blatant appeal to fear.[11]

Only three days later, on October 10, Bush got his wish as the House passed a resolution authorizing the use of force against Iraq by a 296–133 vote, with the Senate following suit the next day in a 77–23 vote (Draper 2007: 184). The White House emphasis on communicating a "fear of what Saddam might do next," along with assertions about Iraq's WMDs and its connections to Al Qaeda as indisputable facts based upon intelligence (rather than mere conjecture), had largely succeeded in clearing away the political obstacles. Yet within the intelligence community, reality was still a different story. Army Major General James "Spider" Marks arranged October meetings with the Defense Intelligence Agency's top experts on Iraq, who presented a list of 946 suspected sites of WMDs that upon closer inspection had little empirical evidence or support (Woodward 2006: 92–96). Indeed, Marks realized "of all the suspected sites on the list, he couldn't say with confidence that there were any weapons of mass destruction or stockpiles at a single site.

Not one" (Woodward 2006: 96). Similarly, Clarke (2004: 241–42) recounts a conversation with Randy Beers, who had replaced him as the senior NSC counterterrorism official, who felt he too needed to resign:

> They still don't get it. Insteada goin' all out against al Qaeda . . . they wanna fuckin' invade Iraq again. We have a token U.S. military force in Afghanistan, the Taliban are regrouping, we haven't caught bin Laden, or his deputy . . . they aren't going to send more troops to Afghanistan to catch them or to help the government . . . secure the country. No, they're holding back, waiting to invade Iraq. Do you know how much it will strengthen al Qaeda . . . if we occupy Iraq? There's no threat to us now from Iraq, but 70 percent of the American people think Iraq attacked the Pentagon and the World Trade Center. You wanna know why? Because that's what the Administration wants them to think!

And while not committing to the certainty of war publicly, the president was privately far more willing to acknowledge he was planning to go to war. A good illustration was a brief thirty-second conversation Bush had with Tenet in the fall of 2002, where the president "made it clear that war with Iraq was necessary and inevitable," emphasizing that "we're not going to wait" because "the risks presented by Saddam would grow with time" (Woodward 2006: 89). After one meeting with Bush on November 4, Tenet told a colleague who asked whether the United States was really going to war, "You bet your ass . . . it's not a matter of if. It's a matter of when. This president is going to war. Make the plans. We're going" (Woodward 2006: 89).

The march toward war picked up further speed in November, when the UN Security Council, after lobbying by the British and American governments, voted 15–0 to find Iraq in "material breach" of previous UN resolutions regarding its WMDs. Iraq was to be given, under the terms of a new resolution (1441), "a final opportunity to comply with its disarmament obligations" by fully cooperating with a series of new, "enhanced" inspections (Isikoff and Corn 2006: 158). Although the Security Council purposefully left the "serious consequences" to be faced by Iraq intentionally vague, Bush immediately declared "any act of delay or defiance" on the part of Saddam would "justify military action" (Isikoff and Corn 2006: 158).

At the same time, the selective gathering of intelligence to demonstrate the threat posed by Iraqi WMDs continued apace. Between July 2001 and 2002, the WINPAC at CIA issued at least nine reports arguing high-strength aluminum tubes being acquired by Iraq were "compelling proof" a "reconstituted Iraqi nuclear program was proceeding," all without mentioning prominent dissents from experts at other agencies (Isikoff and Corn 2006: 41). In fact, top experts at both the Energy Department and State Department had dismissed the connection of the tubes to a nuclear program as entirely baseless—which undoubtedly was the reason they were not shown the WINPAC reports by administration officials pushing the case for war (Isikoff and Corn 2006: 41). A former senior DIA official, observing the "sleight of hand" being applied to intelligence within the Pentagon, noted, "I truly believe that they were making decisions based on their own personal beliefs, and when the intelligence said otherwise, then they would look for intelligence that confirmed their beliefs."[12] For those working at the Pentagon, this alternative source for "confirming intelligence" was to be found in Feith's Office of Special Plans. As another former DIA official noted, "That was the whole deal, the idea behind the Office of Special Plans was to look for intelligence that confirmed their beliefs," and for the White House this worked perfectly since "they wanted to bypass the intelligence community."[13] And for analysts working on the Pentagon side of the intelligence community, the effect of this "selective processing" of intelligence had much the same effect as it had on the CIA analysts. As one former DIA analyst observed, "Analysts felt strong-armed, they felt marginalized, like no one was listening to them if they had an alternative view—then everybody just kind of fell into place after a while."[14] As another senior DIA official observed regarding the debate over whether the administration was "cherry-picking" its intelligence over Iraq:

> I'm really amazed to this day [about that]. You have to be so closed to informa-
> tion to actually make that argument anymore, that it wasn't going on! I don't
> understand why this is a question to some . . . why there is any other answer
> going around out there! [*laughs*] We all know it, we all worked it! There's way
> too many people who are witnesses to it![15]

As Pillar (2006: 17–18) observed, this led to the Bush administration using "intelligence not to inform decision-making, but to justify a decision already made." In the end, these tactics served not only to justify decisions to go to war in Iraq, but were also used by the administration to deflect criticism over the Iraq policy. As Pillar (2006: 19) notes, "The Bush administration deviated from the professional standard not only in using policy to drive intelligence, but also in aggressively using intelligence to win public support for its decision to go to war" by selectively "cherry-picking" among the facts.

BLAME AVOIDANCE: LINDSEY'S SEPTEMBER 2002 ESTIMATE OF WAR COSTS

In September 2002, Lawrence Lindsey, who served as the head of the White House Economic Council, ignited a controversy during an interview with the *Wall Street Journal* when he estimated the likely costs of an Iraq war (and regime change) would range between $100 and $200 billion—far above previous White House estimates seeking to downplay the numbers. As McClellan (2008: 122) observed, "Lindsey had violated the first rule of the disciplined, on-message Bush White House: don't make news unless you're authorized to do so. Lindsey's transgression could only make the war harder to sell." It was a real opportunity for war critics, and the administration required immediate action to avoid blame for proposing a costly policy. Lindsey was criticized for his estimate, which was argued to be considerably "off the mark" and in December was forced to leave his post, which from a blame-avoidance perspective was an attempt to decrease the credibility of the messenger. But this was not sufficient to drown out the controversy. Seeking to rebut Lindsey's estimate, the administration sent Office of Management and Budget Director Mitch Daniels to provide a new estimate in December 2002, suggesting the cost of a war with Iraq would be in the range of $50 billion to $60 billion, roughly in line with the costs of the first Gulf War in 1991.[16] Yet, this effort at blame avoidance was not entirely successful because Daniels failed to provide minimally credible numbers to support his claim of a far cheaper war. In the end, Lindsey's departure did not discredit the higher number, as the administration had hoped, but wound up being supported by other sources.

BLAME AVOIDANCE: THE CONGRESSIONAL REQUEST FOR A NATIONAL INTELLIGENCE ESTIMATE ON IRAQ

As the White House sought to garner political support by emphasizing the danger posed by Saddam, opponents in Congress, who were unconvinced by the claims, began demanding a new National Intelligence Estimate (NIE) on the issue of Iraqi WMDs. As a result, in September 2002 the Senate Select Committee on Intelligence asked the CIA to produce a written assessment of Iraq's WMD programs. From a blame-avoidance perspective, the stakes were quite high for the administration, since an NIE failing to support its claims would open it to considerable criticism and greatly complicate the political environment. Given Bush's desire to confront Saddam as soon as possible, unlike most NIEs, which take considerable time to compile (since they are supposed to be the consensus opinion of the nation's sixteen intelligence organizations), this NIE would be rushed to meet a very short congressional deadline. Acknowledging NIEs usually require several months of preparation in order to coordinate all of these views, Tenet (2007: 321–22) later admitted that "an NIE on Iraq should have been initiated earlier, but at the time I didn't think one was necessary. I was wrong."

As a result of congressional pressure, Tenet (2007: 322–23) subsequently directed the National Intelligence Council on September 12 to "initiate a crash project to produce an NIE on the 'status of and outlook for Iraq's weapons of mass destruction programs'" that would seek to produce the report in only three weeks (rather than the normal six- to ten-month process). Due to time pressures, "analysts lifted large chunks of [twelve] other recently published papers and replicated them in the Estimate," which combined with the highly technical nature of the material involved "pushed standard procedures to the breaking point" (Tenet 2007: 324). On the issue of Iraqi WMDs, Tenet (2007: 330) acknowledges that "inevitably, the judgments were influenced by our underestimation of Iraq's progress on nuclear weapons in the later 1980s and early 1990s—a mistake no one wanted to repeat." It contributed to a biasing of the threat assessment process by analysts away from "probable" or "likely" outcomes to ones emphasizing "worst-case scenarios" based on what hypothetically "could" happen—a well-known distortion routinely leading to "threat inflation" during compilation of threat assessments (Cirincione 2000). As Tenet (2007: 332) admits, often the desire of the intelligence community to remedy one "so-called intelligence failure can help set the stage for another."

The NIE delivered to Congress on October 1 generally supported Bush's argument in broad strokes, though there were still caveats and other material congressional opponents seized upon, questioning why these dissents were not more prominently highlighted. After several days of contentious testimony, pressure began to build for an unclassified version of the Estimate to be produced within the next few days that could be used as part of the ongoing domestic political debate over the war. This also presented major problems for the intelligence community, since producing an unclassified document "was virtually impossible in the time allotted" to the agency, leading to yet another major error—taking an unclassified white paper NIC drafted months before on the same subject and modifying it for this purpose (Tenet 2007: 334). Though faster than creating one from scratch, Tenet (2007: 334) acknowledged "a saying that 'if you want it bad, you get it bad,' and that was precisely what we got."

The white paper on Iraq's weapons was released October 4 and, due to the quick editing and use of previously drafted material, produced a report far less nuanced (and more definitive) than the original NIE. It removed the hedging language and contained none of the dissents of the original NIE, and falsely stated all intelligence experts agreed Iraq was seeking nuclear weapons, despite State's pointed dissent (Isikoff and Corn 2006: 138–39). Moreover, it stated "most intelligence specialists" believed the aluminum tubes were part of an Iraqi centrifuge program (leaving out an Energy Department dissent), claimed UAV's could threaten the continental United States (despite Air Force dissents), and completely dropped the admission that the IC had "little specific information on Iraq's chemical weapons stockpiles" (Isikoff and Corn 2006: 138–39).

The response to the white paper by congressional critics was intense, since it was clear the public version to be released had all the various caveats and dissents removed, leaving only seemingly strong statements supporting claims of Iraqi WMDs. In fact, Senator Graham, who had been among those calling for an unclassified version of the NIE, "called Tenet and lit into him, demanding to know how the CIA could have produced two such different documents: a secret NIE filled with dissents and a public 'white paper' that conveyed unanimity and certainty" (Isikoff and Corn 2006: 140–41). Not only would Graham send a letter seeking public release of the specific section of the NIE containing the caveats and doubts about Iraqi WMDs, he also called on Tenet to allow disclosure of a closed-door hearing on October 2 in which his deputy, John McLaughlin, had put the likelihood of Saddam using chemical and biological weapons or attacking the United States as low, and only likely to occur if we invaded him (Isikoff and Corn 2006: 140–41). This Tenet refused to do, instead putting out a statement claiming there was "no inconsistency between our view of Saddam's growing threat and the view expressed by the President," outraging Senator Levin, who later recalled the "head of the CIA was saying there was no difference between that CIA testimony and the administration," which was "a fabrication and bullshit. . . . That was important testimony, and they were lying about it" (Isikoff and Corn 2006: 140–41).

Thus, in seeking to avoid blame from Congress over not being forthcoming in providing an unvarnished assessment of Iraqi WMD development, the intelligence community took a shortcut to appear responsive to the investigative committee. But providing the unclassified white paper for public consumption, which lacked the caveats and couched language of the NIE itself, actually made a stronger, more unequivocal statement supporting Iraqi WMDs than the intelligence community had fashioned in the NIE. This would later, when WMDs were not discovered, result in more blame flowing back toward the community than would have occurred had normal procedures been followed in producing the white paper. As Pillar acknowledges, several elements stand out that should have been handled differently, including a letter to the Democratic senators who had questioned the white paper's conclusions:

> We addressed [the senators' questions] in terms of the estimate. . . . And the key judgment [was] . . . he's got WMD, but he probably will not use that against the United States. He would probably *not* give them to any terrorist group, *ex-*

cept in one case . . . if we try to invade his country and . . . topple his regime. Hardly a case for war! So the Senate Democrats said, "Hey, that's an important judgment! Why the heck don't you make that public? . . . And so we came to an agreement in this session . . . we'll try to go back and . . . craft something that would be in the form of a letter from DCI to the then chairman that would be releasable. Bob and I went back and drafted something. We sent it down the hallway, and we lost control of this. The director's office took over. And the final thing that was released was much different from what Bob and I had drafted. It had the essentials in there, namely . . . testimony from McLaughlin on this or that question, but then it immediately added in some off-setting stuff to obviously sugarcoat it for the administration. But if you read the whole thing, the letter, the impact of it was greatly reduced. It softened it to the point that it was starting to fall apart. And Bob and I were shaking our heads over that. I think it *should* have been handled differently . . . because the Democratic senators were absolutely right, this is an important judgment. . . . If [they] hadn't pressured us on this, the judgment, even in the softened version, would *never* have come out. It was solely in response to the opposition party pressure from these key senators on the Hill that it ever came out at all.[17]

Still, as Isikoff and Corn (2006: 137) observe, "In the end, the actual wording of the NIE probably didn't matter" very much since the White House "had already made extensive use of the faulty intelligence that had been packaged in the estimate" to make their case for the war. Moreover, Bush, who had not been the one to ask for the NIE in the first place, would later admit to not have even read it (Isikoff and Corn 2006: 137). This was not a case of using intelligence to inform or reach a decision, but one of advocacy to justify a course already decided upon.

BLAME AVOIDANCE: THE MEDIA AS "COMPLICIT ENABLERS"

During the latter half of 2002, one of the most effective blame-avoidance strategies utilized by the administration involved the use of the media to amplify its message and downplay those of critics. The coverage on the Fox News Network was, predictably, uniformly supportive of the administration's case for confronting Iraq and seldom voiced any critical analysis (Woodward 2004; Isikoff and Corn 2006; Rich 2006). Isikoff and Corn (2006: 43) note how Judy Miller at the *New York Times* would often "serve as the conduit" for messages crafted in the White House that would later find their way into her reporting on WMD issues, while other "journalists and Iraqi exiles, working in tandem, helped to create favorable conditions for the White House sales campaign." Woodward, who was well known for currying favor with political figures in order to gain access, was seen by the White House as providing the administration with a tremendous public relations success after his very flattering book, *Bush at War* appeared in 2002, leading White House communications officials to "strongly urge" the CIA's cooperation with Woodward on his next book once the Iraq War started (Tenet 2007: 365). Observing the unfolding of this media strategy, McClellan (2008: 125) notes the unquestioning role played by the media, which mostly abdicated its role as a watchdog of the facts, served to dampen criticism, and built political support for the war, thereby serving as "complicit enablers" of the Bush strategy. This media strategy was also seen as one providing very positive political dividends for the president as well. As a leaked presentation by Rove pointed out in June 2002, the main political plan was "to use the war as a way to maintain a positive issue environment" (Bamford 2005: 318). Aside from reinforcing Bush's own political standing, this served as an effective blame-avoidance strategy to deal with any policy reverses and was emphasized by the administration throughout the remainder of its tenure in office.

BLAME AVOIDANCE: "CURVEBALL," "SLAM DUNK," AND POWELL'S UN SPEECH

One of the major sources being relied on to support the administration's case that Iraq was pursuing WMDs was an individual code-named "Curveball"— who for many years had been feeding Western intelligence services with a variety of dire reports relating to WMDs. In an environment in which the intelligence community as a whole (apart from Feith's pseudo-intelligence shop at the Pentagon and WINPAC at CIA) were issuing reports questioning the extent to which Saddam was pursuing or acquiring WMD capabilities, Curveball became a critical source for White House officials seeking any information confirming their views.[18] Strong doubts at the CIA about the reliability of Curveball as a credible source were downplayed or dismissed as the focus remained one of proving the case for war (Drumheller 2006: 78).[19] In fact, German intelligence, which allowed the CIA access to interview Curveball, had already warned he was likely not a reliable source, but this did not result in a cooling of the ardor of those in Cheney's office or at WINPAC for the confirming information on Iraqi WMDs he provided.[20] Drumheller (2006: 82–83) recounts numerous efforts by analysts to convince WINPAC that Curveball was not a reliable source, and likely a fabricator, including one December 19, 2002, meeting in which WINPAC analysts refused to accept these warnings and later wrote a memo pronouncing Curveball credible. For Wilkerson, the behavior of WINPAC, and the way in which memos or intelligence coming from various other parts of the government (like Cheney's office and Feith's DoD shop) read, raised suspicions:

> I'm convinced now that there were people in WINPAC who were working not only for George Tenet and John McLaughlin but also for the vice president and maybe even for Feith's shop. They had similar minds. They had talked. That they felt their bread was better buttered on the side facing the vice president than the side facing the DCI. And that they were in, I won't say in league with them, but they were certainly in mind-meld with them. I'm convinced of that now. Because otherwise, I can't explain how I heard some of the *same language* almost with the same intonation, semicolons, colons, commas, you know, in one place that I heard in the other place. It was almost like they were *memorizing* their talking points, sharing their talking points, and then regurgitating the same thing in decision making, or in this case, in the preparation phase.[21]

A common pattern developed, one observed by many former administration and intelligence officials, of reporting from this one Curveball source being repackaged in reporting coming out of Feith's shop, in memos prepared by Cheney's office, in WINPAC material, and presented to other officials later as intelligence coming from "multiple sources" corroborating each other.[22] What was actually happening was one source was being reported from multiple locations in the government to create the illusion of multiple sourcings—a sleight of hand used to great effect by those seeking to build the case for war with Iraq.[23] And importantly, intelligence calling into question Curveball's credibility or undercutting the building WMD rationale for war was routinely ignored or downplayed.

For example, contrary to the Curveball claims, there was also intelligence prior to the war from a senior Iraqi source, who had direct access to Saddam and his inner circle, informing us that Iraq's WMD programs were nonexistent, essentially a "Potemkin village" without substance—yet this reporting was completely ignored by the administration (Drumheller 2006: 87–98). For CIA analysts, Drumheller (2006: 87) noted, "we all felt under pressure" since it was very obvious the White House was manipulating their reporting "for its own ends," and Tenet himself was setting a tone "whereby people knew what he and the White House wanted to hear"—evidence supporting the WMD case in Iraq (or Saddam's links to Al Qaeda), not disconfirming information. As Drumheller (2006: 87) later remarked, "The bureaucratic imperative was to prove one's worth by supporting the president's case for war." And this pressure and selective use of intelligence would result not only in distortions being included within the writing of the NIE in 2002 but also with claims (based on dubious intelligence) eventually finding their way into presidential speeches and Powell's UN address.

A good illustration of this is the case of the purported "mobile biological warfare facilities" the Iraqis were supposed to possess. As Drumheller (2006: 85) notes, "three of the four sources" for this information were "either fabricators or extremely suspect, and the fourth would later turn out to be a fabricator too," though the NIE would still claim multiple sources for the germ warfare charge. The argument that Iraq was developing mobile biowarfare capability quickly gained political traction and was seized upon as further evidence of the threat posed by Saddam. Hearing that Bush intended to include this Curveball-derived intelligence in his January State of the Union address, Drumheller (2006: 83–84) immediately sent an email to Deputy CIA Director McLaughlin's executive assistant, highlighting all of the credibility problems surrounding the use of this particular source for the president's speech. But as Drumheller (2006: 83–84) discovered, "McLaughlin talked to the WINPAC analysts around this time, apparently in response to this email, and received robust reassurances about the reliability of Curveball." As a result, Bush delivered his January 2003 State of the Union address confidently arguing, "From three Iraqi defectors we know that Iraq, in the late 1990s, had several mobile biological weapons labs. These are designed to produce germ warfare agents and can be moved from place to a place to evade inspectors."[24]

And this was merely the tip of the iceberg regarding the ongoing intelligence distortions. The WMD commission would later note the flow of reporting by CIA to top policy makers—in the President's Daily Brief (PDB) and the Senior Executive Intelligence Brief (SEIB)—were even "more alarmist and less nuanced than the NIE," with repeated "attention-grabbing headlines" giving "an impression of many corroborating" reports, while leaving out that there were "very few sources" and information casting doubts on the their validity (Isikoff and Corn 2006: 137). Another example was the use of material derived from the "enhanced" interrogations of a senior Al Qaeda field commander held at Guantanamo Bay named Al-Shaykh al-Libi, which the administration argued conclusively linked Saddam to Al Qaeda. Yet the actual evidence from these interrogations, and what was used in the NIE, did not support this kind of strong linkage and was being dramatically overstated. As Pillar, who had worked on the NIE later, noted, not only was it found the al-Libi testimony had been fabricated on his part, but the conclusions drawn from what little he had said had been greatly exaggerated by both the intelligence community and administration officials:

> On al-Libi . . . certainly the intelligence community and the people involved in this are to blame, it's not just Tenet, for drawing more specific conclusions . . . than it deserved. Now when I came back to the Powell speech, since they were going over things so carefully, the representation of the Libi stuff was a little more careful. . . . Before that, al-Libi had already been used publicly by

the administration. "Assistance was provided," Condi Rice said. "They got aid in making chemical and biological weapons!" Which goes *way* beyond what the Libi stuff said! Course the whole thing was fabricated anyway. But even if it weren't fabricated, my point is that it had been seized upon well before that fall '02 estimate was written. It had already been seized upon and used publicly, repeatedly by the likes of Rice. Aid in BW and CW [biological and chemical weapons] has been provided! It never said that! Even when it's fabricated, it never said that![25]

The claims of an Iraqi–Al Qaeda connection derived from the al-Libi source was later utilized by Bush in his 2003 State of the Union address to make the case that Saddam posed a continuing, dire threat to America, noting "evidence from intelligence sources, secret communications and statements by people now in custody reveal that Saddam Hussein aids and protects terrorists, including members of Al Qaeda."[26] Bush argued "secretly, and without fingerprints," Saddam could "provide one of his hidden weapons to terrorists, or help them develop their own," inviting his audience to "imagine those 19 hijackers with other weapons or other plans, this time armed by Saddam Hussein"—an explicit linkage of the powerful 9/11 imagery to Iraq.[27] This despite a CIA report titled "Iraqi Support of Terrorism," published the same day as the president's speech, specifically stating available evidence did not support the conclusion Saddam and Al Qaeda had ever moved beyond merely "seeking ways to take advantage of each other" (Tenet 2007: 350). As Tenet (2007: 349) recalled, there was very intense, repeated White House pressure to suppress this analysis (beginning in December), as soon as the final revision of the report had been completed by the agency.

At the same time that the intelligence being used for the State of the Union address was being debated internally, another key speech was also being drafted in parallel that would become perhaps the single most important statement by the administration in its strategy to build public support for war. On February 5, Powell was scheduled to give a speech at the UN laying out the case for taking action against Iraq and its WMD program. Within the administration, it was seen as an opportunity to galvanize international and domestic political support, to have a moment like the one Ambassador Adlai Stevenson had during the Cuban Missile Crisis, where he laid out the clear and unequivocal case against the Soviets as having placed offensive missiles in Cuba.[28] As Powell's staff began working on the substance of the speech, it was quite clear to them why he had been the one selected to make the presentation instead of Ambassador Negroponte. As Wilkerson recalls:

You don't even need to ask that question! John Negroponte doesn't have Mother Theresa poll ratings. Colin Powell does. That's why he's going up there. They're putting him out in the front of the fox hole, because he's the one with all the credits. With the international community, particularly Europe. And with the American people. He's got the credibility. That's the reason he's doing it.[29]

Working at Langley with his closest staff, Powell sought to design a speech using only corroborated intelligence, making charges that could be substantiated, while avoiding statements that would later be proven false. By this point, he and Armitage had seen enough of how Cheney's office and Rumsfeld's Pentagon operated to be suspicious. Unfortunately for Powell, as events would later demonstrate, he was still not suspicious enough. And a tremendous amount of intelligence papers and other products were shown to Powell by the CIA, by the Pentagon, and by Scooter Libby in an attempt to build the strongest case against Saddam possible. The problem was, even for Powell, a lot of this material just lacked credibility. Indeed, as Wilkerson recalls, during one session at Langley,

> [Powell] threw twenty-seven pages of CIA-developed terrorist contacts out! And he said, "That's a genealogy! That's like Deuteronomy . . . from Khartoum to Baghdad! I'm not gonna sit up there and read this crap!" And he threw it out! Then all of a sudden George comes in and starts talking about a high-level Al Qaeda operative who has just been interrogated. We didn't know it was al-Libi, tortured in Cairo with no U.S. personnel present. But that swayed Powell to at least put those substantive contacts between Al Qaeda and Iraq back in there, you know. So he was very frustrated already. So George knew, "Man, I pull one pillar on this guy, he's out of here!" [*laughs*] So there's a lot of pressure on Tenet.[30]

And the Curveball material was there as well, cited numerous times in different products, making it appear as if there was substantial corroboration of his specific WMD claims. Drumheller (2006: 83) recalls that when a draft of Powell's speech appeared in their division at CIA, they highlighted the Curveball language for removal and then warned McLaughlin directly:

> To my astonishment, he appeared to have no idea that there were any problems with Curveball. "Oh my! I hope that's not true," he said, after I outlined the issues and said the source was probably a fabricator. It was then that I began to realize that Curveball was central to the case for war. My fear was confirmed when I said to a colleague at the counterproliferation division that WINPAC must have something else apart from Curveball to back up their case for war. "No," he said. "This is it. This is the smoking gun."

For many within Powell's staff, and throughout the intelligence community, there still exists to this day disbelief that Tenet, and an analyst as experienced as McLaughlin, could have possibly been fooled by the Curveball material. Certainly many former officials throughout the government have expressed, at the very least, healthy skepticism about Tenet's (2007: 373) argument in his memoir that "CIA and State Department officials worked side by side to rid the draft of material that would not stand up," but "despite our efforts, a lot of flawed information still made its way into the speech."[31] But while some questioned whether Tenet was merely telling Bush what he wanted to hear, others supported the notion he really was not trying to distort the intelligence at all, but was just unaware there were problems with it. For example, Armitage observed:

> I'm a friend of George's, and . . . I'll tell you what I think. Secretary told George early on, "You're coming to New York with me. You're gonna sit right in back of me." And Tenet understood from the first minute Powell showed up over there that he was gonna put his, George Tenet's, name on this document. So that's why George sat behind him. So I don't think George *was* aware. He wouldn't have let his name be trashed like this if he'd been aware! He would not allow his name to be dragged through the mud, as it was because of this, if he'd had any idea.[32]

Similarly, other colleagues found another explanation for how he could have been unaware of the problems with the intelligence. Tenet's style of information processing was one marked by impatience, where he tended to avoid detail and going into depth on topics, preferring instead to focus on the big picture. As Kay would later explain:

> George told me one day, "You know, I never read a book in graduate school." Now, he thought that was supposed to impress me? For me, that was an insult! A failure of the education system! George didn't have a computer in his office. I mean, it was a joke around the agency. George would have a hard time going through a two-page document. He just, he absorbed what he absorbed verbally. And so, he was not someone who would dig. If you're ever in a meeting with him, he's shifting around, cigar that's not lit. I mean, he's just a ball of energy. And he never would sit down and go through a deep . . . I mean, I'm absolutely convinced that there was *no* case that I knew of that he had ever read beyond the executive summary page. He just couldn't take it. So I think he did this . . . either he took it on faith, he heard what he had heard, or he knew what the White House wanted to hear. But if he'd told me there were multiple sources . . . I would want someone else's view because I would never trust George.[33]

Yet for Pillar, who believed Tenet was "astute enough to know about the issue of phony multiple sources," the explanation for his behavior is much simpler.[34] It was not that he was necessarily "unaware" of the problems with the materials, though he may have been in some instances. In looking back at the dynamics between Tenet and the administration during this time period, Pillar simply observes, "I think when we're talking about George, it's more of just kind of getting swept up in the moods and desires of his political masters."[35] As for McLaughlin, Wilkerson's experience during the drafting of the UN speech led to a different conclusion:

> John lived with me. John was standing beside me dictating at 2 a.m. in the morning to Lynn Davidson, the speechwriter sitting at the computer. . . . He was changing periods and semicolons, and phrases, to make it perfect. So it wouldn't be a lie. So it wouldn't be unprofessional. He was using an analyst's language, so it'd be. And I go back to some of those late nights when he's sitting there giving Powell a forty-minute exposition on the latest pin with twelve angels on it! [*laughs*] I'm thinking to myself, "Jesus John, you got into the nitty-gritty! I mean, you knew the texture of the metal. You knew the miraging steel caliber. How could *you* have been fooled by all of this crap?" I don't think John was lying. I think he fudged some things. But I don't think he was lying. Part of their problem was they had hand selected the analysts to whom they listened. John had these guys. Bob Walpole was right at the head of that. And so I think they began not only to drink the Kool-Aid, they began to help manufacture it.[36]

But aside from the question of whether Tenet and McLaughlin were themselves unaware of the problems with the intelligence, or part of a conscious administration effort to manipulate the data, the reality is Powell and his staff were highly dependent upon their expertise and analytical judgments. It was not realistic to imagine Powell's staff could, during the course of a few days, independently verify and confirm all of the myriad sources of intelligence on Iraqi WMDs they were being presented with at Langley. As Wilkerson notes, this dependence on Tenet and McLaughlin for confirmation of intelligence products clearly put them in a very difficult position:

> Where they got *me*, and where they got the secretary too was . . . once Tenet vouched for a source, not only did we not have the *expertise* to say, "Bring him here!" It might be an NSA wiretap, it might be an asset, it might be HUMINT. You don't know what it is. But once Tenet vouched for that source, we had to kind of say . . . time constraints wouldn't allow us to look at it either. We take your word for it, Mr. DCI. On occasion, the secretary would say, "Okay. Is that a *consensus* view about that source?" And Tenet would go and look in the computer. Get his DA to go out and do something. They'd come back three minutes later, and he'd say, "Well, there was an Air Force dissent on that and here it is." Or "there was a DIA dissent on that, it was a flip-note in this document, here it is." And the secretary would look at it. But more often than not, due to time constraints and just plain expertise, we had to say, "You vouch for that source? And there are multiple sources, independently corroborating one another, right?" "Yes." On the mobile biological labs, Tenet said there were four

sources. And those four sources independently corroborated one another with regard to the existence of the labs, and two of them independently corroborated one another with regard to the specifications which Tenet's graphics people were actually gonna draw for us so that we'd be able to put it on our screen. And that's why we had those things. Powell didn't like that at all. He said, "I want photos, satellite or otherwise, of these vehicles! I don't wanna put a drawing up there!" And Tenet had to say, "Look, we have been unable to get anybody," and they were running a couple of agents inside of Iraq, "to get ahold of one of these vans and take a picture of it." So we had to go with those graphics. Well, that even, ultimately, made it more convincing, because we sat down with people who drew the fermenters, the pipes, the coolers. . . . And they're telling us, "This is exactly thirty-six inches long." You know. And they were telling us . . . it was an Iraqi major, who was an engineer, who had been in the labs and given them all of these specifics, and he'd been in one of the labs when an accident had occurred. Several people had been injured or killed . . . it was not the explosion, it was the lethal agent released that had killed them. Proving it was a lethal agent. And all this detail apparently, I learned much later, came from Curveball. But it was presented to us as coming from at least two sources, the presence from four, the graphics from two, independently corroborating one another.[37]

When Powell called Armitage to join him and Wilkerson at Langley, it was clear to his deputy the secretary felt "something wasn't right."[38] Over the preceding three days, Cheney and Libby, or Rice and Hadley, had frequently visited Powell's group to provide additional information, and Armitage suspected his boss wanted him there so he "could yell at Condi or Hadley, because he was getting tired of it."[39] So along with Tenet and McLaughlin, Powell was getting input from a range of other people, but a frustrated Armitage would later observe: "Did we know that people in that room knew that a burn notice had already been placed on Curveball? No. No one raised it. You can ask Larry, he was there. Nobody raised it. And they were *in the room*! People knew it!"[40] As Wilkerson later observed, Powell kept asking for verification about specific intelligence to be used in the speech and found nothing but affirmation:

The secretary did this, half a dozen times. And he did it at least twice on the labs, because that was a significant part of the presentation. "You stand by this George, right? You stand by this? There's no doubt in your mind that these exist and that they're for the purposes you've so detailed here, and that I'm being asked to detail to the Security Council?" And on each occasion, John's in the background going like this [*nodding*]. George says, "Mr. Secretary, I fear my oversight committees more than I fear your ire if I'm wrong! I'm not wrong." And the last time he did that was on the top of the UN building, when he turned to Tenet and said, "Now I'm gonna do this tomorrow. You stand behind everything that we have left in this presentation?" And Tenet said, "Yes, I do, Mr.

Secretary." And then Secretary Powell smiled and said, "Well, you're gonna
be with me tomorrow in camera. You're gonna be sitting with me." And Tenet
. . . you know . . . I don't think George knew he was gonna be there! [*laughs*]
Because he's, "Alright, Mr. Secretary!" [*laughs*][41]

The pressure being placed on Powell and his staff from those in Cheney's
office to include material based on dubious sourcing was intense. Pillar, who
was working nearby in the CIA headquarters building when the speech was
being written, remembers his colleague, who was the deputy head of the
policy planning staff at State, stopping by his office carrying in his hand "this
script that came from Libby and the Office of the Vice President on the terrorism point" to show him:

> He said, "Read this." Basically, Barry's question was, do you think this is as
> much crap as we think it is! [*laughs*] And yeah, it is crap! And the secretary
> apparently had similar views. And it was! It was just garbage. "And Zarqawi
> was here, at this point, so that means he was being controlled by the regime!"
> It was all a bunch of nonsense! The part that Powell agreed to stick in right at
> the end of the speech was kind of the minimum he could get away with without
> having OVP jumping all over him for not saying anything about this supposed
> terrorist connection. But that was probably the part that offended me the most.
> The whole purpose was to create an impression that was contrary to professional
> judgments.[42]

And long after the speech had been delivered, members of Powell's staff
continued to discover pieces of information that had been withheld from them
during their time at Langley. For example, after Powell's presentation, Wilkerson discovered "the DIA had dissented on al-Libi's testimony," which was
central to making the argument that there were linkages between Saddam's
regime and Al Qaeda.[43] As he later observed, the explanation for this omis-
sion he eventually received was not at all satisfying: "They told me it was a
complete computer glitch . . . the way it was coded into the computer, when
they put the search criteria in for dissents, that it didn't come up."[44]

Of course, for Tenet, who would be used as a lightning rod by the White
House when WMDs did not turn up in Iraq, the issue of whether or not he was
warned by Drumheller about Curveball's lack of credibility was central to his
own blame-avoidance strategy. In his memoir, Tenet (2007: 380) denies having been warned, or receiving Drumheller's memo, noting his successor, Porter Goss, had his staff run down the Curveball story, and found "the letter, located in the European Division, had not been formally logged in as received,"
and "despite extensive searching, no records" were found showing it had been
"sent to either John McLaughlin or me." This is consistent with what another
former senior Bush administration official, on condition of anonymity, noted

during an interview, recalling, "I've been told that after Drumheller left, his safe was opened, as would always be the case, and there was a memo to the director in there. However, it had never been sent, because when a memo to the director is sent, it gets logged in, and it was never sent. So Drumheller was right that he wrote it, but he never sent it apparently."[45] Going further, Tenet (2007: 378–79) argues the German BND representative who had lunch with Drumheller "denied ever having called Curveball a 'fabricator' and said he only warned that he was a 'single source' whose information the Germans could not independently verify."

At the same time, however, a wide range of former officials, as well as colleagues of Drumheller's in the intelligence community, almost uniformly defend him as an individual who would have no motivation to make the story up and who was a credible witness in their minds.[46] As Wilkerson observes, "someone's lying somewhere," but in the case of Curveball, "I simply can't fathom why Tyler would be lying. I don't see what he gains by lying."[47] And Kay, who notes Drumheller is just "not that sort of guy" and was "the last person you would expect to have an axe to grind in this thing," notes "there is electronic evidence to show that the call was made" to Tenet.[48] But as Wilkerson explains, this particular instance regarding Curveball formed only part of the overall political environment faced by Tenet and the CIA:

> Remember that Tenet . . . and McLaughlin . . . are sitting there at the top of this ivory tower, and they're getting fed all this information. They've got Feith's shop over there analyzing and evaluating everything they're doing. They've got the vice president's office taking the product from Feith and challenging them. Actually coming out there eleven or twelve times to do it! Scooter Libby. And so, George is in this situation, and John is in this situation. I fault John even more than George, because John is a thirty-year veteran of the intelligence community. George is a politico who has some intelligence trappings. But John and George both have all these inputs and pressures. . . . It's not quite as simple as some people try to make it seem. You know, Tyler called him and said, "Secretary of state should not be saying this, it's all false, by God, pull it out!" And George has got to weigh all this. You know, he's gonna say, "Do I wanna do that?" I tell you what would have happened. If you'd come back to Secretary Powell and pulled that out, Powell would have probably thrown that crap at him and walked out of that building! Cause we had already been through some *torturous* moments with the aluminum tubes, with the Al Qaeda contacts with Baghdad, etc.[49]

Indeed, the larger problem faced by officials and analysts alike was the manner in which the administration sought out (or less charitably, manufactured) intelligence supporting a war with Iraq. The pressure the CIA and the State Department found themselves under in countering this tidal wave of "alternative analyses" flowing from Feith's shop and Cheney's office was enormous. While noting the well-known problems with WMD intelligence gathering, Pillar observes "where greater offenses were committed" was in how policy makers used or developed intelligence on the terrorism question itself (the purported link between Saddam and Al Qaeda), with "Feith's people trying to string stuff together."[50] According to Pillar, not only did "the overall judgment depart, in terms of timing and so on from the intelligence community judgment," the reporting coming out of Feith's office "was almost the reverse of it."[51] As opposed to the intelligence community judgment that there had been no alliance between Saddam and Al Qaeda, which had been based on an exhaustive analysis of all the available reporting, Feith's office was circulating material arguing for the definite existence of such an alliance.[52] As Pillar observes regarding the Feith operation and its selective cherry-picking through mountains of raw intelligence, "the whole point was just to have some place to be able to scarf up enough scraps of stuff to stitch together to make a case that was contrary to the intelligence community's judgment."[53] Indeed, for an intelligence professional like Pillar, steeped in the need to conduct analyses through careful, objective tradecraft, Feith's shop was really best understood "as an extension of the speechwriting staff," not as an intelligence organization.[54] As he would note:

> The only thing that was on people's minds was selling policy, not making a policy. So whether you sell it with stuff that came from Langley or Feith's people doesn't make any difference. What matters is how's this gonna play publicly? It doesn't make a damn bit of difference whether it's part of a legitimate intelligence analysis or part of an effort just to scarf up scraps that sell! If they sell, let's use them! I've had people ask me . . . Feith's shop, should that be considered part of the intelligence community?! [*whistles in disbelief*] It's an extension of the speechwriting staff! It has absolutely nothing to do with making policy, it has to do with selling policy. And that's what all the discussions and meetings on Iraq were. There weren't any meetings on making the policy, it was selling and executing, and mostly selling.[55]

Indeed, according to one former intelligence official who "was intimately aware of Feith's operation," having worked in the shop itself, Feith's own legal background led to him approaching the case more like a prosecutor, building the case as an advocate, instead of objectively assessing it to see if there was a case at all:

> It was my experience that there was a departmental frustration with the lack of intel. And the intel we had did, in fact, lend itself towards indicating Iraq had WMD, if you look at disparate pixels in this vast mosaic. It's a classic intelligence problem. How do you connect those pixels? Or should you even connect

those pixels? I can't read Feith's mind. But if you're frustrated with what you got, you try to find good analysts who can relook at the same data and say, well, what do you think? So what you really had by him doing that is an indictment of the system that wasn't paying attention to a key, critical customer. And that was a policy maker. Now, Feith, quite frankly, was a very difficult gentleman to get along with, and unless he had a deep and personal relationship with you, he would just look on with askance at any assertion you make. Clearly, a litigator's mindset. . . . Show me the data, show me this . . . and I think that gets lost in the shuffle that Feith was a lawyer. He thought like a lawyer. You know, make the case for me. But, I think Feith takes too many rounds in the chest when it was the entire administration that had a bias from the get-go! And I suspect it probably was at the presidential level.[56]

Of course, others who dealt with Feith at deputies committee meetings, like Armitage, had a much less charitable view: "I just wanted to kill him! He was an idiot! He *is* an idiot! What can I say? I mean, I think I probably despised him with every fiber of my being!"[57] And it was not just the substance of the issues Feith would raise that infuriated Armitage, but his alliance with Cheney's office—and their single-minded focus on one policy approach— meant it was difficult to have true, objective discussions with "give and take" among advisers:

It was not the fact that he put things on the table, but you had the vice president, and you had Hadley, they were all working together on this stuff. And it was almost like a little fraternity, and they were frightened I'd stand up and not be on the same side with their fraternity brothers. So, you didn't have issues where today I'm with you, tomorrow I'm with them because I'm trying to judge each issue on its merits. No, you're either wholly in or wholly out. I remember one day Feith came into a meeting. Marc Grossman and I were there. And this was after the invasion of Iraq. We were arguing about getting more access to drinking water for the Iraqi people. And he said, "It's a Third World country, give 'em Third World water!" No. We're not gonna do that! That's not what the president wants. The president wants them to have a shot, so we're gonna do this. So we gotta work through these issues. And that kind of stuck. These kind of stupid things that he'd raise.[58]

But the "sales pitch" element in Feith's approach to his job, which mirrored the emphasis within the administration itself, came through quite strongly in other settings. Pillar recounts attending a White House meeting as he was preparing congressional testimony for Tenet:

It was he and Rumsfeld, Powell, all were gonna have congressional testimony in the next week or so. So it was a meeting that Hadley chaired to get everyone on the same page. Hadley chaired the meeting but it was Feith that did most of the talking. And it was a real display of "don't bother me with the facts, we've got a war to sell" approach. And the desire of the room came through quite strong.[59]

For Armitage, the emphasis being pushed within the administration to "stay on message" about certain assertions being used to justify the war (like Saddam's links to Al Qaeda)—often through the use of products originating in Feith's shop—represented a form of the "Big Lie" propaganda approach:

> You know, you keep saying it and saying it, people will believe it. You just keep repeating and repeating. To some extent, you know, it was true. But I don't think that was the deliberate policy they came up with. They didn't sit down and say, "Look, if we say X, even though it's completely wrong, people will start thinking it's right." I don't think they went to that extreme. I think they really believed a lot of this stuff, because they *wanted* to believe it. They wanted to believe it. Mohammad Atta in Prague is the perfect example! Time after time after time.[60]

Indeed, Tenet (2007: 302) acknowledges one of his senior analysts came to him in mid-2002 to complain that "several policy makers, notably Scooter Libby and Paul Wolfowitz, never seemed satisfied with our answers regarding allegations of Iraqi complicity with al-Qa'ida," to which he "told her to tell her analysts to 'quit killing trees.' If the answer was the same as the last time we got the question, just say, 'we stand by what we previously wrote.'" In fact, when the CIA was producing its June 2002 paper, "Iraq and al-Qa'ida: Interpreting a Murky Relationship," which made clear there was no conclusive evidence of links between Iraq and Al Qaeda regarding terrorist operations, Tenet (2007: 344–47) recalls receiving a strange offer from Feith's shop at the Pentagon (a policy, not intelligence shop) to share "their observations on the case for a connection between Iraq and terrorism." Though lacking the professional skills or discipline of real intelligence analysts, Feith's team wanted to brief the CIA on things they felt had been missed in the raw intelligence—"little nuggets" supporting their beliefs, while "never understanding that there might be a larger picture they were missing" or "thousands of other data points that might convey an opposite story" (Tenet 2007: 344–47). One presentation, titled "Iraq and al-Qa'ida—Making the Case," particularly got Tenet's attention, as the briefer argued it was "an open-and-shut case" requiring "no further analysis" or "debate" regarding the Iraq–Al Qaeda relationship (Tenet 2007: 344–47).

Tenet (2007: 348) had no idea this same presentation was also being briefed to officials at the White House, NSC, and the Office of the Vice President, complete with an additional slide (not included in the CIA presentation) titled "Fundamental Problems with How Intelligence Community Is Assessing Information." The slide complained the CIA was too picky and applied standards of proof not normally required of the evidence (Tenet 2007: 348). But as Tenet (2007: 348) observed, "We weren't too impressed with their work either, especially their willingness to blindly accept information that confirmed preconceived notions," which the CIA eventually came to refer to as "Feith-based analysis."

As Armitage later observed, there were Feith-based disciples, or advocates from Cheney's office, in numerous locations: "There were people in WIN-PAC, then you got some at the NSC (you know, with weapons and arms control), and they can exert a lot of pressure on WINPAC."[61] Plus, as Armitage notes, "The vice president of the United States and his top aide come down with several others, once or twice a week, and sits down and pours through intelligence. . . . You're not stupid if you're in the CIA. You know you're in the hot seat! So, you can put pressure on them."[62] Indeed, Tenet (2007: 343–44) recalls a November 2002 briefing of Cheney and Libby over the Iraq–Al Qaeda connection where "Libby approached it like an artful attorney"—throwing in additional hypothetical points after analysts made each statement asking "if this were true, would it change your judgment?" After six "if that were trues" later, Tenet interrupted to note there *were* other pieces of intel out there, but the CIA had looked at these in terms of the whole and they didn't add up to what he was suggesting—that "everything else was just speculation" (Tenet (2007: 343–44).

As one senior intelligence official at the Pentagon observed regarding the use of intelligence by key policy makers, "If your decision-making process is already biased in a certain direction, and I would submit that's probably the case," then those decision makers who feel a decision has to be made are heavily influenced by their own "personal bias coming in contact with ambiguous data and analysis."[63] Reflecting on his own experience working in key areas dealing with the Iraq issue within the intelligence community, the same official noted, "In this case, I think you had an administration almost thinking as one. There were obvious dissenters or skeptics. But everybody was jumping on the train in the face of ambiguous data and saying, 'Yep, I agree, this is how I read it.'"[64] When the Pentagon's own inspector general issued a report in February 2007 calling Feith's efforts in "peddling his alternative intelligence" "inappropriate," Tenet (2007: 348) noted in his mind it was the kindest thing you could say about it: "This was an example of bad government. Policy makers are entitled to their own opinions, but not to their own set of facts."

Yet as Tenet discovered during the run-up to Powell's speech, and his own use as a lightning rod for the purported statement he made to Bush about the case for Iraqi WMDs being a "slam dunk" (see Woodward 2004: 249), it was clear the White House was focused primarily on collecting facts to back up its opinions, not new intelligence. During a December 2002 White House meeting called to gather all the supporting evidence available to make the public case Saddam had WMDs (in the run-up to Powell's speech), Tenet (2007: 360) noted staffers made it clear they were looking for an "Adlai Stevenson moment"—even though his staff warned "our collected intelligence was nowhere near that categorical." After McLaughlin's presentation of existing evidence "underwhelmed" the president, Tenet (2007: 361) recalled Bush replied, "nice try," but it was not likely to convince "Joe Public." Nowhere was there a suggestion that WMDs might not exist and the intel could be wrong.

It was certainly Tenet's view that White House officials set him up as the "scapegoat" when they revealed to Woodward his supposed use of the term *slam dunk* regarding the veracity of WMD intelligence on Iraq—a story later repeated by Cheney, Rice, and others, which Tenet views as "the most despicable thing that ever happened to me" (Linzer 2007). Acknowledging the December gathering had essentially been "a marketing meeting," where the focus was simply on "sharpening the arguments" to be made to the public, Tenet was asked whether we didn't have better information that could be declassified to add to the debate, to which he replied "strengthening the public presentation was a 'slam dunk,'" a phrase later taken completely out of context by Woodward to portray his input as "leading" Bush to go to war—"but that's not the way it was" (Tenet 2007: 362–63).

From a blame-avoidance perspective, emphasizing the "slam dunk" quote was the perfect way to deflect blame away from Bush and toward the intelligence community when WMDs were not found in Iraq and the war became unpopular. Tenet (2007: 366, 480) believes the White House reaction to Woodward's book, and its emphasis on the "slam dunk" passage during its own public statements, was "the perfect public-relations deflection" for the administration and that the "whole Oval Office arm-waving, jumping-off-the-sofa, slam-dunk scene had been fed deliberately to Woodward to shift the blame from the White House to the CIA."

INNER-CIRCLE DYNAMICS AND THE RUN-UP TO WAR

As one senior-level official in the intelligence community observed regarding the administration's use of intelligence and inner-circle dynamics over Iraq, "I have seen dumb decisions made by just about every administration in the last twenty years. And those decisions, inevitably, have been made when the system itself was circumvented and the people were too compartmented."[65] And as many within the administration have noted, the alternative intelligence-influence network established by Cheney and Rumsfeld worked in exactly this fashion, to essentially circumvent the existing intelligence community system, while the NSC under Rice basically abdicated its function to vet information and maintain balance for the president across different policy actors. There were no fair hearings for dissenters, or easy access for information and advice that failed to support the push against Iraq. The disconnect between the Defense and State Departments not only led to bureaucratic conflict between the two over policy, but greatly increased the already substantial influence of Cheney's office (Mann 2004: 275–76). Apart from Powell and Armitage, who were often seen as not being "part of the team" because they raised questions or concerns about policy during meetings, it was clear less senior officials were excluded from meetings or worse for dissenting over policy. Powell, for example, noting Rumsfeld had destroyed Army Chief of Staff General Eric Shinseki's career over his congressional testimony suggesting several hundred thousand troops would be required to invade and occupy Iraq (not the much smaller number being pushed by the White House), observed "dissent simply was not allowed at the Pentagon" and "those who speak up get treated like Shinseki" (Woodward 2008: 50). Indeed, during an interview on ABC in April 2006, former JCS chairman Myers said he felt it had been wrong for administration officials to criticize Shinseki for expressing the view a much larger invasion force for Iraq would be necessary and that he had been "inappropriately criticized" for speaking out.[66] Similarly, Bruce Hardcastle, a widely respected DIA analyst for Near East affairs, found himself "shunted aside, bumped at the last minute from an overseas trip to the Middle East, and uninvited to key meetings" after clashing with a Feith deputy on Middle East issues (Isikoff and Corn 2006: 135–36). It was a common pattern often alluded to during interviews with former officials across the Bush administration.

In addition, the NSC process often not only worked to assist the Cheney-Rumsfeld group in circumventing normal routes for vetting policy advice and information, but provided a setting for blame avoidance, allowing officials to change conclusions after the fact to reflect quite different views. As Armitage recalled:

> I said to Hadley, "This deputies' process is not working. You've got to go back to a more recognizable process. We have to say, here's the agenda. And each side comes ready to speak to the agenda. And you have a discussion. And the deputy national security adviser sums it up and gives the summary of conclusions. That way we can all go back to our bureaucracies and give them a five-minute dump. And everybody would be on the same base. After that, there'd be a written summary of conclusions that would come back a couple of days after the meeting." So Hadley would sum up, give a summary conclusion. We'd

all write it down. You know, it's not brain surgery! And go back and brief it to the staff. . . . About two days after that, the written summary of conclusions recalled would be different! I'd say, "What the fuck is this?" He'd say, "Well, on that, you know, Doug called up and he had a different recollection." "So wait a minute! Steve, if you had a different recollection, you raise it while we're in the meeting!" He [Feith] went back, I would say, and got a different recollection because he got there with his hommies, and they're saying, "We don't want that, that's not good enough! Let's change it!" So, that kind of stuff went on all the time! And if you took a show of hands, you had Scooter, you had Feith, you had nothing in the military. This is the dog that's not barking! They never played. Meyers and Pace never played.[67]

Not only did Rice abdicate the impartial arbiter role previous national security advisers had performed in favor of an advocacy role, she too was often shut out by more senior players like Rumsfeld—adding to the dysfunctional dynamics in the inner circle. As Woodward (2006: 109–10) revealed, when Rice had questions about war planning or troop deployments, Rumsfeld at times would not even return her phone calls, responding to her complaints with the observation that "the chain of command did not include the national security adviser." When Rice subsequently complained to the president about Rumsfeld's behavior, "Bush's response was to try to be playful with Rumsfeld. 'I know you won't talk to Condi . . . but you've got to talk to her'" (Woodward 2006: 109–10). Armitage had gone so far as to tell Rice directly he felt the NSC system was "dysfunctional" because the "deputies committee was not carrying its load, policy was not sufficiently coordinated, debated and then settled," and she needed to be a "good, knock-down-drag-out fighter to be a strong security adviser and enforce discipline" (Woodward 2004: 414). When Rice responded by complaining to Powell, after the *Washington Post* published an article describing the NSC as "dysfunctional" only days later, the secretary replied:

> "You can blame Rich if you want," Powell said. "Rich had the guts to go talk to you directly about this, so I don't think he is the source." What Armitage had said reflected a general feeling around Washington and in the foreign policy establishment. . . . "Whether you like it or not, that's a view . . . heard around town. And I'm sorry it comes back to the NSC for not making it happen." Powell thought Rice was more interested in finding someone to blame for the public airing of the problem than in fixing it. (Woodward 2004: 415)

Yet Powell also found it difficult to influence the policy debate. Facing increasingly strident positions on Iraq by Cheney, Rumsfeld, and their deputies, Armitage observed: "We in the State Department, by the way the only ones who'd seen any combat ever, were the ones always raising questions.

Asking questions—and seen as "not on the team," we weren't macho! I'm sorry. We're not on the team because someone asked these questions today? The questions were designed to flesh out the difficulties of these endeavors!"[68] But as Powell later observed, there was "no one in the White House who could break through to insist on a realistic reassessment" (Woodward 2004: 415). Though Bush's reliance on Cheney and Rumsfeld for policy advice, the dysfunction within the NSC, and the successful circumventing of the normal intelligence vetting process played a role, it was also Bush's own personality at work—his penchant for seeing the world in absolute, black-and-white terms, often framed by his own ideological beliefs. Indeed, when famously asked by Woodward (2004: 420) whether he ever suffered any doubt about his decisions, Bush replied, "I haven't suffered doubt. . . . No. And I'm able to convey that to the people." But when you never suffer any doubt about your policy decisions or directions, you seldom are open to critiques or revisions of them.

BLAME AVOIDANCE AND THE "SIXTEEN WORDS" FLAP FROM THE STATE OF THE UNION ADDRESS

During Bush's 2003 State of the Union, sixteen words became famous as an example of how faulty intelligence was being used to justify invading Iraq. These words eventually resulted in blame-avoidance tactics being adopted that would ultimately lead to the outing of Valerie Plame by administration officials. Some of these (like Scooter Libby) would later face criminal investigations and prosecution over the matter, though the trail of prosecutions would peter out long before reaching figures like Cheney who had also likely been involved. The sixteen words in question were uttered by Bush as he built the case for war: "The British government has learned that Saddam Hussein recently sought significant quantities of uranium from Africa."[69] This, however, was hardly new information to the administration, which had been briefed on the subject nearly a year earlier.

It was during a CIA morning briefing in February 2002 Cheney first learned about the Niger yellowcake rumors, even though analysts at the time noted "there was nothing to substantiate the report, and parts of it did not make sense" (Isikoff and Corn 2006: 4). Nevertheless, Cheney jumped on the report, demanding the intelligence community get more material on the yellowcake rumors, pressing his interlocutors to find out about it (Isikoff and Corn 2006: 4). As Bush's address and Powell's UN speech approached, an even greater push developed to marshal all the supporting evidence possible against Saddam. During a January 6 meeting in Rice's office focused on building such a case, Hadley noted the Iraq nuclear case was "weak and needed to be 'beefed up,'" to which Walpole bluntly replied, "the draft was weak because the *case* was weak" (Tenet 2007: 371). This was clearly an unsatisfactory answer, and at the January 24 meeting (just days before the State of the Union), Hadley asked Walpole more directly what Saddam would need in order to successfully obtain nuclear weapons—in response to which Walpole faxed twenty-four pages (out of a ninety-page NIE) for background purposes, out of which one paragraph (now taken completely out of context) was used to justify Niger yellowcake and Saddam's nuclear ambitions (Tenet 2007: 371).

In fact, the CIA had already previously warned the White House back in October 2002 that the yellowcake information should not be cited in the president's upcoming Cincinnati speech because it had been based on dis-credited or suspect intelligence (Tenet 2007: 472–73). This finding was based on Ambassador Wilson's fact-finding mission to Niger in February 2002, which reported back the rumored sale of 500 tons of yellowcake to Iraq was dubious in the extreme (Wilson 2004). Nevertheless, in the push to find as much evidence as possible during the run-up to the war, these warnings failed to prevent the yellowcake intelligence from being used in both the State of the Union and Powell's UN speech.

But in the aftermath of the invasion of Iraq (and the inability to find WMDs), criticism of Bush's prewar claims and justifications for the war began to grow rapidly. The need for blame avoidance became clear, and the initial response was to claim its mistake had been an unavoidable, yet honest one, given the highly ambiguous nature of the intelligence it had to work with. Yet by late June, it was apparent this tack was not working, and Cheney met with Bush and White House lawyers to discuss ways to respond to the continuing stream of negative news stories about its use of prewar intelligence. Eventually, the two agreed in order to refute the criticism, they ought to divulge (or leak) to the public select portions of the classified NIE on Iraq presented to Congress in 2002 (Isikoff and Corn 2006: 250). It was a classic blame-avoidance move, deflecting blame away from Bush's deci-sion and back toward the NIE it claimed to believe was accurate at the time. Parts of the NIE were secretly declassified by Bush, who directed Cheney to "get it out" to rebut the charge they had manipulated intelligence (Isikoff and Corn 2006: 250). The information "would be used selectively—not to inform the public but to buttress a political argument" (Isikoff and Corn 2006: 250).

The continued assertions that Iraq had sought yellowcake from Africa for its nuclear weapons program (an assertion also appearing in the British white paper the Blair government used to justify Britain's participation in the war) drew fire from Ambassador Wilson, who had gone on the fact-finding mis-sion to Niger in February 2002—and reported back, by way of the CIA, to

Cheney's office that such a sale had been unlikely (Wilson 2004). Concerned the administration was distorting or misrepresenting intelligence to justify an invasion of Iraq, Wilson went public in a scathing editorial in the *New York Times* on July 6, 2003, in which he outlined the details of his Niger trip. He had found that Niger's uranium business, run through a foreign consortium, overseen by the IAEA, and requiring approval from a number of government officials for any transaction of the type described in the Iraq yellowcake rumors, made it impossible for such a transaction to have occurred without notice—a view shared by the American ambassador in Niger as well (Wilson 2003).

Wilson's editorial was a bombshell, one directly targeting Bush's "sixteen words" and the administration's motivations and use of intelligence prior to the war. The critique was blunt and threatened the underpinnings of Bush's blame-avoidance strategy, with Wilson asking if his reporting "was ignored because it did not fit certain preconceptions about Iraq, then a legitimate argument can be made that we went to war under false pretenses," and "questioning the selective use of intelligence to justify the war in Iraq is neither idle sniping nor 'revisionist history,' as Mr. Bush has suggested" (Wilson 2003).

The morning after Wilson's editorial, the buzz within the White House press corps was all about Wilson's charges, and Press Secretary Fleischer responded to the barrage of questions by emphasizing, "There is zero, nada, nothing new here. . . . This is old news" (Isikoff and Corn 2006: 256). It was a blame-avoidance strategy routinely employed by every administration seeking to downplay new revelations as irrelevant old hat. Fleischer not only emphasized the White House had already admitted "repeatedly the information on yellowcake did indeed turn out to be incorrect" but insisted no one in the administration had any reason to suspect the veracity of the Niger charge prior to the State of the Union address (Isikoff and Corn 2006: 256).

Of course, this argument was becoming far more difficult to sell to the public as time went by, as new revelations were heard and the surrounding political environment (on both sides of the Atlantic) became more skeptical. While still considering how to respond to the "sixteen words" controversy, White House aides closely followed the political crisis faced by the Blair government after BBC reporter Andrew Gilligan broadcast a report quoting intelligence officials suggesting the British white paper on Iraqi WMDs (released the previous September) had been "sexed up" by Blair's government (Isikoff and Corn 2006: 248). Skeptics within the United States quickly drew their own parallels between the Bush and Blair governments on the intentional distortion of prewar intelligence—making the blame-avoidance strategy of seeking to dismiss the reports as "old news" or "honest mistakes based on faulty intelligence" far less effective.

As the controversy continued to build, Rice informed Tenet that while it had not been her decision, the White House had decided against issuing any statements saying the Niger materials shouldn't have been used in the State of the Union (Tenet 2007: 455). Recognizing the weakness in this approach, Tenet (2007: 458–59) recounts phoning Hadley to tell him he was going to take responsibility for the passage making it into the president's speech, to which Hadley admitted the process had not worked well at the White House either and they would join in taking shared responsibility for it. But Tenet's mea culpa statement did not elicit the kind of positive response he had hoped for from the administration. Indeed, as Tenet (2007: 470–71) later observed, "One of the reasons some people in the White House were unhappy with my 'mea culpa' statement was that the details in it might lead some of the journalists who received background briefings on the NIE—without our knowledge—to discover that they had been misled regarding the importance we attached to intelligence reports alleging Iraq had vigorously pursued yellowcake in Niger." Moreover, it was quite plain in Tenet's statement that the CIA had "put little stock" in the Niger reporting and "did not rely on it for our judgment regarding whether Iraq was reconstituting its nuclear weapons program" (Tenet 2007: 471).

For the White House, sharing blame with the CIA was not exactly a preferred solution given the more traditional use of the intelligence community as a lightning rod to deflect blame away from policy makers. Tenet (2007: 463) quickly found "no signs of that 'shared responsibility' that I had been promised by Hadley. Reporters kept calling our press office with accounts from 'senior administration officials' on Air Force One who continued to insist that the CIA's share of the fault was 100 percent." As the administration continued placing blame for use of the Niger material squarely at the feet of the intelligence community, some within it were provoked to fight back in the press. After one story on the *CBS Evening News* reported CIA officials had previously warned the White House about the unreliability of the Niger reporting, but they had gone ahead with it anyway, Tenet received an irate phone call from Rice. As Tenet (2007: 466) recalls, she was "furious," and when he reminded her that he had intervened earlier to get similar language out of Bush's Cincinnati speech that still found its way back into the State of the Union, the "conversation ended uncomfortably."

One of the most important attributes in any actor selected to be a lightning rod is their willingness to serve as a conduit for the bolt descending from above. To the extent the lightning rod fights back, or seeks to deflect the bolt in other directions, the less convincing and valuable it is for blame-avoidance purposes. For the White House, the CIA's refusal to "go quietly into the night" on this matter was one that provoked an effort to force Tenet back into line. As Tenet (2007: 469) remembers, a few days after his tense phone conversation with Rice, he received a call from Powell, inviting him to come over to his house—where he delivered a message from Bush to "keep your building quiet" and an account of a fierce debate aboard Air Force One (led by Cheney) over whether he should be let go.

Rice and NSC officials repeatedly requested CIA officials declassify se-lected paragraphs from the NIE dealing with the Niger uranium issue, which senior agency officials resisted doing, arguing it would be "misleading" and make it incorrectly appear to have been a major part of their thinking when, in fact, the material had never been stated in the report as being among the reasons the intelligence community had believed Saddam was reconstituting his nuclear program (Tenet 2007: 470). Eventually, the agency relented and the Key Judg-ments and the Niger paragraphs from the NIE were released to the press. As Tenet (2007: 471) recalls, their intent was obviously to suggest the intelligence community had given Bush "every reason to believe" Saddam had WMDs, and spokesmen were soon suggesting the material left out of the Cincinnati speech at the CIA's request was different from that in the State of the Union. "That simply wasn't so. . . . It was clear that the entire briefing was intended to convince the press corps that the White House staff was an innocent victim of bad work by the intelligence community. . . . Apparently, I was expected to go along with the notion that *only* we had screwed up (Tenet 2007: 471).

Thus, a critical component to the use of lightning rods is simply this: if you are using someone involuntarily as a lightning rod, it is important to ascertain beforehand whether or not they have the ability to credibly defend themselves against your efforts to direct blame at them. For the White House, this required the CIA to have no recourse but the familiar "he said, she said" situation where only each side's word is available as evidence to prove the truth behind the events. Unfortunately for the administration, Tenet's staff discovered two memos in their files that had been sent to the White House in October 2002 explaining in detail why the president should not cite the yel-lowcake information in his Cincinnati speech (Tenet 2007: 472–73). Taking these with him to the president's PDB on July 22, Tenet presented copies of the memos to Hadley and Card, noting that he had sent "two follow-up memos to make sure the NSC got the point" (Tenet 2007: 472–73). Ac-knowledging Hadley, Rice, and chief speechwriter Michael Gerson had read the memos last October (and known about the CIA's objections to the Niger information), Card asked why he was being given the memos now, to which Tenet (2007: 472–73) replied:

"I wanted to double-check on my end to make sure that not only did we write the memos, but that they were received as well. I had my staff confirm with the folks who keep the secure fax machine logs that the memos were in fact sent and received," I said. Just to remove any doubt, I passed Andy a slip of paper indicating the precise times each memo had arrived at the White House Situation Room. "Besides . . . I presume you were doing the same thing . . . looking for the facts. If I have the memos, surely your staff gave them to you, too, didn't they?" Andy shook his head and simply said, "I haven't been told the truth."

With the "smoking gun" now pointing directly at the White House, it was clear the blame-avoidance strategy of casting all of it at the CIA over the "sixteen words" was no longer tenable. Though Hadley told his colleagues he "had simply forgotten about the memos" and offered to resign (which the president refused), it was determined Hadley would have to "come clean" over the memos or risk the CIA leaking them (Isikoff and Corn 2006: 299). Thus, during a White House press conference on July 22, on the very day Tenet revealed his evidence, Hadley and Bartlett admitted to having received the memos and that they had "described weakness in the Niger uranium evidence and the fact that Iraq's effort to procure the yellowcake was not particularly significant" (Tenet 2007: 474–75). Hadley was also forced to admit the memos he and Rice received stated the CIA had been telling Congress the "Africa story was one of two issues where we differed with the British intelligence" (Tenet 2007: 474–75).

After Hadley's mea culpa, Isikoff and Corn (2006: 300) described vividly how Bush aides perceived the nature of the White House–CIA environment: "We should never have gotten into a knife fight with the CIA," John Gibson, the White House speechwriter, recalled. "Making Tenet say that statement [accepting fault for the sixteen words] was like opening up a hornet's nest. [The CIA's] job is to screw you." But for Tenet, the view was different. As he reflected on Bartlett's ducking of a reporter's question during the press conference about whether or not this meant the mess was not Tenet's fault, as Hadley suggested the week before, Tenet (2007: 475) observed, "That, I suppose, is what the White House meant when it promised to 'share' the blame."

BLAME AVOIDANCE AND THE "PLAME GAME"

Connected to the flap over the "sixteen words" was the case of Valerie Plame. Her husband, Ambassador Joseph Wilson, had been sent on a fact-finding mission to Niger and reported back there was no basis for believing any Iraqi purchases had occurred—which was then transmitted to the White House. Wilson's analysis was later backed up by IAEA Director Mohamed ElBaradei. When the administration finally showed the IAEA its Niger materials in February 2003 (despite already having shown these to Congress months earlier in October 2002), the IAEA staff experts quickly concluded the documents were nothing more than elaborate forgeries.[70] But by that point, the case for war had already been made.

Much later, after the war had begun and the administration continued to refer to the Niger reporting as a justification for invading Iraq, Wilson finally wrote his July 2003 *New York Times* article, provoking the subsequent efforts to release the NIE and blame Tenet and the CIA. It also resulted in another blame-avoidance tactic being employed, that of attempting to "discredit the messenger as being biased"—and for Wilson, this meant revealing his wife, who was a covert CIA officer in the Clandestine Service, had played some role in his selection for the mission. Given the administration's ongoing attempts to blame the CIA, there was a certain logic to attempting to link Wilson's wife at the CIA to the issue, since it would make it seem possible (at least when presented to the public) that the agency had been actively trying to undercut Bush on Iraq. And anything calling into question the ambassador's motives for going public with his critique could help to dampen the impact of his attacks.

But the problem with taking such a step was a profound one due to a simple fact—revealing Plame's identity was a felony, a revelation of top-secret information not only undercutting her ability to work in the Clandestine Service but endangering all of her network of contacts she had worked with undercover over her twenty-year career (Leiby 2005; V. Wilson 2007). It was a plainly illegal action. Nevertheless, Plame's identity was revealed by administration officials to reporters, including Bob Novak, who outed her as working for the CIA in his July 14, 2003, column—unleashing a political firestorm (J. Wilson 2004; V. Wilson 2007).[71] Eventually, a special prosecutor, Patrick Fitzgerald, was appointed to conduct a criminal investigation of the leak, an investigation that would lead directly to Cheney's inner circle.

For Bush, the appointment of a special prosecutor and the trail that led him to senior officials posed a serious danger politically—especially if it could be proven the administration had targeted Plame in retaliation, intentionally revealed classified information to out her, or willfully sought to discredit her husband to hide the fact they had knowingly used faulty intelligence. The Fitzgerald investigation strongly suggested (though could not conclusively prove) the authorization to reveal Plame's identity came from Cheney himself and found a number of senior White House officials (Libby, Rove, and Armitage specifically) as being involved in the leaks.[72] A lightning rod (or fall guy) was required to prevent those closest to the president (like Cheney and Rove) from being indicted, and this individual would prove to be Libby. During his trial, Libby's attorney stated White House officials were trying to blame him to protect Rove.[73] Recounting Libby's end of the conversation, defense attorney Theodore Wells noted his client felt betrayed by the White House: "They're trying to set me up. They want me to be the sacrificial lamb. . . . I will not be sacrificed so Karl Rove can be protected."[74]

In the end, however, Libby would be the only official found guilty in the probe and sent to prison for his role in the Plame affair. Fitzgerald would not pursue charges against either Rove or Armitage, though each had been found to be the source of leaks to Novak, due to an inability to find criminal intent behind what each had claimed was only inadvertent comments.[75] Fitzgerald did, however, find Libby had been involved in an effort to beat back criticism of the Iraq War and discredit Wilson by intentionally revealing his wife's identity.[76]

Libby's conviction for perjury, obstruction of justice, and making false statements to investigators—though not reaching Rove or Cheney directly— provided further ammunition to critics. In reality though, the Plame case was not nearly as damaging as it might have been, due to the fact there existed a buffer, or "shock absorber," to assist in minimizing the blame that might have attached more easily in its absence. Namely, the strength of partisan defenders in the mass media (like the Fox News network and talk radio programs, hosted by the likes of Rush Limbaugh and Bill O'Reilly), which served to reduce the credibility even of Libby's conviction by issuing a constant drumbeat of assertions the entire case had been "politically motivated" and was purely the work of those opposed to the administration. In a complex environment where the details of a case are complicated and nuanced, and in some cases open to interpretation, this additional background noise proved to be quite effective in reducing the impact of Libby's conviction on the general public by providing a rival, competing message to discredit it. But while Cheney could not be proven to have authorized the leaks, Libby's testimony differed significantly from his boss's. For example, though Cheney testified that "no one ever told him of a desire to share key judgments" of the NIE with the press, Libby testified Cheney had directly authorized sharing the report with Judith Miller in July 2003 because he thought it was "very important" to get out the message about Saddam and the uranium.[77] According to Libby, "the vice president instructed me to go talk to Judy Miller to lay this out for her."[78] But with no direct paper trail, it was just one person's word against another's.

Opening Pandora's Box:
Blame Avoidance during the Iraq War

BLAME AVOIDANCE:
THE DISBANDING OF THE IRAQI ARMY

The strong belief held by Bush and his key inner-circle advisers that the operation to topple Saddam would be a relatively easy one, allowing U.S. forces to avoid a lengthy occupation of Iraq, was an error similar to those made by many leaders who ignored Clausewitz's dictum—"Everything is very simple in war, but the simplest thing is difficult." In fact, Thucydides reminds us in *The Peloponnesian War* that the Athenians imagined their war with Sparta would only require three years rather than the twenty-seven it eventually lasted. In 1914 British and French leaders believed the war against Germany would be over in as little as three months, with their troops "home in time for Christmas," instead of envisioning the four long years of slaughter that lay in wait (Tuchman 1962; Keegan 1998). For the Bush administration, a similarly optimistic view held sway. It was one that led General Mike Jackson, the former British chief of general staff, to observe that Rumsfeld and those around him took it "as an ideological article of faith that the coalition soldiers would be accepted as a liberating army" by the Iraqis, resulting in what he viewed as an "intellectually bankrupt" handling of postwar Iraq (Jordan 2007: 27). Yet as Packer (2006: 147) notes, the policy failure was "not entirely the result of constraints and mistakes" but in a sense "deliberate" since there was never a coherent postwar plan beyond rapidly handing off to the Iraqi exiles and letting them "deal with the messes that came up."

This "certainty" by Bush that regime change and bringing democracy to Iraq would allow an easy departure for American troops set the administration up for considerable blame when the ease of the initial military operations was not followed up by an effective postwar plan. As civil order rapidly deteriorated and violence spread across Iraq, the administration's response did little to damp down criticism, especially after Rumsfeld's famous dismissal on April 11 of media reports of bedlam in the country with his "stuff happens" remark (Isikoff and Corn 2006: 213). It was clear, at least from the intelligence community's perspective, that the administration had been warned. It had just failed to take seriously warnings about the destabilizing consequences and blowback likely to result after an invasion of Iraq, which had been covered in both the CIA's August 2002 "Perfect Storm" paper and the NIC report of January 2003 (Woodward 2004; Tenet 2007). Though the State Department had been heavily involved at a number of levels in developing postwar plans, including the "Future of Iraq Plan," it would soon lose control over policy to an assertive Department of Defense. As one former senior State Department official later remarked, after all of the work done on the plan and other humanitarian initiatives, they were summarily informed by the White House (without prior consultation) that everything would be handed over to the Pentagon![1] As the official observed:

> The presidential directive set up a whole structure that superseded everything we were doing. And we were told that there had been no coordination . . . that Rumsfeld had just walked into the president and he'd signed it. . . . Then Rumsfeld went out and hired a bunch of personnel out of headhunters, and hired a whole bunch of Republican kids (some of whom had to go get passports). Not exactly professionals. It had not been coordinated with anyone! Just Rumsfeld to the president! And even the embassy didn't know about it.[2]

Indeed, as Armitage would observe, the "Future of Iraq Plan" "was a checklist if you will of everything that could go wrong, [raising] every issue, from looting to all the things that could happen—not a bad starting point—but we were frozen out."[3] In fact, Armitage notes the Department of Defense made certain to remove as many State Department staff as possible from Garner's staff in Iraq (especially any with ties to those at State who were not quite as gung-ho as the Defense staffers):

> We were frozen out. There were eleven people who were gonna go in initially with Jay Garner. And they were all frozen out. Megan Shaw for example. Megan was frozen out because she was close to Richard Haass. Tom Warrick was frozen out because he knew that Ahmed Chalabi was full of bullshit! The vice president told Rumsfeld no. Still, when they got in a jam, they still had to turn to us sometimes—because we need the language, we need this or that. But mostly we were frozen out.

Lieutenant General Garner himself, a political moderate who had been appointed to lead the Coalition Provisional Authority (CPA) in Iraq after the invasion in March, was replaced less than two months later by Rumsfeld's own choice, the far more political Paul Bremer. It was Bremer who would subsequently make one of the most controversial (and disastrous) decisions of the entire Iraqi occupation—the disbanding of the Iraqi military in the name of de-Baathification. Yet in fairness, it was Bush's own style and delegation to subordinates (like Bremer and Rumsfeld) that played as big a role in these events—and the manner in which they were handled. Bremer's CPA Order 2, disbanding the entire 400,000-strong Iraqi Army, along with his orders forbidding former Baath Party members from taking any jobs in the new Iraqi government or in public service (like teaching), alienated huge segments of the Iraqi population. It also made the challenge for postwar reconstruction far more difficult, since most of the experienced, technically or bureaucratically trained individuals had, under Saddam's regime, been members of the Baath Party—much like being a member of the Communist Party had been a requirement for holding many jobs in the Soviet Union. Banning all of these individuals, many of whom had been in the Baath Party purely for employment purposes under Saddam, now meant they had no-where to go—other than the insurgency.

It was a decision that would raise concerns not only in the United States but also in Britain, where former defense minister Geoffrey Hoon acknowledged the strong disagreement between the British government and Bush over Bremer's decisions to disband the Iraqi Army and pursue de-Baathification. As Hoon observed, "Sometimes . . . Tony [Blair] had made his point with the President. I'd made my point with Don [Rumsfeld] and Jack [Straw] had made his point with Colin [Powell] and the decision actually came out of a completely different place. And you think: what did we miss? I think we missed Cheney."[4] Indeed, key aides to Blair later acknowledged he had "repeatedly and unsuccessfully raised his concerns with the White House" about what he believed were inadequate prepara-tions for postwar reconstruction in Iraq.[5] Moreover, Blair's concerns over the lack of planning were so vexing to him he sent Sir David Manning, one of his most senior foreign affairs advisers, to Washington a full year before the invasion to get answers to questions such as how difficult and long the operation would be, what would the postinvasion plans be, and others.[6] Upon his return, Manning wrote in a memo to Blair warning, "I think there is a real risk that the [Bush] administration underestimates the difficulties. . . . They may agree that failure isn't an option, but this does not mean that they will avoid it."[7]

It was not just the State Department and the Blair government left out of the planning. The intelligence community, strongly disliked and distrusted by the administration, was also largely frozen out of postinvasion planning.[8] Bush, who was not a huge consumer of information or the details of policy beyond "big picture" generalities, also did not push his NSC to objectively explore or sift through the inputs from other actors who might have other views. It was a closed advisory system, much like Johnson's in Vietnam, and it would fail Bush much as LBJ's had failed him. As Tenet (2007: 447–48) later observed, "US policy operated within a closed loop," with bad news ignored and CIA reporting dismissed because the "NSC did not do its job" and "became too deferential to a postwar strategy that was not working."

Though Bremer initially took the lion's share of the blame for his two controversial orders—much to his own chagrin (Bremer 2006)—it's fairly clear these actions were not taken without consultation. As Andrews (2007: 11) notes, Bremer was unhappy about being portrayed as a "renegade" by White House officials in search of a lightning rod. Indeed, Bush was later quoted by Draper (2007) as saying he believed at the time the actual decision he had made was "to keep the army intact" in Iraq, but that this "didn't happen"—a statement clearly seeking to shift the blame for the disastrous decision to Bremer. But as with Tenet, lightning rods that fight back tend to reduce their effectiveness in dissipating blame. As Bush officials steadily distanced themselves from his order over the following months, Bremer had been "smoldering," noting to Andrews (2007:11) that "this didn't just pop out of my head"; he had sent drafts of the order to top Pentagon officials and discussed it "several times" with Rumsfeld. Later, after the decision was largely blamed for aiding in igniting the insurgency (providing masses of disaffected former soldiers to the cause), Bremer finally released previously undisclosed letters to the *New York Times* in September 2007 showing Bush was told in advance (in May 2003) of the plan to "dissolve Saddam's military and intelligence structures" (Andrews 2007). In fact, after being briefed on the plans to disband the Iraqi Army, Bush sent a short thank you letter to Bremer stating, "Your leadership is apparent. . . . You have quickly made a positive and significant impact. You have my full support and confidence" (Andrews 2007). But as was often the case in the Bush White House, many senior players (including State and the joint chiefs of staff) were left out of the decision—which ended up being made by a small group led by Rumsfeld and Cheney (with Bush's concurrence). As Andrews (2007: 11) observes, Powell notes he "did not know about the decision ahead of time," and Pace confirms "the decision to disband the Iraqi Army was made without the input of the joint chiefs."

BLAME AVOIDANCE: THE FAILURE TO FIND WMDS

An even greater threat still lay in wait for the administration. In addition to the disastrous decisions to disband the Iraqi Army and pursue de-Baathification, which served to amplify the conflict in-country, the subsequent failure to find any WMDs posed a far greater challenge to manage—especially given that Saddam's possession of WMDs had been the primary justification for going to war in the first place. In fact, Bush's domestic political problems over Iraq began materializing nearly as rapidly as his promises of a quick, easy victory (complete with piles of WMDs stacked high for inspection) dissipated like a morning fog. According to the Marist College Institute for Public Opinion, between April and November 2003, public support for Bush's handling of Iraq dropped a full 28 percent to only 48 percent of registered voters.[9] And the problem was obvious from a blame-avoidance perspective. Bush had publicly expressed such *absolute certainty* in the existence of the threat—and the link of Saddam to Al Qaeda—that failure to find these weapons was a political disaster. The White House had essentially argued the evidence proving these weapons existed was irrefutable, having showcased its case for war using intelligence supposedly leaving no other conclusions in Powell's UN speech. Thus, the failure to find Iraqi WMDs undercut the administration's credibility and justification for the war, as well as stoked the fires of those who suspected it had manipulated the evidence to support its position.

As U.S. forces spread out across Iraq searching for WMDs, the White House began fending off questions regarding the failure to find them, with officials still emphasizing their confidence in a successful outcome. Rumsfeld claimed during a March 30 press conference, "we know where they are," while Ari Fleischer stated on April 10, "We have high confidence they have weapons of mass destruction. This is what this war was about and is about. And we have high confidence it will be found" (Isikoff and Corn 2006: 214). Yet despite the administration's assurances, doubts were beginning to be raised. Carl Ford Jr., the assistant secretary in charge of the State Department's Bureau of Intelligence and Research (INR), recalled that as interrogations and polygraphs of captured senior Iraqi officers and scientists continued to indicate no WMDs, the administration was "in denial" and assumed they were all "good liars"—while "our common reaction was . . . Holy shit, we're in trouble" (Isikoff and Corn 2006: 215).

David Kay, who previously had led UNSCOM inspections during the 1990s (after the first Gulf War), was tapped to lead a new Iraq Survey Group (ISG). It seemed a safe choice by officials, since Kay had demonstrated his tenacity and competence in finding such weapons before and was known (due to frequent press interviews) to believe Saddam still possessed WMDs.[10] As

Kay would later reflect, "In the run-up to the war, I was heavily influenced by the period of the nineties in which there was deceit, denial, disruption, frustration of the inspection effort. . . . That did play a role, quite clearly, in my conclusions prior to the war."[11] And it was Kay's prior background that likely smoothed the path for his appointment to the ISG. "In 1991 my first experience with Iraq, when we actually did find WMD, the CIA had said it didn't exist," Kay explained. "So I found stuff that CIA had been telling Cheney, as Secretary of Defense, wasn't a concern—so I think that's partly the reason I got Cheney's clearance to get this job. I found stuff when people said it couldn't be found."[12]

But despite his prior history and preexisting belief Saddam possessed WMDs, once he returned to Iraq to lead the ISG, Kay was forced to begin revisiting his beliefs almost immediately given what he found on the ground:

> It was the first time I'd been back in Baghdad since the UNSCOM days. And I was just shocked at how much physical deterioration had taken place. . . . It had nothing to do with the bombing, because the bombing campaign actually did very little. . . . I was really struck with how this country had fallen apart . . . and the level of corruption was clear. When I went back with ISG, I really tried to put everything that had occurred in the nineties behind me because it was a very different situation. . . . In the nineties, if we'd wanted to talk to someone, we told the Iraqi security people, and they either brought them or they didn't bring them. Now . . . we had to go out and find them! The chaos was so different. And mostly what they were afraid of at that point wasn't Iraqi security. . . . They were afraid of the general level of violence and crime. . . . So they were more than willing to talk . . . a cascade of explanations about how they hadn't been able to do anything after we left. Either we'd destroyed so much, or people weren't very interested in it. So they'd been driving cabs or doing other things.[13]

For Kay, a specialist in the physical requirements of running a sophisticated WMD program, the deterioration of the Iraqi infrastructure that occurred over the previous decade (quite aside from what his contacts were saying) made finding WMDs unlikely in his mind. But it was not just his *own* previous experiences in Iraq that played a role in his own initial mindset. A similar dynamic existed in Bush officials he reported back to in Washington:

> I'll tell you the person that the nineties made a huge difference for. . . . It was the vice president. The vice president came away from the first Gulf War with a deep suspicion of the CIA. Rumsfeld had it also, and it goes back to the missile plan reviews. I mean, there was just a level of suspicion of intelligence. . . . I mean, I've got a low opinion of the way we conduct human intelligence. But they just didn't trust anything. And the fact that we had found them in '91, '92, they thought meant that they were there and we just hadn't found them yet. And

that was just sort of based on that experience. They had a hard time in looking at new evidence and new things. I tried to describe in one of the briefings for the President the changed social situation and all . . . and it didn't seem . . . it was just, whoosh [*gestures with hand going over head*]. Over the head! They didn't understand the implications of the culture of corruption, the way the process itself . . . you can't run a WMD program, which is after all, a scientific program with this engineering. You can't run it when the corruption is so pervasive that nothing gets done.[14]

Soon Kay was discovering even more problems with the administration's case for WMDs, as the tubes presented as evidence of centrifuges were found to be (just as earlier Department of Energy dissents had argued) nothing more than efforts to build conventional artillery rockets. Even prior to going to Iraq, Kay had his doubts about many of the nuclear claims being made, noting, "I was never certain the evidence on nukes that I saw was ever compelling—I mean, I didn't doubt that they were trying to resurrect their nuke program, but I didn't think they were very far along."[15] On the other hand, Kay believed claims about chemical and biological programs made more sense, since "it was easy to do and they'd done it very well before."[16] Yet even here, Kay found little evidence of any CBW program—and some of the more sensational claims involving mobile bioweapons production trailers were quickly found to have no basis in fact. Indeed, a team of Pentagon and State Department Intelligence and Research analysts had already disputed the findings of an earlier CIA team that the discovered trailers were designed to produce anthrax and other bioagents—a dissent Kay's ISG now confirmed (Isikoff and Corn 2006: 307). Interestingly, this earlier CIA field team's report that the items *were* biotrailers is an interesting example of how intelligence was being distorted to satisfy what senior officials wanted to hear. One senior member of this team, who was an expert in microbiology and biowarfare pathogens, recalled that upon first examining the purported biotrailers he knew "instantly that these were not capable of producing BW" because the equipment was all wrong for that purpose and the trailers lacked many of the essential elements that would be required.[17] Yet upon expressing this view (which was supported by British experts on the team as well), the scientist was essentially "slapped down by the senior CIA officer on our team," who then reported back to Washington a biotrailer had indeed been found.[18]

Even in the area of chemical weapons, where the Iraqis had developed extensive production capabilities and an impressive arsenal by the early nineties, Kay's team was finding nothing. Upon interviewing surviving members of Saddam's inner circle, the most that was being uncovered were reports that just prior to the war, Saddam and his sons had asked people if they could restart the CW programs, regain certain capabilities, but as Kay notes regarding Saddam, "I'm absolutely convinced that he did not think that he had WMD!"[19] Indeed, for Kay, it was increasingly apparent as the ISG moved forward with its investigation that Saddam had seen WMDs as a bluff to deter the West and maintain his own prestige in the region:

> I'm absolutely convinced he saw it as a bluff. I spent hours with Tarik Aziz about this. Saddam had essentially three things. First of all, he was fearful of his military. He knew these were the guys, if anyone was going to overthrow him, it was the guys with the guns. And he went to great lengths to either buy them off or emasculate them, by keeping ammunition out of their hands if they had guns. But he also knew that if they thought he'd given up WMD, his belief was they would view him as a less powerful Arab man . . . and the senior military, by and large, those we interrogated, thought they had WMD. They thought they had, up until the end, when there was this final meeting with Saddam and his commanders, when he told them, "We don't have it!" I mean he *told* them! We've got multiple sources for that meeting. There are no WMDs. The second reason was he thought his status in the Arab nations was increased by the thought that he had WMD . . . [that] he was given deference by the Syrians and the Egyptians and others because he'd managed to maintain that capability. And the third reason definitely was the fear of a Shia/Kurd uprising. He knew they thought he had it and would use it. It wasn't a bluff vis-à-vis us, because he actually believed we would never be so stupid as to do what we did. He had the French and Russians telling him, up until the end, it won't happen. The Russian special envoy told him, "The Americans will never do it. At most they'll do an air campaign. And we'll stop it in the Security Council, etc., etc." And so, on the first two days of the war, when the ground campaign kicked off . . . he didn't allow his forward units to take up any offensive operations because he thought it was a bluff. . . . Saddam thought the U.S. had not gone to Baghdad for the reasons many American decision makers had said we didn't go to Baghdad. We didn't want to take over responsibility for the country; we'd never get out. He believed that really ensured we wouldn't do it again. And for him, bombing wasn't a big threat. He'd had a lot of that before. And he knew that, by and large, it increased his political power in the country.[20]

But as Kay's frequent reports and briefings back to Washington continued to emphasize a lack of evidence supporting the existence of WMDs, officials from DoD, and especially Cheney's office, began pressing the ISG to look at the evidence again—and search harder. Moreover, the pressure was on Kay not only to find evidence of WMDs but to uncover anything that could justify the Saddam–Al Qaeda link. While leading the ISG, Kay recalls receiving calls more than once a week from Wolfowitz, pushing him for any material supporting 9/11 connections in the materials the ISG was uncovering—convinced "somewhere, buried in those documents, would be the smoking gun that would show" Saddam had been involved.[21] Kay later remarked, "It was a mystery to all of us in Baghdad, because we knew the evidence in there, and there *just was not* a connection there!"[22] Kay's deputy, Major General Keith Dickey, also found himself fielding frequent calls not only from Wolfowitz but from other DoD officials like Stephen Cambone, who were told, "We have looked; it's just not there."[23] As Kay recalls, "Paul came to Iraq fairly often in the early days," but during those visits, it was the 9/11 connection that was "all he seemed to be interested in."[24] In fact, Kay found it "amazing" that after three weeks on the ground, Wolfowitz "showed *absolutely no interest* in the failure to find WMD," leading him to wonder if he really "knew there were no WMDs there," or "more likely, how weak the case was."[25]

Others within the administration, however, were not giving up on WMDs so easily. As Kay recalls, "The vice president's shop was digging directly into primary intelligence forms," noting, "the funniest one for me has always been this phone call, at 3 a.m., giving me a set of coordinates that I should go look at because there was some indication on intelligence that there was WMD buried there—it turned out to be in the middle of the Bekkaa Valley [in Lebanon], not in the middle of Iraq!"[26] Similarly, Kay recounts being called by Cheney's office regarding some "executive intercepts" (very high-level NSA communication intercepts), which are not generally distributed throughout the government because they represent "a very thin layer" of raw intelligence usually devoid of the context that would give them meaning.[27] As Kay remembers:

> I had this call from Cheney's office in the middle of the night asking me if I'd seen this communication intercept. And my answer was, "No, but I'll dig it out." . . . It was just a piece of chatter. No geocoordinates from either end of the conversation. No knowledge of who they were. And like most chatter, it didn't mean anything to anyone . . . unless you were convinced there was WMD there and this must have been code for it. I continued to be amazed throughout my period at how deep his office . . . and the vice president himself asked about these things! . . . I just thought, "My God, don't you have anything better to do than read the crap at the primary level?" Because it's, I mean it's like drinking from a fire hose, there is so much out there! And he just didn't believe that the community, the intelligence community, could filter it adequately. He thought they were incompetent on this issue.[28]

What Kay was discovering firsthand as head of the ISG was the way in which the administration was selectively using intelligence to drive its case. It was the same pattern that had occurred in the prewar period. But the issue now was no longer merely selling the use of force against Saddam, but actually proving the threat marketed to the public really existed after the fact. Kay noted "each new raw piece" of intelligence Bush officials raised with him often had little substantive support behind it, and in many cases "the evidence was sort of immaterial to it" because "they just believed it."[29] By the end of July, Kay was reporting back to Tenet and McLaughlin at the CIA that his ISG was unlikely to find any actual WMD stockpiles and would probably only be able to uncover evidence of a "production surge capacity" allowing for the quick manufacture of limited quantities of chemical or biological weapons if an order was given (Isikoff and Corn 2006: 306). It was certainly not a report that would help the White House avoid blame over its justification for the war.

In late July 2003 Kay returned to Washington to brief the Senate Intelligence and Armed Services Committees, and while there he accompanied Tenet to Bush's morning intelligence briefing—attended that day by a larger than normal group, including Cheney, Rumsfeld, Wolfowitz, Rice, and Card (Isikoff and Corn 2006: 310). Reporting he "had found nothing," Kay was surprised to discern "no disappointment coming from Bush," who instead seemed "disengaged" (Isikoff and Corn 2006: 310). In fact, Kay later noted that "the president *never* pressed me . . . when I said we hadn't found it. That was it . . . never heard it again."[30] In looking back, Kay observed, "I'm not sure I've spoken to anyone at that level who seemed less inquisitive. . . . He was interested but not posing any pressing questions" (Isikoff and Corn 2006: 310). Instead, Bush merely asked what he needed and replied to Kay's response he needed "patience" with the observation, "I have a world of patience" (Isikoff and Corn 2006: 310). Meeting later with Cheney and Libby, Kay was asked whether he was "relying on intelligence from the CIA" or "finding his own facts" and asked if he "had seen the intelligence—signals intercepts and satellite imagery—indicating there had been prewar movement of Iraqi trucks and aircraft across the Syrian border," perhaps carrying Saddam's WMDs there (Isikoff and Corn 2006: 311). As Kay would later recall about Cheney's questioning, "He kept remembering little facts that he thought proved big conclusions. The problem with intelligence is that little facts often don't prove anything, let alone something big. They're just pieces of puzzles—sometimes just pieces that don't even make a puzzle" (Isikoff and Corn 2006: 311).

Upon returning to Iraq in August, Kay found even his earlier "surge capacity" theory for production of chemical weapons didn't hold up to the evidence he was finding—which he reported back to Tenet (Isikoff and Corn 2006: 312). But as the word coming from the ISG continued to grow less positive, Tenet (who had been in weekly communication with Kay) now stopped responding, and Kay only heard from McLaughlin (Isikoff and Corn 2006: 312). After briefing McLaughlin in September about the negative ISG findings regarding the aluminum tubes and mobile weapons labs, McLaughlin wouldn't accept Kay's findings and "just refused to believe that it wasn't part of the nuke program!"[31] As Kay recalled:

John didn't know a damn thing about the nuke program. He knew even less about the technical requirements of centrifuge design. And, you know, it was just, "close my eyes, I don't want to hear it!" And so, it just shut down all communications. There was a bunker mentality.[32]

As far as Tenet was concerned, Kay viewed him as a "very likable guy" who "ought to be selling used cars or insurance," because he was such "a relationship guy," but noted these qualities did not prepare him to deal with the pressures he found himself under over Iraq.[33] Indeed, as Kay would observe about Tenet:

He was under tremendous pressure. The search for WMD was not producing the evidence that it should. The lack of intelligence capacity about the insurgency. The military was constantly on his back. The White House was on his back. So, I mean, he was under *tremendous* pressure. And the agency he represented was under pressure. . . . And he understood how vulnerable . . . that the agency might be held as a scapegoat. And you have to remember, when you get back to late 2003, early 2004, this war . . . that was the period where it was going like this [gestures *sharply down with hand*] . . . down. . . . So George . . . he was just not a "tower of power" in terms of integrity under pressure.[34]

In his memoir, Tenet (2007) would later suggest he had been shocked at the negative feedback Kay's ISG reported back from Iraq—and that the absence of WMDs took him by surprise—almost suggesting Kay had not been in enough contact to forewarn him. From Kay's perspective, this version of events is likely a result of Tenet's own blame-avoidance needs:

I was sending him emails. I'd been talking to him on the telephone. . . . He called *all the time*! And I sent emails every week! We had a teleconference every week. And so there was *absolutely* no surprise as to what was going on there. None. You know, I think he acted surprised because . . . George was concerned that the White House would hold him responsible, instead of hold me responsible. [*laughs*][35]

As he would later tell Isikoff and Corn (2006: 312), Kay believed both Tenet and McLaughlin were "in denial" and just didn't want to hear bad news. Eventually, both "just stopped talking to me," which Kay described as the "agency way": "You cut people off, you don't have to kill 'em. Just cut 'em off."[36] As Kay later observed:

I mean, George told me, "I don't care what you say. I will never believe that there was not chemical weapons in Iraq." And John and I had a real tiff over the aluminum tubes, because on that point I discovered that not only were the aluminum tubes not associated with the nuke program, but that the way the agency had come to the conclusion that they were was, I think, there's no other way to describe it, it was dishonest. That is, they had excluded people who *knew* something about centrifuges, and they'd used a handpicked team out of WINPAC that never explained how they came to their conclusions.[37]

When Kay returned to Washington in October to provide closed-door briefings to the House and Senate Intelligence Committees on his interim findings, it was quickly apparent to those who viewed the draft report that the administration would find no support for its prewar claims. Though WINPAC, along with Tenet and McLaughlin, continued to support Curveball's reporting (at least for a while longer), Kay's investigators had concluded "Curveball was nothing but a fabricator and that his reporting was all false" (Isikoff and Corn 2006: 327). After viewing the draft ISG report, Tenet "urged Kay not to say anything too definitive about the empty-handed weapons hunt," but Kay disagreed (Isikoff and Corn 2006: 328). Not only did he report ISG had not "been able to corroborate the existence of a mobile BW production effort," but he also reported "Iraq's chemical weapons stockpiles had apparently been destroyed after the first Persian Gulf War and that he'd found no evidence of any ongoing major nuclear program. . . . On every key prewar claim—a revived nuclear program, WMD-carrying unmanned drones, stockpiles of chemical and biological weapons—Kay had uncovered nothing" (Isikoff and Corn 2006: 327–28). After the hearings, Tenet and McLaughlin informed Kay they had received calls from Bush officials who asked why Kay "had started out by saying weapons had yet to be found," instead of suggesting they might "have been buried" (Isikoff and Corn 2006: 328–29).

After Kay's final Senate testimony in January 2004, where he famously noted, "We were almost all wrong" on the WMD issue and none were there, he briefed a Bush full of questions on "how we got it wrong"—but he didn't show anger, disappointment, or challenge Kay's conclusions: "[Bush] was at peace with his decision to go to war. I don't think he ever lost ten minutes of sleep over the failure to find WMDs" (Isikoff and Corn 2006: 349). The reaction of Bush's political opponents to Kay's report was to call for the appointment of an "independent commission" to review the WMD intelligence failure—a move the White House initially resisted, fearing damage to Bush's reelection efforts. But as calls from Democrats (and the party's prospective presidential candidates) for an independent commission grew more intense, Bush eventually relented, appointing an "independent" commission (with the White House picking all of the commission's members), along with an order not to issue any report until March 2005, well after the presidential election (Isikoff and Corn 2006: 349). As a creature of the White House, it was understood by those appointed that the enquiry was to focus on the failure of the intelligence community and its prewar intelligence—not on how intelligence was used by Bush and his advisers to make the case for war.[38] From a blame-avoidance standpoint, it was the perfect composition and tasking orders for creating a thoroughly "housebroken" commission, one unlikely to bite its creator. Bush's preemptive move in creating the WMD Commission also prevented it from being modeled on the 9/11 Commission (as Democrats wanted), which would have allowed Congress to appoint half of its members (Woodward 2006: 286–87).

The White House was never enamored with the idea of fact-finding commissions, having unsuccessfully fought to block the creation of the 9/11 Commission (as well as public congressional hearings of pre-9/11 intelligence failures) until being forced to relent (after enormous political pressure from victim's families) in November 2002 (Shenon 2008). Cheney warned then Senate majority leader Daschle in January 2002, "We've got our hands full," and raising questions about intelligence failures would be a "very dangerous and time-consuming diversion for those of us who are on the front lines of our response today" (Shenon 2008). Once the commission was established, the executive director, Philip Zelikow (who would later work in the administration), pushed his staff to include material on links between Saddam and Al Qaeda (until being forced to retreat by their threats to resign). "He wanted to put the commission's staff on record saying there was at least the strong possibility bin Laden and Saddam had collaborated to target the U.S. before 9/11" (Shenon 2008). Indeed, the day after the 9/11 report came out, saying no such connection existed, Bush still insisted "there was a relationship between Iraq and al-Qaeda," with Cheney arguing in interviews that "the Atta-in-Prague report might be credible—even though the CIA, FBI, and the 9/11 Commission had found there was nothing to support it" (Isikoff and Corn 2006: 363). The report had done nothing but complicate Bush's prewar efforts to make the case against Saddam, and he wanted no similar problems from a WMD commission.

With Kay resigning as ISG head in January 2004, Bush appointed former UN weapons inspector Charles Duelfer as his successor, holding out hope a fresh set of eyes could perhaps succeed where Kay's had failed. From a blame-avoidance perspective, the appointment of Duelfer allowed Bush to buy a little time by publicly suggesting we should wait to "see what Duelfer can find" in Iraq. Officials, like Cheney, were still arguing Saddam's WMDs might have been smuggled out of Iraq and into Syria (though this had also been discounted by Kay's investigations) and that just because they hadn't been found *yet* doesn't mean they don't exist, still hidden or buried in the sands of the Iraqi desert.[39] But in reality, it was a mere stanching of the political wound at this point, with even Duelfer acknowledging (prior to his departure for Iraq) that the chances of finding chemical or biological weapons in Iraq was "close to nil at this point."[40] When Duelfer returned to Washington to issue the final ISG report in October 2004, the findings would support and be even *more* definitive on the lack of Iraqi WMDs than Kay's had been. Unlike the WMD Commission, which would not report back its findings until after the presidential elections, Duelfer (2009: 442) was determined to issue his final report before that date, observing, "I was convinced that for the report to be considered an objective compilation of data and analysis, it had to be produced before the elections. If the report were issued after the elections, it could too easily be dismissed as a politically driven product."

The ISG was shut down for good in January 2005 without ever finding WMDs in Iraq. In response to public criticism about its failure to find what had been used as the primary justification for going to war, the administration would employ the classic blame-avoidance tactic of stating it was "looking ahead rather than backward to the past." Responding to a press corps question regarding whether there would be "consequences" given it was now clear the WMD information had been wrong, McClellan replied simply that the president's "focus" was "on helping to support those in the region who want to move forward" (Isikoff and Corn 2006: 379–80). For the White House at least, it was time to move on.

BLAME AVOIDANCE AND THE "RUMSFELD PROBLEM" (FROM ABU GHRAIB TO THE REVOLT OF THE GENERALS)

As the controversy over the use of prewar intelligence grew and a full-blown insurgency erupted across Iraq, the man who had quite visibly taken charge publicly of day-to-day Iraq operations, Rumsfeld, almost inevitably was going to attract increasing amounts of criticism and blame. Rumsfeld held frequent press conferences where he downplayed negative news and confidently fenced with reporters, dismissing critics with a style delighting conservatives and enraging others. And just as the Vietnam War eventually became known to critics of the time as "McNamara's War," Rumsfeld's similar high-visibility role at the Pentagon leading and defending the campaign led many people (supporters and opponents alike) to see the conflict as "Rumsfeld's War" (Scarborough 2004).[41] Further, Rumsfeld's actions during the run-up to the war—like insisting on a "light" footprint and small invasion force, resulting in too few troops on the ground to prevent the lootings and disorder that occurred, and his aggressive sidelining of the State Department to assert Pentagon control over day-to-day operations—meant that when the situation deteriorated, it was hard for Rumsfeld to avoid becoming the target of blame.

Indeed, much later, during his testimony before the Iraq Study Group in 2006, a furious Powell "just exploded" and was "mad as hell" when asked why the invasion had gone in with so few troops (Woodward 2008: 47). Powell recounted having raised the issue of force size with Franks in September 2002, who relayed this to Rumsfeld: "Franks reported that 'Rumsfeld chuckled,' but wanted to make sure that Powell's doubts were aired. 'I want him to get them on the table in front of the president and the NSC. Otherwise, we'll look like we're steamrolling'" (Woodward 2008: 47). It was a concern Rumsfeld easily dismissed at the time, knowing he had enough support with Bush to push through his preferred strategy regardless of Powell's reservations. When Powell's fears were realized after the invasion, Rumsfeld publicly dismissed questions about whether a lack of adequate U.S. forces were to blame with his famous reply, "Stuff happens" (Woodward 2008: 48–49). Rumsfeld's Pentagon would not involve State, which had done a great deal of postwar planning, preferring instead to send inexperienced operators to Baghdad who responded in an ad hoc manner to events, while pushing for expat Iraqis, who lacked significant bases of indigenous support (like Ahmed Chalabi), to assume leadership positions (Woodward 2008: 48–49).[42] As the insurgency grew, Rumsfeld dismissed this as the work of a "pocketful of dead-enders" and refused to use the word *insurgency* to describe events in Iraq.[43] The Pentagon did not actively consult with others over major actions, such as Bremer's de-Baathification or the disbanding of the Iraqi Army (Woodward 2008: 48–49). Whether talking to frustrated officials in State Department, the intelligence community, or senior military officers themselves who were dealing firsthand with Rumsfeld and his lieutenants, his abrasive, controlling style was one that provoked frequent complaints internally.[44] Indeed, top officials would note Rumsfeld's "destructive arrogance," with one frustrated adviser lamenting, "You have no idea what it's like to deal with the United States of Rumsfeld" (Dickerson and Cooper 2004).

But for the White House, Rumsfeld's "big" personality and loyalty to Bush were major assets—especially in the early days of the war. Rumsfeld's uncompromisingly confident demeanor while defending policy during his press conferences set the desired tone and was a highly effective communications channel to the public. He was in charge of the largest government department during a time of war, which greatly increased his bureaucratic and political clout. Bush liked Rumsfeld, and he had a long history with Cheney stretching all the way back to their days together in the Ford administration (Woodward 2008: 194). All of these factors served to increase Rumsfeld's prominence and influence within the president's inner circle. Yet it was this very closeness to Bush and Cheney, and his prominence on Iraq policy, that would later pose significant problems for the White House when controversies involving

Rumsfeld's stewardship of the Pentagon arose. Indeed, from a blame-avoidance perspective, Rumsfeld was a very poor lightning rod for Bush because he was not distant enough from the president to effectively divert the current away. And while Rumsfeld was already channeling a growing charge as the Iraq situation deteriorated, two events significantly increased the voltage of that current: Abu Ghraib and the so-called revolt of the generals. The White House would eventually be forced to respond to these events and try to shift blame away from Bush, all while trying to hold on to Rumsfeld—further reducing his ability to serve as an effective lightning rod.

On April 28, 2004, the Abu Ghraib scandal became public as explosive photos—depicting extreme, dehumanizing abuse by American military personnel of Iraqi prisoners held at the US-run detention facility in Iraq—were broadcast on the news program *60 Minutes II*, followed the next day by an online article in the *New Yorker* magazine by Seymour Hersh providing even more graphic details of the case.[45] The sadistic, grotesque nature of the abuse (e.g., simulated executions, sexual assaults, the use of dogs, the stacking of naked prisoners into human pyramids, etc.) created a political firestorm overnight for the administration (at home and abroad) while provoking widespread revulsion in the American public.[46] Aside from angry Senate Republicans, Democrats like Joseph Biden (the ranking Democrat on the Foreign Relations Committee) launched attacks on the administration, calling Abu Ghraib "a disaster of significant proportions" that called for quick "accountability."[47] Stopping just short of calling for Rumsfeld's resignation, Biden warned if the blame went all the way to the secretary's office, he should resign.[48] For a White House that long had portrayed itself as being the toughest on terrorism and refusing to compromise or hold back on the use of force, the Abu Ghraib scandal was a political disaster, ripping away its moral credibility abroad while providing ammunition to domestic critics to charge it with recklessly overstepping its authority by authorizing the torture of inmates during interrogations (Danner 2004; Hersh 2004; Greenberg and Dratel 2005).[49]

The White House itself was said to have been caught unawares regarding the more sordid details surrounding Abu Ghraib until after the story broke, though it would later be found to have authorized "enhanced interrogation techniques" of prisoners (including water-boarding), encouraged defense and intelligence officials to make use of such enhanced techniques at Abu Ghraib (and other detention facilities), and engaged in "extraordinary rendition" that secretly moved detainees to foreign prisons where they could be tortured by other countries for information (Danner 2004; Hersh 2004; Greenberg and Dratel 2005; Woodward 2006, 2008). The ensuing furious debate over torture, water-boarding, rendition, and detainee abuse would never abate for the remainder of Bush's tenure, becoming a frequent topic of congressional hearings and investigative journalism. While the official military investigation concerning Abu Ghraib, the *Taguba Report*, would find senior intelligence and military officials had pressed for the use of enhanced techniques on the detainees, no senior members of the administration were directly charged with misconduct.[50] Only eleven lower-ranking enlisted personnel were eventually court-martialed and sent to prison, while the commander of the 800th Military Police Brigade, Brigadier General Janis Karpinski, was demoted in rank to colonel for dereliction of duty. They would take the blame and be held up as examples of fact-finding and punishment of transgressors by the administration, a few "bad apples" whose actions had nothing to do with the orders of senior officials. And while this defense worked to a degree, the other controversial actions being taken in the name of the war on terror made selling the notion that no one more senior than a brigadier general was culpable a difficult one—especially given the public perception of Rumsfeld as being fully engaged and in charge of handling military operations in Iraq.

The immediate public response by Rumsfeld to the release of the Abu Ghraib photos was to downplay their importance (typical of his usual style of dismissing negative stories coming out of Iraq), noting while he "did inquire about the pictures," he had been "told that we didn't have copies" (Woodward 2006: 305). Recognizing Rumsfeld's response was hardly helpful and needing to quickly stop public blame from reaching the White House, word leaked (with authorization from Bush himself) through aides that "the President had expressed his displeasure to Mr. Rumsfeld during a meeting in the Oval Office because of Mr. Rumsfeld's failure to tell Mr. Bush about photographs of the abuse" that had so enraged the Arab world.[51] Not only would the story recount how Bush had "admonished Rumsfeld over the Abu Ghraib scandal"; it would emphasize that the president "was unsatisfied and unhappy with Rumsfeld's handling of the matter" (Woodward 2006: 305). Further, as Dickerson and Cooper (2004: 37) observe, the leak was "a presidential shot" across the Pentagon's bow, where officials "were insisting the White House had been kept in the loop about the abuse investigation."

On Capitol Hill, Rumsfeld was met with calls for his resignation over the scandal as he testified during congressional hearings, acknowledging, "If there's a failure, it's me. . . . These events occurred on my watch. As Secretary of Defense I am accountable for them, and I take full responsibility."[52] After offering his "deepest apology" to the victims of Abu Ghraib and promising compensation to them, Rumsfeld responded to inquiries about whether he would resign as being "a fair question" given the circumstances: "Since this firestorm started, I have given a good deal of thought to the question. If I thought that I could not be effective, I certainly wouldn't want to serve. And I have to wrestle with that."[53]

The following day, a *New York Times* article quoted an unidentified aide to Rice as saying Rumsfeld had "become a liability for the president" and had "complicated the mission in Iraq" (Woodward 2006: 306). With a presidential campaign already underway, and public uproar regarding Abu Ghraib building, Rumsfeld decided to offer Bush his resignation during the latter's visit to the Pentagon on May 20 (Woodward 2006: 306). Not only did Bush refuse Rumsfeld's offer to resign (the first of two), he appeared the same day in public with the secretary (alongside Cheney, Powell and General Myers), turning to Rumsfeld to say, "You're doing a superb job. You are a strong secretary of defense, and our nation owes you a debt of gratitude" (Woodward 2006: 306).[54] It was certainly a show of personal loyalty by a president who valued the trait as highly as any other in an adviser. But it was also a recognition that, from a blame-avoidance perspective, a senior member of Bush's own inner circle could hardly be fired without appearing to justify those who sought to attach blame at the highest levels of the administration. It should be recognized that the Abu Ghraib scandal was not occurring in a vacuum but was now part of broader criticisms over the use of prewar intelligence, the failure to find WMDs, and an unpopular war. So acknowledging blame at such a senior level certainly held the danger of very easily becoming the "thin end of the wedge" for Bush. Though White House Chief of Staff Card kept trying to convince Bush to fire Rumsfeld during 2004, Woodward (2006: 367–68) notes Cheney continued to argue Rumsfeld's departure (no matter how spun) would be seen "as an expression of doubt and hesitation on the war" and only give critics encouragement to then go after the president himself. Bush decided he couldn't fire him. The communications process between the military and civilian leadership was misfiring, and Rumsfeld still held a tight grip on day-to-day management of Iraq operations by dominating the senior military leadership (like Generals Pace and Abizaid).

The White House continued to take further steps at blame avoidance over the WMD fiasco with the assistance of its Republican allies in Congress. In July 2004 the Senate Intelligence Committee issued a 511-page report focused mainly on the failures of the intelligence community, while carefully avoiding any criticisms of Bush, Cheney, or other administration officials for having stretched the flawed intelligence community assessments (Isikoff and Corn 2006: 363–64). The chairman of the Senate Intelligence Committee, Republican Pat Roberts of Kansas, not only decided to put off looking at how Bush had used the faulty intelligence until after the 2004 elections, but afterward ditched this investigation in favor of one focusing on what Democrats and Republicans had said over the previous decade on Iraqi WMDs, while slow-tracking any further examination of the White House (Isikoff and Corn 2006: 363–64).

But a more impressive blame-avoidance attempt was yet to come. In December 2004, in a starkly self-confident dismissal of his critics, Bush chose to award the Presidential Medal of Freedom (the highest civilian honor) to two of the main individuals involved in several of the biggest controversies over Iraq: one who had been blamed for contributing to the faulty WMD intelligence in Iraq (Tenet) and the other who had made the disastrous decisions to dismantle the Iraqi military and institute de-Baathification in Iraq (Bremer). It was a blatant, very public denial of the validity of the criticisms directed at the two men, and by extension, Bush. And it was a clear refusal to give one inch in publicly accepting any blame for the reverses in Iraq. Indeed, much as Bush would later publicly tell FEMA Director Michael Brown, during the Hurricane Katrina disaster, that he was doing "a heck of a job," a largely similar statement was now being made for Tenet and Bremer (Preston 2008; Boin et al. 2010).

Still, there were now limits to how far Bush could go in convincingly pushing certain interpretations of events. For example, the Pentagon found itself having to distance itself from assertions being made by Feith's shop after he sent the Senate a classified report in October 2004 rehashing his earlier claims of fifty contacts between Saddam and Al Qaeda, the Atta-in-Prague allegation, and al-Libi's claims about poisons training—all of which had already been discounted or dismissed by intelligence analysts (Isikoff and Corn 2006: 334–35). Though Feith's report was leaked to the neoconservative *Weekly Standard*, which concluded "there can no longer be any serious argument about whether Saddam Hussein's Iraq worked with Osama bin Laden and al Qaeda to plot against Americans," the Pentagon quickly announced it did not stand by the report (Isikoff and Corn 2006: 334–35).

The Department of Defense also sought to prevent other embarrassing reports from surfacing, such as a RAND study prepared for the army on planning for postwar Iraq titled "Rebuilding Iraq," which it submitted in the summer of 2005.[55] After discovering the study's wide-ranging critique had heavily criticized the White House, Defense, and a number of other government agencies, the Pentagon decided to keep the report under "lock and key."[56] It criticized Bush and Rice for never mediating the tensions between Defense and State during the planning process, of giving the Pentagon the lead in overseeing the postwar period despite its "lack of capacity for civilian reconstruction planning and execution," and Bush's unchallenged assumption that reconstruction requirements would be minimal.[57] In addition, it criticized Franks and Central Command for having a "fundamental misunderstanding" of what the military needed to do to secure Iraq (and assuming American civilian agencies would do most of the work rebuilding the country).[58] Given the RAND study was submitted just as the White House was teeing up the president's November 2005 announcement of his "National Strategy for Victory in Iraq," it is hardly surprising the Pentagon sought to keep the report under wraps.[59] But with critics becoming more emboldened throughout the administration, the report quickly leaked to the *New York Times*, adding another example to Tenet's (2007: 434) knowing observation that leaks "are the improvised explosive devices of inside-the-Beltway warfare."

The beginning of the end for Rumsfeld came in the form of the so-called revolt of the generals in April 2006, when six retired senior generals went public with their criticisms of Rumsfeld and called for his resignation. It was not only highly unusual but unprecedented for so many senior military men to make such a call. And these were hardly unknown officers. The group included high-profile officers such as General Anthony Zinni, former head of Central Command; Lieutenant General Gregory Newbold, former director of operations on the Joint Staff; Major General John Batiste, former commander of the First Infantry Division in Iraq; Major General Charles Swannack, former commander of the 82nd Airborne Division in Iraq; and Major General Paul Eaton, who commanded training of Iraqi security forces. Moreover, given their recent personal involvement in Iraq operations, it was also a group that couldn't be characterized as being out of touch with the current situation.

The White House initially tried to dismiss the criticism as simply reflecting tensions over the war, with Press Secretary McClellan adding, "The president believes Secretary Rumsfeld is doing a very fine job during a challenging period in our nation's history."[60] However, potential political damage from this highly visible criticism in the months leading up to midterm elections (and the attention the generals were receiving from the media) forced Bush to interrupt a family holiday at Camp David to give yet another defensive statement: "Secretary Rumsfeld's energetic and steady leadership is exactly what is needed at this critical period. . . . He has my full support and deepest appreciation."[61] White House surrogates, like retired generals Myers and Franks, quickly appeared on cable news programs to criticize their former colleagues for publicly questioning the civilian leadership—with Myers noting on CNN, "My whole perception of this is that it's bad for the military, it's bad for civil-military relations, and it's potentially very bad for the country, because what we are hearing and what we are seeing is not the role the military plays in our society."[62] Rumsfeld himself countered that "out of thousands and thousands of admirals and generals, if every time two or three people disagreed we changed the secretary of defense of the United States, it would be like a merry-go-round."[63] Yet such statements were quickly rebutted by still other former Pentagon officials, weakening the response. Former army secretary Thomas E. White chimed in with his own defense of the generals, observing, "Rumsfeld has been contemptuous of the views of senior military officers since the day he walked in as secretary of defense. It's about time they got sick and tired."[64]

The "revolt" began to pose a particularly difficult problem for the White House from a blame-avoidance perspective. Since long before the war in Iraq, and certainly during it, Bush had consistently argued publicly he "relied on the judgment of his generals" in guiding his policy decisions (Ricks 2009: 40). But given the generals in revolt had essentially *been* those whose judgments he relied upon and were ones with personal experience with both Iraq and Rumsfeld, it was difficult to "swipe aside their collective judgment" without deepening "the public's lack of faith in Bush and those around him" (Ricks 2009: 40). And Bush wasn't yet prepared to abandon his secretary of defense. Responding to a question about whether Rumsfeld might be forced out by the generals' criticisms during a press conference, Bush flatly remarked:

> I don't appreciate the speculation about Don Rumsfeld. . . . He's doing a fine job . . . [and as for the generals] I listen to all the voices, but mine's the final decision. . . . I hear the voices, and I read the front page, and I know the speculation. But I'm the decider, and I decide what is best. And what's best is for Don Rumsfeld to remain as the secretary of defense. (Ricks 2009: 40)

At the same time, the White House decided to launch a counteroffensive against critics following time-honored blame-avoidance tactics of questioning the motives of opponents or suggesting they didn't truly understand the situation as clearly as the administration did. But as Ricks (2009: 54–55) observes, the characterizations were crudely done, with Rumsfeld saying they were "morally and intellectually confused" (like those who opposed confronting Hitler in the 1930s), Cheney arguing they were "abetting terrorists," and Bush saying detractors could "not be more wrong." These attacks only increased the growing public perception that Bush was "divorced from the realities of Iraq and dismissing the legitimate worries of those who believed—with ample evidence—that the war was being mishandled" (Ricks 2009: 55). To a great extent, this approach to blame avoidance—with its emphasis on presenting an image of absolute certainty and confidence in the White House view of events—was driven by Bush's own leadership style. He was a leader driven by absolutes, by his own idiosyncratic views on policy that were illuminated by ideology—and he firmly believed in the need to be decisive, to be "the decider." And while commendable in many ways, it had a destructive effect on Bush's national security decision making, a process requiring open-minded, objective analysis and a willingness to consider alternative courses of action. As Woodward (2008: 38) observes, "a 'no doubt' president can swamp any process" by not "allowing much reconsideration," and "the president and his team had become marketers of Bush's certainty. . . . A president so certain, so action-oriented . . . almost couldn't be halted." And like Johnson's inner circle during Vietnam, the Bush response to critics tended to be purely defensive and one refusing to consider their critiques. As former White House counselor Dan Bartlett remarked, recalling his efforts to tell Bush he needed to show he was listening to critics, to acknowledge when their intentions were good, and avoid "coming off as pigheaded" with his expressions of resolve and determination, "All of this flew in the face of Bush's natural tendencies. . . . It would take time to wean the president from his zero-defect proclamations" (Woodward 2006: 406).

BLAME AVOIDANCE AND THE "DOWNING STREET MEMO"

Adding to the administration's public woes over its use of prewar intelligence was the May 2005 publication of a secret memorandum in the London *Sunday Times* written by Sir Richard Dearlove, head of Britain's MI6 (roughly the equivalent of the American CIA). The memo detailed Dearlove's report on talks he had conducted with American officials during a July 2002 meeting with Blair and other senior officials in London. In the memo, Dearlove noted that among White House officials:

> There was a perceptible shift in attitude. Military action was now seen as inevitable. Bush wanted to remove Saddam, through military action, justified by the conjunction of terrorism and WMD. But the intelligence and facts were being fixed around the policy. The NSC had no patience with the UN route, and no enthusiasm for publishing material on the Iraqi regime's record. There was little discussion in Washington of the aftermath after military action. (Danner 2006: 88–89)

Obviously, this reference to "fixing the intelligence and facts" around the policy immediately called into question administration assertions it had not manipulated intelligence during the run-up to the war. Moreover, given the clear problems with postwar planning during the time this memo came out (May 2005), its acknowledgment that "there was little discussion" about the aftermath of military action was also very damaging from a blame-avoidance standpoint. Yet there was still more in the Downing Street memo that undercut the Bush administration's damage-control efforts. Despite White House denials it had *not* already decided the matter long beforehand, in the memo there was a clear recognition (in July 2002) that Bush had already made up his mind to go to war with Iraq, "even if the timing was not yet decided" (Danner 2006: 90).

The memo seemingly supports the recollections of many former Bush administration officials who have suggested the decision to go to war had essentially been made in 2002, long before the final push to justify it at the United Nations in February 2003.[65] It would also potentially help to explain Bush's initial lack of interest in going to the UN for that last resolution on Iraq—since Saddam's acceptance of its terms would short-circuit the ongoing war planning. Indeed, Armitage recalls a meeting in which both he and Powell explained to the president that the resolution "means no war if Saddam agrees," to which Bush replied simply, "I got it. But I won't help you. I'll allow you to go, but I won't help you."[66] Similarly, Woodward (2008: 432) recounts, during the sixteen months prior to the war, Bush received a dozen detailed briefings on Iraq invasion plans from Rumsfeld and Central Command but failed to have any meetings to discuss the question of *whether* to go to war. In fact, Woodward (2008: 432) noted Bush acknowledged, during later interviews, that he did not seek recommendations about going to war from his father, Powell, Tenet, or Rumsfeld because essentially "the president had never questioned its rightness, and its rightness made it the only course."

BLAME AVOIDANCE AND THE RETURN OF THE BIOTRAILERS

Although Iraq Survey Group reports by both Kay and Duelfer had found no credible evidence to support the existence of mobile biowarfare trailers, these had nevertheless been one of the key WMD claims made before the war (having featured prominently in Powell's UN speech). And for some within the administration, it was not an element that would be easily given up, especially with the blame-avoidance need to demonstrate at least some of the prewar case might have been justified. As a result, the CIA issued a six-page report in May 2006 declaring the trailers found earlier in Iraq were, in fact, mobile bioweapons labs—thereby proving part of the prewar intelligence had been correct. But as Isikoff and Corn (2006: 227) noted, inside the intelligence community, the paper "generated fierce controversy," with most intelligence professionals viewing it as "a shoddy piece of work that had been prepared more for public relations purposes than legitimate analysis." Indeed, weapons analysts observed the trailers couldn't have been used to produce bioagents given the simple fact the supposed fermentation tanks lacked any drains whatsoever allowing lethal materials to be removed afterward (Isikoff and Corn 2006: 227).

Moreover, the manipulation of the intelligence process employed to produce the new CIA biotrailer report, upon closer inspection, appeared to be similar to how earlier prewar intelligence had been distorted, with State's Intelligence and Research excluded and DIA contractor reports concluding the trailers were not labs left out, and when DIA analysts refused to sign on to the CIA assessment, a sympathetic DIA analyst was approached by WINPAC to allow the DIA logo to be used on the paper (Isikoff and Corn 2006: 228). As one senior DIA analyst later exclaimed, "We were tricked . . . that report was bogus . . . that was not one of the finest moments in intelligence analysis" (Isikoff and Corn 2006: 228). Given the open revolt among so many within the intelligence community over the report and the clear weaknesses in its analysis, it would not be used to defend the administration's case for war. But like many earlier products, word of the dispute would leak out to the press, further damaging the administration's credibility.

BLAME AVOIDANCE, THE IRAQ STRATEGY REVIEW, AND THE IRAQ STUDY GROUP

By mid-2006 the basic problem for the administration, as it sought to retain control over the direction of its Iraq policy, was it no longer was the only game in town. Reacting to growing public disenchantment, Congress had appointed in March 2006 an independent, bipartisan commission known as the Iraq Study Group (ISG) (not to be confused with the earlier Iraq Survey Group), cochaired by James Baker and Lee Hamilton and tasked with evaluating the situation in Iraq and making new policy recommendations by the end of the year. And unlike with the earlier WMD Commission, the White House had very little ability to rein in or constrain what this group chose to focus on regarding Iraq. Though the White House maintained its official posture that everything was under control and progress was being made, privately senior officials were beginning to have their doubts—and were growing increasingly worried about the political damage that would arise if the ISG issued a harsh critique of current policy or their handling of the war. Bush himself would later acknowledge to Woodward (2008: 12) that "despite his outward optimism, he had realized even then, in June 2006, that the strategy wasn't working" in Iraq.

While there had been some internal discussions regarding the feasibility of holding an official Iraq strategy review (to reexamine their approach and consider what changes should be made), such reviews are always politically dangerous from a blame-avoidance perspective, since they often open up current policies to even greater external criticism. Almost inevitably, these kinds of reviews end up being perceived by observers as an acknowledgment that existing policies have failed. As a result, engaging in an official, highly publicized internal review was a particularly dangerous path for Bush to take, especially given his previous strategy of proclaiming the effectiveness of Iraq policy and completely dismissing any bad news or reverses. But now, whether Bush liked it or not, at least one *very* public review of Iraq policy would occur at the end of the year when the Iraq Study Group issued its report. Within the NSC, Hadley and Meghan O'Sullivan "realized that conducting an Iraq strategy review was risky, even under the greatest secrecy," since any "leak that the White House was questioning its strategy could be devastating," especially with congressional elections only months away, Republican majorities in both houses of Congress in jeopardy, and Iraq likely to be the main campaign issue (Woodward 2008: 71). O'Sullivan's creative blame-avoidance solution was to find "a way to have a review without calling it that, suggesting to Hadley that "he send a series of broad questions" to key Iraq policy players (like Rumsfeld, Casey, and Khalilzad) requiring them to reflect upon the pros and cons of the current policy approach in Iraq (Woodward 2008: 71). It was an effective, "under the radar" way of eliciting feedback and reflections on how to improve or reshape Iraq policy without labeling it as a strategy review.

The blame-avoidance strategy suggested by O'Sullivan led not only to Hadley's submission of questions to key players but to several other unofficial reviews being conducted at other locations. Not only was there a lack of coordination across these reviews given their unofficial nature, but often those involved in them were unaware other reviews were in progress. While these were being conducted, General Casey (the commander in Iraq) was not even included in any of the discussions (Woodward 2008: 172). JCS Chairman Pace set up a so-called council of colonels, composed of the best and brightest minds on his staff, to look at Iraq, while Rice organized a different one doing a similar task at the State Department. At the NSC, Hadley organized a third review in October using William Luti, a senior director for defense on the NSC staff known for his hard-line views and support for a troop "surge" in Iraq (Woodward 2008: 161).

Yet after receiving Luti's report (which focused on using a surge in Iraq), it was apparent a study by one lone NSC staffer would have difficulty successfully advocating a strategy committing even further to the Iraq War when Casey and Rumsfeld had both begun advocating a plan accelerating a departure from Iraq (Woodward 2008: 170). There were also political problems to overcome. Not only had Hadley failed to inform O'Sullivan he had requested the Luti report, but the NSC and White House staffs were not supposed to undertake military planning strategies—which Luti's analysis clearly was (Woodward 2008: 170–71). Finessing the problem, Hadley decided to "hide it in plain sight" by meeting with Pace to personally hand him a copy of the paper, observing in a helpful tone the report merely represented "ideas from our staff," but since "you're the military planners . . . running your own process," he hoped the ideas might be of use (Woodward 2008: 170–71). In fact, what Hadley hoped was Pace would take on board the surge idea and eventually present it as the military's own idea (Woodward 2008: 171). Later, Pace requested a private meeting with Rice—a meeting where both discovered the other had been engaged in a review process (with Pace outlining the council of colonels and Rice admitting she had her own staff conducting a similar assessment)—but as Woodward (2008: 172-173) recounts, "Rice saw no way she and Pace could join their efforts at the moment, because it might leak and generate 'hothouse' news stories about an administration second-guessing its strategy."

Finally, in mid-October 2006 Hadley got authorization from Bush to start an informal review of Iraq policy using a small NSC staff run by O'Sullivan (Woodward 2008: 177). Rice's representative to this group from State, David Satterfield, was pushed by the secretary to think about radical change to the Iraq policy, emphasizing, "This cannot succeed, this will not succeed . . . and no amount of fine-tuning around the edges is going to fix it" (Woodward 2008: 178). Of course, for the White House, the most visible element that would show progress on the ground in Iraq would be the ability of Casey to reduce the number of combat troops deployed in the field, coupled with their successful replacement by Iraqi forces. But Casey's plans to cut the number of U.S. troops had repeatedly been delayed for more than a year, and "both the president and his advisers knew the stand up/stand down approach . . . wasn't working" in Iraq (Woodward 2008: 128). This failure to show progress was becoming increasingly difficult to defend as "progress," as illustrated by Bush's clear efforts at blame avoidance during a September 2006 press conference when challenged by reporters on whether the "goalpost" was moving, since the training of Iraqi forces was expected to be complete by the end of the year, but no U.S. troops were coming home (Woodward 2008: 127). Bush replied that was not the case, but "the enemy is changing tactics, and we're adapting," and Casey had told him he had what he needed to deal with the problem, "and that's the way I will continue to conduct the war. I'll listen to generals" (Woodward 2008: 127).

During an August 2006 White House meeting, Hadley gave Bush a summary of the questions and answers he received back from Casey, Khalilzad, and Rumsfeld—answers contradicted by more pessimistic, analytical reports Bush received from O'Sullivan at NSC (Woodward 2008: 101). In looking across all the reporting, a clearly unhappy Bush was unable to get past the negative trends being pointed to in Iraq, noting that "the situation seems to be deteriorating" and he wanted to "be able to say that I have a plan to punch back," but "we have to fight off the impression that this is not winnable" (Woodward 2008: 88–89). But Casey's focus on reducing troop numbers in Iraq did not appear to address the problem of increased insurgent violence, and when Bush asked if he needed more troops, Casey replied he didn't (Woodward 2008: 106–7). In NSC meetings without Bush present, Rice blasted Casey's optimistic reports in front of Cheney, Pace, and Hadley, noting, "We've had years of over-confident briefs by the military, gliding past the emergent problem" (Woodward 106–7). Yet it was another illustration of how Bush's style served to short-circuit the sharing of unvarnished information—Rice never brought her complaints about Casey's reports directly to Bush because everybody had "a tendency toward optimism," with the president almost demanding optimism, and "he didn't like pessimism, hand-wringing or doubt" (Woodward 2008: 106–7).

But even as many generals were publicly criticizing Rumsfeld, others were criticizing the administration's overall handling of the war, which greatly complicated Bush's blame-avoidance efforts. For example, upon retiring in 2006, Lieutenant General Ricardo Sanchez, the former top commander of American forces in Iraq, blamed Bush for a "catastrophically flawed, unrealistically optimistic war plan," while strongly denouncing the addition of more troops as a "desperate" move that would not achieve long-term stability.[67] Sanchez went on to state there had been "a glaring and unfortunate display of incompetent strategic leadership" on the part of Bush officials, who had been "derelict in their duties" and guilty of a "lust for power."[68] Taking broad aim at Bush's approach to Iraq, Sanchez concluded, "National leadership continues to believe that victory can be achieved by military power alone. . . . Continued manipulations and adjustments to our military strategy will not achieve victory. The best we can do with this flawed approach is stave off defeat."[69] Although not saying so publicly, these sentiments also reflected those of General Casey and the difficulty he perceived in carrying out the draw-down approach given Bush's black-and-white views, which he felt reflected the "radical wing of the Republican Party that kept saying, 'Kill the bastards! Kill the bastards! And you'll succeed' (Woodward 2008: 4). Casey felt that Bush had always viewed the war in terms of how many enemies had been captured and killed (much like LBJ in Vietnam), but that the real battle "was to prepare the Iraqis to protect and govern themselves" (Woodward 2008: 4).

Indeed, noting Casey's superior, General Abizaid, head of U.S. Central Command, agreed with Casey's view, Woodward (2008: 5–6) observed, "Casey was troubled by the thought that the president simply didn't get it, didn't understand the war and the nature of the fight they were in. . . . The president often paid lip service to the importance of these political and economic elements, and winning over the people. But then he would lean in with greater interest and ask about raids and military operations, grilling Casey about killings and captures. . . . Bush emphasized . . . 'I want everybody to know we're not playing for a tie.'" Yet with the midterm elections approaching and an increasingly skeptic public failing to accept the argument progress was being made, by mid-October 2006 even GOP congressmen were pleading with Bush to tone down his rhetoric (Woodward 2008: 193).

Thus, on October 25, just weeks before the midterm elections (and in the face of falling poll numbers and greatly increased violence in Iraq), Bush for the first time acknowledged at a news conference "missteps" in his policy, while calling on the public to look beyond the violence on their televisions and becoming disillusioned over a war that was being won.[70] While noting the emphasis on "committed to getting the job done," Rutenberg observed Bush's comments represented a rhetorical evolution in which he moved from "vowing to 'stay the course' in Iraq to promising flexibility."[71] At the same time, Bush continued to express public support for Rumsfeld and promised there would be no major changes in overall Iraq strategy. At the Pentagon, there were plans to ramp up its ability to respond to negative news via a "rapid response unit" that would react to news reports (often using their media surrogates within minutes of a report going out) to put a more positive spin on events in Iraq (and the beleaguered Rumsfeld).[72] Cheney, whose influence had waned along with Rumsfeld's, was pulling back and made no attempt to lead O'Sullivan's NSC review, and no one from his office attended her meetings (Woodward 2008: 194).

Within weeks, after the midterm elections brought a stinging defeat and loss of the Senate to Republicans, Rumsfeld was replaced by Gates—a move made necessary by Rumsfeld's increasing unpopularity, the generals' revolt, and his inability to serve as an effective lightning rod to divert blame away from the White House. Bush's own blame-avoidance explanation for getting rid of Rumsfeld sought to link it to the change of policy he was about to adopt, not the failure of his prior one in Iraq: "When I decided on a new strategy, I knew that in order to make the strategy work, for people to understand that it was new, there had to be new implementers of the strategy" (Woodward 2008: 196–97). Recognizing the Iraq Study Group would be issuing its own report in December, the White House pushed ahead with its own reviews so it could present its own reassessment at the same time. From a blame-avoidance standpoint, a White House Iraq policy review allowed the administration to deflect the charge it was unresponsive to criticism of its policies and inflexible, hopefully decreasing the impact of the Iraq Study Group report. Moreover, if the ISG came back with recommendations Bush didn't care for, having his own competing analyses would allow him to argue he was taking into account both assessments and choosing the best course from among them.

But it was still a steep hill to climb with the public, who were increasingly skeptical of the administration's pronouncements. For example, a majority of Americans in an April 2005 Gallup poll believed Bush had "deliberately misled the American public about whether Iraq possessed weapons of mass destruction," a figure that remained at 52 percent in May 2006 (Cannon 2007: 58). Indeed, by the eve of his 2007 State of the Union, a *Washington Post/ ABC News* poll found only 42 percent of respondents believed Bush could be trusted in a crisis (the first time a majority had given him this negative rating during his presidency), nearly two-thirds stated the war had been a mistake, 65 percent opposed the proposed surge of additional troops, and only 29 percent approved of his handling of the Iraq War against 70 percent disapproving![73]

The confused state of the administration's policy in 2006 and the rapidly deteriorating situation on the ground militarily also provided an opening for advocates of the surge strategy (led by retired former army vice chief of staff Jack Keane) to influence policy through effective bureaucratic maneuvering. Much as Cheney and Rumsfeld had bypassed the normal intelligence community and national security process in the run-up to the Iraq War (with assistance from Rice's inept handling of the NSC), Keane and his allies bypassed the normal military chain of command to gain support for the surge. Keane believed the history of most counterinsurgency campaigns—from the British in Malaya to the American experience in Vietnam—had shown it was necessary to protect and separate the population from the insurgents, which in Iraq required the deployment of more, not less, troops (Ricks 2009: 81–84). So "with no official backing, and nothing but his credibility and persuasive abilities to go on," Keane helped shape the development of the surge idea (with assistance from the American Enterprise Institute (AEI) and General Ray Odierno in Iraq) behind the back of Casey, who told Keane not to visit Iraq (Ricks 2009: 79–80). Through force of will, Keane eventually maneuvered an invitation to pitch the idea to Bush, later won approval of his own choice to lead the Iraq campaign under a surge (General David Petraeus), and by late 2006 Keane "was the one driving the planning" for the surge (Ricks 2009: 79–80). Keane spoke daily with Odierno, and jumping the chain of command, Odierno bypassed the commanders above him to talk directly to White House officials and aides to the JCS to express his own support for the increase (Ricks 2009: 91–92).

Yet despite these backchannel efforts, at the time the surge was being debated within the administration, there was also a great deal of doubt among some senior officials regarding whether it would be effective. In fact, during his testimony before the Iraq Study Group in November 2006, Michael Hayden, the new CIA director, said, "I cannot point to any milestone or checkpoint where we can turn this thing around. . . . Given the level of un-controlled violence . . . the most we can do is to contain its excesses and pre-serve the possibility of reconciliation in the future" (Woodward 2008: 218). Similarly, while Hadley was arguing the surge was the "best chance" to get violence in Iraq down, Rice was highly dubious about the strategy's chances for success and was fearful of putting the U.S. Army in the untenable position between the Shia and Sunnis (Woodward 2008: 246–48).

Ironically, it marked one of the first times during the entire Iraq policy debates within the Bush administration that such a strong disagreement was aired in front of the president within his inner circle. During previous disagree-ments—such as Powell and Armitage's objections to the push to attack Iraq be-ing advocated by Cheney and Rumsfeld—it had never been about the benefits of removing Saddam (there had been general agreement on this point); it had only been about the means to achieve those ends (and their timing).[74] Neither Powell nor Armitage opposed toppling Saddam as an overall strategic objective for U.S. policy. But in this case, Rice was firmly opposed to pursuing the surge strategy. Indeed, during a November 26, 2006, White House meeting reviewing Iraq strategy, in which the surge was being advocated by Hadley, Rice strongly argued against adopting the new approach, warning Bush he wasn't getting "a clear picture" of what was happening on the ground and the military briefings presented such a blurred, incomplete picture "it was hard to judge the truth" (Woodward 2008: 245). Whether it was her new position as secretary of state (since she had *never* been as forceful as NSC adviser) or the absence of players like Rumsfeld and the weakening of Cheney, Rice continued to challenge the policy in ways she never had before. At a mid-December 2006 NSC meeting, Rice again told Bush she didn't believe the current circumstances permitted success based on either the surge or the status quo and that a surge would be meaningless if the Iraqi Shia government wasn't willing to take on the Shia militias (Woodward 2008: 291–92). Though Bush pushed back, saying her strategy was to "redeploy for failure" rather than "surge for success," Rice responded it was also possible to "surge for failure" if we don't know what the additional troops could accomplish (Woodward 2008: 291–92).

Rice's doubts about the strategy continued during her interactions with Bush over the coming weeks. In fact, after concluding a trip to Iraq in De-cember, Rice met with Bush and, in response to his question about whether or not we can win, Rice replied, "I can tell you . . . we're not winning it now" (Woodward 2008: 259). Rice was not alone as a doubter, with JCS Chairman Pace warning regarding the surge that "the U.S. military might not have the ability to pull it off," and "from a military point of view, the dangers were so great that the task would be virtually impossible" (Woodward 2008: 248).

But a counterargument was also being made in other quarters. During a meeting with outside experts (including academics Eliot Cohen, Stephen Biddle, and others) arranged by Keane for Bush and Cheney on December 11, 2006, the retired general warned Bush time was running out in Iraq and a new strategy was required (Ricks 2009: 98–101). After Cohen advised Bush he needed to replace the current team of generals managing the operation (with Keane helpfully suggesting the name of Petraeus), Cohen drew on the "lessons of Vietnam" to bring home the point to the president: "Generals disagree, sometimes profoundly. . . . Civilian leaders need to discover these disagreements, force them to the surface, and probe them. This is what Lincoln and Roosevelt did. LBJ's failure in Vietnam was not micromanagement, but failure to force serious strategic debate" (Ricks 2009: 99).

As the surge notion gained more traction and the frustration of the JCS at being cut out of the debate became more profound, Pace suggested Bush should "sit down with them . . . hear from them directly," which Bush and Cheney did in the tank at the Pentagon on December 13, 2006 (Woodward 2008: 286). Yet this was not a meeting to which Bush went with an open mind to hear the chiefs' objections and their disagreement with the notion that a surge of five brigades could be maintained in Iraq; rather it was one intended to "just hear them out, try to point out they weren't on top of the situation, and that they were going to do it anyway" (Woodward 2008: 287–89). Along with Casey in Iraq, Army Chief of Staff Peter Shoomaker continued to make arguments against the surge, going so far as to tell Bush, "No, I don't agree with you," during the meeting (Woodward 2008: 289). And the news from Iraq the generals pointed toward in trying to convince Bush against the surge was demonstrably bad. By December 2006 the Pentagon's own assessment of security conditions in Iraq concluded attacks against American and Iraqi forces had surged to their highest levels to date between early August and early November, with almost 960 attacks recorded every week (a 22 percent increase from the period from May to August).[75]

Yet while the administration largely ignored the opposition of its top generals in Iraq (and the JCS), the Iraq Study Group's final report was influenced by their comments to William Perry, who as a member of the ISG met with Casey and General Peter Chiarelli in late 2006. As Ricks (2009: 53–54) notes, though Perry had broached the surge argument to them, both Casey and Chiarelli forcefully argued against the surge, leading the group's final report to straddle the idea—rejecting a major increase while conditionally supporting "a short-term redeployment or surge of American combat forces to stabilize Baghdad . . . if the U.S. commander in Iraq determines that such steps would be effective" (Ricks 2009: 53–54).

Indeed, once the Iraq Study Group report and its recommendations came out to great public fanfare on December 6, 2006, Bush understood attempting to maintain the status quo was politically impossible. The ISG report had essentially stated the administration's current approach to Iraq had been a failure and the situation in the country was continuing to rapidly deteriorate (Baker and Hamilton 2006). In addition to proposing a range of solutions Bush had heretofore resisted, such as direct negotiations with Iran and Syria, it suggested that a surge in U.S. forces (an idea originally proposed by ISG member Chuck Robb and later adopted by surge advocates like Keane) was the only way to potentially allow Iraqi security forces to stand up and secure the country (Baker and Hamilton 2006).[76] For a leader who viewed the world in absolute terms like Bush, who was naturally predisposed to look for big dramatic moves rather than seeking the nuances of details, the idea of a surge had overwhelming appeal. And as Woodward (2008: 264) notes, it became clear to Hadley, once the ISG report came out, despite doubts by Rice and the joint chiefs, Bush was going to go ahead with the surge.

Once Bush made up his mind, Rice, ever mindful of loyally maintaining her close relationship with the president, quickly dropped her resistance and acquiesced to his decision.[77] In fairness to Rice, it is quite possible she read the writing on the wall as well, that given the Iraq Study Group report, the only option remaining for the White House (if it hoped to salvage any success from the ruins and maintain enough domestic political support to continue) was to embrace the surge and run with it. At a dinner in Crawford, Texas, with Bush on December 27, 2006, Rice seemed to recognize this reality, telling him she was now in favor of the surge, but it was "going to be one of the most consequential decisions of all time" and it was important to "find a way to bring as many people along" as possible given it was "not going to be popular"—and if it didn't work, "it'll be the last bullet . . . the last card" (Woodward 2008: 303–4).

Interestingly, just as Rice's behavior illustrated how she perceived her adviser role within Bush's inner circle—and how her emphasis on loyalty and preserving her personal relationship influenced the advice she gave to him—the testimony by a number of former Bush advisers before the Iraq Study Group also highlighted how the inner circle functioned. For example, Powell's testimony described the dysfunction created by Bush's delegation of authority to Rumsfeld over Iraq policy. In addition to expressing his deep frustration at having gone into Iraq with such a small force (due to Rumsfeld's insistence), Powell recounted a private meeting with Bush in September 2002 where he laid out his "pottery barn" warning about invading Iraq—the "if you break it, you own it" notion—that he felt the president and his inner circle were not considering (Woodward 2008: 47–48). Powell noted that while he warned Bush "once this happens, you're the one who is going to have to pick up the pieces and put it back together again," and it won't be an easy task to accomplish, his advice was ignored, and when the United States invaded Iraq, "We not only did not have enough troops to stabilize the country and act like an occupying force, we didn't *want* to act like an occupying force. But we *were* the occupying force" (Woodward 2008: 47–48).

Rice's handling of the NSC process was also a focus of Powell's ire, noting while the "whole purpose of the NSC was to present issues and options for debate and decision," the huge issues were never brought to Bush's attention and "the NSC had no apparatus to make sure things happened. . . . There was no follow-through, no discipline" (Woodward 2008: 50). Similarly, for more than a year, Powell noted Bremer ran the Coalition Provisional Authority overseeing Iraq "outside of anyone's control," recalling he first "learned of Bremer's seven-point plan for Iraq in the *Washington Post*" (Woodward 2008: 50). Powell also expressed frustration with officials who lacked proper credentials, like Bernard Kerik (the troubled former New York City police commissioner Bush named to head the Iraqi national police and intelligence agency): "Bernie Kerik is in charge of police?" Powell asked, with a mixture of mock surprise and disgust. "Where did Bernie Kerik come from?" (Woodward 2008: 48–49).

The Iraq Study Group met with Bush on several occasions during its investigations and "found him engaged but far more upbeat than the realities in Iraq seemed to warrant," arguing to the group (after his recently completed secret trip to Baghdad) "the strategy was working" (Draper 2007: 402). On other occasions, Bush told the ISG, just as Truman had eventually been rehabilitated by historians, "Iraq would be judged by history to be a success," leading one member of the group to observe that "the President did not so much want to hear their views as convince us that we should be writing a report that would reflect *his* views" (Draper 2007: 402). After a meeting with the group on November 13, 2006, participants recalled Bush was "both passionate and overbearing," with Perry noting, "He was not seeking advice from us. . . . He was telling us what his view of the war . . . how important the war was, and how it was tough, how we stay together. It was a Churchillian kind of thing" (Woodward 2008: 214).

Despite the Iraq Study Group findings, during his December 20, 2006, traditional year-end news conference, Bush warned the war in Iraq would require "difficult choices and additional sacrifices" in the year ahead, but vowed "victory in Iraq is achievable" and the United States would not be "run out of the Middle East" by extremists and radicals—emphasizing positive developments like twelve million Iraqis voting in free elections.[78] And the blame-deflecting answer given by Pace during a press conference that "we are not winning, but we are not losing" in Iraq was seized upon by Bush to counter calls for a change in policy direction.[79] It was the formulation used by Bush in acknowledging, for the first time, that the United States was "not winning" in Iraq—an admission reported under the headline, "U.S. Not Winning War in Iraq, Bush Says for 1st Time" in the *Washington Post* (Woodward 2008: 294). In a somewhat Orwellian statement seeking to avoid blame for the current situation, Bush agreed with Pace's notion "we're not winning, we're not losing" in Iraq (Woodward 2008: 294). It was an acknowledgment of the reality in Iraq (we're not winning), while seeking to avoid acceptance of the ISG findings—that the United States was currently losing the conflict in Iraq—which would be his fault.

BLAME AVOIDANCE AFTER ADOPTION OF THE SURGE

In February 2007 Petraeus took command in Iraq to oversee the surge and, in typical administration fashion, established a secret back-channel line of communication around the military chain of command (through Keane and Cheney) directly to Bush (Woodward 2008: 331). Having gambled on a surge, Bush now found himself playing for time politically. In May 2007 House Republican moderates bluntly warned Bush that the war was risking the future of the Republican Party and he couldn't count on GOP support for many more months.[80] In June two senior GOP senators, George Voinovich of Ohio and Richard Lugar of Indiana, who had expressed concerns about the surge also expressed the view that Bush's war strategy was a failure.[81] By July a *USA Today*/Gallup poll showed Bush's approval rating reaching a new low of 29 percent, with 62 percent saying it had been a mistake to send troops to Iraq.[82] In response to this growing GOP revolt and falling poll numbers, the White House rejected calls to change course, but launched a campaign emphasizing the president's intention to draw down U.S. forces in 2008 and move toward "a more limited mission if security conditions improve."[83] Although several prominent Republican senators (like Lugar and Voinovich) had already broken with Iraq policy, after days of intense internal deliberations the White House decided against their proposals to begin withdrawing troops as early as summer 2007, instead calling on Congress to wait for a fuller assessment on the surge's effectiveness due in September.[84]

This desire to shift the focus to the September rather than the July assessment became understandable when it was released a few weeks later. The twenty-five-page White House document—which had been ordered by lawmakers as an interim report card on the troop-increase strategy—found Iraqi progress toward meeting eighteen benchmark political and military goals mixed over the preceding months, with slow advances toward some of the targets and even reverses in other areas.[85] In particular, movement toward new elections, reversal of existing de-Baathification laws limiting Sunni participation in the government, and legislation to more fairly distribute oil revenue were all judged to be "unsatisfactory"; the ability of Iraqi security forces to operate independently of the U.S. military was judged to have actually declined; and important areas, such as eliminating sectarian-based operations and decision making within the Iraqi security forces, received failing grades.[86] The immediate blame-avoidance tactic employed was to argue the new strategy was still in its "early stages" and there were some "encouraging signs that should, over time, point the way to a more normalized and sustainable level of U.S. engagement in Iraq."[87] In other words, it was too soon to reach conclusions about the success of the strategy and final judgment should await future, much better data.

But in an ominous foreshadowing of the long-term consequences the administration's Iraq War was to have on the counterterrorism fight in places like Afghanistan and Pakistan (which continues to this day), the White House found itself fending off renewed criticism after a new National Intelligence Estimate (NIE) was released on July 17, 2007, that concluded Al Qaeda had "protected or regenerated key elements of its Homeland attack capability" by reestablishing bases in Pakistan and reconstituting its top leadership.[88] Not only did the NIE note Al Qaeda had been able "to recruit and indoctrinate operatives" by associating itself with an Iraqi subsidiary that had not existed prior to the American invasion (thereby calling into question Bush's decision to focus on Iraq); it concluded that the United States was "losing ground on a number of fronts in the fight against Al Qaeda and describes the terrorist organization as having significantly strengthened over the past two years."[89]

Now the White House was forced to address renewed accusations it had been distracted by Iraq from the broader terrorism fight, and necessitated Bush rebuffing calls to withdraw troops from Iraq for redeployment to Afghanistan, noting, "The same folks that are bombing innocent people in Iraq . . . were the ones who attacked us in America on September the 11th, and that's why what happens in Iraq matters to the security here at home."[90] Though Bush usually went to extreme lengths to avoid Vietnam references when discussing Iraq policy, he couldn't resist the Vietnam analogy in defending the need to remain in Iraq during an August 2007 speech in Kansas City: "One unmistakable legacy of Vietnam is that the price of America's withdrawal was paid by millions of innocent citizens whose agonies would add to our vocabulary new terms like 'boat people,' 're-education camps' and 'killing fields.'"[91] Bush's analogy suggested the same bloodshed and chaos would result from a pullout from Iraq.

As Petraeus's September report to Congress approached, Bush made an enormous push to frame the upcoming discussion of Iraq policy—and at the same time was forced to rebut a report issued by the General Accounting Office a week beforehand that offered an extremely bleak portrait of Iraq's political and security situation. Though the top military command in Baghdad protested the GAO report, calling it flawed and "factually incorrect" and having rejected several changes proposed by the Pentagon, the GAO concluded, "Iraq had failed to meet all but two of nine security goals Congress had set as part of a list of 18 benchmarks of progress."[92] Preempting a planned White House progress report on Iraq by only a few days, the GAO argued that "only one of eight political goals—safeguarding minority rights in the Iraqi parliament—had been met" and found "little if any substantive movement on key legislation, including measures to clarify the distribution of oil revenue, schedule provincial elections and change de-Baathification laws."[93] The White House immediately responded with its own report arguing Iraq had made "satisfactory progress" toward meeting nine of the eighteen political, economic, and security benchmarks, gaving Iraqi leaders higher marks than they had received in the July interim report, and citing "encouraging signs" of conditions allowing a reduction in U.S. forces.[94] By having its own report available for release to counter the GAO report, the White House had inadvertently used the blame-avoidance strategy of weakening the impact of a bad external report with a positive one. And it allowed the congressional testimony by Petraeus and Ambassador Ryan Crocker to be pushed as the objective third-party view. Indeed, after visiting a Marine base in Quantico, Bush told reporters, "I call upon the United States Congress to listen very carefully to what General Petraeus and Ambassador Crocker report and support the troop levels that these two men think are necessary to achieve our objective," and he warned that if the United States were driven from Iraq, "the Middle East could be in chaos, and chaos would embolden Sunni extremists like al-Qaeda, and chaos would embolden Iran."[95] But it was a tough sell to a skeptical public, even if the message was coming from the popular Petraeus, with a majority feeling he would try to make the situation seem rosier than it really was in his testimony.[96]

Fittingly, given the importance it played in making the case to go to war in the first place, the use of 9/11 imagery was again put on display by the administration to support the need to stay the course in Iraq. On September 11 (as Petraeus was testifying before Congress) an advocacy group allied with the White House launched a $15 million media blitz featuring television commercials explicitly linking the need to stay in Iraq with 9/11. "The television commercial is grim and gripping: A soldier who lost both legs in an explosion near Fallujah explains why he thinks U.S. forces need to stay in Iraq. 'They attacked *us,*' he says as the screen turns to an image of the second hijacked airplane heading toward the smoking World Trade Center on Sept. 11, 2001. 'And they will again. They won't stop in Iraq.'"[97] And the imagery persisted inside the Senate chambers during the Petraeus and Crocker testimony, with Republican John McCain asking Petraeus to repeat his belief that Iraq was the "central front in the war on terror," while Democrat Barack Obama complained the timing of the hearing perpetuates the "notion the original decision to go into Iraq was directly related to the attacks on 9/11."[98]

The administration now wasted little time in claiming its surge had been successful, with Bush announcing on September 14 the "return on success" now achieved would allow him to gradually begin withdrawing some troops for the first time since the war began, while warning this success "could be squandered by the deeper and speedier reductions that the war's opponents have demanded."[99] Now describing Iraq as "a vital part of a strategy in the Middle East to defeat al-Qaeda and counter Iran," Bush's eighteen-minute address to the nation was the finishing touch on "several weeks of political stagecraft," including several speeches, a presidential trip to Iraq, and heavy reliance on Petraeus to make the more optimistic public case.[100] But even with Petraeus's testimony, Bush decided to take a blame-avoidance path by refusing to reappoint Pace to a second term as JCS chairman—thereby avoiding the spectacle of his being grilled over Iraq policy during hostile confirmation hearings in a Democratic-controlled Senate.[101]

By March 2008, with continued progress beginning to be seen on the ground, Bush declared the United States was on the cusp of victory in Iraq, and the surge had "opened the door to a major strategic victory in the war on terror."[102] In a classic blame-avoidance move, Bush also sought to portray the success of the surge tactic as validation and justification for the Iraq War itself—in the clear hope of distancing himself from the five previous years of policy reversals, the questionable rationale for entering the conflict in the first place, and the broader consequences of the action upon the counterterrorism campaign in Afghanistan and Pakistan. Indeed, Bush argued the increase in troops had helped "turn the situation in Iraq around" and made the "high cost in lives and treasure" worthwhile.[103]

Reinforcing the president's message, Cheney gave similar assessments during interviews and speeches, arguing the war had been "a successful endeavor" that was "well worth the effort."[104] Cheney even went so far as to compare Bush to Lincoln, who had been "willing to withstand the slings and arrows of the political wars" to win the Civil War.[105] In making the case that Bush's leadership had been one of making tough calls in the face of adversity, Cheney noted while being interviewed on ABC's *Good Morning America* it didn't matter that two-thirds of the public felt the war had not been worth fighting, since "you cannot be blown off course by the fluctuations in the public opinion polls."[106]

BLAME AVOIDANCE AND THE FINAL CRITIQUES
OF THE USE OF PREWAR INTELLIGENCE

Once Republicans lost control of the Senate in November 2006, the oversight role of Congress, which had been put into neutral during the first part of the administration, now shifted firmly back into gear as Senate committees explored questions that had been put onto the back burner by the GOP leadership. A February 2007 report issued by the Pentagon's acting inspector general, Thomas F. Gimble, strongly criticized the administration's handling of prewar intelligence and particularly the activities of Feith. In the report, Gimble criticized Pentagon officials for conducting their own intelligence analysis to find links between Al Qaeda and Saddam Hussein, concluding Feith's group "developed, produced and then disseminated alternative intelligence assessments on the Iraq and Al Qaeda relationship, which included some conclusions that were inconsistent with the consensus of the Intelligence Community, to senior decision-makers" (Cloud and Mazzetti 2007: A8). Though no laws had been broken in doing so, Gimble would subsequently testify before the Senate Armed Services Committee that Feith's team had "made dubious interpretations of intelligence reports and shared them with senior officials without making clear that its findings had already been discounted or discredited by the main intelligence agencies" and these actions "were inappropriate" (Cloud 2007: A5). Gimble testified that captured Iraqi documents and interrogations of Saddam and his aides "all confirmed" the regime was not directly cooperating with Al Qaeda before the war (Smith 2007: A1).

But this initial critique of Bush's use of prewar intelligence was just a runup to a more damaging final report issued by the Democratically controlled Senate. Originally, after the invasion of Iraq and lack of WMDs, the GOP-controlled Senate had responded with a series of reports on intelligence failures leading up to the war. With Republicans in charge during the writing of the first report, its focus was restricted and deliberately avoided the question of whether Bush had deliberately distorted or misused intelligence. Instead, the July 2004 report focused purely on flaws in the intelligence gathering and analysis provided by the U.S. intelligence community.[107] As a result, the earlier report concluded unanimously that the "U.S. intelligence agencies had botched the task of assessing Iraq's capabilities regarding weapons of mass destruction" and that "key intelligence reports made unwarranted assumptions and overstated what was then known about Hussein's weapons programs," and faulted "the CIA and other agencies for failing to cultivate reliable informants and for basing key assessments on extrapolation and inference."[108]

However, by the time the final report was being put together in June 2008, Democrats controlled the Senate and now were in a position to push past previous GOP stonewalling of efforts to look at how the administration used the intelligence. The June 2008 report concluded, "Bush and top administration officials repeatedly exaggerated what they knew about Iraq's weapons and its ties to terrorist groups," and while most of its claims about Iraq reflected discredited intelligence reports, the "White House crossed a line by conveying certainty about the threat that Saddam Hussein posed to the United States."[109] Senator John Rockefeller, the committee chairman, noted "in making the case for war, the administration repeatedly presented intelligence as fact when it was unsubstantiated, contradicted or even nonexistent."[110] Only two of the seven Republicans on the fifteen-member Senate panel (moderates Olympia Snow of Maine and Chuck Hagel of Nebraska) voted to approve the report, with five dissenting Republicans first trying to kill it, then attempting to force a vote to delete most of its conclusions, and finally (when these efforts failed) settling for appending objections to the report's final findings.[111]

In the face of the damaging report, Bush immediately sought to employ the blame-avoidance strategies of dismissing the report as partisan and arguing it provided nothing new. White House Spokesman Dana Perino called the report a "selective view" and noted the administration's public statements were based on the same "faulty intelligence" given to Congress and endorsed by foreign intelligence services.[112] The committee's top Republican, Christopher Bond, called the report a "waste of committee time and resources" and argued the "real story" was the CIA had failed by providing flawed intelligence.[113] Nevertheless, given the long-existing public skepticism regarding Bush's case for war, the finding of the report that "Bush and his aides built the public case for war against Iraq by exaggerating available intelligence and by ignoring disagreements among spy agencies about Iraq's weapons programs and Saddam Hussein's links to Al Qaeda" fell into place with what many already believed to be the case.[114] The 170-page report by the Senate Select Committee on Intelligence represented close to five years of partisan squabbling over the use of prewar intelligence and represented "the most comprehensive effort to date to assess whether policy makers systematically painted a more dire picture about Iraq than was justified by the available intelligence."[115] The report accused Bush, Cheney, and other senior officials of "repeatedly overstating the Iraqi threat in the emotional aftermath of the September 11th attacks," and in a statement accompanying the report, Rockefeller said, "The president and his advisers undertook a relentless public campaign in the aftermath of the attacks to use the war against Al Qaeda as a justification for overthrowing Saddam Hussein."[116]

BLAME AVOIDANCE SURROUNDING
IRAQI CIVILIAN CASUALTIES

For the administration, war casualties were always going to be a serious concern from both a political and a blame-avoidance perspective—especially as the war grew more unpopular. Indeed, the desire to avoid the public spectacle of flag-draped coffins of U.S. soldiers being unloaded at Dover Air Base led then secretary of defense Cheney to institute the original ban in 1991 of all photography of these events during the first Gulf War.[117] It was a reversal of a longstanding military tradition, in place since WWII, in which honor guard ceremonies marking the return of the fallen from abroad were covered.[118] For blame-avoidance purposes, it was a way to conceal the visible costs of war from a notably squeamish American public and better maintain support for the war—since people are always more willing to support policies that appear to have little cost to themselves (whether it be wars or tax cuts). With the October 2001 invasion of Afghanistan, the Bush administration reinstituted the ban on photography of returning caskets at Dover, and in March 2003 the ban was extended to include all media coverage of caskets arriving at any other port of entry.[119] Again, from a blame-avoidance standpoint, it was an understandable decision, given the 24/7 media cycle that otherwise would inundate the public with disturbing photos of American war dead returning from Iraq. But it was also a way to avoid blame for the deaths of soldiers in an unpopular war, making it easier for Bush to maintain public support during a lengthy, protracted conflict. Certainly, the constant spectacle of coffins returning to Dover haunted Johnson during Vietnam and provided a focal point for the antiwar movement to point toward in highlighting the costs of the war (Johnson 1971; McPherson 1972; McNamara 1995). It was not a parallel with Vietnam Bush wanted to repeat, and the ban would remain in place until lifted by Obama in February 2009.[120]

The issue of Iraqi civilian casualties, however, was a different kind of problem. Although it would frequently be raised by war critics in condemning the costs of the conflict, it didn't have the direct, emotive impact on the American public photos of its own war dead possessed. It was also an area in which it was difficult to find hard, indisputable numbers to point toward. Though it was impossible to indefinitely conceal from his or her family the fact a given U.S. soldier had been killed or wounded, and a final accounting would inevitably have to be made by the Department of Defense, this was not the case with Iraqi civilian casualties. After Vietnam, the U.S. military ceased providing "body counts" of enemy war dead, and the numbers of civilians killed in conflicts had never really been counted by combatants beyond rough estimates.

Yet with the media reporting daily on widespread sectarian violence and massive car bombs exploding among civilians, more and more attention began to be paid to the question. For Bush, the question of how many innocent civilians had been killed due to his decision to invade Iraq was a loaded one both politically and blamewise. Critics would point to the longstanding "just war" tradition in Western societies, stretching all the way back to Roman times, emphasizing the moral requirements surrounding both the resort to war and its conduct. Paramount within these just war norms was the avoidance of civilian casualties among noncombatants (innocents), that the costs inflicted be "proportional" to the original wrong inflicted, and that war be a last resort (Walzer 1977; Paul 1994). From this perspective, it's easy to see how growing numbers of civilian dead would violate many of these just war provisions, especially those regarding proportionality and the injunction to avoid harm to innocents. Moreover, if one's actions served to create an environment through regime change or war where civilians would die from violence (even if it was not directly by your own hands), you are still culpable according to just war tenets (Walzer 1977; Wakin 1979). Thus, the higher the costs became for Iraqi civilians, the more difficult it was for Bush to make a 9/11 justification for U.S. actions due to the clear lack of proportionality between the cases.

The controversy over civilian deaths gained traction in the fall of 2004 with the publication in the prominent British medical journal, the *Lancet*, of a study done by researchers from Johns Hopkins University in Baltimore putting the first big number behind the question. In their first survey, researchers randomly selected 990 families in representative locations across Iraq who were asked to produce death certificates and lists of family members who had died between January 1, 2002, and the start of the war, and all those who had died afterward (Steele and Goldenberg 2008). Subtracting the former figure from the later produced an "excess" rate that was applied to calculate the excess deaths (above the normal fatality rates in Iraq's total population) caused by the war, which they estimated to have reached over 98,000 deaths by October 2004 (Steele and Goldenberg 2008). This was a statistical technique routinely employed by epidemiologists to analyze how lethal a given flu season has been in the United States by analyzing "excess" deaths due to influenza above the normal rate usually killed by influenza annually.

Nevertheless, the *Lancet* report was dismissed by both the White House and the British government as using a flawed methodology greatly overstating the number of civilian casualties. In responding to the *Lancet* study, Blair's spokesman instead argued for using rather dubious (but much lower) Iraqi Ministry of Health (IMH) figures—that were based purely on incomplete hospital reports (collected only since April 5, 2004—more than a year after the invasion) that also assumed every casualty in the country would be taken to such facilities.[121] The British government also stated it supported the statement made by the Iraqi Ministry of Health on October 29, 2004, that the most reliable available data showed "between 5 April 2004 and 5 October 2004, 3,853 civilians were killed and 15,517 were injured."[122] Like the Bush administration, the Blair government took issue with the validity of the Iraq Body Count website (which maintained a running estimate of civilian casualties based purely on media and governmental reporting), and its estimate of between 14,000 and 16,000 civilian deaths.[123]

As the debate over the rising civilian death toll continued, Bush was eventually forced to admit to a count of 30,000 in December 2005, using figures from a recently completed study by the Iraqi Health Ministry, which had focused on keeping the numbers low by banning the release of official morgue figures in its count (Steele and Goldenberg 2008). In fact, the new Iraqi health minister, Dr. Salih Mahdi Motlab al-Hasanawi, later acknowledged the ministry survey and the methodology by which it had been conducted had been prompted by controversy over civilian casualties (Steele and Goldenberg 2008). From a blame-avoidance standpoint, it was understandable that the Iraqi government would also want to downplay the true numbers.

Given the criticism of the first study, a follow-up survey by Johns Hopkins researchers was published in the *Lancet* in 2006. Interestingly, at the time the *Lancet* study came out, the Iraqi Health Ministry was putting the total mortality level in Iraq through June 2006 at only 50,000.[124] The new *Lancet* study, in contrast, placed the figure at over 655,000 excess deaths (or 2.5 percent of Iraq's total population, amounting to a little more than five hundred deaths per day since the invasion) (Steele and Goldberg 2008).[125] The explosive estimates in the report were widely reported around the world, forcing Bush to inform reporters, "I don't consider it a credible report," and Blair's spokesman to note the figure "was not one we believe to be anywhere near accurate" (Steele and Goldenberg 2008). In response to the uproar, Iraqi Prime Minister al-Maliki ordered the country's medical authorities to stop providing the UN with monthly figures on the number of civilians killed and wounded—with UN envoy to Iraq Ashraf Qazi warning that "the prohibition may hinder the ability of his office to give accurate accounts in its . . . reports on the levels of violence and the effect on Iraqi society."[126] This withholding of the casualty figures by the Iraqi government (because they might undermine public support) was later criticized in an April 2007 UN report suggesting 34,452

Iraqi civilians had been killed in the previous year—with al-Maliki's government subsequently dismissing the report as being "inaccurate" and based on "unreliable sources."[127]

Over the next two years, a number of additional studies, all using differing methodologies, reported a wide range of estimates regarding casualties—some with highly inflated figures and others with lower numbers. And while the validity of these various studies (and their underlying methodologies) can certainly be debated, this argument is essentially beside the point given the blame-avoidance focus of this book. The reason for this is a simple one. For Bush (and his critics), regardless of the validity of any individual study, each casualty figure reported became ammunition for one side or the other—whether the statistics were accurate, underreporting, or overreporting deaths. As the estimates rose, even the lower-end figures were unquestionably showing a great many civilians had died.

For example, in September 2007 the British polling firm Opinion Research Business (ORB) released findings from a highly controversial statistical study of survey results from Iraq suggesting an extremely high maximum total of 1,220,580 deaths since the 2003 invasion (with a minimum toll of 733,158, a total that was still larger than the 2006 *Lancet* figure) (Steele and Goldberg 2008). In contrast, the World Health Organization released the findings of its "Iraq Family Health Survey" in January 2008, which employed statistical survey analysis to conclude an estimated 151,000 civilians had died between March 2003 and June 2006 (with the range estimate being from 104,000 to 223,000 at the top end).[128] The independent group Iraq Body Count (IBC), which collates all media fatality reports corroborated by two or more sources (as well as figures from hospitals and other official sources) reported between 22,586 and 24,159 Iraqi civilians had been killed in 2007, with the grand total in the conflict ranging between 81,174 and 88,585 casualties.[129] This in addition to the two million Iraqis who had fled abroad and the 1.5 million who had become internally displaced persons inside Iraq itself by 2007 (Steele and Goldenberg 2008). By March 2008 these figures grew to 2.7 million Iraqis displaced internally and 2.4 million fled abroad as refugees, mostly to Syria and Jordan, with nearly 20 percent of Iraq's prewar population having been uprooted.[130] As Steele and Goldenberg (2008) rightly observe, with estimates ranging from under 100,000 to over a million, "Inevitably, the issue has become a political football, with the Bush administration, the British government and other supporters . . . seizing on the lowest estimates and opponents on the highest."

Yet for Bush, on the fifth anniversary of the war in March 2008, one consistent blame-avoidance posture remained the same—as it had during all the debates over prewar intelligence and the failure to find WMDs or links to Al

Qaeda: "Five years into this battle, there is an understandable debate over whether the war was worth fighting, whether the fight is worth winning, and whether we can win it. . . . The answers are clear to me. Removing Saddam Hussein from power was the right decision, and this is a fight that America can and must win."[131]

6

Bush and Iraq: Revisiting the Vietnam Analogy

Turning and turning in the widening gyre
The falcon cannot hear the falconer;
Things fall apart; the centre cannot hold;
Mere anarchy is loosed upon the world,
The blood-dimmed tide is loosed, and everywhere
The ceremony of innocence is drowned;
The best lack all conviction, while the worst
Are full of passionate intensity.

—William Butler Yeats, "The Second Coming" (Gardner 1984: 820)

Years later, looking back on his own involvement in Lyndon Johnson's Vietnam decision making, McGeorge Bundy observed a major lesson to be drawn from his experience for future policy makers: "Conviction without rigor is a strategy for disaster" (Goldstein 2008: 144). While obvious differences exist between Iraq and Vietnam that render imperfect the fit of analogy, there are important similarities. Most notably, commonalities between the styles of the two presidents, how they structured their advisory systems, and used information. Both shared insular inner circles shutting out dissenting voices, selectively using information and intelligence to bolster favored approaches. Each lacked foreign policy experience, making them heavily dependent on "expert" advisers. Both shared a less nuanced, more absolute view of the world and were driven by their own, strongly held idiosyncratic beliefs. They possessed a passionate intensity, convinced they were right. And each, like Pandora, unleashed a maelstrom growing in intensity far beyond their expectations that consumed their administrations—continuing long after to harm U.S. interests abroad. Taken with great conviction, these decisions lacked the analytical rigor to avoid disaster. In this final chapter, the appropriateness of the Vietnam analogy, so often employed by Bush's critics, will be explored in more depth—looking at both the similarities and differences between the cases.

HOW APPROPRIATE IS THE VIETNAM ANALOGY? THE DIFFERENCES

In contemplating the fit of the Vietnam analogy (and the dynamics in Johnson's administration) to those found within Bush's, one is immediately drawn to many areas where the cases are clearly mismatched. For example, critics of the Iraq War often note it was a war of *choice* and not one forced on the White House (Bamford 2005; Isikoff and Corn 2006; McClellan 2008). From the morning of September 11 onward, Bush quite purposefully set out on a path to war with Iraq, actively seeking justifications for regime change to remove Saddam. While Bush clearly failed to foresee the immense difficulties of implementing such a policy, Iraq cannot be argued to be a conflict he inadvertently found himself mired in. It was not a war fought as a last resort—but actively sought out, even as Afghanistan remained unsettled. As one former Department of Defense official remarked, "We weren't guided by ideology in Iraq. I think we were guided by the personal biases of the leadership in the administration and the trauma of 9/11, of wanting to strike back, and that happened to be the biggest, baddest target we could find."[1]

In contrast, a former official who worked in both the Johnson and Bush administrations noted LBJ "inherited" the ongoing conflict in Vietnam from Kennedy, while "Bush chose to initiate his conflict directly."[2] Vietnam had been a simmering problem for many years by the time Johnson became president, one slowly sucking the administration into a larger and larger conflict in response to a deteriorating situation on the ground and a belief in the need to contain communist expansion in Southeast Asia (McNamara 1995; Goldstein 2008). As H. R. McMaster (1997: 323) observed, "Vietnam was not forced on the United States by a tidal wave of Cold War ideology" but instead had "slunk in on cat's feet" to ensnare the administration.

Another major difference between Vietnam and Iraq involves the actual strategic importance of the two areas to U.S. national interests. While Vietnam was often viewed by American policy makers of the time as representing a key area of peripheral competition between the superpowers, even those espousing the "domino" theory (positing the collapse of neighboring states to communism if one fell) did not usually see Vietnam as comparable in importance to U.S. interests in places like Europe or Japan (McNamara 1995;

Ambrose and Brinkley 1998). On the other hand, the Middle East (including Iraq), with oil reserves absolutely critical for Western industrial economies to function, has long held a strategic value far outstripping Vietnam. As Lawrence Wilkerson observed:

> The stark difference in my view is that Vietnam, although it was conceived to be of a strategic nature, never was—that is to say, we could have left Vietnam anytime and it wouldn't have made a bit of difference. With Iraq, it was not strategically necessary for us to invade. But now that we're there, with Arab soil under our feet, it is strategically necessary that we be perceived as not having bumped it up so bad that we come home with our heads hung low. The prestige factor, plus there is so much else in the Middle East that is of strategic interest to us, from the flow of oil to the Israelis. . . . We definitely need to have a posture there that is protective of our interests.[3]

There also was a huge difference in the nature of the two insurgencies. In Vietnam the Viet Cong followed a nationalist, charismatic leader (Ho Chi Minh) fighting a war of national liberation, whereas the insurgency in Iraq was fragmented across sectarian lines, lacked any unifying leadership, and was primarily intent upon driving out U.S. forces and securing their own grip on power (Laird 2005: 36). As Biddle (2006: 6) observed: "If the war in Iraq were chiefly a class-based or nationalist war, the violence would run along national, class, or ideological lines. It does not. . . . Defense of sect and ethnic group, not resistance to foreign occupation, accounts for most of the anti-American violence. . . . This should come as no surprise: the insurgents are not competing for Shiite hearts and minds; they are fighting for Sunni self-interest, and hardly need a manifesto to rally supporters." The Iraqi insurgency was "not a Maoist 'people's war' of national liberation" like Vietnam had been but was better understood as "a communal civil war with very different dynamics" (Biddle 2006: 2).

Another major difference was the level of domestic political opposition. Though Bush's poll numbers would nosedive as Iraq became a protracted conflict much as Johnson's had, there was no repeat of the massive public protests against the war like the 1960s. To a great extent, this was due to an absence of the draft, which for Johnson spurred college students to demonstrate. Bush himself would later observe, privately, the critical role the draft had played in sparking protests in Vietnam, noting in the absence of an all-volunteer force, "we could never have sustained this effort in Iraq politically."[4] With Republicans in control of Congress avoiding confronting or embarrassing the administration, Bush didn't face the congressional opposition and hearings over Iraq Johnson had over Vietnam (Johnson 1971; McPherson 1972).

A final difference between the two conflicts was the confidence level (or certainty) of each president that their strategy would ultimately be effective. It was very clear Bush himself was extremely confident and certain he was making the correct policy decision—that regime change was the right thing to do (Woodward 2008). His key lieutenants, Cheney and Rumsfeld, shared Bush's confidence. This policy confidence would continue for years in the face of multiple reverses and the need for blame-avoidance strategies. In contrast, Johnson was actually dubious about intervening in Vietnam from the beginning but felt trapped in a situation requiring some action to prevent its collapse to communists. Bundy recounted a conversation he had with Johnson in mid-1964 illustrating the president's doubts:

> "I'll tell you," said Johnson, "the more that I stayed awake last night thinking of this thing . . . it looks to me like we're getting into another Korea. It just worries the hell out of me. I don't see what we can ever hope to get out of there . . . once we're committed. . . . I don't think it's worth fighting for and I don't think that we can get out. It's just the biggest damn mess that I ever saw." (Goldstein 2008: 112–13)

Similarly, Beschloss (2001: 59), in his examination of transcripts from tape recordings of White House conversations, found LBJ was privately quite the opposite from the publicly confident leader over Vietnam, remarking in one 1965 meeting, "I can't get out [of Vietnam], and I can't finish it with what I have got. And I don't know what the hell to do!" Even as he was ordering Robert McNamara to begin Operation Rolling Thunder in February 1965, he noted, "Now we're off to bombing these people. . . . We're over that hurdle. I don't think anything is going to be as bad as losing, and I don't see any way of winning" (Beschloss 2001: 59). Regarding the Viet Cong, Johnson told McNamara, "I don't believe they're ever going to quit," and worried he didn't have a "plan for victory—militarily or diplomatically" (Sanger 2001: A15). As he told his friend Richard Russell, chairman of the Senate Armed Services Committee, "The great trouble I'm under [is that] a man can fight if he can see daylight down the road somewhere. But there ain't no daylight in Vietnam. There's not a bit" (Beschloss 2001: 60). In fact, in response to Bundy and McNamara's January 1965 "Fork in the Road" memo (arguing for more aggressive military intervention), LBJ's reaction, as Bundy's colleague Douglass Cater later recalled, was hardly one of confidence:

> I'd never seen the man in as dejected a mood—he said, "I don't know what to do. If I send more boys in, there's going to be killin'. If I take them out, there's going to be more killin'. Anything I do, there's going to be more killin'." And he never put the "g" on the "killin'," it was Texas "killin'." Then he got up and

walked out of the room, leaving us in a somewhat shattered state." (Goldstein 2008: 154)

It was certainly not a scene paralleled in the Bush White House, where if anything the expectations were the Iraqi operation would be a relatively easy one, with American forces being seen as "liberators" and regime change bringing about a democracy allowing for a quick U.S. withdrawal (Woodward 2004, 2006; Isikoff and Corn 2006). While Johnson actively sought to downplay the chances of war during his 1964 presidential campaign, arguing, "We don't want our American boys to do the fighting for Asian boys" (Goldstein 2008: 129), Bush emphasized his status as a "war president" to gain public support during the 2004 elections (Woodward 2004, 2006; Rich 2006; McClellan 2008). In this respect, Iraq and Vietnam are quite different.

THE SIMILARITIES BETWEEN IRAQ AND VIETNAM

Commonalities across Bush's and Johnson's Styles

For all of the differences making Iraq an imperfect fit for the Vietnam analogy, there are also a great many similarities worth observing—parallels that, while not suggesting Iraq *is* Vietnam, nevertheless show how similar political styles across the two presidents (coupled with their uses of advisers and intelligence) produced analogous policy dynamics. Bush and Johnson shared relatively closed, insular advisory systems making their inner circles difficult to penetrate for dissenting policy voices. Both saw the world in absolute terms and relied heavily on expert advisers in formulating policy. While Johnson differed from Bush in his high need for personal involvement and control over policy and was far more personally engaged on Vietnam policy details than Bush was on Iraq, both still delegated substantial policy formulation tasks to their subordinates. Both had dynamic senior advisers with "strong personalities"—like McNamara and Rumsfeld—who would help drive their administration's policies. And both presidents would establish inner circles that selectively sought out evidence supporting their existing policies and had difficult relations with those who disagreed with them—leading to frequent misuse and distortions of advice and intelligence.

Though Bush received updates and held frequent meetings on Iraq, McClellan (2008: 253) notes he was still "insulated from the reality of events on the ground and consequently began falling into the trap of believing his own spin." More troubling to McClellan (2008: 253) was that Bush "failed to spend enough time seeking independent input from a broad range of outside experts, those beyond the White House bubble who had firsthand experience on the ground in Iraq . . . [or] those with differing points of view." Policy details were of little interest to Bush beyond the big picture format. As Armitage notes, Bush just "wasn't interested in the details, he was interested in the result," so when involved in war planning, the president would ask the generals if they had what they needed, but he wasn't interested in the details of what the requested resources would be used for.[5] In an ironic twist, Bush perceived his lack of focus on details as a "lesson" learned from his predecessor's experiences in Vietnam. As Armitage recalls:

> Part of it, I think, was what he's read about Vietnam. That Vietnam had been run from the president's desk and all that, and you let the generals fight the war. But it's gotta be both. The president commits young men and women to battle and then he wants to be sure that he's fighting in the best possible way. And Mr. Bush, in my view, took a very, too much hands-off view. But it was a reaction to what he sees during Vietnam as too much interference by the president. So no, he wasn't steeped in details.[6]

Similarly, during interviews with Woodward (2008: 93), Bush repeated his understanding of this Vietnam lesson, noting he had always "let the generals run the war," and the main problem during Vietnam had been Johnson and McNamara micromanaging the war. To a gathering of congressmen, Bush again emphasized, "I'm not LBJ. . . . I'm not going to sit around some map room and micromanage the war" (Thomas and Wolffe 2005: 35). But while Bush was certainly no LBJ, who was so engaged he was known to decide upon individual air strikes from the White House basement, it is difficult to discern the difference between Rumsfeld's extremely hands-on efforts to control events in Iraq and McNamara's forty years earlier (Preston 2001). Against the advice of State Department and intelligence officials, as well as experienced individuals who had been on the ground in Iraq (like Jay Garner), Rumsfeld and his lieutenants supported and encouraged Bremer to disband the Iraqi Army, pursue de-Baathification, and crowd out State from reconstruction and postwar efforts (Woodward 2004, 2006; Isikoff and Corn 2006). It was micromanagement of the war from afar, coupled with Rumsfeld's well-known insistence upon controlling his senior military officers and disregarding their advice (Cockburn 2007). The end result, due to Bush's hands-off, delegative style, was not micromanagement by the president himself, but by his subordinates instead.

Moreover, Bush tended to take absolute positions on issues while dismissing intelligence assessments contradicting his views. During the run-up to the January 2005 Iraqi national elections, the CIA repeatedly warned conditions in the country were unfavorable to having the poll—with the likely result being a surge in violence and the exclusion of minority Sunnis from the vote

(Woodward 2006: 381–82). After receiving the warning from his CIA briefer, Bush dismissively remarked, "Is this Baghdad Bob?" referring to Saddam's propagandist. "I'm not hearing that from anyone else but the CIA" (Woodward 2006: 381–82). Bush clapped his hands loudly and slammed his briefing book shut in the Oval Office, stating, "We'll see who's right" (Woodward 2006: 381–82). It turned out to be the CIA, as the Sunnis, who were the backbone of the insurgency and 20 percent of the population, effectively boycotted the elections (Woodward 2006: 383). George Casey, the commander of U.S. forces in Iraq, could not help but draw his own Vietnam parallels in response to Bush's oversimplified framing of the military situation:

> The president repeatedly questioned his commander about whacking the bad guys, as if everything would be okay if they just whacked enough. He summed up Bush's approach for a colleague: "If you're not out there hooking and jabbing with American forces every day, you're not fighting the right fight." The president's persistent questions suggested to Casey that [he] believed in an attrition strategy of simply eliminating the bad guys. The Vietnam War had established that that wouldn't work. (Woodward 2008: 6)

Another similar dynamic shared by Bush and Johnson was how senior military commanders were often excluded from key decisions by their civilian counterparts. During the Iraq War, Casey and General John Abizaid found themselves hearing what their own military strategy was (for the first time) during congressional testimony by Rice in October 2005, who described a "clear, hold, and build" strategy for Iraq to senators that had not even been broached with senior commanders (Woodward 2008: 31–32). Soon after Rice's statement, Rumsfeld became aware it was going to be used in one of Bush's speeches and requested all but "clear" be removed since it was up to the Iraqis to hold and State to work with somebody on building—but Bush gave the same formulation anyway (Woodward 2008: 32–33). Nearly three years later, as General David Petraeus worked to implement the new "surge" strategy (while facing off against doubters at the Pentagon), Bush's delegative style led to a supportive back-channel message being sent to Petraeus (without either Robert Gates or Stephen Hadley's knowledge) but little in the way of direct presidential support in his debates with Central Command (Woodward 2008: 390). Carrying the ball was left to Petraeus.

That disconnect between the White House and senior military officers was also a characteristic of Johnson's administration. As McMaster (1997: 41) observed, Kennedy bequeathed LBJ an advisory system that treated the joint chiefs of staff (JCS) "more like a source of potential opposition than of useful advice." Like Rumsfeld, McNamara insisted upon strict personal control over the Pentagon, often suppressing advice from the JCS in favor of more

supportive views from his civilian analysts (McMaster 1997: 21). He sup-
ported appointment to the JCS of compliant officers whose "loyalty and sup-
port" could be counted upon by Johnson for his policies (McMaster 1997: 45).
And similar to Rumsfeld's relationship with senior officers at the Pentagon,
McMaster (1997: 19) noted, "McNamara's autocratic style and the conde-
scending attitude of his young civilian assistants deeply disturbed the Joint
Chiefs and other military officers," with officers tending to view the "rest of
McNamara's staff as adversaries," not allies.

It was a pattern frequently pointed to by former members of Rumsfeld's
Department of Defense during interviews, from senior officers to civilian officials, who consistently described the condescending approach of Rumsfeld
aides—Paul Wolfowitz, Douglas Feith, and Stephen Cambone—toward the
uniformed military.[7] It was much like the dynamic described by McMaster
(1997: 328), who noted McNamara and his lieutenants disparaging military
advice as "too narrow" and trusting their own "intelligence and analytical
methods could compensate for their lack of military experience and education." This mindset was much in evidence within Feith's two intelligence
operations at the Pentagon, the Office of Special Plans and the Counter
Terrorism Evaluation Group, set up to compensate for the intelligence community's supposed failure to find the "right" evidence on Iraq or WMDs. Just
as McNamara and Johnson "extracted from the JCS acquiescence and silent
support for decisions already made" over Vietnam, Bush also relegated the
chiefs to a "peripheral position in the policy making process," while carefully preserving "the façade of consultation to prevent the JCS from opposing
the administration's policies either openly or behind the scenes" (McMaster
1997: 329).

Much as would occur in Iraq, McMaster (1997: 325–26) noted "the relationship between the president, the secretary of defense, and the Joint Chiefs
led to the curious situation in which the nation went to war without the benefit
of effective military advice from the organization having the statutory responsibility to be the nation's 'principal military advisers.'" But McMaster's
critique goes much deeper. It is in essence an indictment of a senior military
leadership who remained silent and acquiesced to Johnson's conduct of a
war they actually didn't believe could be successful. As McMaster (1997:
333) observes, because "forthright communication between top civilian and
military officials" was never developed, the JCS "became accomplices in the
president's deception and focused on a tactical task, killing the enemy." This
parallel was not lost on some within the Bush administration who observed
a similar dynamic over Iraq policy. Reflecting on McMaster's book, Wilkerson observed the "most dramatic similarity" between Vietnam and Iraq for
him was "Dick Myers, Pete Pace, George Casey, and the uniformed military

leadership essentially did the same kind of deed with regard to Iraq that West-moreland and others had in Vietnam."[8] Noting McNamara's effort to select compliant JCS senior officers, Wilkerson observed:

> I think it's very clear . . . Rumsfeld not only cowed the uniformed military leadership, he handpicked some of it so that it would be very, very predisposed to be bovine. . . . Dick Myers made himself comfortable. Utter nonentity. Partly because air force officers don't understand ground combat and Dick Myers was not in a position to give the best possible advice with regard to Iraq other than to say, "Shock and Awe will do it!" . . . No, Rumsfeld took every opportunity to cut the chairman [of the JCS] out . . . except for those who would be willing sycophants.[9]

Prior to his promotion to chairman, Pace was warned by General Jim Jones that "military advice is being influenced on a political level" and the JCS had improperly "surrendered" to Rumsfeld, adding, "You should not be the parrot on the secretary's shoulder" (Woodward 2006: 404). But as Clarke (2008: 54) later observed, "dissenting publicly with Bush and Rumsfeld would have meant resigning and then being criticized by the administration's media machine," a difficult choice for either senior military or intelligence officers (Yingling 2007). It also meant resigning from your chosen career and, in all likelihood, having no effect whatsoever on the course Bush was setting.[10] Thus, while General Ricardo Sanchez, the former top commander in Iraq, later criticized the "catastrophically flawed, unrealistically optimistic war plan," and "glaring and unfortunate display of incompetent strategic leadership" by national leaders, he did not resign in protest at the time (Clarke 2008: 54). Indeed, Clarke (2008: 49–53) argues, like McMaster, that generals contributed greatly to the war and its ineffective prosecution because they failed to stand up or dissent from the civilian leadership, with only one senior officer, Marine Major General Gregory Newbold, director of operations for the JCS, resigning "before the Iraq invasion because he disagreed with the plan to conduct the war."

Both Conflicts Were Initially Justified Using Flawed Intelligence

Another common theme between Vietnam and Iraq was the use of flawed intelligence to justify the need to use force—the Gulf of Tonkin for Johnson and Iraq's possession of WMDs and links to terrorism for Bush. Each leader was surrounded by advisers who mostly shared a similar mind-set on the preferred strategy of intervention, and neither White House was renowned for broad-based information searches seeking out feedback or advice questioning their desired policies (Preston 2001, 2008). For Bush, the threat was Saddam could attack the United States "on any given day" with WMDs, and going to war was critical for winning the war on terror—likening the threat posed by Iraq to the Cuban Missile Crisis.[11] Connecting Iraq to the 9/11 attacks and Al Qaeda, along with its possession of WMDs, would be Bush's *casus belli*. For Johnson, it was the August 1964 incidents in the Gulf of Tonkin, in which North Vietnamese patrol boats supposedly fired torpedoes at the USS *Maddox*, which set the stage for him to pursue a congressional resolution authorizing the use of military force against North Vietnam. As would later be discovered, the attack on the *Maddox* was as illusory as the WMDs and Al Qaeda connection had been in Iraq.

As part of a covert CIA mission, South Vietnamese patrol boats and commandos had been staging raids on North Vietnamese–controlled islands and coastlines for months, and U.S. naval forces, like the *Maddox*, were assigned to monitor enemy radio transmissions and reactions to better map their defenses (Weiner 2007; Goldstein 2008; Aid 2009). On August 2 the *Maddox*, having been shot at by patrol boats, returned fire and drove the crafts off, suffering no damage (Goldstein 2008: 122). Upon being informed, Johnson asked whether we were "up to any *mischief* out there?"—and upon being told of the CIA operations, ordered no reprisals (Goldstein 2008: 123–24). Two months earlier, Bundy had written a memo anticipating the need in coming months to obtain a congressional resolution approving the expanded use of force against North Vietnam—a sample of which had already been penned by Bundy's brother William (Goldstein 2008: 116). But given the run-up to the November 1964 presidential elections, with Johnson campaigning on a platform of not drastically increasing American engagement in Vietnam, LBJ decided against pursuing Bundy's resolution at that time. The political climate was just not right. But events in the Gulf of Tonkin would soon change the political calculus and provide an opening for increasing Johnson's leverage to use more force after the election.

Despite suggestions from State to postpone further raids to defuse the situation, Johnson ordered the raids continued and intensified since they were "beginning to rattle Hanoi" and represented a way to show U.S. resolve (Aid 2009: 89). Interestingly, prior to the second incident (that would occur later that day), Johnson visited Bundy's office and directed him to "get the resolution your brother drafted" for Congress ready for him—and in response to Bundy's surprised response that perhaps "we ought to think about this," LBJ bluntly replied, "I didn't ask you what you *thought* . . . I told you what to *do*" (Goldstein 2008: 126). Also, Johnson ordered McNamara to identify targets for potential reprisal action: "One of their bridges or something. . . . We've already picked out and just hit about three of them damn quick and go right after them" (Goldstein 2008: 126). McNamara replied the targets would be identified, and he and Bundy would be prepared to recommend the retaliatory response if an attack happens during the next six to nine hours (Goldstein 2008: 126).

Less than an hour later, on August 4, the *Maddox* and another American destroyer, the USS *Turner Joy*, returned to the Gulf of Tonkin and, during stormy, confused conditions, came to believe they were again under attack, leading both ships to open fire at "ghostly blotches in the night" and engage in furious evasive maneuvers (Weiner 2007: 241). Upon receiving word of the new attack, McNamara recommended (backed by the unanimous support of Johnson's other NSC advisers) launching air strikes on North Vietnamese patrol boat bases and oil complexes (Goldstein 2008: 127). Johnson seized on the moment to set in motion his legislative strategy to get approval of the Gulf of Tonkin Resolution—a "blank check" piece of legislation opening the path for whatever expansion of the war in Southeast Asia the administration felt justified. But even as the political strategy was moving forward, evidence was surfacing questioning whether a second attack had occurred. The destroyer captains had discovered only the *Maddox*'s inexperienced sonar operator had heard the twenty-six torpedoes they believed had attacked them, while the experienced operator on the *Turner Joy* had heard nothing but the sounds of the destroyers making their evasive maneuvers (Weiner 2007: 241). Further, given the entire North Vietnamese navy only had twelve PT boats carrying just two unreloadable tubes, it made the high number of supposed torpedo attacks an impossibility (Aid 2009: 95). These concerns were dutifully reported back to Washington, and subsequent searches found no physical evidence of any kind of military engagement at all—no oil slicks or debris from patrol boats supposedly sunk during the skirmish (Aid 2009: 96–97).

The sole remaining piece of evidence supporting the contention that an attack had taken place—which the White House was relying on to support its case—was a National Security Agency (NSA) intercept of signals intelligence (SIGINT) purported to be a North Vietnamese naval communiqué reading, "SACRIFICED TWO SHIPS AND ALL THE REST ARE OKAY" (Weiner 2007: 241). As the declassified NSA history later noted, "The reliance on SIGINT even went to the extent of overruling the commander on the scene. It was obvious to the president and his advisors that there really had been an attack—they had the North Vietnamese messages to prove it" (Aid 2009: 97). So despite growing reservations on the part of both ship captains, Johnson moved ahead with the Gulf of Tonkin Resolution and retaliation against the North.

There is little question McNamara's use of raw SIGINT, without submitting it for further intelligence analyses that would have shown its faulty nature, greatly resembles how raw intelligence was used by Feith's Pentagon shop and Cheney to make the case for Iraqi WMDs or Al Qaeda connections. Both are examples of policy makers bypassing normal intelligence community procedures and tradecraft to make use of "evidence" supporting a preconceived notion. As Aid (2009: 97) notes, the NSA provided Johnson and McNamara with raw intercepts that were then "analyzed and evaluated by civilian and military commanders with little or no background in intelligence, much less SIGINT analysis." Compounding the problem, neither SIGINT specialists at the NSA nor CIA analysts were called on to provide a more professional assessment of the intelligence, and according to the former head of State's Bureau of Intelligence and Research (INR), McNamara's use of the SIGINT "may go down in history as one of the most serious mistakes made by a senior U.S. government official. He ended up seeing what he wanted to believe" (Aid 2009: 97).

Of course, had such analysis been undertaken in a less rushed environment, the assessment would have differed significantly. After the fact, the NSA reexamined the intercept, double-checking the translation and time stamp, and found the message actually read, "WE SACRIFICED TWO COMRADES BUT ALL ARE BRAVE" (Weiner 2007: 241). The message was actually referring to the first clash days earlier and had nothing to do with the events of August 4. Years later when the NSA materials were declassified in 2005, researchers learned—in a classic blame-avoidance move—the NSA's mistake had been covered up and all the incriminating evidence destroyed. As Weiner (2007: 241–42) observed, the NSA "buried" evidence about the faulty translation in all of its after-action reports and official summaries of the event, and destroyed the "smoking gun" intercept McNamara had shown Johnson.

Afterward, even Johnson had doubts about whether the attack had taken place. Recordings of White House conversations show LBJ, only weeks after Congress passed the Gulf of Tonkin Resolution, admitting to McNamara, "when we got through with all the firing . . . we concluded maybe they hadn't fired at all" (Sanger 2001). But as Bundy observed, Johnson shrewdly used "a moment of high feeling" to increase his own power or freedom of action (via the resolution), while burnishing his anticommunist credentials and showing laudable restraint to the initial attack (always popular with the electorate): "Tonkin was very Johnsonian. It's not possible to imagine Kennedy doing that. He wouldn't have thought of the legislative parlay" (Goldstein 2008: 126–35). Still, while a highly effective political tactic, the wording of the declassified NSA history leaves no doubt it was one built on faulty intelligence and poor analysis—with the report concluding the intelligence "was deliberately skewed to support the notion that there had been an attack" (Weiner 2007: 242–43).

But in one sense, there is a potential difference between Bush's and Johnson's use of faulty intelligence. While LBJ's inner circle was clearly looking for justifications to apply greater force to North Vietnam, and jumped to conclusions they shouldn't have, given the spotty nature of the evidence, it seems clear they honestly *believed* there had been a North Vietnamese attack on the *Maddox* given the available intelligence. That there had been no lengthy analyses of the evidence was less a result of Johnson "fixing the intelligence to the facts" as it was one of political necessity to "strike while the iron was hot" to obtain the congressional resolution. The military retaliation and the legislative strategy moved forward at a rapid pace, one not allowing careful analyses to catch up to Johnson's decision making. However, having a bad decisional process making use of faulty intelligence is not the same thing as the *motivated* use of intelligence already understood to be faulty to support a desired policy outcome.

For the Bush administration, which was equally focused on finding justifications for use of force against Iraq, it is far less convincing to argue it was misled and made the decisions it did due to faulty intelligence alone. Especially given the motivated efforts by many in Cheney's office, the Department of Defense, and segments of the intelligence community to distort the available intelligence and select only that which supported a WMD or terrorism connection. It's hard to credit key advisers, like Cheney, Rumsfeld, Rice, and Wolfowitz, as being unaware the available evidence was stacked in favor of reaching certain conclusions—though it should be noted some who worked in the White House at senior levels emphasized during interviews that Bush himself (whether from ideology or the intel case being presented to him) sincerely believed the case against Iraq being made by his advisers.[12] Both administrations engaged in blame avoidance to conceal that faulty intelligence had been used to justify their military actions. This effort proved far more successful for Johnson, due to the classified nature of the SIGINT material and active efforts on the part of the NSA to cover up the evidence. Given the far more public presentation of the evidence against Iraq by the Bush administration, the faults in its own analysis of the intelligence came into the light much more quickly during subsequent congressional inquiries.

Across both administrations, policy makers fell victim to a mind-set leading them to overestimate their own competence in analyzing and making use of intelligence. Like Cheney and Rumsfeld, McNamara had an "intense distrust of intelligence professionals in general" and a belief that "he was a better intelligence analyst than the men and women at the CIA" (Aid 2009: 97). Similarly, Bush, and especially Cheney, didn't trust or value the intelligence community's analytic judgments—a point often acknowledged by senior officials during interviews.[13] It was quite visible during the lead-up to the Iraq War, where Bush officials politicized intelligence and bypassed normal community channels to produce more supportive products. In their jaundiced view of the intelligence community (which they saw as more of a roadblock to policy than an asset), the Bush White House appears to have shared Johnson's sentiments, famously captured in a well-known LBJ quote:

> Let me tell you about these intelligence guys. . . . When I was growing up in Texas, we had a cow named Bessie. I'd go out early and milk her. I'd get her in the stanchion, seat myself, and squeeze out a pail of fresh milk. One day I'd worked hard and gotten a full pail of milk, but I wasn't paying attention, and old Bessie swung her shit-smeared tail through that bucket of milk. Now, you know, that's what these intelligence guys do. You work hard and get a good program or policy going, and they swing a shit-smeared tail through it. (Weiner 2007: 248)

A final similarity between the Gulf of Tonkin and Iraqi WMDs is that, like Johnson, who was able to maneuver Congress into granting a resolution serving as a "blank check" for open-ended operations in Vietnam, Bush was able to obtain his own congressional authorization for war based on equally fake intelligence. After reading Bush's Iraq resolution, Republican Senator Chuck Hagel thought, "My God, this crowd down at the White House is rolling right over the top of us—and we're letting them do it"—especially given the blank-check nature of its call to use "all means" appropriate to enforce UN resolutions, dismantle Iraqi WMD programs, and "restore international peace and security in the region" (Isikoff and Corn 2006: 64). In its sweep, the Iraq resolution was just as much a blank check as the Gulf of Tonkin Resolution had been.

Both Conflicts Were Marked by Policy Makers Not Understanding the Regional Context and How to Fight a Counterinsurgency

One of the major challenges for any intervention is correctly ascertaining the nature of the opposition and what the political-military environment "on the ground" requires. For both administrations, this posed significant hurdles, especially in how to fight a counterinsurgency campaign. As Wilkerson observed regarding the Iraq-Vietnam comparison, a major similarity was "our inability to do counterinsurgency worth a shit," a problem having its roots in decisions made post-Vietnam that "we're not gonna do these Vietnam things" ever again.[14] As a result, counterinsurgency thinking was deemphasized, almost as a "lesson learned" that would not have to be repeated by the military. And as Wilkerson remarked, "We let all the experience that we did gather from Vietnam, which was quite a lot, just fade into the distant past, atrophy, fall away, and we didn't pay any attention to it."[15] It was a view seconded by former Iraq Survey Group and UNSCOM leader Dr. David Kay:

If you go back to Vietnam, the military was unprepared for a counterinsurgency war, and in fact, the doctrine was, we don't want to do one of those wars. It goes back to Marshall—we don't want to get involved in a war in Asia. We certainly don't want to fight in jungles. And this time [in Iraq], the military hadn't remembered any of the lessons of counterinsurgency, and organized itself in a way that wasn't relevant to the counterinsurgency campaign. . . . The CIA after 9/11 called back a lot of their retirees, and they were gray-badge retirees who were working, a lot of them in Baghdad. And we'd sit around in the evening talking, and they would just bemoan the fact—because they'd all been involved in Vietnam. And none of the people understood how you dealt with counterinsurgency in the military. The big army just didn't understand special ops—didn't like special ops. So I think there was a similarity.

An additional problem lay in each administration's misdiagnosis of the underlying problem and how it should be addressed. For Johnson, the reality was his inner circle viewed the conflict primarily through the prism of the Cold War and the need to contain communism (Goldstein 2008).[16] It was a perspective driven by an acceptance of containment policy and the belief that the fall of states in a region to communism would bring about the collapse of neighboring ones (Ambrose and Brinkley 1998; Preston 2001). For Johnson, who lacked any in-depth knowledge of foreign affairs (or Southeast Asia), this simple template of containment policy framed his views and showed the correct policy path. Indeed, Bundy later explained, Johnson "was intrinsically, basically, a believer that the right thing to do was to stand and deliver," and if you start from that understanding, his Vietnam policy "isn't really that complicated!"[17]

For Bush, the perception of Iraq wasn't one based on a long-standing doctrine like containment, but based on events after 9/11, a "war on terror" dividing states into those "with us or against us," and neoconservative notions of the value of regime change in creating democratic transitions in countries to create regional stability. It was a perspective many foreign policy experts, like Brent Scowcroft, believed to be unrealistic and out of touch with the political and cultural context in the region (Goldberg 2005: 62). Yet for neoconservatives, regime change was the magical silver bullet to solve the region's multifaceted problems, and heavily influenced the administration's thinking regarding Iraq (Woodward 2004, 2006; Isikoff and Corn 2006). This neocon argument was well illustrated by former CIA director James Woolsey's observations prior to the Iraq War in April 2002:

I would accept the formulation that we are now in World War IV. World War III having been the Cold War. And that the objective really should be to democratize the Middle East. . . . We really need to finish the work of the first three world wars, and the major area . . . is the Middle East, particularly the Arab Middle East. Essentially, the only way to solve this problem is to change the governments. And I think Iraq is first in the crosshairs. . . . Dictators that want to try to stay in power and they need to be aggressive often to keep people repressed. And democracies turn to military matters last not first. . . . We've basically democratized three-quarters of the world already. . . . In the Arab world . . . there are none. What we really need to do for the Middle East is what we've done for much of the rest of the world and change the face of the government. . . . You can't just keep swatting mosquitoes, you got to drain the swamp! And the swamp is the dictatorial and autocratic governments of the Middle East.[18]

With Iraq representing unfinished business in the minds of many neoconservatives, regime change seemed an appropriate means for eliminating Saddam while moving the region more toward U.S. interests (Mylroie 2000). But as Richard Perle, who led Bush's Defense Policy Board and advocated the overthrow of Saddam, later ruefully observed: "Rather than turn Iraq over to Iraqis to begin the daunting process of nation building . . . we blundered into an ill-conceived occupation that would facilitate a deadly insurgency from which we, and the Iraqis, are only now emerging. . . . I had badly underestimated the administration's capacity to mess things up."[19] It soon became apparent those advocating regime change as the solution to all the region's problems operated under the simple notion that all that was required was to topple the leader and walk away—rather than Colin Powell's "pottery barn" understanding that if you break something, you had to buy it. Yet as former defense secretary Laird (2005: 34–35) later acknowledged, in both wars, the United States "sought to establish a legitimate indigenous government," which in the case of Iraq was to be a "democratic government, whereas in Vietnam the United States would have settled for any regime that advanced our Cold War agenda."

Armitage also notes historical and cultural differences separated Iraq from Vietnam and was never a matter as simple as the regime-change crowd insisted on believing. As Armitage remarked, Vietnam, far more than Iraq, "had the colonial overhang—the division of the country in 1954 after Dien Bien Phu—which you didn't have in Iraq. But the similarities in both was that the overwhelming military might of the United States was rendered equal by people who used very low-tech weaponry, but who were fighting for their home turf—we weren't."[20] And just from the standpoint of how the United States got into each war, and the understanding by policy makers of the cultural differences in each country, Kay points to other interesting parallels:

The real difference in the case of Vietnam, we slid into it. . . . Vietnam was really a slippery slope that you sort of slid into. Iraq was a conscience decision. It wasn't a slippery slope. He decided to go in and go do it. In both cases, I think they didn't understand the foreign societies. . . . An example . . . one of the major translators the press relied on, but also the diplomatic community used as well, was all the time a senior Viet Cong officer. We just didn't understand brothers and cousins, and arrangements that were more powerful than states. And in the case of Iraq, we really didn't understand the power of secularists versus religion in Iraq. And the role that played, and I'm not sure even now it's penetrated. It's quite clear that was really far from senior decision makers' understanding.[21]

The Politicization of Intelligence

The Bush administration pursued an elaborate strategy of bypassing normal intelligence channels to gather evidence to back up their Iraq policy preferences. Moreover, as the war, and the administration's prewar use of intelligence, became more controversial, intelligence was further politicized in White House efforts at blame avoidance. It is indicative of the point Churchill stressed to Stalin at the Tehran Conference in 1943: "In wartime, truth is so precious that she should always be attended by a bodyguard of lies" (Cannon 2007: 57). For the Bush administration, this was true not only from a policy advocacy standpoint but from a blame-avoidance one as well.

The Johnson administration also politicized intelligence and worked to have only positive news reported to the White House press corps. In this, there is again a marked similarity between Iraq and Vietnam. Of course, during Vietnam, the focus of the politicization had not been to create a false case for intervening in the conflict to sell the war to the American people (as it had been for Bush), but rather it was an exercise in seeking to maintain public support for an unpopular conflict and "convince the people that the war was going well" (Weiner 2007: 269). There was also a more political concern on Johnson's part (one often shared by Bush) regarding how dissent by subordinates or negative intelligence reporting might later be used against him. As McNamara would later observe regarding Johnson:

I don't want to say he didn't encourage dissent or didn't want to hear dissent. But he was very sensitive to the political environment that he was in, whether it was on civil rights legislation or Vietnam decisions or whatever it was. And he knew that under certain circumstances, if his opponents knew that some members of his administration had dissented from Johnson's views or opposed a particular action he was about to put forward, that his opponents would use that dissent to weaken Johnson's position. And therefore, it was almost a tool of his management style to—I wouldn't say stifle dissent—but to ensure that it wasn't expressed in a way that his opponents could use to his disadvantage.[22]

Johnson was well known (like Bush) for excluding advisers or subordinates from policy meetings when it was clear their views would be at odds with current policy (McPherson 1972; Preston 2001; Goldstein 2008). Both presidents tended to see such disagreement as disloyalty—whether it be Hubert Humphrey, Bill Moyers, and McNamara during the 1960s, or Powell and Armitage in 2003 (Preston 2001).[23] Certainly organizations within the intelligence community, like the CIA, were quickly seen as problems when their analysis did not support the administration's policy views.[24] In fact, Johnson's national security adviser, Walt Rostow, was constantly ordering the CIA to produce good news about the war, asking CIA Director Richard Helms, "Whose side are you on anyway?" (Weiner 2007: 269). Helm's predecessor, John McCone, also had warned Johnson in April 1965 of the dangers of intervening in Vietnam, but had no impact on LBJ's thinking and only stayed on the additional year due to the president's concern over the appearance of "loyalty" prior to an election (Weiner 2007: 248). Johnson subsequently appointed a Texas political crony, Ray Raborn, to the CIA director job in April 1965—a military yes-man who lacked any intelligence experience but who was a clear LBJ loyalist (Weiner 2007: 249).

When McNamara famously resigned as secretary of defense in 1967 due to his disagreements over the war, Johnson would describe him (in a good example of blame-avoidance tactics) as having suffered a "mental breakdown"—an explanation widely reported and believed (inaccurately) by the press (Preston 2001). It was Johnson's way of weakening the political impact of dissenters within his inner circle and joined a larger repertoire of tactics including not inviting dissenters (like Humphrey) to meetings; temporarily cutting them out of meetings and giving them the "silent treatment" as a corrective measure (like with McPherson); or dismissing the actual criticism (such as that by Ball) as mere "devil's advocacy" on the part of his adviser (McPherson 1972; Preston 2001; Goldstein 2008).

And when dealing with critical analyses undercutting existing policy (such as Helm's 1967 memos reporting the utter failure of U.S. bombing efforts or McNamara's 1967 critique of existing policy, which called for a bombing halt and de-escalation of the war), Johnson, and gatekeepers like Rostow, prevented wide circulation of the documents (Preston 2001). Indeed, the first "Wise Men" group meetings in November 1967—composed of senior foreign policy luminaries assembled to provide a public, external review of Vietnam policy for Johnson—were prevented from seeing either the CIA reports or McNamara's memo, and in the absence of the negative information announced their support for the administration's policies (Clifford 1991; Preston 2001).[25]

Another example of the politicization of intelligence is found in the pressure placed on the intelligence community in 1967 to support the Pentagon's estimates that "fewer than 300,000 communist fighters" were in the field in Vietnam, rather than the 500,000 CIA analysts were estimating (Weiner 2007: 267). In the "eyes-only memos" General Westmoreland and his aide Robert Komer sent to Johnson promising "victory was at hand," the lowball figure was treated as "an article of faith"—despite the fact CIA analysts disagreed strongly with it (Weiner 2007: 267–68). Finally, Komer warned the CIA, "You guys simply have to back off," because the truth would "create a public disaster and undo everything we've been trying to accomplish out here" (Weiner 2007: 267–68). The military was trying to convince an increasingly skeptical press and public the United States was winning the war, and an acknowledgment of the far higher CIA numbers would undercut them. Especially after having been consciously presenting an image of steady progress and declining Viet Cong capabilities over the previous year (McNamara 1995). Eventually, feeling the pressure from the Pentagon and White House to get on the team, Helms caved in and trimmed the CIA's reporting to fit the Defense estimate of 299,000 enemy forces or fewer, noting the number "didn't mean a damn" (Weiner 2007: 268). Similar politicization also surrounded the issue of body counts in Vietnam, which the Pentagon also used to demonstrate progress in the war.[26]

Yet in looking at comparisons across Iraq and Vietnam regarding the use of intelligence and its politicization, those who served during the Bush administration have some interesting takes on the question. For example, Pillar notes in the case of Vietnam (unlike in Iraq), "intelligence was used a lot," and there was a process that incorporated intelligence from the community in policy making, even if it "wasn't heeded necessarily."[27] As Pillar observes:

> One respect in which those of us in the Iraq episode had it much harder was . . . at least they were *asked*! Throughout much of this period in the sixties, the White House, and even more so the McNamara Pentagon, particularly a couple of years into the war after McNamara was starting to have his own second thoughts, was *peppering* the agency and intelligence community with request after request after request. Give us an assessment of what you think will happen if this happens. Give us an assessment of what you think will happen if we do that. And so you had this total stream of special national intelligence estimates and a whole bunch of other kinds of papers in response to policy-maker requests. There was *absolutely nothing like that*! Nothing like that in Iraq! Certainly not before the war began. So that's a huge difference. A huge difference . . . the questions being asked of intelligence, it was like night and day.[28]

Armitage had a similar view to Pillar regarding the notion intelligence on Vietnam had been "quite good"—especially when compared to the "quite bad" intelligence on Iraq, which due to the way it had been "rendered" had seriously "interfered with decision making" by the administration.[29] Recalling Wolfowitz's later statement that "WMD had been the only thing all of us could agree on," in terms of justifying the war, Armitage noted:

> That's true! Cause we didn't agree on Mohammed Atta. We didn't agree on Ahmed Chalabi. We agreed that weapons of mass destruction in Iraq was a problem? Yeah! Guys already used it on the Kurds. So, of course, we thought that was a problem! Had we known, absolutely, there was nothing there, that would have *changed* the dynamic a little, but I'm not sure it would have changed it a lot. You know why? We were telling the president, North Korea and Iran. They either have or are heading to a nuclear bomb. We weren't going to invade them! So there was a head of steam on this one.[30]

And the quality of the intelligence assets available to the community in assessing the situation in Iraq differed greatly from those available to policy makers during the Vietnam War. As Kay would observe:

> Now, in intelligence, the thing that was different in Vietnam was that it was before the era of big technology for intelligence collection assets, so we still had a pretty good human capacity. Now it was not adequate for Vietnam, but by and large, the reporting out of Vietnam showed very early on, we can't win. And it was based on human intelligence. When we started out in Iraq, in the period I was there, the intelligence community wanted to continue to rely on big assets, national collection assets, and had no human capacity. A handful of people spoke Arabic, and we didn't send out these young officers to go into the neighborhoods, they had to go with a translator! Come on! So I think the difference was the relatively robust, human intelligence capacity that existed in Vietnam was gone by the time we came to Iraq.[31]

However, in looking back at the general atmosphere of politicization in the intelligence community, it is interesting to note one longtime CIA veteran sees less of a parallel with Vietnam than with the political pressures of the 1980s. As Pillar observes:

> For intelligence officers in my generation . . . the time that is most reminiscent of the atmosphere on Iraq and the lead-up to the war was the earlier part of the Reagan administration in the eighties—when there was this similar kind of pressure to find Moscow behind every little bit of trouble in the world. And a very strong appetite by policy makers for anything that supported that picture of the world. That was the environment that came closest in the twenty-eight years of my career to the environment that we had in the lead-up to the Iraq War. Even that, though . . . was not as intense, not as suffocating as the Iraq one . . . and I truly believe the difference was there wasn't a war riding on it. There was a set

of policies in terms of military buildup and that kind of stuff in the Reagan administration. But what the Bush group was trying to do was launch an offensive war, a major offensive war. I mean, that's a hell of a departure![32]

In the face of these failures of intelligence and Bush's White House leadership, what steps were taken to fix the problem? Have reforms, such as creating a director of national intelligence (DNI), improved the intelligence community and lessened the potential for politicization, or had little impact? Off-the-record interviews and informal conversations with senior intelligence officials as well as analysts from across the community generally betray the common view it made no difference at all—that it was primarily political window dressing to "appear to be doing something" rather than being a true reform.[33] In fact, as one senior Defense intelligence official observed, "Reformation in the analytical process has been a big thing since 9/11, but I would tell you, it's name only."[34] Another Defense intelligence official remarked the setup of the DNI had merely represented "our traditional panacea, let's add another bureaucracy!"[35] It was similarly the view of Richard Clarke, who felt the reforms, while not making politicization worse, had no real impact.[36] Indeed, as one senior Defense intelligence official observed:

Honestly, I don't think there were any more structural improvements to the intelligence process instituted by the DNI that weren't already there under the community management staff. It's just that they ballooned up to bazillions of people . . . trying to peer back down. But I didn't see any structural improvement! You still had multiple agencies around the table with their own resources, all insisting they have an equal voice. You had an NIE process that remained largely intact under different names. But nothing *changed* structurally for the product! So, that's one of the things I condemn, as a card-carrying Republican, I condemn the Bush administration—it took an election to get them off their butts to reform the intelligence process. And they did it by simply adding another level of bureaucracy! What were we doing in the intervening two years, you know, after the worst surprise attack in U.S. history? We finally got around, and literally it was in a matter of days, come up with the DNI concept.[37]

Longtime CIA veteran Pillar agrees, noting the DNI "basically makes no difference" to how the intelligence community actually operates since "the DNI is fundamentally the same position as the old DCI [Director of Central Intelligence] was."[38] Observing the DNI and DCI are both presidential appointees who work for the White House, Pillar sees the reform as "mainly a charade" making no difference at all regarding the problem of politicization.[39] As Pillar notes, "It's a changing of the lines of the chart and pretending we've accomplished something, but as far as the political relationships with policy makers goes, the DNI is basically the same place where George Tenet worked—which has problems of its own. . . . We certainly didn't address the problem."[40]

As far as pressure on the intelligence community goes, there are limited protections in place to prevent politicization. Although the CIA has an ombudsman tasked with responding to individual analyst complaints of pressure to alter analyses, there are no similar protections in other branches of the intelligence community—nor protection against the kinds of subtle pressure on analysts that frequently occurred during the Iraq case (Clarke 2004; Bamford 2005; Pillar 2006; Drumheller 2006). While the CIA ombudsman for politicization concluded no undue pressure had been placed on analysts, it seemingly dismissed during its investigation that a quarter of analysts questioned (six of twenty-four) mentioned "pressure from the administration" (Isikoff and Corn 2006: 112).

Indeed, noting there is no mechanism like the CIA ombudsman for politicization at the State or Defense Department intelligence shops, one senior Defense intelligence official observed "there is no institutional value to dissent," and if you don't rock the boat and "take care of the party line," you will "get promoted and recognized."[41] Bush's replacement of Tenet as DCI by the politically partisan congressman Porter Goss led to even more overt politicization, as part of a broader blame-avoidance effort to muzzle dissent and leaks to the press. As Drumheller (2006: 159–60) recalls, Goss's staff drew up lists of analysts (among them some of the most experienced officers in the CIA) who "were not deemed politically loyal" to the administration, accused upper echelons at the agency of "harboring political affiliations none of us had," and laid out new "rules of the road" in a November 2004 memo ordering all staff "to distance themselves from any and all criticism of the administration and its policies."

For analysts, politicization places them in a nearly impossible position. Analyses swimming upstream against political currents from the White House tend to result in criticism to superiors and a lack of authored product being requested or published—causing obvious problems for promotion and raises.[42] As many senior intelligence analysts observe, in an environment where analysts need to have the "comfort zone" to "think outside of the box," to challenge preconceptions in producing the best analysis of problems or regions, politicization stifles their effectiveness.[43] As Pillar notes:

How are you supposed to react when you know that your *stuff*, the stuff from the organization, is being used to create an impression of something that is, in the judgment of the community, false? Even if the specific item, each one, is nearly factually true. I don't have a good answer to that question. It is certainly not professional or proper for an intelligence officer to say, "Well, I'm not gonna give you that stuff because I know what use you're gonna make of it." That's the intelligence officer intruding with his own policy preferences essentially. I think all you're left with is what McLaughlin and the rest of us did, which was to do our level best to make sure that everything's factually correct. And that we haven't signed on to judgments we disagree with. But beyond that, what we can do about it, short of resigning or making a stink, which I think in this case wouldn't have made any difference anyway. What do you do?[44]

In response to the "brouhaha about the sixteen words" in Bush's State of the Union address, Pillar recalls new procedures were set up so upcoming presidential speeches would be vetted for inaccuracies (though often only days ahead at the "draft number fourteen" stage).[45] Yet this was more of a blame-avoidance strategy than an effort to glean the best from the intelligence community. And the continued manipulations of the intelligence product remained fairly subtle, as Pillar recalls:

My typical reaction to the stuff in my area was, okay, I didn't see any one statement that was factually wrong. However, in my judgment, this whole paragraph, or this whole passage, was crafted to create an incorrect impression about the conclusion that should be drawn. So I would typically write my comment and send it to whoever in the director's office was collating these things. And it would say basically that. And, not unexpectedly, I didn't . . . see any real difference in the delivered version a day or two later. . . . Basically what I was doing was placing on the record, okay, there's no factual error here, but in my professional judgment this creates an impression, clearly was intended to create an impression, that is incorrect. Whether it was on a terrorism connection thing, or something else, maybe on one of the weapons things. Intelligence officers are not presidential speech writers, nor should they pretend to be such. So I don't know what else you can do. But it is a source of frustration.[46]

Both Conflicts Lost Public Support after Becoming Protracted Wars

An obvious parallel between Iraq and Vietnam is the way public support, which initially supported each conflict, rapidly diminished over time as the wars became protracted, harming each president's political standing. During the first eight months in office prior to 9/11, Bush averaged a respectable 58 percent approval rating, which subsequently soared to 85 percent after the terror attacks. In fact, one CBS News poll showed Bush with an "approval rating of 90 percent—the highest of any president—following the Sept. 11 attacks."[47] Yet even early on, there were some warning signs. Though a *Washington Post*/ABC News poll in December 2001 gave Bush an approval rating of 86 percent, it also showed the public believed, by a two to one margin, the war on terror would only succeed with *both* the death or capture of bin

Laden *and* overthrow of Saddam (Rich 2006: 234). Thus, while White House efforts to link Saddam to the 9/11 attacks certainly resonated with the public, and eventually helped build the public case for war, it also tightly coupled the effectiveness of the Iraq campaign to the overall war on terror. This held the potential of being a positive thing if the war went well (given the difficulties in capturing bin Laden), but represented a highly dangerous move politically if the conflict went poorly.

Still, with the White House emphasizing the image of a decisive war president at every opportunity (Rich 2006; McClellan 2008), Bush's popularity was still at 71 percent the following year, giving him a first-term average approval rating of 64 percent, one of the best on record.[48] In retrospect, had the administration avoided the Pandora's box of Iraq, those approval ratings might have remained solid throughout Bush's tenure. Yet by mid-2004, as the war became more controversial and the insurgency showed no signs of abating, approval for the war barely held a majority at 51 percent—and was becoming increasingly problematic during an election year (McClellan 2008; Langer 2009). Support for both Bush and the war continued downward steadily after 2004, with the majority of Americans coming to believe it had not been worth fighting.[49] Eventually, Bush would leave office in 2008 as the most unpopular departing president in American history, with a *CBS News/ New York Times* poll showing a final approval rating of only 22 percent.[50] Indeed, Bush's final Gallup approval rating of 20 percent was the lowest for any outgoing president since the organization began asking the question in 1938 (seventy years earlier) and far exceeded the previous record holder's low score—Truman's during the Korean War at 32 percent.[51] Thus, while the "war president" image and the patriotic fervor following 9/11 no doubt buoyed Bush politically—greatly aiding his victory in 2004—these same elements (in light of Bush's mishandling of the war and misuse of intelligence) later boomeranged to result in a final Gallup poll showing 73 percent of the public disapproved of the way he had handled his job over his entire eight-year term.[52]

Similarly, for Johnson, the initial polling numbers were very good, with 74 percent of the public approving of LBJ's performance after Congress passed the Gulf of Tonkin Resolution in 1964.[53] And in terms of support for the war, Gallup in August 1965 (immediately after the massive forty-four battalion deployment of U.S. forces to South Vietnam) found 61 percent of the public felt it was not a mistake to become involved in Vietnam.[54] By May 1967, however, half of respondents felt the war had been a mistake—a figure that rose to 59 percent by March 1968 (when Johnson announced he would not run for reelection).[55] By 1968 Johnson's own personal approval numbers had fallen from a high of 74 percent in 1964 to only 35 percent.[56]

Like Bush, Johnson launched a public relations campaign to improve public support for the war, bringing Westmoreland home in mid-1967 to become the focal point of a campaign to convince the public we were winning the war—often using his infamous "body count" metric to demonstrate progress.[57] Westmoreland suggested U.S. troops would begin withdrawing from Vietnam "within two years or less," noting "we have reached an important point where the end begins to come into view."[58] Johnson also organized a number of political committees to promote the war's progress, such as the Committee for Peace with Freedom and the Vietnam Information Group, which monitored public support and sought to counter negative developments as they formed (Brigham 2006: 107). As Brigham (2006: 108) notes, in 1967 the White House "publicity machine went into high gear, promoting stories about PAVN/PLAF body counts and significant military victories in the Mekong Delta, the heart of the insurgency." For a time, it appeared the PR offensive had worked, with polls showing support for the war, though still below 50 percent, was holding steady—but then the disaster of the Tet Offensive in January 1968 occurred, an event completely discrediting all Johnson's efforts at positive spin (Brigham 2006: 108). It was a lesson in "the importance of not putting the best face on a military situation for political reasons."[59]

Bush engaged in any number of similar PR efforts to maintain support (and avoid blame) for the Iraq campaign, efforts that nevertheless failed to prevent the hemorrhaging of public support (Rich 2006; McClellan 2008). While Bush was not facing a large antiwar movement like Johnson—and enjoyed far more patriotic fervor post-9/11 from a public, press, and political system fearful of appearing unpatriotic by criticizing his wartime policy—these advantages would not be enough. Bush certainly had a far easier time with the press than Johnson, who seldom found a friendly face on network broadcasts during the late 1960s. But the sixties lacked an analog to the unrelenting support of the Fox News Network, which provided Bush with a constant stream of positive PR in its coverage, or the pressure applied to other networks by corporate bosses fearful of public backlash from critical coverage (Stelter 2008). The former head of *CBS News*, Andrew Heyward, acknowledged the trauma of 9/11 and ensuing sense of patriotism "muted press skepticism about the war," while Jessica Yellin of MSNBC noted journalists were "under enormous pressure from corporate executives, frankly, to make sure that this was a war presented in a way that was consistent with the patriotic fever in the nation" (Stelter 2008). Katie Couric, anchor of the *CBS Evening News*, remembers feeling pressure from government officials and corporate executives to cast the war in a positive light and "really squash any kind of dissent or any kind of questioning of it" (Stelter 2008). For Couric, the "lack of skepticism shown by journalists about the Bush administration's case for war amounted to one of the most embarrassing chapters in American journalism" (Stelter 2008).

The Wise Men Group of 1968 and the Iraq Study Group of 2006

Another interesting parallel between Iraq and Vietnam involves the eventual gathering of a group of outside foreign policy elites to assess each administration's war policies. For Bush, this took the form of a bipartisan, congressionally appointed panel, the Iraq Study Group, tasked with independently assessing the situation in Iraq and reporting back policy recommendations. Unlike Johnson's Wise Men group, which was organized by the White House to report directly to LBJ, the Iraq Study Group was an outside policy "competitor"—a group that from the very beginning posed a challenge to Bush's Iraq policy.[60] Though the ISG very studiously avoided "pulling back the curtain" on White House deliberations and avoided criticizing or assigning blame to the executive branch over the conduct of the war (much to the frustration of critics), the very need for an ISG in the first place was seen by many as an implicit criticism of the administration.[61]

For an administration already deep in blame-avoidance mode, the ISG represented, in essence, a political landmine that would eventually go off with the release of its final report[62]—especially if the findings differed significantly from the administration's preferred approach. For one former ISG member, while the comparison between the Wise Men and ISG is interesting, there was still one big difference: "The Wise Men were convened by or for him [Johnson], as opposed to this other group [the ISG], which was convened by Congress to force him [Bush] to take another look at Iraq policy. It's a very important distinction between the two I believe."[63]

For Johnson the Wise Men formed part of an intentional, well-planned political blame-avoidance strategy, whose clear goal was to deflect growing domestic criticism of the war by Congress and the public. It was already known beforehand (after careful checking by Johnson and Rostow) that most of the invited individuals had previously expressed strong support for the war (Preston 2001). It was assumed this handpicked group, once provided all the positive news by Westmoreland, would once again come out expressing strong and loyal support (Berman 1989; Preston 2001). This support would then be announced to the press and presented as an example of Johnson's openness to outside advice and willingness to consider alternatives. But more importantly, it would be external validation—by a group of objective, impartial senior foreign policy experts—of the merits of Johnson's strategy (McPherson 1972; Berman 1989; Clifford 1991; Preston 2001).[64] Bush certainly lacked the ability (with the ISG) to rig the game the way Johnson did by preventing access to the most pessimistic assessments (Berman 1989; Clifford 1991; Preston 2001). As McNamara later observed about his own critical memo calling for a change of direction and de-escalation of the war, and how Johnson limited its circulation to only critics (while preventing circulation to the Wise Men):

> He believed he knew how Fortas and Clifford would respond, and therefore he sent it to them to get on the record their response. . . . He sent it to Walt Rostow too . . . and I think he asked Walt to write a rebuttal for the file. . . . That was *typical* of the way Johnson reacted. . . . He was really thinking of his place in history and how history would look at this. . . . As for the Wise Men . . . my memo was dated November 1. I delivered it to [LBJ] on November 1. I believe the first meeting that fall of the Wise Men was in the evening of November 1 and it carried over to November 2. So he had ample opportunity to give it to the Wise Men. He did not. He did not disclose to them. . . . Had the Wise Men *had* a copy of my memo, I'm certain they would have come to a different conclusion. . . . Bundy, when he was notified of the Wise Men meeting and invited to attend . . . wrote Johnson a memo . . . stating that he believed Johnson was on the right course. And I'm sure Mac would not have written that memo . . . had he been exposed to . . . my memo.[65]

The first Wise Men meeting, just as Johnson hoped, came back with a strong endorsement. McNamara, recognizing there was no way to change LBJ's mind, tendered his resignation and was replaced Clark Clifford—who unbeknownst to Johnson had also experienced a change of heart and now had similar views to those of his predecessor (Clifford 1991; Preston 2001).[66] With the Tet Offensive and visual evidence on every television that the Viet Cong were not a spent force, contrary to Westmoreland's optimistic predictions, Johnson decided a second Wise Men meeting was needed to bolster support (Berman 1989; Preston 2001). This time, however, Clifford organized the sessions and made sure negative intelligence and analyses on the deteriorating situation in Vietnam were available to the group—resulting in their finding the war was unwinnable and a new strategy of de-escalation was required (Clifford 1991; Preston 2001). It was the end of the road for Johnson, who announced only weeks later he would not seek reelection. It had been a spectacular cascading effect—the Tet Offensive, an already unpopular war, the discrediting of the administration's optimistic claims about the war, and the final failure of its blame-avoidance strategy relying on the credibility of the Wise Men group.

For Bush, however, the ISG was not a pillar of its blame-avoidance strategy, nor was it at that point facing a situation analogous to Tet in Iraq. The administration still had allies in Congress who prevented the group from targeting White House failures of leadership or misuses of intelligence, and it continued to have the unquestioned loyalty of significant segments of the national media (including Fox News and the conservative radio networks). It was support LBJ could only have dreamed of. And while Bush strongly disagreed with the Iraq Study Group's issued findings (such as the need to open negotiations with Iran and Syria and to begin reducing ground forces), it also proposed a lifeline the White House firmly grasped. As former members of the ISG would later describe, though a reduction in forces was being recommended, there was also support for what would become the surge (a temporary increase to stabilize the country to better allow a handover to the Iraqis).[67] Ironically, while Bush couldn't be seen (for blame-avoidance purposes) to uncritically accept all of the ISG's recommendations, he eventually adopted most of them (including negotiations with Iran and Syria and the surge).[68]

Interestingly, both of the outside groups ended up essentially providing Bush and Johnson with potential off-ramps from their existing policies—and the chance to change policy direction. For Johnson, it was the option of following the Wise Men's recommendation to de-escalate the war, institute a bombing halt, and begin negotiations with the North (Preston 2001). For Bush, who was looking for one last shot at salvaging his disastrous management of the war, the ISG's mention of a temporary surge to stabilize the situation was seized upon to justify his desire (against public opposition) to send more troops to Iraq.[69]

Final Reflections on Vietnam-Iraq Similarities

There are a number of other similarities between Iraq and Vietnam that bear at least passing mention. For example, much as the Nixon administration later pursued a policy of "Vietnamization," in which responsibility for managing the war and handling security was slowly transferred back to the South Vietnamese (Laird 2005: 28–29), the essential logic of the Bush surge in Iraq was that of a modern-day, "Iraqization" of the conflict. As the security situation stabilized and Iraqi forces were shown to be able to maintain the situation, U.S. forces were to be withdrawn from the country. Yet, as the promise of downsizing U.S. forces in Iraq became linked to pursuing the surge, it put tremendous pressure on Bush to withdraw troops from Iraq as soon as security improved. In this respect, the dynamic was similar to concerns Kissinger expressed to Nixon in his "salted peanut" memo of September 1969, where he warned the more the fight was turned over to the South Vietnamese, the more it would increase pressure to end the war because the public wants a quick resolution: "Withdrawal of U.S. troops will become like salted peanuts to the American public; the more U.S. troops come home, the more will be demanded" (Woodward 2006: 409). In Iraq a very similar pressure to remove U.S. forces as soon as possible emerged, especially as violence began to subside.

There was also an echo of Johnson's and Nixon's rhetoric over Vietnam in Bush's over Iraq. In November 1969, for example, Nixon charged the antiwar movement with being "irresponsible" and called on the "great silent majority" to support Vietnam in its hour of need, warning, "North Vietnam cannot humiliate the United States. Only Americans can do that" (Brigham 2006: 112). This was not unlike the rhetoric espoused by Bush questioning the "patriotism" of critics who challenged his war on terror policies, or the charge that opponents were "sending the wrong signals to the enemy" (Woodward 2002, 2004, 2006; Bamford 2005; Isikoff and Corn 2006). For Wilkerson, it was further evidence of how U.S. foreign policy, more and more, has become based on domestic politics—noting Bush's rhetoric surrounding the war on terror of "building terrorism into a politics of fear" to maintain political power was "not unlike what Joseph McCarthy did during the early years of the Cold War."[70] In fact, if one traces Bush's own statements regarding the situation in Iraq, the progression over time of his blame-avoidance strategy becomes clearer, as new explanations are provided regarding the growing violence, coupled with justifications for "staying the course":

April 13, 2004—"It's not a civil war. It's not a popular uprising. Most of Iraq is relatively stable."

December 18, 2005—"Not only can we win the war in Iraq, we are winning the war in Iraq. . . . To retreat before victory would be an act of recklessness and dishonor and I will not allow it."

September 11, 2006—"Whatever mistakes have been made in Iraq, the worst mistake would be to think that if we pulled out, the terrorists would leave us alone. They will not leave us alone. They will follow us. The safety of America depends on the outcome of the battle in the streets of Baghdad."

January 10, 2007—"The situation in Iraq is unacceptable to the American people—and it is unacceptable to me. . . . Where mistakes have been made, the responsibility rests with me. It is clear that we need to change our strategy in Iraq."

March 19, 2007—"It can be tempting to look at the challenges in Iraq and conclude our best option is to pack up and go home. That may be satisfying in the short run, but I believe the consequences for American security would be devastating."[71]

For the White House during Vietnam, it was the "global war against communism" framing the issues, a struggle against a ruthless opponent who would take any opportunity to attack the freedom of the Western world. Forty years later, it was a "global war on terror" framing the issues, with an opponent perceived to be equally ruthless in attacking the Western world. Unlike the Cold War, which had a clearly defined bad guy in the USSR, the war on terror became a bushel basket into which any actor disliked by Washington was cast (Al Qaeda, Saddam, the "axis of evil" states, etc.). This perception by policy makers that Vietnam and Iraq were the very center stage of those global conflicts was yet another clear similarity across the two cases.

While Bush did not lose as many staff to resignation as Johnson did (with Moyers, Ball, and McNamara being most prominent), it is known that Haass left his position at State and Clarke resigned as counterterrorism czar due to their disagreements over Bush's policies (Alfonsi 2006: 9). In both inner circles, there were also a handful of dissenters (whether over Vietnam or Iraq) who sought to argue against the war or modify the extremes being adopted. In Vietnam it was Humphrey, Ball, Moyers, and much later McNamara and Clifford who battled against the core advisers surrounding Johnson. In the Bush administration, aside from less senior officials like Clarke and Haass, few directly opposed the push toward war, though Powell and Armitage often sought (to little avail) to moderate policy. Concerning Vietnam and Iraq, dissenters were marginalized, not invited to key meetings, and steamrolled by the dominant group. It points to a weakness, or dysfunction, in how each president's advisory system functioned.

There was also a similarity between Vietnam and Iraq in how officers reacted to the civilian leadership. As Wilkerson recalled, former Israeli prime minister Ariel Sharon once opined that all "generals lie to themselves when they lie to politicians," and he believed he would be effective as prime minister because he would "know when they are lying to me."[72] For Wilkerson, Sharon's observation brought home to him a further insight regarding the comparison between Iraq and Vietnam—the tendency among those in the military to emphasize a "can-do attitude" toward superiors despite their doubts:

> I mean, there is a tendency. It's part of this "can-do attitude" of the military, which got us in trouble in Vietnam and got us in trouble initially in Iraq. They don't want to acknowledge problems, because you win stars, you win promotions, by overcoming, by accepting. So I think that was very, very common in both cases.

Finally, both conflicts became lengthy, protracted wars, lasting far longer, and becoming more costly, than either administration ever imagined. In this, both the Bush and Johnson administrations fell victim to over-optimism, to ignoring (as many political leaders throughout history have done) the age-old lessons of war. In *On War*, Clausewitz (1985) observed that "everything in war is simple" but that the "simplest things are difficult"—a warning to students of war that factors like "friction," the "fogs of war," or even pure chance often stand in the way of clear implementation of war plans. It was a call to never underestimate the difficulties of the task at hand during wartime or assume the road will be an easy one. It was a warning ignored by generals and politicians in World War I, who assumed the war would be over in only a few months, much as Athenian leaders during the Peloponnesian War believed the war with Sparta would last but three years (instead of the twenty-seven it ran). By finding themselves in protracted campaigns of occupation, Johnson and Bush demonstrated the truth behind Sun Tzu's (1971) dictum that there had "never been a protracted war from which a state had benefited," and such conflicts should be avoided at all costs since they weaken the state, drain the treasury, and destroy morale. Each of the conflicts was ruinously expensive. By February 2007, economist Joseph Stiglitz put the total cost of Iraq at $700 billion in direct costs, and more than twice that in indirect expenditures, leading to a total of more than $2 trillion (Stiglitz and Bilmes 2008). Even if one only counts the direct costs appropriated so far (and ignores all the indirect or future costs), by the end of Bush's second term, Iraq had surpassed the total cost of Vietnam ($686 billion in inflation-adjusted dollars) to become (at $694 billion in April 2009) the second most expensive war in U.S. history (after World War II at $4 trillion).[73]

Essentially, both administrations fell into an "over-optimism" trap—one believing U.S. forces could stabilize the situation in Vietnam, the other holding they would be greeted as liberators by Iraqis, who would quickly take over security, allow troops to withdraw, and pay for all the war costs through their oil revenues. In each case, policy makers quickly found themselves entrapped in the quicksand of their policies as each conflict dragged on, becoming more and more dependent upon blame-avoidance strategies.

CONCLUSIONS AND IMPLICATIONS FOR FUTURE POLICY MAKERS

Throughout this volume, we have explored the potential fit of the Vietnam analogy to the war in Iraq. And while there are many areas where the analogy was an imperfect match (which is to be expected, given any two historical cases are never going to be completely identical), there were, nevertheless, a number of important parallels. But it is worth repeating: though suggesting there are substantial areas of "fit" across the two cases, it must be understood that this book in no way suggests *Iraq is just like Vietnam*—merely that in some important respects, there are some common links useful in both understanding the conflicts and guiding future policy makers. Analogies are always best used only as heuristics, to highlight areas of comparison across cases, rather than as exact guides (Tetlock and Belkin 1996).

The clearest fit across the two cases was the leadership styles of the two presidents and how their advisory systems gathered and used information and advice. It is also perhaps one of the most important areas holding implications for future policy makers. For leaders with relatively closed advisory systems, which are very selective in how they gather information and effectively shut out dissenting views, the dangers of stumbling into complex, protracted conflicts are far more pronounced than those with more open advisory systems. In both the Bush and Johnson inner circles, a dominant group of like-minded advisers framed the policy problem and potential options for the president—with opponents being dismissed as being disloyal or not part of the team. This dynamic was compounded by presidents who were personally less sensitive to context, more absolute and black-and-white in their views of the world, and lacked foreign policy expertise of their own. For such leaders, their delegation to subordinates of policy formulation, and their dependence upon group "experts" to understand the environment, made them far more vulnerable to one dominant in-group view. With such styles, there is also a marked tendency to not have these dominant in-group views countered during policy debates by alternative or dissenting viewpoints. This was certainly the case during the Vietnam policy debates, just as it was during Bush's deliberations over Iraq, from the aftermath of 9/11 on through to the actual invasion in March 2003. *Leaders matter!* Their styles and personalities play a major role in how their advisory systems and inner circles function—and how they deliberate over policy choices. Indeed, across interviews with many senior advisers who worked for both Kennedy and Johnson, the author has yet to find one who argues Kennedy, had he been in Johnson's place in 1965, would have made the same decisions to intervene in Vietnam or pursued the policy directions LBJ later did.[74] Similarly, it is hard to find many who worked in the Bush administration who believe a Clinton or Gore administration would have pursued the same policies in Iraq and Afghanistan.[75] As Wilkerson observed:

> I don't think Clinton would have gone to war with Iraq post-9/11. I don't think *any* president would have gone to war with Iraq post-9/11! I think a president that has his act together, or her act together, would have gone after Afghanistan, and gone after it tooth-and-nail until bin Laden was captured, until most of his lieutenants were captured. Al-Zawahiri, for example, was dead or swinging.[76]

One implication for those serving as advisers to future leaders is the importance of recognizing that leader styles sharing similar weaknesses to those of

Bush and Johnson will find it very difficult to recognize or adapt to changing policy environments and are more likely to become trapped in protracted conflicts, allowing policy to continue along a similar path even as available feedback (if gathered) shows deteriorating situations. Those who worked for Kennedy routinely noted he was very sensitive to the broader environment around him and would become deeply uncomfortable if all the advisers within his inner circle were agreeing with him or arguing the same point (Preston 2001). He would set up groups to play devil's advocate, to argue against the dominant group position—and not just to create a show of being open-minded (as Bush and Johnson often did) but rather as a real attempt to flesh out the pros and cons of a policy (Preston 2001). Sensitive leaders who search broadly for information and feedback from the environment have their antennae up and, as a result, are more likely to pick up on negative information, intelligence warnings, or other indicators policy is not moving according to plan. They are more adaptive to their environment, more able to modify their policies to respond to changing circumstances (Preston 2001). Because of this, they are far more likely to be able to recognize and adjust to the constantly changing nature of war as described by Sun Tzu (1971):

> An army may be likened to water, for just as flowing water avoids the heights and hastens to the lowlands, so an army avoids strength and strikes weakness. And as water shapes its flow in accordance with the ground, so an army manages its victory in accordance with the situation of the enemy. And as water has no constant form, there are in war no constant conditions. Thus, one able to gain the victory by modifying his tactics in accordance with the enemy situation may be said to be divine.

Less sensitive leaders who are more rigidly focused on their preferred policy directions are more prone to selectively use intelligence to support their policies—and view dissent as disloyalty (whether it be inner-circle advisors or actors like the CIA or State Department). The unfortunate reality in Washington is when such dynamics are in place, often those advising presidents "go with the flow" and "don't rock the boat," given all the disincentives flowing from such actions. Yet whether it be "silent generals" during Vietnam, "cowed" ones over Iraq, or inner circles that dismiss negative reporting from the intelligence community as if it were enemy broadcasts, the end result is a dysfunction within the proper workings of the advice and intelligence networks serving the White House. If these tendencies to cut out dissent or "bad news" are not counteracted by influential advisers around the president (or by an enlightened president himself), a "feel good" feedback loop develops, creating group pathologies and faulty decision making greatly increasing the chances of policy fiascos ('t Hart et. al. 1997; Preston and 't Hart 1999; Boin et. al 2010).[77] Inner-circle advisers have the ability to either compensate for a leader's style weaknesses or exacerbating them. As Powell and McNamara both discovered, sometimes the leader won't listen to counsel or allow them to compensate for too narrow a debate. But in cases where they can have an impact, such advice can help leaders avoid becoming trapped in their own narrow perspectives and open the advisory process to greater amounts of information, both pro and con.

Further, just as the styles of presidents make a big difference for policy—influencing how much information is sought out, whether intelligence is used properly, and the types of advice that receive a hearing—the blame-avoidance strategies selected by leaders also play a large role in policy outcomes. Certainly a major lesson to be drawn from both Iraq and Vietnam is a warning for leaders not to become trapped by their own blame-avoidance strategies. In other words, while many blame-avoidance strategies can be used by policy makers to deflect blame away from themselves or their policies, in order to make situations seem better and less dire than they really are, it is important for leaders not to fall into the trap of "believing their own cover stories" and failing to adapt or change failing policy positions.

Obviously, the political environment any White House operates in often necessitates the use of blame-avoidance strategies. It goes without saying that "Got You" is a perennial Washington pastime between political opponents. At the same time, however, it is important for policy makers to recognize relying too much on blame-avoidance strategies can sometimes stabilize political situations temporarily, thereby allowing them to proceed even further down a given path than they would otherwise be able to do, regardless of the wisdom of doing so. Though it is a difficult choice to make, sometimes taking some political lumps by reconsidering policy positions or admitting mistakes—and avoiding the seduction of shifting blame—is preferable to a policy of denial and positive messaging that only results in becoming bogged down in an even more intractable problem.

Kennedy again provides a vivid example. After the failure of the Bay of Pigs in 1961, rather than seeking to rescue the failed policy with a costly invasion of Cuba, he pulled the plug on the operation and took personal responsibility for the fiasco. It was an example of political courage, but also one of pragmatism. It was a recognition that blame-avoidance strategies, like the lies we tell children to avoid, often grow bigger and bigger over time—and more impossible to control. And when these blame-avoidance strategies eventually fail, like a snowballing lie eventually backfiring on the teller, the damage to a leader's credibility and political viability is often catastrophic. Moreover, the policy or political situation being protected or concealed by such strategies may actually have reached the point of failure due to a lack of corrective actions that might otherwise have been taken. For leaders, these consequences can be immense. For Johnson, it resulted in a failed presidency, the collapse of his Great Society dreams, and a hobbling of U.S. foreign policy activism for decades. In the case of Bush, the insistence on linking Iraq to the 9/11 attacks and the eventual war resulted in his own failed presidency, a diminishment of America's prestige and reputation worldwide, and (through its policy of neglect) a prolonged conflict in Afghanistan that now shows no signs of ebbing.

Indeed, just as the "ghosts of Vietnam" haunted American policy makers for decades, it is likely the "ghosts of Iraq" will haunt not only the current Obama administration but its future successors in their efforts to tamp down the growing instabilities now spreading from Afghanistan into Pakistan, creating one of the most difficult foreign policy challenges faced by the United States in the past seventy years. Bush, like the Pandora of mythology, fell into a trap—brought about by his own style, uses of information and intelligence, and blame-avoidance strategies—unleashing unforeseen miseries and evils upon the world. And like Pandora, at the end of the day, future policy makers will be left with only the "hope" that the situation will eventually get better—and by using information and intelligence more wisely, and blame-avoidance strategies more responsibly, the trap set for Pandora may at last be avoided.

Notes

PREFACE

1. See also, Billings-Yun, Melanie. *Decision Against War: Eisenhower and Dien Bien Phu, 1954.* New York: Columbia University Press, 1988.

2. Off the record conversations with Obama administration officials and government personnel who have had direct access to the President and his inner circle officials, and who have direct insight into how information is received and processed.

3. The Hermann LTA technique has been incorporated into a highly sophisticated, automated computer 'expert system' called *Profiler-Plus*. This expert system, developed by Michael D. Young at Social Science Automation, Inc. in Columbus, Ohio (http://socialscience.net/Default.aspx) allows the user to rapidly code millions of words from scanned texts of leader interviews and speeches to develop detailed personal profiles across a number of measured traits (need for power, conceptual complexity, self-confidence, locus of control, in-group bias, task/interpersonal orientation, distrust of others). Capable of employing several different types of assessment techniques (in addition to LTA), the *Profiler Plus* system eliminates intercoder reliability problems and allows comparison of leader scores to a population of nearly three hundred world leaders.

4. Goodwin, Doris Kearns. *Team of Rivals: The Political Genius of Abraham Lincoln.* New York: Simon and Schuster, 2005.

5. Off the record conversations with Obama administration officials and government personnel who have had direct access to the President and his inner circle officials, and who have direct insight into how information is received and processed.

CHAPTER 1

1. Mark Mazzetti, "Intelligence Chief Says Al Qaeda Improves Ability to Strike in U.S.," *New York Times*, February 6, 2008, A1 and A12.

2. Ben Macintyre, "Bush Will Bring the Troops Home," *Times Online* (London), August 22, 2000, http://www.timesonline.co.uk/tol/news/world/us_and_americas/article988745.ece.

CHAPTER 2

1. The Hermann LTA technique is incorporated into a highly sophisticated, automated computer "expert system" called Profiler Plus. This system, developed by Michael Young at Social Science Automation Inc. in Columbus, Ohio (http://socialscience.net/Default.aspx), allows users to rapidly code millions of words from scanned texts of leader interviews and speeches to develop detailed profiles across a number of measured traits (need for power, conceptual complexity, self-confidence, locus of control, in-group bias, task/interpersonal orientation, distrust of others). Capable of employing several types of assessment techniques (in addition to LTA), the Profiler Plus system eliminates intercoder reliability problems and allows comparison of leader scores to a population of nearly three hundred world leaders.

2. Johnson's LTA scores on need for power and self-confidence are the highest of any modern American president and are considered high when compared to a set of 230 world leaders. Bush, on the other hand, showed relatively lower need for power. Johnson scored high in tasks over interpersonal needs, while Bush is high on interpersonal focus. Both share low complexity scores and were relatively inexperienced in foreign affairs.

3. Richard Armitage interview with the author, December 15, 2008.

4. Paul Krugman, "Don't Blame Bush," *New York Times*, May 18, 2007, A27.

5. Richard Armitage interview with the author, December 15, 2008.

6. Ibid.

7. Ibid.

8. Lawrence Wilkerson interview with the author, June 26, 2008.

9. Ibid.

10. Ibid.

11. Richard Armitage interview with the author, December 15, 2008.

12. "Ex-Aides Say Bush Never Recovered From Katrina," *ABC News*, December 29, 2008, http://abcnews.go.com/id-6545048.

13. Interviews with multiple senior Bush administration policy makers and staff who requested anonymity.

14. Interviews with multiple senior Bush administration policy makers and staff who requested anonymity, as well as briefers from various government departments and agencies.

15. Mike Allen and David S. Broder, "Bush's Leadership Style: Decisive or Simplistic?" *Washington Post*, August 30, 2004, A01.

16. David Kay interview with the author, September 11, 2008.

17. Ibid.

18. Richard Armitage interview with the author, December 15, 2008.

19. Off-the-record interview with senior Bush administration official.

20. Lawrence Wilkerson interview with the author, June 26, 2008.

21. Ibid.

22. Ibid.

23. Off-the-record interview with senior Bush administration official.

24. Ibid.

25. Ibid.

26. Richard Armitage interview with the author, December 15, 2008.

27. Ibid.

28. Ibid.

29. Lawrence Wilkerson interview with the author, June 26, 2008.

30. Interviews by the author with Robert McNamara and McGeorge Bundy.

31. Dana Milbank, "The Chairman and the CEO: In Incoming Corporate White House, Bush Is Seen Running Board, Cheney Effecting Policy," *Washington Post*, December 24, 2000, A01.

32. Ibid.

33. Off-the-record interview with senior Bush administration official.

34. Ibid.

35. Ibid.

36. Richard Armitage interview with the author, December 15, 2008.

37. Ibid.

38. Lawrence Wilkerson interview with the author, June 26, 2008.

39. Off-the-record interviews with senior Bush administration officials.

40. David Kay interview with the author, September 11, 2008.

41. Ibid.

42. Off-the-record interviews with senior Bush administration officials.

43. Lawrence Wilkerson interview with the author, June 26, 2008.

44. Off-the-record interviews with senior Bush administration officials.

45. Lawrence Wilkerson interview with the author, June 26, 2008.

46. Richard Armitage interview with the author, December 15, 2008.

47. Off-the-record interviews with senior Bush administration officials.

48. Off-the-record interviews with intelligence analysts and senior Bush administration intelligence officials.

49. David Kay interview with the author, September 11, 2008.

50. Ibid.

51. Ibid.

52. Off-the-record interviews with intelligence analysts and senior Bush administration intelligence officials.

53. Lawrence Wilkerson interview with the author, June 26, 2008.

54. Off-the-record interviews with senior Bush administration officials.

55. Ibid.

56. Off-the-record interviews with senior Defense Department officials and military officers.

57. Ibid.

58. Off-the-record interview with government consultant.

59. Off-the-record interview with senior Defense Department official.

60. Off-the-record interview with senior Bush administration official.

61. Off-the-record interviews with senior Defense Department officials and military officers.

62. Ibid.

63. Ibid.

64. Off-the-record interviews with senior Bush administration officials.

65. Lawrence Wilkerson interview with the author, June 26, 2008.

66. Off-the-record interviews with senior Bush administration officials.

67. Richard Armitage interview with the author, December 15, 2008.

68. Off-the-record interview with senior Bush administration official.

69. Ibid.

70. Lawrence Wilkerson interview with the author, June 26, 2008.

71. Paul Pillar interview with the author, June 18, 2008.

72. Ibid.

73. David Kay interview with the author, September 11, 2008.

74. Ibid.

75. Ibid.

76. Ibid.

77. Lawrence Wilkerson interview with the author, June 26, 2008.

78. David Kay interview with the author, September 11, 2008.

79. Off-the-record interview with senior Bush administration official.

80. Off-the-record interviews with senior Bush administration officials.

81. Off-the-record interview with senior Bush administration official.

82. Lawrence Wilkerson interview with the author, June 26, 2008.

83. Ibid.

84. Author interviews with Arthur Schlesinger Jr., George Christian, Harry McPherson, McGeorge Bundy, Clark Clifford, Paul Nitze, Paul Warnke, George Elsey, Walt Rostow, and Robert McNamara.

85. Author interviews with Arthur Schlesinger Jr., Harry McPherson, and McGeorge Bundy.

86. Ibid.

87. Off-the-record conversations by the author with many friends and associates of Powell in 2000 and 2001.

88. Lawrence Wilkerson interview with the author, June 26, 2008.

89. Off-the-record interview with senior Bush administration official.

90. Richard Armitage interview with the author, December 15, 2008.

91. Lawrence Wilkerson interview with the author, June 26, 2008.

92. Ibid.

93. Off-the-record interview with senior Bush administration official.

94. Author interviews with Arthur Schlesinger Jr., McGeorge Bundy, Harry McPherson, Paul Warnke, and George Christian.

95. Author interview with McGeorge Bundy.

CHAPTER 3

1. Polls pre- and post-9/11 show President Bush in the low to mid-fifties in terms of public support of his performance in the White House, numbers that would skyrocket in the aftermath of the terror attacks. ABC News/Washington Post polling pre-9/11 showed Bush at 55 percent, rising to 92 percent two weeks later; CNN had Bush at 55 percent pre-9/11 and 88 percent post; NBC News/Wall Street Journal at 50 percent pre, 88 percent post; and Gallup/USA Today showed Bush at 51 percent pre and 90 percent post. See http://www.pollingreport.com/BushJob1.htm for an overview and detailed reporting of all polling numbers across various polls throughout the Bush presidency.

2. Off-the-record interviews with senior Bush administration officials.

3. Off-the-record interview with senior participant in WMD Commission.

4. Ibid.

5. Ibid.

6. Ibid.

7. Ibid.

8. Ibid.

9. Off-the-record interview with senior participant in the Iraq Study Group.

10. Ibid.

11. Ibid.

12. Lawrence Wilkerson interview with the author, June 26, 2008.

13. Ibid.

14. Ibid.

15. Ibid.

16. Off-the-record interviews with senior Bush administration officials.

17. Kathy Frankovic, "Polls, Truth Sometimes at Odds," *CBS News*, September 12, 2007, http://www.cbsnews.com/stories/2007/09/12/opinion/pollpositions/main 3253552.shtml?tag=mncol;lst;1.

18. Lawrence Wilkerson interview with the author, June 26, 2008; off-the-record interviews with senior Bush administration officials.

19. Ibid.

20. Jim Rutenberg and David E. Sanger, "Bush Aides Seek Alternatives to Iraq Study Group's Proposals, Calling Them Impractical," *New York Times*, October 10, 2006, A18.

21. Lawrence Wilkerson and Richard Armitage interviews with the author, June 26, 2008; off-the-record interviews with senior Bush administration officials.

22. Off-the-record interviews with senior Bush administration officials.

23. Ibid.

24. Ibid.

25. Off-the-record interview with senior intelligence official.

26. Off-the-record interview with senior Bush administration officials.

27. Off-the-record interview with senior intelligence official.

28. Paul Pillar interview with the author, July 1, 2008.

29. Off-the-record interviews with former intelligence officials and senior Bush administration officials.

30. Ibid.

31. Ibid.

32. Ibid.

33. Paul Pillar interview with the author, July 1, 2008.

34. Off-the-record interviews with senior Bush administration officials.

35. Author interviews with George Elsey, Clark Clifford, Paul Nitze, Paul Warnke, George Christian, McGeorge Bundy, Robert McNamara, Walt Rostow, Richard Neustadt, Arthur Schlesinger Jr., Harry McPherson, as well as numerous off-the-record conversations with former Clinton and Bush administration officials.

36. Off-the-record conversations with individuals working within the Obama administration.

37. Off-the-record interviews with senior Bush administration officials.

38. Paul Pillar interview with the author, July 1, 2008.

39. Off-the-record interview with senior Bush administration official.

40. Ibid.

41. Paul Pillar interview with the author, July 1, 2008.

42. Ibid.

43. Ibid.

44. Jim Rutenberg, "In Advance of Speech, Bush Seeks Iraq Advice," *New York Times*, December 12, 2006, A14.

45. Gardiner Harris, "Surgeon General Sees 4-Year Term as Compromised," *New York Times*, July 11, 2007, A1.

46. Paul Pillar interview with the author, July 1, 2008.

47. Ibid.

48. Off-the-record interview with senior Bush administration official.

49. Interview by the author with George Christian, August 4, 1993.

50. Ibid.

51. Off-the-record interview with senior intelligence official in the Bush administration.

52. Ibid.

53. Off-the-record interviews with former intelligence officials and senior Bush administration officials.

54. Off-the-record interview with senior intelligence official in the Bush administration.

CHAPTER 4

1. David E. Sanger, "Bush, Focusing on Terrorism, Says Secure U.S. Is Top Priority," *New York Times*, January 30, 2002, A1.

2. Thom Shanker and David D. Sanger, "U.S. Envisions Blueprint on Iraq Including Big Invasion Next Year," *New York Times*, April 28, 2002, A1 and A18.

3. Lawrence Wilkerson interview with the author, June 26, 2008.

4. Off-the-record interview with senior Bush administration official.

5. Ibid.

6. Off-the-record interviews and conversations with intelligence and defense analysts, and other senior Bush administration officials.

7. Ibid.

8. Paul Pillar interview with the author, June 18, 2008.

9. Dana Milbank, "Cheney Says Iraqi Strike Is Justified," *Washington Post*, August 27, 2002.

10. Ibid.

11. George W. Bush speech on October 7, 2002, in Cincinnati, Ohio, http://georgewbush-whitehouse.archives.gov/news/releases/2002/10/20021007-8.html.

12. Off-the-record interview with senior Bush administration intelligence official.

13. Ibid.

14. Ibid.

15. Ibid.

16. Elisabeth Bumiller, "White House Cuts Estimate of Cost of War with Iraq," *New York Times*, December 31, 2002, A1 and A10.

17. Paul Pillar interview with the author, June 18, 2008.

18. Off-the-record interviews with senior Bush administration intelligence officials.

19. Ibid.

20. Ibid.

21. Lawrence Wilkerson interview with the author, June 26, 2008.

22. Off-the-record interviews with senior Bush administration officials and intelligence officials.

23. Ibid.

24. "Text of President Bush's 2003 State of the Union Address," *Washington Post*, January 28, 2003, http://www.washingtonpost.com/wp-srv/onpolitics/transcripts/bushtext_012803.html.

25. Paul Pillar interview with the author, June 18, 2008.

26. "Text of President Bush's 2003 State of the Union Address," *Washington Post*, January 28, 2003, http://www.washingtonpost.com/wp-srv/onpolitics/transcripts/bushtext_012803.html.

27. Ibid.

28. Lawrence Wilkerson interview with the author, June 26, 2008.

29. Ibid.

30. Ibid.

31. Off-the-record interviews with senior Bush administration officials and intelligence officials.

32. Richard Armitage interview with the author, December 15, 2008.

33. David Kay interview with the author, September 11, 2008.

34. Paul Pillar interview with the author, June 18, 2008.

35. Ibid.

36. Lawrence Wilkerson interview with the author, June 26, 2008.

37. Ibid.

38. Richard Armitage interview with the author, December 15, 2008.

39. Ibid.

40. Ibid.

41. Lawrence Wilkerson interview with the author, June 26, 2008.

42. Paul Pillar interview with the author, June 18, 2008.

43. Lawrence Wilkerson interview with the author, June 26, 2008.

44. Ibid.

45. Off-the-record interview with senior Bush administration official.

46. Off-the-record interviews and conversations with senior Bush administration officials and intelligence officials.

47. Lawrence Wilkerson interview with the author, June 26, 2008.

48. David Kay interview with the author, September 11, 2008.

49. Lawrence Wilkerson interview with the author, June 26, 2008.

50. Paul Pillar interview with the author, June 18, 2008.

51. Ibid.

52. Ibid.

53. Ibid.

54. Ibid.

55. Ibid.

56. Off-the-record interview with senior Bush administration intelligence official.

57. Richard Armitage interview with the author, December 15, 2008.

58. Ibid.

59. Paul Pillar interview with the author, June 18, 2008.

60. Richard Armitage interview with the author, December 15, 2008.

61. Ibid.

62. Ibid.

63. Off-the-record interview with senior Bush administration intelligence official.

64. Ibid.

65. Ibid.

66. Jim Rutenberg, "General Defends Rumsfeld, with a Caveat," *New York Times*, April 17, 2006.

67. Richard Armitage interview with the author, December 15, 2008.

68. Ibid.

69. "Text of President Bush's 2003 State of the Union Address," *Washington Post*, January 28, 2003, http://www.washingtonpost.com/wp-srv/onpolitics/transcripts/bushtext_012803.html.

70. "Bush and Iraq: Follow the Yellow Cake Road," *Time*, July 9, 2003, http://www.time.com/time/columnist/karon/article/0,9565,463779,00.html.

71. David Johnston, "In '04 Interview, Cheney Denied Role in CIA Leak," *New York Times*, October 31, 2009.

72. "Libby: White House Sacrificed Him for Rove," *MSNBC*, January 23, 2007, http://www.msnbc.msn.com/id/16770023/.

73. Ibid.

74. Ibid.

75. Jim VandeHei and Walter Pincus, "Role of Rove, Libby in CIA Leak Case Clearer: Bush and Cheney Aides' Testimony Contradicts Earlier White House Statement," *Washington Post*, October 2, 2005; R. Jeffrey Smith, "Novak Accuses Plame Source of Distortion," *Washington Post*, September 14, 2006; "Novak: Rove Confirmed Plame's Identity," *CNN*, http://articles.cnn.com/2006-07-11/politics/cia .leak_1_robert-novak-randall-samborn-leak-probe?_s=PM:POLITICS.

76. "Libby: White House Sacrificed Him for Rove," *MSNBC*, January 23, 2007, http://www.msnbc.msn.com/id/16770023/.

77. David Johnston, "In '04 Interview, Cheney Denied Role in CIA Leak," *New York Times*, October 31, 2009.

78. Ibid.

CHAPTER 5

1. Off-the-record interview with senior State Department official.

2. Ibid.

3. Richard Armitage interview with the author, December 15, 2008.

4. "The Truth about PM's 'Special Relationship' with Bush," *Independent* (London), May 19, 2007, http://www.independent.co.uk/news/world/americas/the-truth -about-pms-special-relationship-with-bush-449524.html.

5. Nicholas Watt, "Blair Knew U.S. Had No Post-War Plan for Iraq," *Guardian* (London), June 17, 2007, 1.

6. Ibid.

7. Ibid.

8. Off-the-record interviews with senior Bush administration officials and intelligence officials.

9. Kenneth T. Walsh, "A Case of Confidence: The President Is Gambling That His Audacious Style of Governing Will Pay Off," *U.S. News & World Report*, November 17, 2003, 20–31.

10. David Kay interview with the author, September 11, 2008.

11. Ibid.

12. Ibid.

13. Ibid.

14. Ibid.

15. Ibid.

16. Ibid.

17. Off-the-record interview with former member of weapons inspection team in Iraq.

18. Ibid.

19. David Kay interview with the author, September 11, 2008.

20. Ibid.

21. Ibid.

22. Ibid.

23. Ibid.
24. Ibid.
25. Ibid.
26. Ibid.
27. Ibid.
28. Ibid.
29. Ibid.
30. Ibid.
31. Ibid.
32. Ibid.
33. Ibid.
34. Ibid.
35. Ibid.
36. Ibid.
37. Ibid.
38. Off-the-record interviews with former members of the Silberman-Robb WMD Commission.
39. David Kay interview with the author, September 11, 2008.
40. *NewsHour with Jim Lehrer*, January 9, 2004, http://www.pbs.org/newshour/bb/middle_east/jan-june04/wmd_01-09.html.
41. For example, aside from the Scarborough (2004) book, which is a highly flattering portrait of Rumsfeld from a supporter of the war, one also has more critical pieces, such as the episode from the PBS documentary series *Frontline* titled "Rumsfeld's War." See http://www.pbs.org/wgbh/pages/frontline/shows/pentagon/view/.
42. Off-the-record interview with senior State and Defense Department officials; Richard Armitage interview with the author, December 15, 2008.
43. "Rumsfeld Blames Iraq Problems on 'Pockets of Dead-enders,'" *USA Today*, June 18, 2003, http://www.usatoday.com/news/world/iraq/2003-06-18-rumsfeld_x.htm.
44. Off-the-record interview with senior State, intelligence community, and Defense officials.
45. See the original *60 Minutes* report on Abu Ghraib, http://www.cbsnews.com/stories/2004/04/27/60II/main614063.shtml; also Seymour M. Hersh, "Torture at Abu Ghraib," *New Yorker*, May 10, 2004, http://www.newyorker.com/archive/2004/05/10/040510fa_fact.
46. For details of the Abu Ghraib abuses, see the *Taguba Report Annexes (AR 15-6 Investigation of the 800th Military Police Brigade)*, http://www.dod.gov/pubs/foi/detainees/taguba/.
47. Elisabeth Bumiller and Richard W. Stevenson, "Rumsfeld Chastised by President for His Handling of Iraq Scandal," *New York Times*, May 5, 2004, A1.
48. Ibid.
49. Seymour M. Hersh, "Torture at Abu Ghraib," *New Yorker*, May 10, 2004, http://www.newyorker.com/archive/2004/05/10/040510fa_fact.

50. For details of the Abu Ghraib abuses, see the *Taguba Report Annexes (AR 15-6 Investigation of the 800ᵗʰ Military Police Brigade)*, http://www.dod.gov/pubs/ foi/detainees/taguba/.

51. Elisabeth Bumiller and Richard W. Stevenson, "Rumsfeld Chastised by President for His Handling of Iraq Scandal," *New York Times*, May 5, 2004, A1.

52. Evan Thomas, "No Good Defense," *Newsweek*, May 17, 2004, 24–30.

53. Ibid.

54. Jim Rutenberg and Mark Mazzetti, "Rumsfeld Gets Robust Defense from President," *New York Times*, April 15, 2006, A1 and A10.

55. Michael R. Gordon, "Army Buried Study Faulting Iraq Planning," *New York Times*, February 11, 2008, A1 and A8.

56. Ibid.

57. Ibid.

58. Ibid.

59. Ibid.

60. David S. Cloud and Eric Schmitt, "More Retired Generals Call for Rumsfeld's Resignation," *New York Times*, April 14, 2006, A1 and A17.

61. Jim Rutenberg and Mark Mazzetti, "Rumsfeld Gets Robust Defense from President," *New York Times*, April 15, 2006, A1 and A10.

62. Ibid.

63. Ibid.

64. David S. Cloud and Eric Schmitt, "More Retired Generals Call for Rumsfeld's Resignation," *New York Times*, April 14, 2006, A1 and A17.

65. Lawrence Wilkerson interview with the author, June 26, 2008; off-the-record interviews and conversations with senior Bush administration officials.

66. Richard Armitage interview with the author, December 15, 2008.

67. David S. Cloud, "Ex-Commander Calls Iraq Effort 'a Nightmare,'" *New York Times*, October 13, 2007, A1.

68. Ibid.

69. Ibid.

70. Jim Rutenberg, "Conceding Missteps, Bush Urges Patience on Iraq," *New York Times*, October 26, 2006, A1 and A12.

71. Ibid.

72. David S. Cloud and Thom Shanker, "Pentagon Widens Its Battle to Shape News of Iraq War," *New York Times*, November 3, 2006, A13.

73. Dan Balz and Jon Cohen, "Confidence in Bush Leadership at All-Time Low, Poll Finds," *Washington Post*, January 22, 2007, A1.

74. Richard Armitage interview with the author, December 15, 2008.

75. David S. Cloud and Michael R. Gordon. "Attacks in Iraq at Record Level, Pentagon Finds," *New York Times*, December 19, 2006, A1 and A14.

76. Off-the-record interviews with members of the Iraq Study Group.

77. Off-the-record interviews with members of Rice's staff and senior administration officials.

78. Sheryl Gay Stolberg, "Bush Asserts That Victory in Iraq Is Still Achievable," *New York Times*, December 21, 2006, A14.

79. Dan Balz and Jon Cohen, "Confidence in Bush Leadership at All-Time Low, Poll Finds," *Washington Post*, January 22, 2007, A1.

80. Shailagh Murray and Jonathan Weisman, "Bush Told War Is Harming the GOP," *Washington Post*, May 10, 2007, A01.

81. Ibid.

82. "Poll: Bush Approval Drops to Low of 29%," *USA Today*, July 9, 2007, http://www.usatoday.com/news/washington/2007-07-09-bush-poll_N.htm.

83. Peter Baker and Karen DeYoung, "Bush Plans to Stress Next Phase in Iraq War," *Washington Post*, July 10, 2007, A01.

84. Ibid.

85. Karen DeYoung and Peter Baker, "White House Gives Iraq Mixed Marks in Report," *Washington Post*, July 12, 2007, A1.

86. Ibid.

87. Ibid.

88. Michael Abramowitz, "Intelligence Puts Rationale for War on Shakier Ground," *Washington Post*, July 18, 2007, A05.

89. Mark Mazzetti, David E. Sanger, and David Stout, "U.S. Intelligence Agencies Offer Grim Assessment of Al Qaeda," *International Herald Tribune*, July 17, 2007, 1.

90. Michael R. Gordon and Jim Rutenberg, "Bush Distorts Qaeda Links, Critics Assert," *New York Times*, July 13, 2007, A1.

91. Ewen MacAskill, "Bush: There Will Be No Pullout from Iraq While I'm President," *Guardian* (London), August 23, 2007, 1.

92. Karen DeYoung and Ann Scott Tyson, "Military Officials in Iraq Fault GAO Report," *Washington Post*, September 5, 2007, A01.

93. Ibid.

94. William Branigin, "White House Cites 'Satisfactory Progress' on Iraq Goals," *Washington Post*, September 14, 2007, A01.

95. Ibid.

96. Jon Cohen and Jennifer Agiesta, "Wide Skepticism Ahead of Assessment," *Washington Post*, September 9, 2007, A18.

97. Peter Baker, "9/11 Linked to Iraq, in Politics If Not in Fact," *Washington Post*, September 12, 2007, A01.

98. Ibid.

99. Steven Lee Myers and Carl Hulse, "Bush Says Success Allows Limited Troop Cuts," *New York Times*, September 14, 2007, A1 and A8.

100. Ibid.

101. Thom Shanker, "Chairman of Joint Chiefs Will Not Be Reappointed," *New York Times*, June 9, 2007, A1 and A13.

102. Dan Eggen, "Bush Is Optimistic Again About Iraq War," *Washington Post*, March 19, 2008.

103. Ibid.

104. Ibid.

105. Ibid.

106. Ibid.

107. Joby Warrick and Walter Pincus, "Bush Inflated Threat from Iraq's Banned Weapons, Report Says," *Washington Post*, June 6, 2008, A03.

108. Ibid.

109. Ibid

110. Ibid.

111. Ibid.

112. Mark Mazzetti and Scott Shane, "U.S. Senate Panel Accuses Bush of Iraq Exaggerations," *International Herald Tribune*, June 6, 2008, 1.

113. Ibid.

114. Mark Mazzetti and Scott Shane, "Bush Overstated Evidence on Iraq, Senators Report," *New York Times*, June 6, 2008, A1 and A11.

115. Ibid.

116. Ibid.

117. Ann Scott Tyson, "Pentagon to Lift Ban on Coffins at Dover," *Washington Post*, February 26, 2009.

118. See "Obama Administration Lifts Blanket Ban on Media Coverage of the Return of Fallen Soldiers," http://www.gwu.edu/~nsarchiv/news/20090226/index.htm.

119. Ann Scott Tyson, "Pentagon to Lift Ban on Coffins at Dover," *Washington Post*, February 26, 2009.

120. See "Obama Administration Lifts Blanket Ban on Media Coverage of the Return of Fallen Soldiers," http://www.gwu.edu/~nsarchiv/news/20090226/index.htm.

121. "Written Ministerial Statement Responding to a Lancet Study on Iraq Casualty Figures," November 18, 2004, http://www.fco.gov.uk/resources/en/news/2004/11/fco_nst_171104_strawiraqcasualty.

122. Ibid.

123. Ibid.

124. Jeff Jacoby, "The Lancet's Overblown Figures," *International Herald Tribune*, January 15, 2008, 1.

125. Sabrina Tavernise and Donald G. McNeil Jr., "Iraqi Dead May Total 600,000, Study Says," *New York Times*, October 11, 2006, A16.

126. Warren Hoge, "U.N. Says Iraq Seals Data on the Civilian Toll," *New York Times*, October 21, 2006, A7.

127. Rick Jervis, "U.N. Says Plight of Iraqis Worsens," *USA Today*, April 26, 2007, 1.

128. Iraq Family Health Survey Study Group, "Violence-Related Mortality in Iraq from 2002–2006," *New England Journal of Medicine* 358, no. 5 (January 31, 2008): 484–93.

129. See Iraq Body Count, "Civilian Deaths from violence in 2007," http://www.iraqbodycount.org/analysis/numbers/2007/.

130. "Mission Still Not Accomplished," *New York Times*, March 20, 2008, A22.

131. Steven Lee Myers, "Marking 5 Years, Bush Insists U.S. Must Win in Iraq," *New York Times*, March 20, 2008, A1 and A11.

CHAPTER 6

1. Off-the-record interview with senior Bush administration official.

2. Off-the-record conversation with former Johnson and Bush administration official.

3. Lawrence Wilkerson interview with the author, June 26, 2008.

4. David Sanger, "On to Vietnam, Bush Hears Echoes of 1968 in Iraq 2006," *New York Times*, November 17, 2006, A13.

5. Richard Armitage interview with the author, December 15, 2008.

6. Ibid.

7. Off-the-record interviews with senior military officers and Bush administration officials.

8. Lawrence Wilkerson interview with the author, June 26, 2008.

9. Ibid.

10. Off-the-record interviews with senior military officers and Bush administration officials.

11. David E. Sanger, "Bush Sees 'Urgent Duty' to Pre-empt Attack by Iraq: Calls It Crucial to the Defeat of Terror," *New York Times*, October 8, 2002, A1 and A13.

12. Off-the-record interviews with senior White House, military, and intelligence officers in the Bush administration.

13. Ibid.

14. Lawrence Wilkerson interview with the author, June 26, 2008.

15. Ibid.

16. Interviews by the author with former Johnson and Kennedy advisers Arthur Schlesinger Jr., George Christian, Richard Neustadt, Paul Warnke, Harry C. McPherson, Clark Clifford, George Elsey, Walt Rostow, McGeorge Bundy, Paul Nitze, and Robert McNamara.

17. McGeorge Bundy interview with the author, November 18, 1993.

18. James Woolsey interview with the author, April 4, 2002.

19. Richard Perle, "Too Heavy a Hand," *New York Times*, March 16, 2008, A13.

20. Richard Armitage interview with the author, December 15, 2008.

21. David Kay interview with the author, September 11, 2008.

22. Robert S. McNamara interview with the author, April 4, 2002.

23. Richard Armitage interview with the author, December 15, 2008.

24. Off-the-record interviews with senior White House, military, and intelligence officers in the Bush administration.

25. Robert S. McNamara interview with the author, April 4, 2002.

26. Paul Pillar interview with the author, June 18, 2008.

27. Ibid.

28. Ibid.

29. Richard Armitage interview with the author, December 15, 2008.

30. Ibid.

31. David Kay interview with the author, September 11, 2008.

32. Paul Pillar interview with the author, June 18, 2008.

33. Off-the-record interviews with senior White House, military, and intelligence officers in the Bush administration.

34. Ibid.

35. Ibid.

36. Response to author question by Richard Clarke at his book signing at the Middle East Institute in Washington, DC, May 2008.

37. Off-the-record interview with senior Defense intelligence official during the Bush administration.

38. Paul Pillar interview with the author, June 18, 2008.

39. Ibid.

40. Ibid.

41. Off-the-record interview with senior Defense intelligence official during the Bush administration.

42. Off-the-record interviews with senior intelligence officials and analysts in the Bush administration.

43. Ibid.

44. Paul Pillar interview with the author, June 18, 2008.

45. Ibid.

46. Ibid.

47. Gary Langer, "Bush Legacy: A Tale of Two Terms," *ABC News*, January 7, 2009, http://abcnews.go.com/PollingUnit/BushLegacy/story?id=6567339&page=1; "Bush's Final Approval Rating: 22 Percent," *CBS News*, http://www.cbsnews.com/stories/2009/01/16/opinion/polls/main4728399.shtml.

48. Gary Langer, "Bush Legacy: A Tale of Two Terms," *ABC News*, January 7, 2009, http://abcnews.go.com/PollingUnit/BushLegacy/story?id=6567339&page=1.

49. Ibid.

50. "Bush's Final Approval Rating: 22 Percent," *CBS News*, http://www.cbsnews.com/stories/2009/01/16/opinion/polls/main4728399.shtml.

51. Ibid.

52. Ibid.

53. Gary Langer, "Bush Legacy: A Tale of Two Terms," *ABC News*, January 7, 2009, http://abcnews.go.com/PollingUnit/BushLegacy/story?id=6567339&page=1.

54. "Explorations: The Vietnam War as History," University of Houston Digital History, http://www.digitalhistory.uh.edu/learning_history/vietnam/vietnam_pub opinion.cfm.

55. Ibid.

56. Gary Langer, "Bush Legacy: A Tale of Two Terms," *ABC News*, January 7, 2009, http://abcnews.go.com/PollingUnit/BushLegacy/story?id=6567339&page=1.

57. James H. Willbanks, "Winning the Battle, Losing the War," *New York Times*, March 5, 2008, A23.

58. Ibid.

59. Ibid.

60. Off-the-record interviews with senior White House officials and staff in the Bush administration; off-the-record interviews with former members of the Iraq Study Group.

61. Off-the-record interviews with former members of the Iraq Study Group.

62. Off-the-record interview with former member of the Iraq Study Group.

63. Ibid.

64. Interviews by the author with former Johnson advisers George Christian, Richard Neustadt, Paul Warnke, Harry C. McPherson, and McGeorge Bundy.

65. Robert S. McNamara interview with the author, April 4, 2002.

66. Interviews by the author with former Johnson advisers George Christian, Paul Warnke, Harry C. McPherson, George Elsey, and Robert S. McNamara.

67. Off-the-record interviews with former members of the Iraq Study Group.

68. Off-the-record interview with former member of the Iraq Study Group.

69. Ibid.

70. Lawrence Wilkerson interview with the author, June 26, 2008.

71. Stolberg, Sheryl Gay and Steven Lee Myers. "Bush to Sell Limited Iraq Pullout as Middle Way." *New York Times*, 13 September 2007, pp. A1 and A11.

72. Lawrence Wilkerson interview with the author, June 26, 2008.

73. Julian E. Barnes, "Cost of Iraq War Will Surpass Vietnam's by Year's End," *Los Angeles Times*, April 11, 2009, http://articles.latimes.com/2009/apr/11/nation/na-iraq-vietnam11.

74. Interviews by the author with former Johnson and Kennedy advisers Arthur Schlesinger Jr., George Christian, Richard Neustadt, Paul Warnke, Harry C. McPherson, Clark Clifford, George Elsey, Walt Rostow, McGeorge Bundy, Paul Nitze, and Robert McNamara.

75. Off-the-record interviews with senior Bush administration officials.

76. Lawrence Wilkerson interview with the author, June 26, 2008.

77. The intentional manipulation of information for political purposes was not limited to Iraq. In February 2004 a group of sixty influential scientists, including twenty Nobel laureates, released a statement claiming the administration systematically distorted scientific fact in areas ranging from environment, health, and biomedical research to nuclear weaponry. James Glanz, "Scientists Say Administration Distorts Facts," *New York Times*, February 19, 2004, A21.

Bibliography

The 9/11 Commission Report: Final Report of the National Commission on Terrorist Attacks upon the United States. New York: W.W. Norton, 2004.

Adorno, T. W., E. Frenkel-Brunswik, D. J. Levinson, and R. N. Sandord. *The Authoritarian Personality.* New York: Harper Books, 1950.

Aid, Matthew M. *The Secret Sentry: The Untold History of the National Security Agency.* New York: Bloomsbury, 2009.

Alfonsi, Christian. *Circle in the Sand: Why We Went Back to Iraq.* New York: Doubleday, 2006.

Allawi, Ali A. *The Occupation of Iraq: Winning the War, Losing the Peace.* New Haven, CT: Yale University Press, 2007.

Ambrose, Stephen E. *Eisenhower: Soldier and President.* New York: Simon and Schuster, 1990.

Ambrose, Stephen E., and Douglas G. Brinkley. *Rise to Globalism: American Foreign Policy Since 1938.* New York: Penguin, 1998.

Andrews, Edmund L. "Envoy's Letters Counter Bush on Dismantling of Iraqi Army." *New York Times,* September 4, 2007, A1 and A11.

Baker, James A., III, and Lee H. Hamilton (cochairs). *The Iraq Study Group Report: The Way Forward—A New Approach.* New York: Vintage Books, 2006.

Baker, Peter. "A President Besieged and Isolated, Yet at Ease." *Washington Post,* July 2, 2007, A01.

Bamford, James. *A Pretext for War: 9/11, Iraq, and the Abuse of America's Intelligence Agencies.* New York: Anchor Books, 2005.

Barber, James D. *The Presidential Character: Predicting Performance in the White House.* Englewood Cliffs, NJ: Prentice-Hall 1972.

Barstow, David. "Behind Analysts, Pentagon's Hidden Hand." *New York Times,* April 20, 2008, A1 and A24–A26.

Berman, Larry. *Planning a Tragedy: The Americanization of the War in Vietnam.* New York: Norton, 1982.

———. *Lyndon Johnson's War: The Road to Stalemate in Vietnam*. New York: Norton, 1989.

Beschloss, Michael. "I Don't See Any Way of Winning." *Newsweek*, November 2001.

Biddle, Stephen. "Seeing Baghdad, Thinking Saigon." *Foreign Affairs* 85, no. 2 (March/April 2006): 2–14.

Boin, Arjen, Allan McConnell, and Paul 't Hart (eds.). *Governing After Crisis: The Politics of Investigation, Accountability and Learning*. Cambridge: Cambridge University Press, 2008.

Boin, Arjen, Paul 't Hart, Allan McConnell, and Thomas Preston. "Leadership Style, Crisis Response, and Blame Management: The Case of Hurricane Katrina." *Public Administration* 88, no. 3 (September 2010): 706–23.

Bonham, G. Matthew, and Daniel Heradstveit. *The "Axis of Evil" Metaphor and the Restructuring of Iranian Views toward the U.S.* Paper delivered at the Middle East and Central Asia Conference, Salt Lake City, September 8–10, 2005.

Bovens, Mark, and Paul 't Hart. *Understanding Policy Fiascoes*. New Brunswick, NJ: Transaction Press, 1996.

Bowen, Mark. *Censoring Science: Inside the Political Attack on Dr. James Hansen and the Truth of Global Warming*. New York: Dutton, 2007.

Brandstrom, Annika, and Sanneke Kuipers. "From 'Normal Incidents' to Political Crises: Understanding the Selective Politicization of Policy Failures." *Government and Opposition* 38, no. 3 (2003): 279–305.

Brandstrom, Annika, Sanneke Kuipers, and Par Daleus. "The Politics of Tsunami Responses: Comparing Patterns of Blame Management in Scandinavia." In *Crisis and After: The Politics of Investigation, Accountability, and Learning*, edited by P. 't Hart, A. Boin, and A. McConnell, 114–47. Cambridge: Cambridge University Press, 2008.

Bremer, L. Paul. *My Year in Iraq: The Struggle to Build a Future of Hope*. New York: Simon and Schuster, 2006.

Brigham, Robert K. *Is Iraq Another Vietnam?* New York: Public Affairs, 2006.

Bruni, Frank. *Ambling into History: The Unlikely Odyssey of George W. Bush*. New York: HarperCollins, 2002.

Brzezinski, Zbigniew. "Terrorized by 'War on Terror': How a Three-Word Mantra Has Undermined America." *Washington Post*, March 25, 2007, B01.

Burke, John P. *Becoming President: The Bush Transition, 2000–2003*. Boulder, CO: Lynne Rienner, 2004.

Burke, John P., and Fred I. Greenstein. *How Presidents Test Reality: Decisions on Vietnam, 1954 and 1965*. New York: Russell Sage Foundation, 1991.

Bush, George, and Brent Scowcroft. *A World Transformed*. New York: Knopf, 1998.

Califano, Joseph A., Jr. *The Triumph and Tragedy of Lyndon Johnson: The White House Years*. New York: Simon and Schuster, 1991.

Campbell, Kenneth J. *A Tale of Two Quagmires: Iraq, Vietnam, and the Hard Lessons of War*. Boulder, CO: Paradigm, 2007.

Cannon, Carl M. "Untruth and Consequences." *Atlantic* (January/February 2007): 56–67.

Cirincione, Joseph. "Assessing the Assessment: The 1999 National Intelligence Estimate of the Ballistic Missile Threat." *Nonproliferation Review* 7, no. 1 (Spring 2000): 125–37.

Clarke, Richard A. *Against All Enemies: Inside America's War on Terror.* New York: Free Press, 2004.

———. *Your Government Failed You: Breaking the Cycle of National Security Disasters.* New York: HarperCollins, 2008.

Clausewitz, Carl Von. *On War.* Harmondsworth, UK: Penguin Books, 1985.

Clifford, Clark. Oral history interview. August 7, 1969. Lyndon Baines Johnson Library, Austin, TX.

Clifford, Clark. *Counsel to the President.* New York: Random House, 1991.

Cloud, David S. "Inquiry on Intelligence Gaps May Reach to White House." *New York Times,* February 10, 2007, A5.

Cloud, David S., and Mark Mazzetti. "Pentagon Group Criticized for Prewar Intelligence Analysis." *New York Times,* February 9, 2007, A8.

Cockburn, Andrew. *Rumsfeld: His Rise, Fall, and Catastrophic Legacy.* New York: Scribner, 2007.

Cooper, Helene. "Blame (Blank) for Iraq." *New York Times,* February 11, 2007, section 4, 1 and 14.

Cottam, Martha. *Images and Intervention.* Pittsburgh, PA: University of Pittsburgh Press, 1994.

Cottam, Martha, and Richard Cottam. *Nationalism and Politics: The Political Behavior of Nation States.* Boulder, CO: Lynne Rienner, 2001.

Cottam, Martha, Beth Dietz-Uhler, Elena M. Mastors, and Thomas Preston. *Introduction to Political Psychology.* 2nd ed. New York: Taylor and Francis, 2010.

Cottam, Richard. *Foreign Policy Motivation.* Pittsburgh, PA: University of Pittsburgh Press, 1977.

Cronin, Thomas E. *The State of the Presidency,* 2nd edition. Boston: Little, Brown and Company, 1980.

Daalder, Ivo H., and I. M. Destler. *In the Shadow of the Oval Office: Profiles of the National Security Advisers and the Presidents They Served—From JFK to George W. Bush.* New York: Simon and Schuster, 2009.

Danner, Mark. *Torture and Truth: America, Abu Ghraib, and the War on Terror.* New York: New York Review Books, 2004.

———. *The Secret Way to War: The Downing Street Memo and the Iraq War's Buried History.* New York: New York Review Books, 2006.

Dickerson, John F., and Matthew Cooper. "What Happened to Bush's Dream Team?" *Time,* May 17, 2004.

Donley, R. E., and David Winter. "Measuring the Motives of Public Officials at a Distance: An Exploratory Study of American Presidents." *Behavioral Science* 15 (1970): 227–36.

Dowd, Maureen, and Thomas Friedman. "The Fabulous Bush and Baker Boys." *New York Times Magazine,* March 6, 1990, 58–64.

Draper, Robert. *Dead Certain: The Presidency of George W. Bush.* New York: Free Press, 2007.

Drumheller, Tyler. *On the Brink: An Insider's Account of How the White House Compromised American Intelligence.* New York: Carroll and Graf, 2006.

Duelfer, Charles. *Hide and Seek: The Search for Truth in Iraq.* New York: Public Affairs, 2009.

Dyson, Stephen Benedict. "Personality and Foreign Policy: Tony Blair's Iraq Decisions." *Foreign Policy Analysis* 2, no. 3 (July 2006): 289–306.

———. *The Blair Identity: Leadership and Foreign Policy.* Manchester, UK: Manchester University Press, 2009.

Dyson, Stephen Benedict, and Thomas Preston. "Individual Characteristics of Leaders and the Use of Analogy in Foreign Policy Decision Making." *Political Psychology* 27, no. 2 (April 2006): 265–88.

Eichenberg, Richard C., and Richard J. Stoll. "The Approval Ratings of George W. Bush." *Journal of Conflict Resolution* 50, no. 6 (December 2006): 783–808.

Ellis, R. J. *Presidential Lightning Rods: The Politics of Blame Avoidance.* Lawrence: University of Kansas Press, 1994.

Etheredge, Lloyd S. *A World of Men: The Private Sources of American Foreign Policy.* Cambridge: MIT Press, 1978.

Feldman, Ofer, and Linda O. Valenty, eds. *Profiling Political Leaders: Cross-Cultural Studies of Personality and Behavior.* Westport, CT: Praeger, 2001.

Fodor, Eugene M., and T. Smith. "The Power Motive as an Influence on Group Decision Making." *Journal of Personality and Social Psychology* 42 (1982): 178–85.

Foyle, Douglas C. *Counting the Public In: Presidents, Public Opinion, and Foreign Policy.* New York: Columbia University Press, 1999.

Franken, Al. *Lies and the Lying Liars Who Tell Them: A Fair and Balanced Look at the Right.* New York: Penguin, 2003.

———. *The Truth (with Jokes).* New York: Penguin 2005.

Freedman, Lawrence. "Rumsfeld's Legacy: The Iraq Syndrome?" *Washington Post,* January 12, 2005.

Gardner, Helen, ed. *The New Oxford Book of English Verse.* London: Oxford University Press, 1984.

Gelbspan, Ross. *Boiling Point: How Politicians, Big Oil and Coal, Journalists, and Activists Have Fueled a Climate Crisis—And What We Can Do to Avert Disaster.* New York: Basic Books, 2004.

Gellman, Barton. *Angler: The Cheney Vice Presidency.* New York: Penguin, 2008.

Gellman, Barton, and Jo Becker. "A Different Understanding with the President." *Washington Post,* June 24, 2007, A01.

Gelpi, Christopher, Peter D. Feaver, and Jason Reifler. "Success Matters: Casualty Sensitivity and the War in Iraq." *International Security* 30, no. 3 (2006): 7–46.

George, Alexander L. *Presidential Decisionmaking in Foreign Policy: The Effective Use of Information and Advice.* Boulder: Westview, 1980.

Goldberg, Jeffrey. "Breaking Ranks: What Turned Brent Scowcroft Against the Bush Administration?" *New Yorker,* October 31, 2005, 54–65.

Goldstein, Gordon M. *Lessons in Disaster: McGeorge Bundy and the Path to War in Vietnam.* New York: Henry Holt, 2008.

Goodwin, Richard. "Making the Facts Fit the Case for War." *New York Times*, February 8, 2004.

Greenberg, David. *Nixon's Shadow: The History of an Image.* New York: W. W. Norton, 2003.

Greenberg, Karen J., and Joshua L. Dratel, eds. *The Torture Papers: The Road to Abu Ghraib.* Cambridge: Cambridge University Press, 2005.

Greenstein, Fred I. *Personality and Politics: Problems of Evidence, Inference, and Conceptualization.* Chicago: Markham, 1969.

———. *The Hidden-Hand Presidency: Eisenhower as Leader.* New York: Basic Books, 1982.

———. "The Contemporary Presidency: The Changing Leadership of George W. Bush: A Pre- and Post-9/11 Comparison." *Presidential Studies Quarterly* 32, no. 2 (June 2002): 387–96.

———, ed. *The George W. Bush Presidency: An Early Assessment.* Baltimore, MD: Johns Hopkins University Press, 2003.

Hearit, K. M. *Crisis Management by Apology.* Malawah, N.J.: Lawrence Erlbaum, 2006.

Heclo, Hugh. "The Political Ethos of George W. Bush." In *The George W. Bush Presidency: An Early Assessment*, edited by F. I. Greenstein, 17–50. Baltimore, MD: John Hopkins University Press, 2003.

Hermann, Margaret G. "Explaining Foreign Policy Behavior Using Personal Characteristics of Political Leaders." *International Studies Quarterly* 24 (1980a): 7–46.

———. "Comments on Foreign Policy Makers' Personal Attributes and Interviews: A Note on Reliability Procedures." *International Studies Quarterly* 24 (1980b): 67–73.

———. *Assessing Leadership Style: A Trait Analysis.* Columbus, OH: Social Science Automation, 1999.

———. "Assessing Leadership Style: Trait Analysis." In *The Psychological Assessment of Political Leaders*, edited by J. M. Post, 178–212. Ann Arbor: University of Michigan Press, 2003.

Hermann, Margaret G., T. Preston, B. Korany, and T. M. Shaw. "Who Leads Matters: The Effects of Powerful Individuals." In *Leaders, Groups, and Coalitions: Understanding the People and Processes in Foreign Policymaking*, 83–131. Boston: Blackwell, 2001.

Hersh, Seymour M. *Chain of Command: The Road from 9/11 to Abu Ghraib.* New York: HarperCollins, 2004.

Hood, C. C. "The Risk Game and the Blame Game." *Government and Opposition* 37, no. 1 (2002): 15–37.

Hood, C. C., W. Jennings, B. Hogwood, and C. Beeston. "Fighting Fires in Testing Times: Exploring a Staged Response Hypothesis for Blame Management in Two Exam Fiasco Cases." *European Journal of Political Research* 48, no. 6 (2009): 695–722.

House, Robert J. "Power and Personality in Complex Organizations." In *Personality and Organizational Influence*, edited by B. M. Staw and L. L. Cummings, 181–233. Greenwich, Conn: JAI Press, 1990.

Hughes, Karen. *Ten Minutes from Normal*. New York: Penguin, 2004.

Isikoff, Michael, and David Corn. *Hubris: The Inside Story of Spin, Scandal, and the Selling of the Iraq War*. New York: Crown, 2006.

Ivins, Molly, and Lou Dubose. *Shrub: The Short but Happy Political Life of George W. Bush*. New York: Vintage, 2000.

Johnson, Lyndon Baines. *The Vantage Point: Perspectives of the Presidency, 1963–1969*. New York: Holt, Rinehart, and Winston, 1971.

Jordan, Mary. "Britain Blames Rumsfeld for Situation in Iraq." *Washington Post*, September 2, 2007.

Kaarbo, Juliet, and Margaret G. Hermann. "Leadership Styles of Prime Ministers: How Individual Differences Affect the Foreign Policy Process." *Leadership Quarterly* 9, no. 3 (Fall 1998): 243–63.

Kearns, Doris. *Lyndon Johnson and the American Dream*. New York: Harper and Row, 1976.

Keegan, John. *The First World War*. New York: Vintage, 1998.

Kennedy, Paul. *The Rise and Fall of the Great Powers*. New York: Random House, 1987.

Kessler, Glenn. *The Confidante: Condoleezza Rice and the Creation of the Bush Legacy*. New York: St. Martin's, 2007.

Khong, Yuen F. *Analogies at War: Korea, Munich, Dien Bien Phu, and the Vietnam Decisions of 1965*. Princeton, NJ: Princeton University Press, 1992.

Kiewe, Amos, ed. *The Modern Presidency and Crisis Rhetoric*. Westport, CT: Praeger, 1994.

Kille, Kent J. *From Manager to Visionary: The Secretary-General of the United Nations*. New York: Palgrave-Macmillan, 2006.

Laird, Melvin. "Iraq: Learning the Lessons of Vietnam." *Foreign Affairs* 84, no. 6 (November/December 2005): 22–43.

Larson, Deborah Welch. "Good Judgment in Foreign Policy: Social Psychological Perspectives." In *Good Judgment in Foreign Policy: Theory and Application*, edited by S. A. Renshon and D. W. Larson, 3–23. Boulder, CO: Rowman and Littlefield, 2003.

Leiby, Richard. "Valerie Plame, the Spy Who Got Shoved Out Into the Cold." *Washington Post*, October 29, 2005.

Levy, Jack S. "Learning and Foreign Policy: Sweeping a Conceptual Minefield." *International Organization* 48, no. 2 (Spring 1994): 279–312.

Linzer, Dafna. "Tenet Says He Was Made a Scapegoat Over Iraq War." *Washington Post*, April 27, 2007, A1.

Mann, James. *Rise of the Vulcans: The History of Bush's War Cabinet*. New York: Viking Penguin, 2004.

Mazarr, Michael J. "The Long Road to Pyongyang: A Case Study in Policymaking without Direction." *Foreign Affairs* 86, no. 5 (September/October 2007): 75–94.

McClelland, David C. *Power: The Inner Experience*. New York: Irvington, 1975.

McClellan, Scott. *What Happened: Inside the Bush White House and Washington's Culture of Deception*. New York: Public Affairs, 2008.

McMaster, H. R. *Dereliction of Duty: Lyndon Johnson, Robert McNamara, the Joint Chiefs of Staff, and the Lies That Led to Vietnam*. New York: HarperCollins, 1997.

McNamara, Robert S. *In Retrospect: The Tragedy and Lessons of Vietnam*. New York: Random House, 1995.

McPherson, Harry. *A Political Education*. Boston: Little, Brown, 1972.

Mitchell, David. *Making Foreign Policy: Presidential Management of the Decision-Making Process*. Burlington, VT: Ashgate, 2005.

Mitchell, Elizabeth. *W: Revenge of the Bush Dynasty*. New York: Hyperion, 2000.

Moens, Alexander. *The Foreign Policy of George W. Bush: Values, Strategy, and Loyalty*. Burlington, VT: Ashgate, 2004.

Moore, James, and Wayne Slater. *Bush's Brain: How Karl Rove Made George W. Bush Presidential*. Hoboken, NJ: John Wiley and Sons, 2003.

Mueller, John. "The Iraq Syndrome." *Foreign Affairs* 84, no. 6 (November/December 2005): 44–54.

Mueller, John, and Karl Mueller. "Sanctions of Mass Destruction." *Foreign Affairs* 78, no. 3 (May/June 1999): 43–53.

Mylroie, Laurie. *Study of Revenge: Saddam Hussein's Unfinished War against America*. Washington, DC: American Enterprise Institute Press, 2000.

Neustadt, Richard E. *Presidential Power and the Modern Presidents: The Politics of Leadership from Roosevelt to Reagan*. New York: Free Press, 1990.

Nitze, Paul C. *From Hiroshima to Glasnost: At the Center of Decision*. New York: Grove Weidenfeld, 1989.

Olmeda, Jose A. "A Reversal of Fortune: Blame Games and Framing Contests after the 3/11 Terrorist Attacks in Madrid." In *Crisis and After: The Politics of Investigation, Accountability, and Learning*, edited by P. 't Hart, A. Boin, and A. McConnell, 62–84. Cambridge: Cambridge University Press, 2008.

Packer, George. *The Assassins' Gate: America in Iraq*. New York: Farrar, Straus and Giroux, 2006.

Parker, Charles F., and Sander Dekker. "September 11 and Post-crisis Investigation." In *Crisis and After: The Politics of Investigation, Accountability, and Learning*, edited by P. 't Hart, A. Boin, and A. McConnell, 255–82. Cambridge: Cambridge University Press, 2008.

Paul, Christopher. *The Ethics of War and Peace: An Introduction to Legal and Moral Issues*. 2nd ed. Prentice Hall, 1994.

Pillar, Paul R. "Intelligence, Policy, and the War in Iraq." *Foreign Affairs* 85, no. 2 (March/April 2006): 15–28.

Post, Jerrold M. *The Psychological Assessment of Political Leaders*. Ann Arbor: University of Michigan Press, 2003.

Powell, Colin. *My American Journey*. New York: Random House, 1995.

Preston, Thomas. *The President and His Inner Circle: Leadership Style and the Advisory Process in Foreign Policy Making*. Ph.D. dissertation, The Ohio State University, 1996.

———. "Following the Leader: The Impact of U.S. Presidential Style upon Advisory Group Dynamics, Structure, and Decision." In *Beyond Groupthink: Group Decision*

Making in Foreign Policy, edited by Bengst Sundelius, Paul 't Hart, and Eric Stern, 191–248. Ann Arbor: University of Michigan Press, 1997.

———. *The President and His Inner Circle: Leadership Style and the Advisory Process in Foreign Affairs*. New York: Columbia University Press, 2001.

———. *From Lambs to Lions: Future Security Relationships in a World of Biological and Nuclear Weapons*. Lanham, MD: Rowman and Littlefield, 2007.

———. "Weathering the Politics of Responsibility and Blame: The Bush Administration and Its Response to Hurricane Katrina." In *Crisis and After: The Politics of Investigation, Accountability, and Learning*, edited by P. 't Hart, A. Boin, and A. McConnell, 33–61. Cambridge: Cambridge University Press, 2008.

Preston, Thomas, and Margaret G. Hermann. "Presidential Leadership Style and the Foreign Policy Advisory Process." In *The Domestic Sources of American Foreign Policy: Insights and Evidence*, edited by Eugene R. Wittkopf and James M. McCormick, 363–80. New York: Rowman and Littlefield, 2004.

Preston, Thomas, and Paul 't Hart. "Understanding and Evaluating Bureaucratic Politics: The Nexus Between Political Leaders and Advisory Systems." *Political Psychology* 20, no. 1 (March 1999): 49–98.

Renshon, Jonathan. *Why Leaders Choose War: The Psychology of Prevention*. Westport, CT: Praeger Security International, 2006.

Renshon, Stanley A., and Deborah Welch Larson, eds. *Good Judgment in Foreign Policy: Theory and Application*. Boulder, CO: Rowman and Littlefield, 2003.

Revkin, Andrew C. "Climate Expert Says NASA Tried to Silence Him." *New York Times*, January 29, 2006.

Rich, Frank. *The Greatest Story Ever Sold: The Decline and Fall of Truth From 9/11 To Katrina*. New York: Penguin, 2006.

Ricks, Thomas E. *The Gamble: General David Petraeus and the American Military Adventure in Iraq, 2006–2008*. New York: Penguin, 2009.

Sanger, David E. "New Tapes Indicate Johnson Doubted Tonkin Gulf Attack." *New York Times*, November 6, 2001, A16.

———. "On to Vietnam, Bush Hears Echoes of 1968 in Iraq 2006." *New York Times*, November 17, 2006, A13.

Scarborough, Rowan. *Rumsfeld's War: The Untold Story of America's Anti-Terrorist Commander*. Washington, DC: Regnery, 2004.

Schafer, Mark, and Stephen Walker, eds. *Beliefs and Leadership in World Politics: Methods and Applications of Operational Code Analysis*. New York: Palgrave-Macmillan, 2006.

Schlesinger, Arthur M., Jr. *A Thousand Days: John F. Kennedy in the White House*. Boston: Houghton Mifflin, 1965.

Shanteau, James. "Competence in Experts: The Role of Task Characteristics." *Organizational Behavior and Human Decision Processes* 53, no. 2 (November 1992): 252–66.

Shenon, Philip. *The Commission: The Uncensored History of the 9/11 Investigation*. New York: Twelve, 2008.

Smith, Charles P., John W. Atkinson, David C. McClelland, and Joseph Veroff, eds. *Motivation and Personality: Handbook of Thematic Content Analysis.* Cambridge: Cambridge University Press, 1992.

Smith, R. Jeffrey. "Hussein's Prewar Ties to Al-Qaeda Discounted: Pentagon Report Says Contacts Were Limited." *Washington Post*, April 6, 2007, A01.

Steele, Jonathan, and Suzanne Goldenberg. "What Is the Real Death Toll in Iraq?" *Guardian* (London), March 19, 2008.

Stelter, Brian. "Was Press a War 'Enabler'?: Two Offer a Nod from Inside." *New York Times*, May 30, 2008, A17.

Stern, Eric K. "Probing the Plausibility of Newgroup Syndrome: Kennedy and the Bay of Pigs." In *Beyond Groupthink: Political Group Dynamics and Foreign Policymaking*, edited by P. 't Hart, E. Stern, and B. Sundelius. 153–89. Ann Arbor: University of Michigan Press, 1997.

Stewart, Dennis D., and Garold Stasser. "Expert Role Assignment and Information Sampling During Collective Recall and Decision Making." *Journal of Personality and Social Psychology* 59, no. 4 (1995): 619–28.

Stiglitz, Joseph, and Linda J. Bilmes. *The Three Trillion Dollar War: The True Cost of the Iraq Conflict.* New York: W. W. Norton, 2008.

Strasser, Steven, ed. *The Abu Ghraib Investigations: The Official Independent Panel and Pentagon Reports on the Shocking Prisoner Abuse in Iraq.* New York: Public Affairs, 2004.

Suedfeld, Peter, and A. D. Rank. "Revolutionary Leaders: Long-Term Success as a Function of Changes in Conceptual Complexity." *Journal of Personality and Social Psychology* 34 (1976): 169–78.

Suedfeld, Peter, and Phillip Tetlock. "Integrative Complexity of Communications in International Crisis." *Journal of Conflict Resolution* 21 (1977): 169–84.

Suskind, Ron. *The Price of Loyalty: George W. Bush, the White House, and the Education of Paul O'Neill.* New York: Simon and Schuster, 2004.

Taysi, Tanyel, and Thomas Preston. "The Personality and Leadership Style of President Khatami: Implications for the Future of Iranian Political Reform." In *Profiling Political Leaders: Cross-Cultural Studies of Personality and Behavior*, edited by O. Feldman and L. O. Valenty, 57–77. Westport, CT: Praeger, 2001.

Tenet, George. *At the Center of the Storm: My Years at the CIA.* New York: HarperCollins, 2007.

Tetlock, Phillip. "Integrative Complexity of American and Soviet Foreign Policy Rhetorics: A Time-Series Analysis." *Journal of Personality and Social Psychology* 49 (1985): 565–85.

Tetlock, Philip E., and Aaron Belkin, eds. *Counterfactual Thought Experiments in World Politics: Logical, Methodological, and Psychological Perspectives.* Princeton, NJ: Princeton University Press, 1996.

Thacker, Toby. *Joseph Goebbels: Life and Death.* Basingstoke, UK: Palgrave-Macmillan, 2009.

't Hart, Paul, E. Stern, and B. Sundelius, eds. *Beyond Groupthink: Political Group Dynamics and Foreign Policymaking.* Ann Arbor: University of Michigan Press, 1997.

Thomas, Evan, and Richard Wolffe. "Bush in the Bubble." *Newsweek*, December 19, 2005, 31–39.

Thucydides. *The Peloponnesian War*. Harmondsworth, UK: Penguin, 1985.

Tjosvold, Dean, R. Nibler, and P. Wan. "Motivation for Conflict Among Chinese University Students: Effects of Others' Expertise and One's Own Confidence in Engaging in Conflict." *Journal of Social Psychology* 141, no. 3 (June 2001): 353–63.

Tuchman, Barbara W. *The Guns of August*. New York: Macmillan, 1962.

Tzu, Sun. *The Art of War*. London: Oxford University Press, 1971.

US Senate Select Committee on Intelligence. *Report on Intelligence Activities Relating to Iraq Conducted by the Policy Counterterrorism Evaluation Group and the Office of Special Plans within the Office of the Under Secretary of Defense for Policy*, June 2008.

Vertzberger, Yaacov. *The World in Their Minds: Information Processing, Cognition, and Perception in Foreign Policy Decisionmaking*. Stanford, CA: Stanford University Press, 1990.

Voeten, Erik, and Paul R. Brewer. "Public Opinion, the War in Iraq, and Presidential Accountability." *Journal of Conflict Resolution* 50, no. 6 (December 2006): 809–30.

Wakin, Malham M. *War, Morality, and the Military Profession*. Boulder, CO: Westview, 1979.

Wallace, M. D., and P. Suedfeld. "Leadership Performance in Crisis: The Longevity-Complexity Link." *International Studies Quarterly* 32 (1988): 439–52.

Walzer, Michael. *Just and Unjust Wars: A Moral Argument with Historical Illustrations*. 2nd ed. Basic Books / HarperCollins, 1977.

Wayne, Stephen J. "Bad Guys and Bad Judgments." In *Good Judgment in Foreign Policy: Theory and Application*, edited by S. A. Renshon and D. W. Larson, 103–24. Boulder, CO: Rowman and Littlefield, 2003.

Weaver, R. K. "The Politics of Blame Avoidance." *Journal of Public Policy* 6, no. 4 (1986): 371–98.

Weiner, Tim. *Legacy of Ashes: The History of the CIA*. New York: Doubleday, 2007.

Wilson, Joseph C. "What I Didn't Find in Africa." *New York Times*, July 6, 2003.

———. *The Politics of Truth: Inside the Lies that Led to War and Betrayed My Wife's CIA Identity: A Diplomat's Memoir*. New York: Carroll and Graf, 2004.

Wilson, Valerie Plame. *Fair Game: My Life as a Spy, My Betrayal by the White House*. New York: Simon and Schuster, 2007.

Winter, David G. *The Power Motive*. New York: Free Press, 1973.

———. "Leader Appeal, Leader Performance, and the Motive Profiles of Leaders and Followers: A Study of American Presidential Elections." *Journal of Personality and Social Psychology* 52 (1987): 196–202.

Winter, David G., and Abigail J. Stewart. "Content Analysis as a Technique for Assessing Political Leaders." In *A Psychological Examination of Political Leaders*, edited by Margaret G. Hermann, 21–61. New York: Free Press, 1977.

Wittenbaum, G. M., S. I. Vaughan, and G. Stasser. "Coordination in Task-performing Groups." In *Applications of Theory and Research on Groups to Social Issues*, edited by R. S. Tindale, L. Heath, J. Edwards, E. J. Posvoc, F. B. Bryant, and T. Suarez-Balcazar, 177–204. New York: Plenum, 1998.

Woods, Kevin, James Lacey, and Williamson Murray. "Saddam's Delusions: The View from the Inside." *Foreign Affairs* 85, no. 3 (May/June 2006): 2–26.

Woodward, Bob. *The Commanders*. New York: Simon and Schuster, 1991.

———. *Bush at War*. New York: Simon and Schuster, 2002.

———. *Plan of Attack*. New York: Simon and Schuster, 2004.

———. *State of Denial: Bush at War, Part III*. New York: Simon and Schuster, 2006.

———. *The War Within: A Secret White House History, 2006–2008*. New York: Simon and Schuster, 2008.

———. *Obama's Wars*. New York: Simon and Schuster, 2010.

Yingling, Paul, Lt. Colonel. "A Failure of Generalship." *Armed Forces Journal* (May 2007), http://www.armedforcesjournal.com/2007/05/2635198.

AUTHOR INTERVIEWS

Off-the-record interviews and conversations with senior White House, Defense Department, State Department, military, and intelligence officials who served during the Bush administration.

Armitage, Richard, Washington, DC, December 15, 2008.
Bundy, McGeorge, New York, NY, November 18, 1993.
Christian, George, Austin, TX, August 4, 1993.
Clifford, Clark, Washington, DC, March 29, 1994.
Elsey, George, Washington, DC, March 28, 1994.
Kay, David, Washington, DC, September 11, 2008.
McNamara, Robert, Washington, DC, April 4, 2002.
McPherson, Harry C., Washington, DC, July 7, 1995.
Neustadt, Richard, New York, NY, November 16, 1996.
Nitze, Paul, Washington, DC, July 7, 1995.
Pillar, Paul, Washington, DC, June 18, 2008.
Rostow, Walt, Austin, TX, August 3, 1993.
Schlesinger, Arthur, Jr., New York, NY, November 15, 1996.
Warnke, Paul, Washington, DC, July 6, 1995.
Wilkerson, Lawrence, Washington, DC, June 26, 2008.
Woolsey, James, Washington, DC, April 4, 2002.

Index

About the Author

Dr. Thomas Preston is the C. O. Johnson Distinguished Professor of Political Science in the Department of Politics, Philosophy, and Public Policy at Washington State University. He currently serves as associate departmental chair and director of graduate studies, director of the M.A. in Global Justice and Security Studies (GJSS) program, and as a member of the board of directors for the Institute for the Study of Intercommunal Conflict at WSU. He received his M.A. at the University of Essex (United Kingdom) and his Ph.D. from The Ohio State University (Columbus, Ohio). He is a faculty research associate at the Moynihan Institute of Global Affairs at the Maxwell School, Syracuse University, New York, and at CRISMART (The National Center for Crisis Management, Research and Training), part of the Swedish National Defense College, Stockholm, Sweden. A specialist in security policy, foreign affairs, and political psychology, Professor Preston joined Washington State University and the Department of Political Science in 1994. He teaches undergraduate courses on international relations, American foreign policy, U.S. national security policy, and political analysis. At the graduate level, he offers seminars on international security and the psychology of leadership and decision making. In 2003, he was awarded the prestigious William F. Mullen Excellence in Teaching Award by the WSU College of Liberal Arts, was named a WSU faculty Innovator by the university in 2007, and received a Fulbright Senior Scholar Award in 2010 from the U.S. State Department and the Fulbright New Zealand Programme. He is the author of four books: The President and His Inner Circle: Leadership Style and the Advisory Process in Foreign Affairs (2001), 'From Lambs to Lions': Future Security Relationships in a World of Biological and Nuclear Weapons (2007/2009), Pandora's Trap: Presidential Decision Making and

Blame Avoidance in Vietnam and Iraq (2011), and coauthor of Introduction to Political Psychology (2004/2010). He has also written numerous refereed journal articles and book chapters on leadership, international security, the use of active-learning simulations in the classroom, and foreign policy analysis. His current research involves a number of projects on nuclear/biological weapons proliferation, the effect of expertise on political leaders, and the psychology of bioterrorism. He frequently serves as an independent consultant for various U.S. governmental departments and agencies.

CPSIA information can be obtained at www.ICGtesting.com
Printed in the USA
BVOW07s2259221113

337102BV00002B/5/P